Implementing Term Limits

Today, 70 percent of the American public supports reforms that would limit the number of terms a state legislator may serve, and the organization U.S. Term Limits advocates for this reform at the national level as well. But do term limits actually ensure that citizens dedicated to the common good—rather than self-serving career politicians—run government, as advocates claim? Or does the enforced high rate of turnover undermine the legislature's ability to function, as opponents assert?

Marjorie Sarbaugh-Thompson and Lyke Thompson bring 13 years of intensive research and 460 interviews to assess changes that have occurred since Michigan's implementation of term limits in 1993 and explore the implications of those changes for government and governing. Paying special attention to term limits' institutional effects, they also consider legislative representation, political accountability, and the role of the bureaucracy and interest groups in state legislatures.

Their thorough study suggests that legislators are less accessible to officials and that there is a larger gap between legislators and their voters. Moreover, legislators become much more politically ambitious after term limits and spend more time on political activities rather than policy making. At the institutional level, top chamber leaders appear to gain clout. The selection of these leaders is complicated by newcomers' lack of knowledge about and experience working with the leaders they select—a vote they make before being sworn in. As a result, term limits in Michigan fail to deliver on many of the "good government" promises that appeal to citizens.

Implementing Term Limits makes a unique and valuable contribution to the debate over the best means by which to obtain truly democratic institutions.

Marjorie Sarbaugh-Thompson is a Professor of Political Science at Wayne State University.

Lyke Thompson is the Director of the Center for Urban Studies at Wayne State University and also a Professor of Political Science.

LEGISLATIVE POLITICS & POLICY MAKING

Series Editors

Janet M. Box-Steffensmeier, Vernal Riffe Professor of Political Science,
The Ohio State University

David Canon, Professor of Political Science, University of Wisconsin, Madison

IMPLEMENTING TERM LIMITS

The Case of the Michigan Legislature

Marjorie Sarbaugh-Thompson
and Lyke Thompson

University of Michigan Press
Ann Arbor

Published in the United States of America by the
University of Michigan Press
Manufactured in the United States of America
⊚ Printed on acid-free paper

2020   2019   2018   2017   4   3   2   1

A CIP catalog record for this book is available from the British Library.

Library of Congress Cataloging-in-Publication data has been applied for.

ISBN 978-0-472-07342-9 (hardback : alk. paper)
ISBN 978-0-472-05342-1 (paper : alk. paper)
ISBN 978-0-472-12273-8 (e-book)

Dedicated to Michigan's State Legislators who let us interview them, some even five times. We are grateful for your time and willingness to educate us about the real world of state legislatures. We have done our best to let voters and other interested readers understand what you taught us.

And to Annie

Contents

Acknowledgments

We are deeply indebted to many, many people. This project survived for 15 years with almost no funding. That it persisted is a testament to the willingness of many people to donate their time and energy in the hope that we would improve the political process and the quality of government in Michigan.

First and foremost, we are especially grateful to the legislators who shared their time and knowledge with us. We have, in turn, tried to share their insights with our students, other scholars, and readers of our work.

We had help from many wonderful Wayne State University graduate and undergraduate students over the 15 years of this project. The project would not have been possible without their efforts. We recognized many of them in our earlier book. Here we acknowledge those who contributed specifically to this volume. Emily Dozier is a Master's in Public Administration graduate student who demonstrated her administrative prowess by keeping us on point on reference lists and citations. Her administrative help in producing the final manuscript is deeply appreciated. We thank the graduate students who appear as coauthors on individual chapters in this volume: Robert J. Mahu, Justin Rex, Catherine Schmitt-Sands, and Laurel Sprague. Their help was essential to completing this project. Additionally we recognize the earlier and enduring contributions of our faculty colleagues, Charles D. Elder, Richard C. Elling, and John Martin Strate.

Finally, we thank our family members and friends for tolerating the seemingly endless demands of the "term limits project."

ONE

Introduction

More than two decades after term limits surged across the political landscape, the time is right to assess this reform. Proponents persuaded voters in state after state to pass measures limiting the service of elected officials. They told voters that limiting elected officials' years in office would restore democracy by severing cozy relationships between legislators and lobbyists, increasing the number of citizen legislators, and making elections more competitive (Niven 2000). These proponents also said that term limits would attract Burkean trustees motivated by the general welfare instead of their own electoral fortunes (Will 1992). Yet term limits proponents also claimed that these legislators would be more responsive to constituents' needs and concerns (Petracca 1991) despite their affinity for the common good. Voters were even told that removing the "drag of incumbency" would diversify state legislators because women and ethnic minority group members would win more seats after entrenched white males were purged from office.

This and more was promised, but what was delivered? With limits implemented in all 15 states that still have them, it is time to examine whether limiting tenure fulfills advocates' hopes or spawns dire consequences, as opponents warned (Polsby 1993). We attempt to answer this question by drawing on 13 years of research about Michigan's legislature based on 460 interviews with the state's representatives and senators.

But we want to know more than just whether term limits achieve their promises. We want to understand how term limits interact with existing political and institutional structures in a state. Early studies of term limits, including some of our own, allowed advocates' rhetoric to set the research agenda. Term limits' promises drove these evaluations, with little attention paid to unintended and unanticipated consequences of term limits. These consequences often alter institutional arrangements, such as the distribution of influence within a chamber or relations between the legislative and executive branches. These are not the touted benefits of term limits that led voters to adopt them. Although Carey et al. (2006) conclude that institutional effects are the most profound changes wrought by limits, there is a major gap in our knowledge about these effects. This is because they are especially difficult to investigate.

Given the depth and extent of our research, we can address some of these questions. To ensure that we delve into unanticipated institutional effects, we probe three levels of term limits effects: direct impacts, related changes in legislators' behaviors or processes, and systemic adjustments in political institutions and legislative chambers. In thinking about these levels, one can compare term limits to a rock thrown into a lake. There are questions about the impact of the rock—does it produce waves or merely ripples? There are also questions about the patterns of the waves and ripples, from which we may learn about the temperature of the water and the depth of the lake. Finally, there are questions about whether the waves are strong enough to reach the shore, and if so what impact do they have on the shoreline? We illustrate this approach using one promise made to voters—term limits' ability to attract citizen legislators.

With a surge in open seats and only a short time to serve, term limits advocates hoped to attract citizen legislators, whose service would be motivated by the common good rather than self-interest (Petracca 1991; Will 1992). Treating term limits first like a rock thrown into a lake, we explore the impact of the limits themselves. At this level of analysis, we assess whether post-term-limits lawmakers resemble the idealized citizen legislator or whether politically ambitious careerists still inhabit the halls of the state capital. As we describe in chapter 2, we find that post-term-limits newcomers are even more politically ambitious than their predecessors. Citizen legislators are rare.

Moving to the next level, term limits trigger waves that reveal systemic effects. Continuing our example, what happens when there are more politically ambitious newcomers in a legislature? As waves of politically ambitious newcomers ripple through the legislature, we compare their behavior to that of their less ambitious colleagues. How do they allocate their time? For example, in chapter 4 we find that politically ambitious legislators prioritize bringing money and projects (aka pork) to the district.

Finally, we use term limits' impact to fathom the lake—learning about institutional facets of Michigan's legislature by observing how it absorbs or is transformed by term limits. Extending our example, we consider how the different behaviors of politically ambitious newcomers alter the legislature itself. For example, do these politically ambitious legislators elect caucus leaders who focus on the external image of the party—media relations, fundraising, and other facets of reelection seeking rather than policy making and bipartisan compromise? Not only do we find that they do, but by examining this we broaden our understanding of legislative leadership and factors that militate against legislating when there is an influx of politically ambitious legislators.

As we point out below, these broader institutional effects tend to be mediated by the political environment and context of the state. This makes them particularly difficult to isolate in cross-sectional studies but a little easier to detect across time in a single state. For instance, the influence that caucus leaders and committee chairs exert over the work of a chamber is likely to differ in the face of strong or weak governors (Miller, Nicholson-Crotty, and Nicholson-Crotty 2011), a state's budget debates, and a host of other factors that vary by state as well as over time within a state. Consequently, we believe our study of term limits in Michigan makes its most unique contributions in the area of institutional effects.

The Need for Further Research

Research about term limits proliferated almost as soon as voters adopted these ballot proposals, peaking around 2002. But there are three problems with much of this work. The first is timing. Often term limits were evaluated before they were implemented and before their effects were fully felt. The second is variation in the limits themselves. Term limits are often treated as a binary variable despite their diversity. Finally, state context appears to interact with term limits. Based on their research, Miller, Nicholson-Crotty, and Nicholson-Crotty (2011) suggest that some of the null findings in cross-sectional term limits research could reflect opposing state effects that neutralize each other at the aggregate level.

Timing of Term Limits Research

Some scholars apparently assumed that term limits would change state politics even before the "new breed" of term-limited legislators populated state capitols (Carey, Niemi, and Powell 1998). This implies that shortening the tenure of sitting legislators alters their incentives and thereby their behavior or that a few newcomers have free rein despite the presence of career veterans. Consequently, states anticipating term limits were often treated as term limited along with states that had implemented their limits. Although this facilitated early research by providing a larger cohort of states that had received the treatment (term limits), it conflated term limits' ability to alter veteran legislators' behaviors with the effects of expelling these veterans and replacing them with a "new breed" of post-term-limits legislator.

Even as newcomers gradually join the legislature after term limits were adopted, veterans retain control while they are still in office. They chair committees, they lead the caucus, and they socialize newcomers into the norms of the chamber. This inhibits term limits effects until the first mass exodus from a chamber. And even then, many legislators termed out of the lower chamber migrate to the upper chamber in term-limited states. So, these upper chambers tend to be controlled by veteran legislators with decades of experience in the lower chamber. Consequently, state governments are shielded from the full force of term limits for many years as implementation ripples through both legislative chambers. And in many states with lenient limits, this lasts for more than a decade.

The rush to judge term limits before they were fully implemented in most states led some scholars to conclude that term limits had little effect on legislatures. For example, Wright's (2007) discussion of partisan polarization uses roll call voting data from 1999–2000 and treats 13 states as term limited.[1] But of these 13 states, 6 had not yet purged veterans from either chamber by the 1999–2000 session, and 3 (Arkansas, Michigan, and Oregon) had expelled them only from their lower chamber. His null findings may well have dissuaded many scholars from pursuing the impacts of term limits on these two important topics, especially given the demands of assembling roll call data and of linking those data to citizen ideology in state legislative districts. But these results should be treated as exploratory, not definitive, because term limits were only partially in place.

Based on similarly precipitate studies, political scientists may have accepted false negatives—term limits have little or no effect—on a host of questions. This issue of timing is important because, as Miller, Nicholson-Crotty, and Nicholson-Crotty (2011) demonstrate, some term limits effects can be found only after the limits are implemented, not after they are adopted. Indeed, in contrast to Wright's (2007) findings, we report in chapter 3 that term limits appear to affect roll call voting in Michigan once they are implemented, and other scholars find increasing polarization in states that have implemented limits (Masket and Shor 2014). Therefore, we argue that it is crucial to evaluate a phenomenon after it is fully implemented and to treat earlier investigations as exploratory or baseline findings.

Recognizing this problem with term limits research, Mooney (2009) highlights three phases of the term limits reform: *anticipation*, which occurs after voters adopt limits but before they are implemented; *transition*, which occurs as a spike accompanying the first mass expulsion of veterans; and *equilibrium*, which involves long-term patterns of turnover and movement between political offices after a state fully implements term limits. Though the equilibrium stage will persist long after the limits are implemented, this phase has received little scholarly attention.

Our longitudinal study of Michigan's legislature encompasses all three phases of term limits implementation: anticipation, transition, and equilibrium. Michigan by the end of our investigation had entered the equilibrium stage, so we can shed some light on this lacuna in term limits research. But even with the sustained effort of more than a decade of research, we only just reached the equilibrium stage at the end of our investigation. Thus, patience and persistence is required to realize the full research potential of term limits. After years of waiting, the time is ripe to investigate the term limits equilibrium in many states. One purpose of this book is to renew interest in and guide efforts into promising areas of term limits inquiry as more and more states enter the term limits equilibrium.

Variation in Term Limits Laws

Term limits research is also plagued by the marked variation in the stringency of service limits. Although scholars often treat term limits as a dichotomy—states either have limits or they do not—in reality some limits are very severe and others are so generous that they could actually increase the average length of state legislative service (Heberlig and Leland 2004). As Sarbaugh-Thompson (2010b) points out, measures of "term-limitedness" that account for this variation should be used in cross-sectional analyses of term limits. Increasingly, scholars (for example, Miller, Nicholson-Crotty, and Nicholson-Crotty 2011 and Erler 2007) add information about the nature of the limits. But this is still rare.

As we show in table 1.1, only three states, Arkansas (from 1998 to 2014), California (from 1996 to 2012), and Michigan, limit service in the lower chamber to six years, and these are lifetime bans. In contrast, Louisiana's lenient limits allow legislators to serve for 12 years in one chamber and then move to the other chamber for 12 more years, and these limits apply only to consecutive years of service. Other states fall between these extremes.

Nationally, 21 states have adopted various limits on legislative service.[2] Today, only 15 of these still have state legislative term limits[3] and seem likely to retain them in their current form for the foreseeable future.[4] A majority of the term-limited states, nine of the 15, only limit consecutive years of service. So term limits in these nine states force legislators to take a "time out," but then they can run for the same office again. The length of the service break depends on state law. Also, depending on the state's law, the "time out" in one chamber can include time spent in the other chamber. So, for example, after spending eight years in the Ohio House, a legislator could run for and possibly win a seat in Ohio's Senate, serve there for eight years, and be eligible to run for the state House of Representatives again. Thus, in Ohio, some legislators could cycle continuously between chambers as long as they win elections.

Michigan has extremely stringent term limits, so it is an especially good laboratory in which to measure the effects of term limits. In Michigan, a state house member can serve six years (three terms) in the 110-member

TABLE 1.1. State Term Limits Provisions and Level of Professionalization

Limit in Years	Consecutive	Lifetime Ban
8 Total	*Nebraska (2006)*	
12 Total		*Oklahoma (2004/2004)* **California (2012)**[a]
16 Total		Arkansas (2014)
6 House/8 Senate		Arkansas (1998/2000)[b] **California (1996/1998)** **Michigan (1998/2002)**
8 House/8 Senate	*Arizona (2000/2000)* *Colorado (1998/1998)* *Florida (2000/2000)* Maine (1996/1996) Montana (2000/2000) *Ohio (2000/2000)* South Dakota (2000/2000)	*Missouri (2002/2002)*
12 House/12 Senate	Louisiana (2007/2007)	Nevada (2008/2008)

Note: Numbers in parentheses indicate year of impact in the House first and Senate second. States listed in bold type are those with highly professionalized legislatures, those in italics have moderately professional legislatures, and those in regular type are part-time legislatures. Levels of professionalism are based on Squire 2007.
[a] In 2012 California voters revised the state's term limits so that legislators may serve 12 years total in either chamber.
[b] In 2014 Arkansas passed a ballot measure extending limits to a 16-year lifetime total. Based on National Conference of State Legislatures.

lower chamber, and then run for (and possibly win) one of the 38 seats in the upper chamber. Those who win a state senate seat can serve for eight more years (two terms). A Michigan legislator's lifetime quota for state legislative service is exhausted at 14 years, but six years is the likely tenure for the vast majority who enter the House. Given these stringent limits, effects we find in Michigan can direct attention toward more promising lines of research about term limits.

Interaction between Term Limits and the State Context

In addition to the variation among term limits laws themselves, we argue that the states with term limits are fundamentally different from the non-term-limited states. It appears that ballot initiative states are distinctive, and most states with term limits (14 of the 15) provide citizens with the ballot initiative. Only seven ballot initiative states lack term limits. Of the 35 non-term-limited states, 28 do not provide the direct democracy opportunities available to citizens in the term-limited states.[5]

Tolbert, Grummel, and Smith (2001) find that the ballot initiative states have different political cultures. And despite the debate about whether ballot initiatives *cause* differences in state fiscal conditions (see, for example, Day and Boeckelman 2012; Keele, Malhotra, and McCubbins 2013; Matsusaka 2004), there appear to **be** fiscal differences between states with and without the ballot initiative Yet it is rare to find cross-sectional analyses of term limits (or other state political phenomenon) that control for the ballot initiative states.

Second, we concur with Miller, Nicholson-Crotty, and Nicholson-Crotty (2011) that some of the null findings in cross-sectional term limits research may reflect countervailing trends across states that neutralize effects in the aggregate. For example, these authors find that in some term-limited states governors gain power, and in others they lose power. The starting point appears to be the key factor—strong governors versus weak governors or strong legislatures versus weak ones. Similarly, they find that the strength of interest groups after term limits depends on the relative historical power of the actors involved. State context appears to be an exceedingly important predictor of term limits effects, so they infer that contrasting state effects could produce false negatives in cross-sectional studies.

We consider this issue of the state's starting point to be crucial in investigating term limits effects. Indeed, our proposed measure of "term-limitedness" (Sarbaugh-Thompson 2010b) is predicated on the assumption that in states with high turnover prior to term limits, moderately strict limits might produce little or no effect on the political environment. Conversely, the same limits in states with very low turnover historically might trigger a political tsunami. Therefore, some ratio of term limits effects compared to the pre-term-limits status quo seems likely to provide a better assessment of the "treatment." For example, in drug trials it would be routine to record both the dosage of the drug and the physical state of the patient. We argue that term limits research needs to follow this model by determining what the dosage is (how much the rate of turnover changes) and the status of the patient—strong or weak with respect to the economy, legislative power, executive power, interest group power, and so on.

Although most cross-sectional research controls for the level of professionalism in a state's legislature, other facets of state context seem likely to interact with term limits. An obvious difference is the state's political opportunity structure, which is affected by the number of seats in the legislative chambers. To illustrate this, Ohio and Colorado have nearly identical term limits. In Ohio, 99 Representatives can compete for 33 State Senate seats if they are interested in cycling back and forth between chambers. At most only one-third of the House members will win seats in the Senate. In Colorado, with 65 seats in the lower chamber and 35 in the upper chamber, more than half of the representatives might be able to participate in a game of musical chairs between chambers. These are clearly different political opportunity structures. States also have different numbers of congressional seats that might attract politically ambitious legislators to move up the electoral food chain. And states vary widely in the opportunities available in large cities for a lucrative political career as mayor or on the city council. These options provide the context in which politically ambitious state legislators operate. And this context could affect legislators' political aspirations.

Similar sources of variation among the states are myriad including different political cultures, various levels of partisan competition, staggered or mass turnover in upper chambers, and a host of other institutional features that complicate cross-sectional analysis of term limits. We find, as do Miller, Nicholson-Crotty, and Nicholson-Crotty (2011), that the chamber matters within the same state. Indeed, throughout this book we report that Michigan's two chambers sometimes move toward each other or diverge from each other after term limits are implemented. So, even within a single state, the effects of term limits could be masked if chamber differences are not considered. This level of background noise is exceptionally hard to identify in multistate research. Given our current level of understanding about term limits effects—especially the institutional effects—single-state studies, especially across time, provide valuable information about factors that interact with term limits. Once these are identified, it is easier to control for them in multistate studies. Michigan is especially suited to this task because its limits are so stringent, and it is one of only two term-limited states (California is the other) with highly professional legislatures.

We do not dispute the value of detailed cross-sectional studies in term limits research. But as we argue above, it is important to control for a host of factors that are likely to affect the results. Moreover, even when researchers consider the state-level factors that interact with term limits, it may not be feasible to control for all the variations and the interaction between the term-limits dosage administered and the relevant conditions in the state. Studying term limits in an individual state across times holds constant many of the state-level sources of variation described above allowing us to capitalize on many advantages of a pretest/post-test quasi-experimental design.

On the other hand, a single-state study constrains generalizability, and changes across time might simply reflect national changes. For example, it is hard to know whether increasing polarization among Michigan's legislators during our study period reflects term limits, national trends, or some combination of the two. Additionally, the effects we find might be unique to Michigan; both cross-sectional and case study research have advantages and disadvantages.

Our investigation provides fertile ground for identifying more and less promising lines of investigation. There are two reasons for this. First, Michigan limits are among the most severe. Second, most other term-limited states (with the obvious exception of California) have less professional legislatures. This should magnify some of term limits effects in Michigan because limiting tenure tends to reduce professionalism in state legislatures (Kousser 2005). In other states with term limits, the level of professionalism is already lower, so the change could be much less noticeable. If we find no evidence to support a specific effect in Michigan, it is unlikely that scholars will find evidence of that effect elsewhere. Thus, an added benefit of our work is that it can alert researchers to lines of investigation that are unlikely to produce results.

Michigan Government during Our Investigation

Given the potential for term limits to interact with state circumstances, we provide an overview of Michigan's political institutions and politics during our study. Michigan's legislature is highly professional (Squire 2007) and its leaders have extensive powers (Battista 2011). Committee chairs historically dominated policy making in its lower chamber with the caucus exerting influence in its upper chamber (Francis 1985). Its governor has a line-item veto and can make appointments as long as the upper chamber does not reject them. On the other hand, the secretary of state and attorney general are both elected separately, as are judges and Michigan Supreme Court justices. Michigan's Governor can only make judicial appointments in case of a vacancy and then only until the next statewide election. In the 21st century, the state's economy is fairly evenly divided between tourism, agriculture, and manufacturing, although in a bygone era manufacturing was king. Reflecting this industrial heritage, both labor unions and the Chamber of Commerce wield political clout.

During our first round of interviews, Michigan's House was controlled by Democrats and its Senate by Republicans. In the 1999–2000 session Republicans controlled the lower chamber and retained this control through our 2003–04 interviews with representatives. Although the Senate remained under Republican control for all three sets of interviews, during our final post-term-limits Senate interviews (the 2007–10 session) Democrats regained control of the House. Although we did not interview representatives after Democrats regained control of the lower chamber, we did ask senators questions about their relationship with the lower chamber and how divided government affected their work.

In the early 2000s Michigan entered a one-state recession, facing high unemployment and plagued by chronic budget cuts and revenue shortfalls. Some observers argue these fiscal outcomes resulted from the continuing decline in manufacturing as corporations moved factories out-of-state and overseas. Others decry an ill-timed income tax cut passed in 1999 after term limits took effect in the House.[6] Regardless of the causes of Michigan's budgetary woes, which are most likely multiple, budget shortfalls coincided with the implementation of term limits in the state. Thus, Michigan's novice legislators confronted a thorny economic and political thicket.

During the first two post-term-limits sessions in the House, Michigan's governor was John Engler, a career politician who entered the state legislature in 1970. He moved from the lower to the upper chamber in 1978, serving as senate majority leader from 1983 to 1990, before defeating an incumbent governor. Widely acclaimed as a skilled politician, Engler was a powerful governor serving his third term in office when the implementation of term limits began in 1999 in the House. Due to staggered implementation of term limits in Michigan, during his tenure the state senate remained in the hands of veteran senators, many of whom were his former chamber colleagues.

In 2002, Michigan's staggered implementation of term limits expanded to include its governor and state senators. The new governor, Democrat Jennifer Granholm, had no legislative experience. Her state government experience consisted of two terms as attorney general. Although she was a charismatic campaigner, she was judged by many opponents and supporters alike to be a political novice. Michigan's state senate continued to be the home of experienced legislators, as termed-out House veterans with decades of experience in the lower chamber migrated to the upper chamber.

In 2007 both the executive and legislative branches of Michigan's government were fully term limited. At the start of the 2007–10 Senate session, Governor Granholm was serving her second term and the Senate's legislative leaders had risen through the lower to the upper chamber, amassing at most 10 of their 14 years of permitted service. (Some legislators left the House early to run for an open state senate seat. So, several Senate newcomers had less than six years of experience, but all had at least some House experience.) Table 1.2 summarizes key features of this political landscape during our research project.

Overview of Our Research Project

In 1998, faculty and graduate students at Wayne State University seized the opportunity to gather data during all three phases of term limits implementation: anticipation, transition, and equilibrium. The implementation of term limits in Michigan was staggered, affecting the lower chamber in 1999 and the upper chamber in 2001, enabling use of a nonequivalent control group design (Campbell and Stanley 1963). Given the findings we report throughout this book, we have, however, become more attentive to chamber differences than we were at the outset of our research.

We began our investigation in 1998, before veteran legislators were purged from office. We conducted face-to-face interviews with legislators to gather baseline data about the way the Michigan House worked before term limits. We collected comparable data in 2002 about the work of the pre-term-limits state senate to establish a baseline before veterans were purged from that chamber. Although technically our baseline interviews occurred during the anticipation phase of term limits implementation, Miller, Nicholson-Crotty, and Nicholson-Crotty (2011) find very few effects of term limits after adoption and before implementation. This comports with our judgment as well. But when we refer to the pre-term-limits legislature, we refer to the period after voters adopted the law, but before anyone was termed out of office—technically pre-term-limits implementation, not pre-term-limits adoption. It is important to keep this caveat in mind.

Continuing our research, we followed both chambers as Michigan implemented its limits, returning to conduct biennial face-to-face interviews with the post-term-limits representatives in 2000, 2002, and 2004 and every four years with the post-term-limits senators in 2006 and 2010.[7] This means that, consistent with the stages identified by Mooney (2009), we amassed some of our post-term-limits data during the transition to term limits and some during the equilibrium stage, which is likely to typify Michigan's term-limited legislature for the foreseeable future. Our final set of interviews in the House (2003–04) is especially valuable because these

TABLE 1.2. Overview of the Political Context of the Research Project

	Chamber	Phase of Term Limits Adoption in House	Phase of Term Limits Adoption in Senate	House Leader Experience and Party Control	Senate Leader Experience and Party Control	Governor Experience and Party
1997–98	House Baseline	Anticipation	Anticipation	Veteran leader D 58 R 52 25 newcomers	Veteran leader R 23 D 15 8 senators entered from the House	Veteran Engler (R)
1999–2000	House Second	Transition	Transition	Novice leader R 58 D52 62 newcomers		
2001–02	House Third & Senate Baseline			Novice leader R 58 D52 22 newcomers		
2003–04	House Fourth	Equilibrium		Veteran leader R 63 D 47 51 newcomers	Veteran leaders, who transitioned from House R22 D 16 29 from House 1 from Congress	Novice Granholm (D)
2005–06	Senate Second			Novice leader R 58 D 52 37 newcomers		
2007–08			Equilibrium	Novice leader D 58 R 52 32 newcomers	Novice leader R 22 D 16 8 newcomers from the House	Veteran Granholm (D)
2009–10	Senate Third			Veteran leader D 67 R 43 44 newcomers		

representatives did not serve with the veterans who might have socialized them into the norms of the pre-term-limits House. In Mooney's terms, the 2003–04 House represents the *post-term-limits equilibrium*. So too does the 2007–10 State Senate. A few of these senators did serve briefly with House veterans, however, and three 2003–04 representatives served in the Senate before moving to the House.

Generally, we combine the transition to term limits and our equilibrium session into the post-term-limits sessions. We do this to take advantage of a larger number of responses, which increases the likelihood that our findings are robust. But we often analyze the equilibrium session in each chamber separately. For the most part, the results are similar for the transition and equilibrium sessions. We report separate effects when we find substantial differences. We discuss these briefly either in the text or endnotes. Three chapters, 7–9, focus heavily on legislative relationships using network analysis. We examine the transition and equilibrium sessions separately in these chapters.

Our interview subjects include many veterans who served for decades before term limits took effect in Michigan and many newly elected legislators, especially after term limits. We scheduled these interviews near the end of each two-year House or four-year Senate term so that even newly elected legislators had enough experience to respond to our questions. The interviews, which include open and closed-ended questions, typically took about an hour, and we asked most of the same questions of each cohort. The questions elicit representatives' self-reports about a wide range of topics (e.g., the extent to which they consult local and state actors for information, their reasons for seeking office, and the grades they give the chamber for several activities).

Though we ask, toward the end of the interview, about the effects of term limits, we concentrate on finding out how they do the job of *legislator* and compare changes in their job perceptions across cohorts. For example, we ask how much time they devote to 11 different tasks, such as studying proposed legislation, monitoring state agencies, or attending events in their district. Other questions probe who they consider to be the most influential members of the chamber and what makes them influential. The interview schedule appears in appendix A.

Instead of sampling Michigan House members and senators, we tried to interview all of them. This reflects our interest in the institutional effects of term limits and our desire to use network analysis to explore these effects. The quality of network analysis declines as missing cases increase. To improve the quality of our network data, we invested heavily in follow-up contacts, driving hundreds of miles to meet legislators at a location of their choice and at their convenience. As a result we exceeded an 80 percent response rate for all four sessions of the Michigan House. For the three sessions of the Senate our response rate fluctuates between 92 percent before term limits and 74 percent and 71 percent, respectively, for the post-term-limits 2006 and 2010 interviews.

Not only does our high response rate facilitate our use of network analysis, it substantially increases the probability that the evidence we provide accurately portrays the Michigan legislature. With such a high response rate, we believe that there is more risk of rejecting true positives than of accepting false ones. As a result, we discuss results with a 90 percent probability that we can reject either one-tailed or two-tailed null hypotheses instead of the usual 95 percent probability (Gill 1999).[8] And occasionally we discuss "noteworthy" results, that is, ones that are substantively large despite lacking statistical significance. This occurs more often in the Senate, which has only 38 seats. Small numbers pose a chronic problem in that chamber even with a very high response rate.

To analyze our interview data, we create a database entry for each legislator for each session in which he or she served from 1998 to 2004 in the House and 2000 to 2010 in the Senate. We enter values for the closed-ended responses for legislators we interviewed, and for all legislators we enter personal characteristics such as gender, political party, education, prior work experience, age, and so on. We code open-ended responses, transforming them into nominal categories, and adding those to the database. We include information from the Michigan Secretary of State's office about the electoral competitiveness of each legislator's district and the base partisan voting strength of each district as reported by long-time state political commentator Bill Ballenger in *Inside Michigan Politics*.[9] We also incorporate district demographic data (e.g., poverty levels and education levels), calculated for each State House and Senate district by the Wayne State University Center for Urban Studies using U.S. Census data. This dataset allows us to test hypotheses about term limits effects using a wide array of control variables and explanatory variables, and it enables us to investigate general phenomena, such as margins of electoral victory, that supplement our interview questions.

Our longitudinal design holds constant many of the institutional rules and political contexts (e.g., political culture, levels of partisan competition, rules of the chamber) that make it difficult to isolate institutional effects in cross-sectional studies of term limits. Additionally, we interviewed 119 respondents (of the 460 interviews overall) more than once, so we are able to trace changes in their responses across sessions and chambers. We do this for changes in the behavior of legislators after term limits and to trace the evolution of relationships of friendship, influence, and vote cuing among legislators. For example, is friendship in one session a leading indicator of influence in the next session?

Without venturing into a discussion of the nature of social reality, we are well aware of the argument that our interview data reveal subjects' perceptions rather than "reality." We hope that our critics on this point will also acknowledge that people often act based on what they believe to be real. So there is value in trying to examine events from their perspective when explaining their actions.

Moreover, we see limitations in using data that are devoid of the intentions, plans, and perceptions of the individuals being studied. Some scholars, media outlets, and political pundits track the actual career paths (winning or at least running for election) of state legislators as a proxy for their political ambition. Without the opportunity to ask about career plans, they are likely to miss the effect on a legislator's behavior of **planning or wanting** to run—that is, their political aspirations or ambition.

For example, some legislators are recruited to run for another office, deciding to do so reluctantly late in their tenure. They might appear to be politically ambitious based on this, but they might have told us they planned to return to their family business. Their behavior in the chamber is more likely to reflect this plan than their eventual run for another office.

Other legislators try to run for statewide office but are thwarted. Candidates vying for some of these positions do not show up in tallies of primary elections. For example, Michigan nominates candidates for attorney general and secretary of state at the party caucus. We know of multiple legislators within the same party in the same chamber who sought these statewide offices, competing to win their party's nomination against one another. Only the nominees are listed as primary candidates. If we simply tallied whether these legislators ran for office based on the official list, we would not find their names. We might conclude that they were not politically ambitious. Their behavior in the chamber, however, was conditioned by their future plans and by competition with their colleagues for the nomination. This was the behavior of politically ambitious legislators with an eye on their next position. Therefore, we argue that political career **plans** may have as much if not more effect on the internal dynamics of the chamber than the career path subsequently traveled.

Plan of the Book

To organize this book, we build on a framework established by Carey, Niemi, and Powell (1998). First we consider the composition of the legislature, then the behavior of its members, and finally the institutional relationships and structures in which legislators work. In our previous book, we evaluated the effects of term limits by assessing whether they fulfilled the promises (intended consequences) made by their advocates when they convinced voters to pass Michigan's term limits law—Proposal B—in 1992. We refer to those findings in this book, but it is not a major emphasis here.

Instead, we explore more general questions about state legislatures using term limits as a probe. Yet it is necessary to establish what effects term limits have if we are to explore the implications of those effects. So we move back and forth between identifying term limits effects and assessing their broader implications. Some readers may wonder why we occasionally describe facets of Michigan's legislature not affected by term limits. Our reply is that resilience in the face of such a dramatic reform provides information about the institutional robustness of a legislature. Moreover, even when we find no effects, the detailed information about one legislature across time contributes to the general reservoir of knowledge about state legislatures. This is especially true in chapter 3 as we explore different ways to measure representation.

Clearly there are myriad facets of the political system that we could examine through the lens of term limits. We focus our energy here on the unique opportunity our face-to-face interviews provide. Unlike anonymous surveys, we know who our respondents are—although we promised them confidentiality and carefully omit details that might identify them. But because we know who they are, we can combine interview responses with characteristics of their specific state legislative district rather than using state averages, compare their voting record with the partisan affiliation of voters in their district, and use their specific margins of victory in primary and general elections to see how vulnerable legislators behave.

We cannot archive our data in their full richness because it would be an easy matter to determine who our respondents are by using the Secretary of State website and so on. Therefore, we concentrate on questions that can be answered only by those of us with Human Subjects Investigation Committee approval to use these data. That we ignore other interesting questions does not indicate a lack of interest on our part, but rather a strategic choice about how best to channel our time and resources. We have often expressed our willingness to collaborate with other scholars, and we remain open to those possibilities. But time, space, and energy focus our efforts here primarily on our interview data.

Contents of the Book

Term limits advocates assumed that, by changing the payoffs for legislative service, term limits would attract legislators with different goals and incentives to seek and hold office. They predicted two types of change: the first internal—involving the motivations and orientation toward the job and toward voters. In this they envisioned an increase in citizen legislators—those motivated by public service, planning to serve briefly and then return to their community. The second compositional change they envisioned was external—involving the physical characteristics of legislators. In chapter 2 we examine both these predictions about the compositional effects of term limits, considering gender and ethnicity as well as legislators' reasons for seeking office.

We find that there are indeed differences in post-term-limits legislators' motives for running and their future political plans, but not the ones that term limits proponents hoped for. It appears that Michigan's legislators after term limits are more, not less, politically ambitious, and also that they are more likely to have been recruited to run for office. We trace these two compositional changes throughout the rest of the book to determine what effect these have on legislators' behavior. For example, in chapter 4 we include a categorical variable designating politically ambitious legislators as we investigate how legislators allocate their time. We find several ways in which politically ambitious legislators allocate their time differently than their less ambitious colleagues do.

On the second compositional characteristic—physical differences—the field of political science has largely reached consensus that term limits make little if any difference. We concur. As we report in chapter 2, even the few early differences in the physical characteristics of post-term-limits legislators are transient adjustments in a game of musical chairs played by veterans termed out of one chamber and jumping into the other. Carey et al. aptly characterize compositional effects of term limits as "the dog that still won't bark" (2006, 113).

But in chapter 2 we move beyond merely documenting null effects to consider why removing the "drag of incumbency" did not help women and ethnic minority group candidates win elections. In this we follow our strategy of probing the effect of term limits' waves and ripples on the larger system. To do this we examine primary election candidacy for clues to the declining number of women in Michigan's legislature after term limits. We discover that both rates of participation in primary elections and success in winning seats are implicated in the declining political fortunes of post-term-limits women in Michigan, and political party mediates these effects.

In chapters 3 through 6 we consider the behavioral effects of term limits. A new breed of legislator was meant to be a means to other ends for term limits advocates, who assumed that a new breed would act differently. Career politicians, motivated by the need to win reelection, are presumed to be more susceptible to influence from special interests whose money can fill campaign war chests (Mitchell 1991). Promised behavioral changes from term-limited legislators included more independence from lobbyists, better policy making, and more responsiveness to voters. But this was predicated on the assumption that these would be citizen legislators, which proved false. So we examine the impact of political ambition as well as the effects of term limits on legislators' behavior.

In chapter 3 we examine whether term limits alter legislators' responsive to their district. To explore this, we consider their representational role orientations and also their roll call voting behavior. We then link their role orientations and their voting behavior with the legislative tasks they spend the most time doing. We find that representation is contingent rather than overarching. We also explore the possibility that representation is a multifaceted concept best assessed by using a variety of measures of its different facets.

In chapter 4, we combine data on district characteristics with legislators' personal attributes to probe changes in their behavior. Does time spent on various parts of their job reflect legislators' political ambition, the amount of political homogeneity among their voters, or possibly the poverty or wealth in the district? In this chapter, we also briefly explore whether the priority legislators place on various activities changes the longer they serve. To do this, we rely on the subset of 119 legislators that we interviewed more than once.

In chapter 5 we explore term limits effects on elections. We compare changes in general election competition nationally and in Michigan, seeking to understand whether term limits alter electoral competition. We also consider the interaction between Michigan's primary elections and term limits. It appears that open primaries interact with term limits to produce two electoral strategies, one if the primary leads to a safe seat and another if the general election contest will be competitive. Finally, we consider how term limits and open seats affect the campaign coffers of legislators in Michigan. For example, do candidates recruited by interest groups raise more money than their colleagues? And do open seats attract less money when there are lots of them (i.e., after term limits)?

Sometimes legislators describe their first encounter with the flood of information in a professional legislature as the proverbial "drink from a fire hose." In chapter 6 we explore how term-limited legislators manage this feat. To do this we analyze responses to a series of questions about 16 sources of information legislators might consult on an issue "seriously considered" in a committee on which they served. We also ask about sources of information our respondents would consult about two ongoing issues that might hypothetically reach a floor vote. Information is valuable in policy making and sources that provide information gain access to the policy process (Kingdon 1989; Mooney 1991). We consider whether colleagues in the chamber, organized groups and lobbyists, or local sources have gained or lost policy-making access under term limits.

We turn to the institutional impacts of term limits in the remainder of the book, chapters 7–11, digging deeper into the implications of term limits for governing in Michigan. We focus on patterns of interaction, the distribution of influence, feelings of trust and friendship, and the formal roles and rules of an organization. These relationships tend to grow and evolve over time, but time is a scarce resource when legislative tenure in limited.

In chapters 7 through 9 we rely heavily on network analysis to explore flows of information, influence structures, and friendship networks. In chapter 7 we find substantial differences in institutional patterns of issue consulting within the legislature after term limits. We identify paths along which information might be disseminated, contrasting the pattern before term limits with those afterward. We compare these patterns for a politically salient issue and a technically complex one. What we find differs by chamber, but these chamber differences diminish after term limits.

Social interaction, or friendship, has been connected with influence in a legislature (Francis 1985). In chapter 8 we compared the number of friends per legislator, finding, unexpectedly, that the average remains stable after term limits. But when we examine patterns of friendship using network analysis techniques, we find a stunning transformation of clusters of friends as term limits are implemented in the Michigan House. In this chapter, we also connect friendship and vote cuing to see whether legislators rely more on friends for information about two specific issues that might reach the floor of the chamber. We find that friendship rather than expertise explains consulting when turnover is higher.

In chapter 9 we explore the structure of influence within the chamber. We asked our respondents to name colleagues they considered to be particularly influential and to explain what makes these colleagues influential. We compare formal and informal influence in the chambers, finding that informal influence is more sensitive to term limits effects. In this chapter, we explore the evolution of influence as a function of other network relationships such as friendship and recognized issue expertise, testing some of the hypotheses advanced by Francis (1985).

Legislators choose their own "bosses" by voting for caucus leaders shortly after they are elected. Chapter 10 examines the choice of these caucus leaders and their behavior. We use cluster analysis to classify the types of leaders that veteran legislators and newly elected legislators seek. In this same chapter, we also examine the work of committees, focusing on the chair's "control over the work of the committee," committee conflict, and the ways this conflict is managed. Finally, we investigate where the most important decisions about two issues are made. Changes in decision making within the chamber after term limits appear to provide an opening for the governor and outside groups to interject themselves more actively in legislative policy making.

Moving beyond the confines of the chamber, in chapter 11 we explore term limits effects on legislative oversight. Bureaucrats or political appointees in state agencies are important sources of information that legislators often rely upon. But legislators also are responsible for monitoring or overseeing the performance of those agencies (Woods and Baranowski 2006). Democratic theory characterizes legislative oversight (see Aberbach 1990, for example) in ways that do not comport with the reality we discovered in Michigan's House (Sarbaugh-Thompson et al. 2010a) where some House members insist that monitoring state agencies is **not** something a legislature does.

Continuing our analysis of outside relationships we explore two others: between the legislature and the governor and between the two chambers. We have data covering several different conditions: experienced leaders in both chambers, experienced leaders in only one chamber, and inexperienced leaders in both chambers combined with an experienced and inexperienced governor. Governors and legislatures have to work together to pass a budget. Moreover, the two chambers need to negotiate and compromise on budgets and to pass legislation. We find that both these relationships are sensitive to the experience of the actors involved.

In our 12th and final chapter, we first summarize our findings. Then we use several cross-cutting themes to integrate strands of our research, discussing the state legislature more broadly. One of these themes is the electoral connection, which we examine using roll call voting in chapter 3, and the behaviors of lame ducks in chapter 4 and electoral vulnerability in chapter 5. Based on this synthesis of our findings we describe what we increasingly see as the myth of ballot box accountability. Other themes include the transformation of friendship and influence when time is short, legislative specialists versus generalists, the importance of contingent effects and chamber differences. A particularly important theme is the chamber differences that permeate the book. Many scholars assumed that most of term limits effects would be isolated in the lower chambers as they absorbed waves of inexperienced newcomers. That we find extremely powerful effects in the upper chamber should reinvigorate interest in term limits research as limits gradually are implemented in upper chambers across the nation.

Purposes of the Book

While this book is about the effects of term limits in one state, the questions it addresses broaden and deepen our understanding of state legislatures more generally. These broader questions have implications not just for other term-limited states but also for wave elections and high turnover in legislative chambers. Among these questions: What happens when the electoral connection is altered? How do legislators learn about complex issues when time and experience are short? What happens in a legislature when friendship and influence are transient? What happens to the incumbency advantage when the maximum time to serve is short? Who performs complex tasks with limited electoral payoff when turnover is high? The list could clearly go on.

Another purpose of this book is to focus other scholars' attention on questions that are more and less likely to reveal term limits effects. In the course of reporting our findings, we distilled promising areas of investigation and highlighted the context in which we discovered these effects. The effort needed to do state politics research is substantial because it is hard to assemble uniform data, especially for multiple states. A rational scholar needs some reassurance that his or her effort will be rewarded before expending hundreds of hours of time to pursue the effects of term limits. Our work can provide a roadmap of promising questions to pursue and contextual factors that are important to consider.

Additionally, as we mentioned earlier in this introduction, we hope to renew interest in term limits research now that many states have finally reached the term limits equilibrium and limits have been implemented in all the other states that have them. It is rare that social scientists in any subfield have the opportunity to compare populations that have and have not experienced an institutional change. Term limits provide political scientists with a chance to do that—and we argue that the discipline should use the opportunity to its fullest.

Despite having PhDs in political science, we learned much from the thorough and candid explanations provided by veteran legislators. Some of them spent several hours patiently answering our questions, and then explaining to us how a legislature really works. It was an incredible education. This book is our effort to share some portion of the insights they provided.

TWO

Is There a New Breed
of Term-Limited Legislator?

Advocates asserted that by removing the "drag of incumbency" term limits would attract citizen legislators motivated by public service rather than reelection seeking (Will 1992). Voters were told that this "new breed" of legislator would serve briefly, then return to their community to live under the laws they passed. Additionally, political scientists (Petracca 1991; Thompson and Moncrief 1993) as well as term limits activists (Will 1992) anticipated that this new breed would include more women and ethnic minority legislators. Indeed, term limits were sold to voters both in Michigan (Yes on B) and nationally (Niven 2000) as a way to diversify legislatures.

This prediction of diversity seemed reasonable because the historical dominance of white men in many state legislatures means that the incumbency advantage favors them disproportionately. By expelling entrenched incumbents, limiting tenure was supposed to herald gains in descriptive representation, which means that elected officials look more like the constituents they represent. (In contrast substantive representation, which we consider in the next chapter, focuses on policy and ideological agreement between elected officials and voters.)

In this chapter we assess whether term-limited legislators differ from their predecessors enough to constitute a new breed. Are they citizen legislators devoid of political ambition? Are they more diverse with respect to gender and ethnicity? Most investigations of these "compositional" effects of term limits focus on physical characteristics only, such as age, gender, and ethnicity. In contrast, we expand our exploration of the "new breed"

23

to include their internal qualities, probing whether they are self-starters or were recruited and their goals and motivation for seeking office, including their political ambition.

By identifying differences between pre- and post-term-limited legislators, we not only assess compositional changes in Michigan's legislative chambers, but we determine a series of legislator characteristics to guide our analyses throughout the book. We use these characteristics (e.g., gender and political ambition) when we examine legislators' behavior and orientation toward their job. For example, do "politically ambitious" legislators allocate their time differently than their less ambitious colleagues? We begin our investigation first with the physical characteristics and then examine legislators' aspirations and reasons for running.

Gender and Ethnic Diversity in State Legislatures

Fueled by the equal rights movements of the 1960s, women and ethnic minority group members made great strides in winning state legislative seats. In 1960 women held 3 percent of these seats nationally. By 1975 they had more than doubled their ranks in state legislative chambers, winning 8 percent of the seats and steadily increasing their presence at a rate of 1 to 2 percent per year until 1993. Many in the United States assumed that the country would inexorably march toward greater descriptive representation. Subsequent gains *and losses* can, however, be described as "decimal dust." From 2002 to 2012, the proportion of women holding state legislative seats increased by only 1 percent nationally (Center for American Women and Politics 2012), an increase that is not statistically significant.[1] Consequently, more than 50 years after the equal rights push of the 1960s, white males are still substantially overrepresented in most state legislatures compared to their proportion of the population. By purging state legislatures of these entrenched white males, term limits rekindled opportunities to diversify state legislatures.

The effect of term limits on women's electoral prospects nationally is ambiguous, however. Colorado, with term limits, is among the states with the largest proportion of women legislators. So too is Arizona. But both were among those the states with the highest percentage of women legislators before term limits. Maine and Michigan, both early implementers of term limits, had more women in their chambers in 1992 than in 2012, after fully implementing term limits. Hence, the effects of term limits appear mixed.

The number of white men who represent majority-minority legislative districts has also been attributed to incumbent advantages. Most observers assumed that minority candidates could win these seats without the "drag of incumbency" (Thompson and Moncrief 1993). But evidence that more open seats resolve this is equivocal. Five of the seven states nationally in 2009 in which African-Americans were "overrepresented" (i.e., the proportion of state legislative seats held by minority legislators exceeds their share of the population) also have term limits.[2] Yet other term-limited states are among those in which African-Americans are most severely underrepresented, according to data compiled by the group All Other Persons (2013).[3] Such mixed evidence lends little support to the notion that term limits *cause* minority group members to gain legislative seats (Caress and Kunioka 2012). The confounding influence of district boundaries on the electoral fortunes of ethnic minority legislators makes it very hard to isolate the effects of term limits.

Although we consider both gender and ethnic diversity equally important, we spend more time in this chapter and throughout the book discussing and analyzing gender rather than ethnic diversity. This is a function of available data and the complications introduced by gerrymandered districts. The Michigan Secretary of State's office does not list gender or ethnicity for candidates seeking office, but first names reveal the gender of most candidates. Gerrymandering has fewer implications for the electoral fortunes of women, because they are residentially integrated with men, making it impossible to pack them into a few legislative districts. Partisan map drawing can have some impact on the gender diversity, however, if one political party is more or less likely to field female candidates—which is indeed the case.

In 80 percent of state legislatures nationally Democratic women outnumber Republican women (Lawless and Fox 2005, 78). Consistent with this national trend, most of Michigan's women legislators are Democrats.[4] This disparity alerts us to potential partisan differences in the effect of term limits on diversity. Therefore, we consider the two major parties separately in some analyses in this chapter and elsewhere in this book.

Term Limits and the Gender Composition of Michigan's Legislature

Considerable evidence demonstrates that during the transition to term limits gender diversity increases in upper chambers of state legislatures

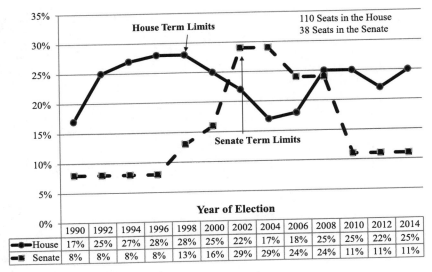

Fig. 2.1. Women in Michigan's Legislature by Chamber

	1990	1992	1994	1996	1998	2000	2002	2004	2006	2008	2010	2012	2014
House	17%	25%	27%	28%	28%	25%	22%	17%	18%	25%	25%	22%	25%
Senate	8%	8%	8%	8%	13%	16%	29%	29%	24%	24%	11%	11%	11%

as some women expelled from lower chambers migrate to open seats in upper chambers. Gains such as these are ephemeral, however, unless there is a steady supply of women entering the lower chamber (Carroll and Jenkins 2001a; Bernstein and Chadha 2003; Schraufnagel and Halperin 2006). Given that several states are still in what Mooney (2009) calls the transition to term limits, it is impossible to assess the national impact of term limits on the gender of state legislators. Michigan, however, has fully implemented term limits and, as figure 2.1 illustrates, the larger number of women initially elected to its legislature during the transition to term limits was indeed an ephemeral change.

This is particularly apparent in the Michigan Senate in 2002 when a wave of open seats provided opportunities for female House veterans termed out of that chamber to run for state senate seats. But, as Bernstein and Chadha (2003) predict, without a "conveyor belt" of local political experience and targeted recruiting efforts to move women into the lower chamber, the surge of women moving into upper chambers receded in Michigan. The number of post-term-limits women senators in Michigan declined almost to the pre-term-limits level by 2010, remaining there through 2015.

After term limits, Michigan appears to have had trouble replacing the women termed from the House to maintain women's marginal share of

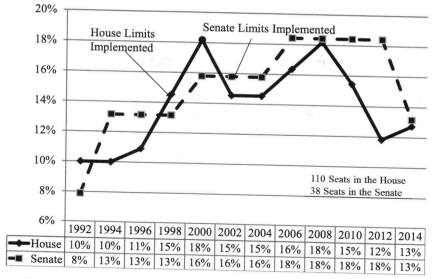

Fig. 2.2. Michigan's Ethnic Minority Group Legislators

seats there, let alone expand their representation. In 2014 the number of women elected to Michigan's House was identical to the number in 1992, the year voters passed term limits, and below the level in 1998, the year term limits were implemented.

Just as we saw with the election of women during the transition to term limits, gains for ethnic minority legislators are fleeting in Michigan. As figure 2.2 demonstrates, the proportion of ethnic minority senators increased to 18 percent shortly after term limits expelled Senate veterans, but fell back to its pre-term-limits level of 13 percent in 2014. Most of this increase in ethnic minority senators occurred in the Democratic Party. Despite declines in the number of Democrats in the Senate, in the 2012 election ethnic minority legislators won a majority of the seats held by the 12-member Senate Democratic caucus, which included 6 African American men and 1 Asian American man. But we see in figure 2.2 a decline in the proportion of ethnic minority legislators the House after 2009. Without a pool of ethnic minority representatives to draw from, it appears that it was only a matter of time before the proportion of ethnic minority senators declined as well.

But, as we noted earlier, one cannot ignore the effects of gerrymandering when considering the electoral fortunes of minority group legislators in Michigan. District maps after both the 2000 and 2010 census were drawn exclusively by Republicans, who packed minority voters, most of whom vote for Democrats in Michigan, into fewer districts. Although Michigan voters have elected minority legislators from districts in which minority group members do not constitute a majority,[5] this phenomenon remains rare. The number of ethnic minority legislators in Michigan's legislature depends heavily on the district boundaries, with or without term limits.

Substantial evidence demonstrates that removing the drag of incumbency is not a silver bullet destined to diversify state legislatures in general (Caress and Kunioka 2012; Carey et al. 2006) or as we find here in Michigan. Compositional changes in Michigan tilt slightly toward increasing the number of white men holding seats. If this constitutes a new breed, then it is more homogenous, not more diverse.

Although district lines explain much of the decline in Michigan's ethnic minority legislators, we wondered why women have lost ground in Michigan's legislature with the full implementation of term limits. Are they sitting on the sidelines or are they losing more of the contests that they enter?

Women Running in Michigan's Elections

As many scholars point out, if women are going to win elections they have to run (see, recently, Lawless and Fox 2013), and primary elections are the first hurdle in the race. We explore women's participation in primary and general elections from 1988 to 2012 using data available through the Michigan Secretary of State's office to see whether women's participation in primary contests explains their electoral misfortune after term limits. We have no way to determine candidates' skin color or ethnic heritage in Michigan's elections data, so we analyze gender only.[6] Additionally, we focus on House seats because these biannual elections are numerous enough to reveal more stable patterns, and term limits in Michigan's House are more fully implemented. The Senate is just barely beyond the transition to term limits.

Term limits were especially devastating for Republican women in Michigan's lower chamber, so we consider the two major political parties separately here. At one point there were only four Republican women in Michigan's lower chamber—down from a high of 12 before term limits. Democratic women began the term limits era at 17 representatives and have yet to fall below 13, even rising briefly to 22 in 2010. The partisan gap persists, with 17 Democratic women and 10 Republican women in the House in 2016, but it is less pronounced currently than it was for a few years immediately after the implementation of term limits in Michigan.

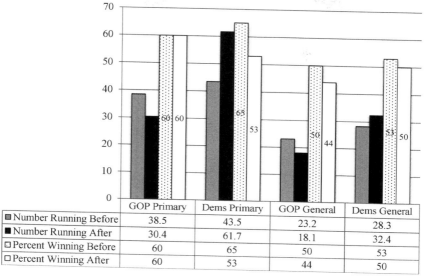

	GOP Primary	Dems Primary	GOP General	Dems General
■ Number Running Before	38.5	43.5	23.2	28.3
■ Number Running After	30.4	61.7	18.1	32.4
□ Percent Winning Before	60	65	50	53
□ Percent Winning After	60	53	44	50

Fig. 2.3. Michigan House Primary Participation and General Election Success Rate of Women

Part of the difference in women's electoral fortunes arises from their participation in primary elections. Although the number of women throwing their hats into the ring differs by party before and after term limits, a moderate pre-term-limits difference (averaging 39 women per primary election cycle for Republicans and 44 for Democrats) expands after term limits to a twofold advantage for Democratic women entering primary election contests. Looking at figure 2.3, we see that a plunge in Republican women running in primary elections for state house seats after term limits corresponds to their dwindling ranks in the legislature. Before term limits Republican women competed in an average of 23 percent of general elections for House seats. After term limits, this falls to 18 percent. The primary success rate for Republican women is unchanged, however—60 percent before and after term limits. But after term limits this is 60 percent of the smaller cohort of Republican women who run in the primaries. Thus, fewer Republican women advance to the general election contests after term limits.

Not only do fewer Republican women compete in general election contests after term limits (about five fewer), they are less likely to win. Republican women only win 44 percent of the seats for which they compete after term limits, compared to a general election victory rate of 50 percent before term limits. The result is far fewer Republican women serving in the Michigan House after term limits.

Lack of participation does not explain the problems Democratic women face. More Democratic women enter House primary competitions after term limits—about 18 more per primary election cycle. The problem for Democratic women is losing elections. Democratic women win only 53 percent of their primary contests after term limits, a decline of 12 percent. But their primary losses are only part of the story. Some of this large decline in primary victories arises ironically from their increased participation, because more Democratic women compete against each other after term limits. And because they enter more primary contests, Democratic women compete in about four more post-term-limits general contests. But after term limits, Democratic women's general election success rate declines by 3 percent. Thus, Democratic women are less likely to win elections after term limits.

Prior to term limits, women in both political parties won general election contests at a slightly higher rate than their party as a whole. This fed the assumption that more open seat elections would help women win more seats. After term limits, Republican women's general election success rate is not only lower than the rate for Republican women before term limits, but lower than that of their party as a whole (44% compared to 51% for the party). Democratic women win seats at a rate nearly identical to their party as a whole (50% compared to 49% for the party), but Democrats won fewer elections after term limits, and Democratic women are no exception to this trend. This reveals that women are not more likely to win general elections without the friction of incumbency. Indeed, they win less often than they did previously.

One factor that might explain women's electoral success rate (or lack thereof) is a phenomenon called sacrificial lambs—candidates who represent their party in general election contests that they stand virtually no chance of winning due to the partisan composition of the district. These are not viable candidates. Evidence from our own research and others (Carroll 1994) suggests that some candidates, often Republican women, run as sacrificial lambs. If women are running for seats that a member of their party is almost certain to lose, it might explain their unexpectedly low success rate in the wake of a flood of open seats due to term limits.

We use a stringent criterion to classify a candidate as a sacrificial lamb—winning less than 20 percent of the vote. In other words, our definition of a sacrificial lamb is a candidate whose opponent won in a landslide of more than 80 percent of the ballots cast. Using this criterion, it is extremely rare for Democratic women to run as sacrificial lambs either before or after term limits. For Republican women, however, the number of sacrificial lambs is still three or four per general election cycle after term limits, falling only slightly from about five per election cycle before term limits. Limiting our analyses to viable candidates only strengthens our findings. When we exclude sacrificial lambs from our calculations, we find that 65 percent of viable Republican women were victorious prior to term limits while 55 percent of them win after term limits. Viable Democratic women emerged victorious 55 percent of the time before term limits, but only 50 percent afterward.

Thus we conclude that Republican women's lack of participation as well as their losses in general elections led to a decline in their ranks despite the success of their political party in controlling the House more often after term limits. Due to their surge in primary participation, Democratic women managed to maintain their pre-term-limits share of the chamber's seats despite losing general elections a little more often in a political climate and with district maps that favor Republicans.

Removing the drag of incumbency does not appear to help women win more seats in Michigan's legislature. This could arise from changes in the "conveyor belt" cultivating quality candidates for office when the need for them increases dramatically. To understand these dynamics more fully, we consider next whether candidate recruiting has changed overall and then we consider differences in recruiting by gender, ethnicity, and political party.

Reasons for Running

When we interviewed legislators, we began by asking about their reasons for seeking office, whether they were asked to run and by whom.[7] We concluded the interview by asking what they planned to do next. We prompted for plans to run for other elected offices if they did not volunteer this. We asked this question at the end of each interview to see whether political ambition increases among lame ducks or dissipates as freshmen confront the reality of being a legislator. (See questions 1 and 2 and 26 in appendix A.) We analyze responses to these open-ended questions in the remainder of this chapter, beginning with candidate recruitment.

Recruiting Candidates

The assumption that large numbers of seats that open on a predictable cycle will automatically attract candidates, especially quality candidates, is not borne out by Michigan's experience with term limits.[8] According to mem-

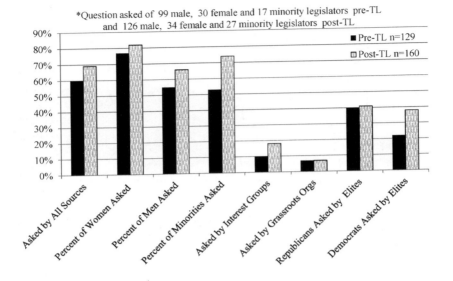

Fig. 2.4. Recruiting before and after Term Limits

bers of the State Officers Compensation Commission (personal conversation), term limits and the difficulties it produced in attracting candidates was one reason they approved a 35.8 percent pay increase for legislators in December 2000, just two years after Michigan expelled the first crop of veterans from the House (Citizen's Research Council 2002). If it is hard to attract candidates even when they are already among the best paid legislators in the nation, then a flood of open seats probably exacerbates the need to recruit more candidates to fill them. And indeed that is what we find.

The proportion of our respondents who say someone asked them to run increases by 8 percent after term limits, an increase that is statistically significant ($p < 0.10$). Consistent with this, some party leaders told us that they had a hard time finding high-quality candidates for some open seats. In a state with such stringent limits on service, persistent waves of open seats appear to increase the need to recruit candidates, as we illustrate in figure 2.4.

Who Is Recruited?

Fox and Lawless (2005) report that women and African Americans are 15 percent less likely than comparably qualified white men to express nascent political ambition—that is, to say that they have considered running for any elected office, including local offices such as school board member. So recruiting is likely to matter more for women and ethnic minority group members. With the post-term-limits increase in recruiting that we see in figure 2.4, the opportunity provided to diversify state legislatures might be realized by concerted efforts to recruit candidates from underrepresented groups.

After term limits, the proportion of winning candidates who say they were recruited increases for all groups: men, women, white, and minority, but these differences are statistically significant only for men. Although it is still true that a larger proportion of the legislature's women than its men are recruited, this gender gap shrinks from a 22 percent difference before term limits to 16 percent afterward. More of the post-term-limits increase in recruiting targets men, not women. On the other hand, a much larger proportion of ethnic minority candidates is recruited after term limits—21 percent more. With few minority candidates among our respondents (44 total), we caution readers that percentages magnify small absolute changes, and this change is not statistically significant, reflecting the small number of cases involved.

The message is clear, however. Recruiting is increasingly important after term limits, but its potential to diversify the Michigan legislature is compromised if the recruiting efforts target the most overrepresented group—white men—which is what we find. Although we do not show white men separately in figure 2.4, the proportion of them who say they were recruited rises by 5 percent after term limits, compared to a 3 percent increase for white women. So we find that men in general, but white men in particular, benefit more than women do from recruiting after term limits—at least among winning candidates.

Who Does the Recruiting?

Term limits provide an opportunity to see who does more recruiting when a flood of open seats increases the demand for candidates. In this section, we examine who asked our respondents to run. We consider this important because it may reflect close ties between legislators and other actors in the political environment, and these sources of influence could change with term limits. We are especially interested in recruiting by interest groups given the claims term limits advocates made about attenuating these ties.

One caveat is important to note. Financial support tends to increase the likelihood that candidates win elections, particularly in expensive races.

Candidates that interest groups or party elites recruit are likely to have more money than their opponents. Therefore, they are more likely to win. Given that we are interviewing sitting legislators (i.e., winners only), our respondents might overrepresent the proportion of all candidates recruited by these actors. Additionally, we note that we classify all groups with economic clout, labor unions and chambers of commerce, specific businesses or professional associations, as interest groups. We distinguish these well-heeled groups from *grassroots organizations*, which we reserve for neighborhood groups and others that lack substantial financial resources. But we recognize that these groups can seek special treatment, too.

Candidate Recruiting by Interest Groups

Lack of money can be a major obstacle for prospective candidates, especially when elections are expensive. We demonstrate elsewhere that Michigan's elections for legislative seats became more expensive after term limits and that interest groups are an important source of campaign funds (Sarbaugh-Thompson et al. 2002).[9] Apollonio and La Raja (2006) argue that interest groups engage in vote buying (postelection donations to winning candidates serving on committees relevant to the group) rather than simply donating to like-minded candidates. If groups convince candidates who share their views to run by offering to support them, it melds these two approaches.

We find that interest groups are more heavily involved in candidate recruiting after term limits, with 6 percent more of our respondents saying that one of these groups recruited them.[10] This implies that the deep pockets of many interest groups enable them to persuade their preferred candidates to seek office. Examining this more closely we find that women are the chief beneficiaries of this increased interest group involvement. Prior to term limits, only 10 percent of women serving in Michigan's legislature[11] say that any of a wide variety of interest groups (e.g., business groups, labor unions, law enforcement or education associations) asked them to run for office. After term limits, this increases to 27 percent of Michigan's sitting female legislators. The corresponding increase for men is only 3 percent. Interest groups do not appear to be more involved in recruiting minority legislators after term limits, at least not among winning candidates.

This gender difference might, as Jenkins (2007) argues, arise from the challenges women face in funding their campaigns. It appears that women more than men worry about raising the large sums needed to run a winning campaign (Witt, Paget, and Matthews 1994). Jenkins (2007) finds that women are more likely than men to say both labor unions and other interest groups were very or extremely helpful with fundraising, while men are more likely than women to say these groups were not at all helpful. The confluence between women's evaluation of interest group fundraising support and the level of concern women express about fundraising provides a credible reason why these groups could be persuasive recruiters of women.

We thought that perhaps interest groups concentrated their recruiting efforts on legislators already in the House considering a move to the Senate. This is plausible because legislators who were interest group allies in the lower chamber might be asked by these groups to consider running for the upper chamber. And this was the pattern before term limits (only 10% of representatives compared to 18% of senators were recruited by interest groups before term limits).

We find, however, that after term limits the so-called "cozy" relationships with interest groups are more likely to arise *before* the legislator reaches the "corrupting atmosphere" of the state capital. After term limits 18 percent of representatives say that interest groups asked them to run, while there is a slight post-term-limits decline of 2 percent in the proportion of our Senate respondents who say interest groups asked them to run for the upper chamber. This 8 percent increase in the House is statistically significant ($p < 0.10$). This is important because term limits advocates claimed that limiting tenure would sever cozy ties with special interests. The pattern of interest group recruiting we find does not support this claim. Indeed, it indicates the opposite. After term limits representatives are more likely to arrive in the state capital with ties to these outside interests.

Recruiting by Grassroots Groups

Grassroots organizations (e.g., citizen groups or community organizations) tend to recruit candidates from underrepresented groups. Only 30 percent of the candidates these groups recruit are white men. The proportion of our respondents saying that these groups recruited them increases by only 2 percent after term limits, however. In the context of an 8 percent increase in recruiting overall, grassroots organizations become smaller players, muting the potential they have to diversify the chambers.

Recruiting by Party Elites

Endorsements from party elites are valuable in elections (Dominguez 2011), so their support could persuade a candidate to throw his or her hat into the ring. Political parties can offer money, and so may be just as persuasive as interest groups in convincing candidates to run. Additionally, legislators serving their final term might recruit someone who could maintain ideological and issue continuity for the district, such as a staff member or family member. Among our respondents 28 percent of Republicans and 19 percent of Democrats said that a current or former state legislator specifically recruited them.

We see readily in figure 2.4 that recruiting by party elites has always been important, but the proportion of legislators recruited by these actors increases after term limits (sig. $p < 0.10$). Although we did not include the chamber breakdown in figure 2.4, recruiting by party elites is more common overall in the Senate than in the House, and the overall chamber difference is large enough to be statistically significant (sig. $p < 0.10$). Proportions before term limits are 27 percent in the House and 41 percent in the Senate, increasing to 37 percent in the House and 52 percent in the Senate afterward. This is a statistically significant increase in recruiting by party elites for House seats (sig. $p < 0.10$).

Partisan Facets of Candidate Recruiting

Prior to term limits, Republicans were much more active than Democrats in candidate recruiting. There are two plausible reasons for this. First, evidence shows that Democrats view the role of government more positively than do Republicans (Pew 2013). Consequently, the argument goes, there is less need to convince Democrats that they should run for office. They are more likely to be self-starters—as we found earlier in this chapter when looking at primary participation of Republican and Democratic women. So, Republican aversion to government may create a greater need for recruiting.

Second, before term limits more Democrats made state legislative service a career, serving longer than Republicans. Lower turnover meant less need to recruit Democrats. Term limits changed this in Michigan. Given that limiting tenure increases turnover more for Democrats than Republicans, it is reasonable that the two parties respond differently.

As we see in figure 2.5, Democratic Party elites ramped up their recruiting game after term limits. Before term limits, nearly twice the proportion of Republicans as Democrats said that party elites recruited them. This disparity nearly vanishes after term limits due to a 16 percent increase (sig. $p < 0.05$) in Democrats saying that party elites recruited them.[12]

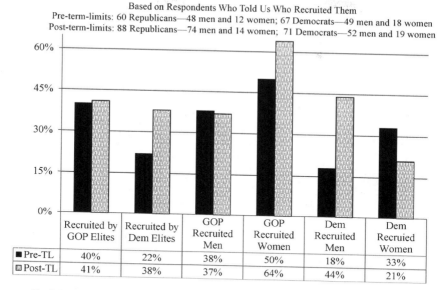

Based on Respondents Who Told Us Who Recruited Them
Pre-term-limits: 60 Republicans—48 men and 12 women; 67 Democrats—49 men and 18 women
Post-term-limits: 88 Republicans—74 men and 14 women; 71 Democrats—52 men and 19 women

	Recruited by GOP Elites	Recruited by Dem Elites	GOP Recruited Men	GOP Recruited Women	Dem Recruited Men	Dem Recruied Women
■ Pre-TL	40%	22%	38%	50%	18%	33%
▨ Post-TL	41%	38%	37%	64%	44%	21%

Fig. 2.5. Recruiting by Political Elites for Each Party by Gender

But we also see in figure 2.5 that much of the increased recruiting by Democratic Party elites targets men, not women. Indeed, the proportion of women recruited by Democratic Party elites falls after term limits. This might be another incumbency advantage that persists even after incumbents depart if white men recruit other white men to fill their shoes. The resulting post-term-limits gender gap (sig. $p < 0.10$) between Democratic men (44%) and Democratic women (21%) supports evidence from Sanbonmatsu (2002) and Lawless and Fox (2005) about a male recruiting bias within the Democratic Party. Prior to term limits this was not the pattern in Michigan, however. Although there was a 15 percent gender gap in recruiting before term limits, it favored Democratic women. This substantial shift coincides with the implementation of term limits.

Party Elites and Recruiting Ethnic Minorities

Minority group members appear to receive even less attention than women from elites in the Democratic Party. Before term limits skin color did not affect the proportion of legislators who said party elites recruited them. After term limits the proportion of white legislators recruited by party elites increases—by 11 percent. So here, too, the dominant group is recruited more heavily after term limits. Given that nearly all minority legislators are Democrats, a partisan comparison is not feasible. There were only three ethnic minority legislators in the Republican Party during our entire 13-year investigation. All three say they were recruited by party elites, however.

Summary of Candidate Recruiting

We find that recruiting is increasingly important after term limits. Republicans still appear to do more recruiting in general than Democrats do—at least we can say with certainty that they recruit more candidates who win. But Democrats are catching up after term limits, seemingly motivated by the need to find quality candidates to run for a steady stream of open seats. But after term limits, recruiting by Democratic Party elites focuses on men. This bodes poorly for increasing diversity in Michigan's legislature because the Democratic Party in Michigan, as well as nationally, has more underrepresented group members from which it can solicit candidates. Despite increased attention in the Republican Party on recruiting women and ethnic minorities, the small pool of underrepresented groups in their party constrains its impact.[13] We conclude that merely increasing the number of open seats does not diversify state legislatures. Rather, choices about which prospective candidates to recruit mediate the effect of open seats.

Interest groups appear to concentrate their recruiting on women, while grassroots organizations recruit both women and ethnic minority legislators. These efforts have some potential to ameliorate the homogenizing effects of recruiting by party elites. But how does this comport with term limits advocates' claims that purging entrenched incumbents would sever "cozy relationships" between legislators and special interests? Increased interest group recruiting challenges this assertion and raises questions about the motives of these legislators, a question we address next.

What Motivates Legislators to Seek Office?

Term limits advocates claimed that limiting time in office would attract "citizen legislators" motivated by public service. This extension of ambition theory (Schlesinger 1966; Ehrenhalt 1992; Fiorina 1996) implies that, by changing the electoral opportunity structure, term limits alter the incentives motivating candidates to seek office. As we noted earlier, we open our interviews by asking our respondents, "When you first ran for the [*chamber*], what were your reasons for running?" Replies were open-ended, and many respondents provided more than one reason. We coded their comments into 50 detailed categories, several of which overlap, so we combine them into broader themes to facilitate analysis.

The same five themes surface most often before and after term limits. They are *a career path in politics* at 52 percent (including a natural progression to higher office and variations on that theme); to *make a difference* at 46 percent (including public service and variations on that theme); an *opportunity* at 43 percent (including an open seat); *issues* at 37 percent (issues in general and any of several specific issues); and the candidate's positive assessment of his or her *personal qualifications* at 36 percent (e.g., I'm the most knowledgeable candidate, I have a unique background). This consistency indicates that term limits have little or no effect on candidates' reasons for seeking office.

We find one reason for seeking office among our respondents that differs substantially before and after term limits, although it was not among the top five themes. Post-term-limits legislators' sole distinguishing characteristic is that they are more likely than their predecessors to have served their community in some way (6% before and 15% after term limits, sig. at $p = 0.01$). Local service seems to be part of the post-term-limits conveyor belt producing a pool of candidates who are then targeted by various recruiters.

Thus, we find that pre- and post-term-limits legislators not only look alike, but they are inspired by similar objectives. In this we support conclusions of other scholars (Carey et al. 2006, for example) that term limits do not produce a distinctive "new breed" of legislator motivated to seek office by different incentives. There is one caveat, however, that we explore below. Some differences in men's and women's reasons for running diminish after term limits.

Do Open Seats Motivate Candidates to Run for State Legislature?

There is widespread acceptance that the "drag of incumbency" depresses the candidacy of women (Darcy, Welch, and Clark 1994). But the argument that waves of open seats wrought by term limits will motivate more women to seek office fails to recognize that when open seats are rare, they may have different effects than when they are plentiful. As figure 2.6 illustrates, we do not find that open seats in Michigan motivate women to run

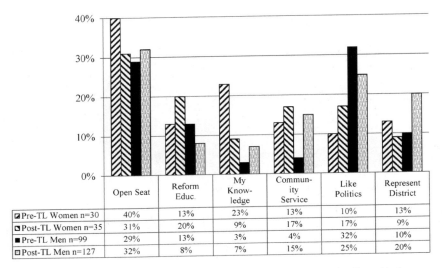

	Open Seat	Reform Educ.	My Know-ledge	Commun-ity Service	Like Politics	Represent District
☑ Pre-TL Women n=30	40%	13%	23%	13%	10%	13%
◪ Post-TL Women n=35	31%	20%	9%	17%	17%	9%
■ Pre-TL Men n=99	29%	13%	3%	4%	32%	10%
☐ Post-TL Men n=127	32%	8%	7%	15%	25%	20%

Fig. 2.6. Gender Differences in Reasons for Running before and after Term Limits

for office after term limits. Although the difference is not statistically significant, the proportion of women who say an open seat motivated them to run declines by 9 percent after term limits, rather than increasing. The proportion of men motivated by an open seat is nearly constant.

The predictable cycle of open seats under term limits could permit women, as well as men, to fit their political ambition around their other roles, such as a career or parenting. If a prospective candidate knows that a seat will be open again in six years, it might be easier to wait until one's children are older before running for office. But when it is unlikely that a seat will open again for decades, a candidate might want to seize the rare opportunity to pursue an open seat regardless of competing priorities. So we speculate that the pull of an open seat declines when it recurs frequently.

Reasons for Running

Descriptive representation matters more if there is evidence that gender or ethnicity make a difference in legislators' behaviors and motivation to hold office. Thus we compare here the motives of men and women and also minority legislators. Nationally and in other states, there is ample evidence that women legislators have different policy priorities and goals and approach their job differently (Thomas 1992; Richardson and Freeman 1995; Kathlene 1994, 1995; Swers 1998; Reingold 2000; and Bratton 2005, among many others). Socialization is often credited with producing these gender differences. For example, recent evidence (Lawless and Fox 2013) demonstrates that life and family experiences, such as playing on high school sports teams, are associated with a woman's willingness to run for elected office. Frequently discussed gender differences include women's alleged lack of interest in politics, lower nascent political ambition, different professional and political experience, and greater family responsibilities (see Dolan et al. 2007 for a cogent summary of these).

Given the persistence and ubiquity of these differences in society, we were surprised to find that some gender differences diminished among our respondents after term limits. In short, referring again to figure 2.6, post-term-limits male legislators' reasons for running resemble women's reasons more closely than they do their male predecessors. For example, after term limits a much higher proportion of men ran because of their community experience. Before term limits this was a characteristic that differentiated women and men. Our findings do not discount gender differences many other scholars find in the general population in terms of interest in politics and in nascent political ambition. They do suggest, however, that among the small subset of people who run for state legislative seats, these gender differences are waning.

To make sense of this we speculate that post-term-limits legislators' gender socialization differs from their predecessors. One possible source of this variation involves a slight change in the age of post-term-limits male legislators. Before term limits, the average age for male legislators was 49.2 years while for women it was 50.4 years—virtually identical. After term limits the average age for men is 46.6, younger than the average for women—51.3 (but not quite sig. at $p < 0.12$).[14] Although this might seem like a very small change, it could affect the socialization of post-term-limits men. If changes in gender roles alter the reasons men seek public office, term limits might indirectly reduce gender differences by attracting younger male legislators.

But not all these changes involve shifts in men's motivation—women change too, resembling men more than they did before term limits. Pre-term-limits women were especially confident in their capabilities, specifically about their superior knowledge. This is consistent with the work of Sanbonmatsu (2006), who finds that women who decide to compete in an election see themselves as uniquely qualified to run. This distinction evaporates after term limits, with neither women nor men especially likely to say their superior knowledge motivated them to seek office.

Although we find some evidence that gender differences in the motivation to seek office narrow, this trend should not be overstated. Two new gender differences surface among our post-term-limits respondents. First, men are more likely and women are less likely to say they ran to represent the district after term limits. They were quite similar in this respect before term limits.

Second, post-term-limits women are statistically significantly more likely than men to say that they ran to do something about the issue of education. Before term limits there was no gender difference on this issue. We looked at several specific issues and also combined all issues to hunt for gender differences. Although there is ample scholarly evidence that women focus more on issues while in office, we find that only this one issue—reforming education—motivated more women than men to run for office.

Differences in Minority Legislators' Motivation for Seeking Office

Minority legislators often represent more constituents who are poor, disenfranchised, or disadvantaged politically. Therefore, they may feel a greater need to give voice to the needs and concerns of their voters (Burden 2007; Mansbridge 1999). We find evidence of this. More than half (58%) of minority legislators say they ran to make a difference and 36 percent say they ran to represent the district. Among white respondents 44 percent and 11 percent provide these reasons, respectively. These reasons distinguish ethnic minority legislators with or without term limits.

Ethnic minority legislators' only other distinctive characteristic is their modesty. They are less likely to consider themselves especially well qualified for elective office (24% compared to 38% of white respondents). And this confidence gap expands after term limits with 21 percent of minority legislators listing their personal qualifications as a reason they ran—compared to 40 percent of white respondents.

Political Ambition

Various advocates envisioned term limits as a prescription for an idealized citizen legislature (see Will 1992, for example). This image was widely popularized by media outlets and pundits during term limits ballot campaigns. Niven (2000) summarizes these headlines, which assert that ordinary citizens will serve briefly and then return to their community to live under the laws they passed. We test this tenet of term limits rhetoric using our respondents' comments about their reasons for running and about their

Size of Cohort Appears Above Each Bar

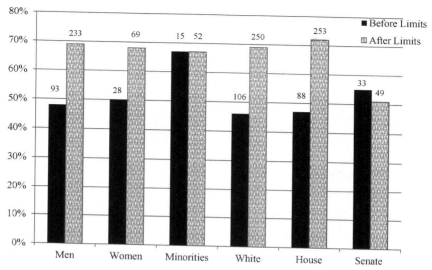

Fig. 2.7. Political Ambition

career plans after they are termed from office. Roughly half of our respondents said that the reason they ran for state legislature was as a stepping-stone on their political career path, often volunteering that "it was the next logical career move for me" (interview notes).

Thus, contrary to predictions of pundits and term limits advocates alike, we find that after term limits more of Michigan's legislators are politically ambitious. The increase is large (20%) and statistically significant ($p < 0.01$). As figure 2.7 shows, term limits increase political ambition in both genders about equally. There is no effect on the political ambition of minority legislators, a larger proportion of whom were already politically ambitious. After term limits, the rest of the chamber catches up to them.

Most of the increase in political ambition occurs in the lower chamber. Roughly the same proportion of newcomers and lame ducks in the House express political ambition before term limits (52% of both lame ducks and newcomers). The political ambition of both cohorts increases similarly after term limits (69% of lame ducks and 68% of newcomers). So not only do most lame ducks hope to continue their political careers, this desire increases after term limits. Tenure in the lower chamber does not appear to sate legislators' ambition, particularly not after term limits. Moreover, we find that more House newcomers arrive after term limits planning to run for another office. A move to the upper chamber is a popular rung on representatives' political career ladders. So too are positions in local government (e.g., large city mayors and county commission seats), and positions in the judicial branch (Michigan elects all its judges), as well as statewide offices and congressional seats—and these are usually not term limited.

This increase in political ambition is the most distinctive characteristic of the new breed of term-limited legislator. Most of them do not aspire to be citizen legislators. On the contrary, they seek a career in politics, and they arrive in the state capital with plans for how to accomplish this. This fundamentally alters Michigan's legislature, making it into a springboard that elected representatives use to reach the next rung on their career ladder. This political ambition will prove an important predictor of their behavior in coming chapters.

Lame Ducks and Newcomers

One of the obvious changes accompanying stringent term limits is higher turnover. This produces waves of newcomers, and these freshman legislators have attracted a lot of attention (Arceneaux 2001; Berman 2004; and Richardson, Valentine, and Stokes 2005, among others). Term-limited freshmen, however, strongly resemble other freshmen except that there are more of them. Their distinctive characteristic is that they are inexperienced, and they need to learn the ropes. We so rarely find any other newcomer effects in the subsequent chapters that we often exclude them from our analyses.

But every newcomer corresponds to a lame duck, and term-limited lame ducks are a unique breed. Typically the status of lame ducks is not known until they announce their planned retirement or lose an election. Often this happens near the end of their final term. With term limits, lame ducks are known as such from the minute they win their seat in their final permitted term of service. They and everyone else know this for the entire duration of that term. That is to say, post-term-limits lame ducks are fundamentally different from pre-term-limits lame ducks.

We argue that term-limited lame ducks provide an opportunity to see what happens when the electoral connection is severed early and publicly. Do lame ducks shirk? Are they shunted to the side? To examine this, we investigate the effects of being a lame duck on legislators' behaviors and perceptions of their job throughout the rest of the book. We find, as we report in coming chapters, that they are often shunted to the side, but they only occasionally engage in shirking.

Conclusions

The most profound difference between the new and old breeds of legislator is their political ambition. Term limits appear to transform legislative service in Michigan from a political career to a stepping-stone on a political career path. Many term-limited legislators do not even stay in the House for their full six-year allotment, choosing instead to run for the state senate if a seat opens there. State senate elections are held every four years in Michigan, and representatives who will be termed out in the middle of a state senate election cycle often leave the House early to avoid waiting for two years until the next Senate election. But, as we noted earlier, there are many other tantalizing local, statewide, and national political opportunities in Michigan.

Political ambition is important because it could alter the behavior of state legislators. Legislators with one eye on their next office may consider their future ambitions when they decide how to vote on issues and how to allocate their time among the competing demands of a state legislator. We explore this and other possible effects of political ambition more thoroughly in coming chapters.

Term limits are not just about expelling veteran legislators, but also about selecting new ones. The "new breed" of post-term-limits legislator is more likely to have been asked to run for office. Finding an adequate supply of quality candidates appears to require some sort of "conveyor belt" to groom a pool of quality candidates, some of whom are then asked to seek state legislative office. Not only is candidate recruiting more common after term limits, it is driven by different groups.

Although partisan elites recruit the largest share of winning candidates, we find that recruiting by interest groups is next, especially for women. This is an intriguing difference between pre- and post-term-limits women serving in Michigan's legislature—the new breed of woman legislator is more likely to arrive with ties to an interest group.

It is also important to mention that the role of interest groups in recruiting candidates, male or female, is much larger in the House than in the Senate—indicating that first-time candidates rather than experienced legislators moving to higher office provide more fertile ground for interest group recruiting efforts. Given the strong term limits rhetoric about attenuating cozy relationships between elected officials and special interests, this expanded role for interest groups is clearly an unintended consequence of limiting tenure in office. Given its prominence in the rhetoric selling term limits, we return to legislators' relationships with interest groups at several points in this book.

We find that grassroots community organizations maintain their role in recruiting legislators from underrepresented groups. The efforts of these groups offer the greatest hope for increasing diversity among Michigan's state legislators. However, as other actors (e.g., interest groups and party elites) expand their recruiting, grassroots groups become proportionately smaller players. Thus, their ability to change of the composition of Michigan's legislature diminished with term limits.

Historically, Republicans outperformed Democrats in candidate recruiting. Prior to term limits Democrats had less need to recruit candidates. There were two reasons for this. First, Democrats are more likely to be self-starters than are Republicans. Second, before term limits Democrats served longer than Republicans so turnover in their ranks was lower. Recruiting by Democrats increases substantially after term limits—nearly reaching the same level as Republicans. But it is mainly men in the Democratic Party who are the beneficiaries of this added effort. Hence, the post-term-limits bias among Democratic Party elites toward recruiting men undermines the opportunities that open seats provide to diversify the chambers.

But recruiting only partially explains the failure of women to make gains in Michigan's legislature. After term limits, women win seats in Michigan's legislature at a lower rate than they did before term limits. Removing the drag of incumbency does not improve their electoral fortunes. Indeed, in Michigan sometimes men replace women who were termed out of office, and occasionally white legislators replace minority legislators. The latter is especially true if minority legislators serve in districts in which their minority group is also a minority among the district's voters,[15] but this happens in so called majority-minority districts too.[16]

Finally, we stress that lame ducks in a term-limited legislature occupy a unique position in which everyone knows during their entire final term that they will not return. This could lead them to shirk, or it could encourage colleagues to shun them—passing them over for valuable committee assignments, for example. In a legislature short of experience, this treatment of its most experienced veterans (aka lame ducks) has the potential to produce profound effects. Therefore, we examine the role of lame ducks throughout the remainder of the book.

We establish that term limits effects on descriptive representation in Michigan's legislature are at best a slight increase in ethnic minority legislators, a decrease in women, and a very small decrease (2.5 years) in the age of male legislators. Legislators are generally motivated to run for similar reasons, with a few possible gender differences after term limits. Therefore, we conclude that the new breed in Michigan looks a lot like the old breed. In this assessment we concur with others (Carey et al. 2006; Caress and Kunioka 2012). The major compositional changes we find are the increase in political ambition, the prevalence of recruiting, and changing nature of lame ducks' final term of service. We explore in coming chapters whether these characteristics of this "new breed" of term-limited legislator are associated with other changes in Michigan's legislature.

THREE

Legislative Representation

A fundamental tenet of representative democracy is that elected officials represent their constituents. Although this sounds simple, it is hard if these constituents happen to be a diverse lot whose preferences conflict. Legislators cope with this dilemma by relying on, in their words, "conscience, constituents and caucus" (interview notes). They do this while being largely oblivious to the enduring debate about representation among political thinkers from Edmund Burke (1790) to Hannah Pitkin (1967),[1] including present-day scholars, who continue to extend and nuance the complexities of political representation (Mansbridge 2003; Guinier 2008; Rehfeld 2009). In this chapter, we add the voices of Michigan's legislators to this discussion.

In chapter 2 we considered term limits effects on descriptive representation—that is, the physical similarity between constituents and their representatives. There we found that the new breed of term-limited legislator resembles the state's voters **less**, not more. From this we infer that term limits decrease descriptive representation, particularly for women. But there are other ways to assess representation. In this chapter we explore two of these—representational roles and roll call votes.

The first of these, a legislator's orientation toward *representational roles*, quantifies how legislators balance two conflicts: (1) doing what their constituents want versus what they think is best, and (2) choosing between the welfare of the district and of the state as a whole. The second approach,

---

Laurel Sprague and Robert J. Mahu are coauthors on this chapter.

roll call voting behavior, compares legislators' voting record with the partisan composition of their district. We weigh the empirical value of these approaches in this chapter with respect to three questions. First, are these reliable, valid measures of representation? Moreover, can we predict how legislators represent constituents either using personal qualities or district and political contexts? And finally, does a legislator's approach to representation affect how he or she performs other parts of the job? Throughout the chapter, we assess whether term limits alter the answers to these questions.

To answer the first of these questions, we examine the strengths and weaknesses of measuring representation using a pair of scaled-response questions that resemble ones political scientists often ask about representational roles. Because we have both scaled responses and open-ended comments, we can examine the validity of these questions by comparing respondents' comments to the scaled values they chose. To assess the reliability of these questions, we explore the continuity of responses across time for respondents we interviewed more than once. Finally, we contribute to the debate about how to measure representation by comparing respondents' representational role orientations and their roll call voting behavior.

Second, we explore whether we can predict legislators' representational role orientations or their roll call voting behavior based on the political, social, or institutional context of the district or by using individual legislators' characteristics and personal experiences. Voters would no doubt like to know if these factors can help them choose candidates. Likewise, reformers trying to foment political and institutional change would be likely to value this information. We examine district-level social and political environments as well as legislators' personal characteristics and experiences to test several theories of representation advanced by other political scientists. We do this using a model based on these theories to predict legislators' representational role orientations and the fit between their votes and their constituents' viewpoints.

Our third line of inquiry examines what effect, if any, a legislator's approach to representation has on his or her other behaviors. For example, do delegates (i.e., legislators who see their role as voting the way their constituents want) devote more time to casework than do trustees (i.e., legislators who rely on their own judgment)? We use interview questions about the priority legislators place on 11 tasks to identify associations between legislators' approach to representation and their other job behaviors.

Term limits advocates, such as George Will (1992), allege that limiting tenure alters legislators' electoral connection and thereby attracts Burkean trustees who use their judgment to advance the common welfare rather than attracting delegates, who in his view are legislators who pander to the district in order to win reelection. Due to the longitudinal design of our research, the combination of open- and closed-ended questions, and our access to district-level partisanship and selected roll call votes for 1997 through 2010, we are uniquely positioned to shed light on this and other claims about representation. Although there is some evidence of a Burkean shift among term-limited legislators nationally (Carey et al. 2006), we demonstrate in this chapter that term limits across time in Michigan have very little effect on legislators' representational role orientations. An underlying theme in this chapter is why altering the electoral connection does so little to change legislators' representational role orientations. We do, however, find that legislators' roll call votes diverge more from their district's partisan ideology after term limits.

Data and Methods for Exploring Representation

In our interviews, we asked legislators what they would do if they confronted conflicts between what they felt was best and what their constituents wanted. We then handed them a seven-point response scale anchored at "always do what you think best" (7 = trustee) and "always do what the district wants" (1 = delegate), asking them to place themselves somewhere along this continuum. We call this conflict *representation style*. We used a similar scale for conflicts between what they believed to be best for their district versus best for the state as a whole, which we call *representational focus* (1 = district-focused; 7 = state-focused). The exact wording of these two questions appears in appendix A, questions 22 and 23. In addition to their quantitative responses, many legislators provided comments about these questions either in lieu of a numerical answer or to elaborate on their scaled response. They often explained factors that might make them go against their preferred approach to representation and identified concerns they find important when deciding how to vote. We coded several of these into categorical variables denoting whether the comment was made or not.

We measure legislators' voting behavior using data compiled and published periodically by *Inside Michigan Politics*. The editor of this newsletter, Bill Ballenger, is a former Republican state representative and a frequent political commentator. At least once per legislative session he selects two to three dozen bills, identifies the liberal and conservative positions, and tabulates the percentage of liberal votes for each state legislator, arraying the legislators along a continuum ranging from 0 percent to 100 percent liberal.

Ballenger selects votes with the intent of differentiating among legislators. This is especially valuable given the frequency of straight party-line votes in a legislature such as Michigan's with exceptionally strong majority party control. Additionally, these data provide a pre-term-limits baseline, allowing us to explore the effects of term limits on roll call voting. The resulting level of polarization that we find using Ballenger's data is consistent with assessments of other scholars (Shor and McCarty 2010) based on roll call votes and issue surveys of state legislators. This increases our confidence that these data provide a realistic assessment of the voting behavior of Michigan's legislators.

Inside Michigan Politics also publishes data on base party strength in Michigan's House and Senate districts. Ballenger calculates these using a rolling average of votes for state board of education candidates and for the officers of the state's three major research universities, all of which are partisan positions.[2] Many voters skip these candidates because they appear at the end of a long ballot, and most voters have little idea of what these positions involve, let alone who the candidates are and what they stand for. Therefore, straight-party voters are the major contributors to the electoral fortunes of candidates for these "bottom of the ballot" positions. Ballenger argues that the results of these races provide a solid estimate of the party strength for each district—that is, those who identify strongly enough with a political party to vote a straight party ticket. After decades observing Michigan politics, we agree.

We calculate two measures of representation based on a legislator's voting record and his or her district's partisan composition. First, we subtract the district's percentage of Democrats from the legislator's percent liberal votes to assess whether a legislator's voting record is more liberal (positive difference) or conservative (negative difference) than his or her constituents. We call this the *partisan disparity*. In the aggregate, positive and negative values for partisan disparity can offset each other giving the misleading impression that overall legislators' voting records are aligned with views of the state's constituents. To avoid this, we compute the absolute value of the mismatch between legislators and their district's voters to measure the size of the gap between legislators' votes and their constituents' partisan preferences. We call this the *voting mismatch*.

Question One: How Should We Measure Representation?

Scholars debate the value of the concepts *delegate* and *trustee*, often using roll call voting as a benchmark against which to assess the value of these representational role orientations. Hadley (1977) finds that self-identified delegates are generally no more likely to vote their constituents' wishes than are self-identified trustees. Friesema and Hedlund (1974) argue that this disparity between a delegate role orientation and voting behavior means that representational roles are useless. Miller and Stokes (1963) explain this discrepancy by demonstrating that legislators are often wrong about the wishes of their constituents, so even if they try to act as delegates their voting records may diverge from constituents' preference. Other work shows that a delegate orientation, in particular, leads to a better fit with constituent preferences if it is consciously adopted and the issues are salient to voters (Kuklinski and Elling 1977; McClone and Kuklinski 1979).

In our reading of this literature, usage of the terms *delegate* and *trustee* vary, and they often blur two conflicts that legislators might confront: whether to rely on one's own judgment (trustee) or the wishes of one's constituents (delegate) and whether to advance the district's welfare (delegate) or the common good (trustee). This conflation might explain some of the conflicting empirical results about representational roles. In an effort to distinguish between these two conflicts, we adopt a distinction advanced by Eulau et al. (1959) in which *representational style* distinguishes between relying on one's own judgment or deferring to constituents' preferences and *representational focus* describes a greater concern for the welfare of the district or for the state as a whole.[3] Accordingly, we restrict our use of the terms delegate and trustee to discussions of representational style, using *trustee* to refer to a legislator's tendency to rely on his or her own judgment and *delegate* to refer to deference to constituents' wishes. When we discuss conflicts between the state and the district, we refer to legislators who prioritize the state's welfare as *state-focused* and those who emphasize district needs as *district-focused*.

Before using representational style and focus we want to see whether they are empirically as well as conceptually distinct. First, we assess the validity and reliability of these two concepts. Then, we measure the association between all three measures of representation (style, focus, and voting mismatch) to determine the amount of overlap between them.

Representational Style and Focus—Are They Different?

In the aggregate our respondents appear to treat representational style and focus independently, tilting slightly away from the district on one and a bit toward the district on the other. The mean for our respondents' representational style is 4.3 (sd 1.6). This is narrowly above the midpoint (4) on the 7-point response scale for these questions. Results before and after term limits are nearly identical: 4.5 and 4.3, respectively. Turning to representational focus, we find a tilt toward the district, with a mean of 3.4 (sd 1.5), slightly below the midpoint on that 7-point scale. Term limits do not appear to alter legislators' representational focus—averages are 3.4 before and 3.5 after term limits.

To test the distinction between style and focus at the individual level, we examine two combinations that would suggest that these concepts are identical—district-focused delegates and state-focused trustees. To see how common these "pure" combinations of the representational roles are, we divided our 7-point scale into three groups (one to three, greater than or equal to three but less than or equal to five, and greater than five). Only 25 percent (60 of 318) of our respondents answered both scaled questions with these two combinations. These 60 respondents include 35 self-identified district-focused delegates—32 in the House and 3 in the Senate—and 25 state-focused trustees—19 in the House and 6 in the Senate. We also correlated legislators' scaled responses to these two questions. We find a statistically significant association between a legislator's style and focus, but the size of the association is not overly large (0.38 sig. $p < 0.01$).

On the other hand, very few respondents approach these conflicts completely independently—district-focused trustees and state-focused delegates. We find only 24 district-focused trustees—23 in the House and 1 in the Senate. Our data contain only 1 state-focused delegate—in the House.[4] We find that legislators' role orientations are rarely orthogonal—fewer than 10 percent. But with only 25 percent reporting the same orientation toward both style and focus when we trifurcate the scale and only a modest correlation between a legislator's scaled responses, we consider these concepts distinct enough to recommend separating them empirically. And we follow our own advice throughout this chapter.

Comparing Scaled Responses and Comments about Role Orientations

Using these role orientations to study legislators' approach to representation assumes that they embody meaningful categories that reflect legislators' experiences. Given the debate about these concepts that we summarized above, we compare respondents' open-ended comments to their scaled responses. Many scaled responses cleave to the midpoint, and comments typically indicate that context matters. Therefore, we find that legislators' approach to representation is more contingent than overarching.

Nearly one-third of our respondents (92 in the House and 9 in the Senate) place themselves at or near the midpoint of both our scales. And many respondents (35%) say that representation depends on the issue (especially moral or core issues); political considerations (e.g., who in the district supported or opposed the issue); and the intensity of constituents' support or opposition. Yet the average scale value for these pragmatic legislators was 4.4, barely different from overall mean of 4.3 that we reported above.

Respondents who placed themselves close to either end of our continua make comments that seem consistent with their scaled responses. And often our respondents' comments echo themes common in the literature about delegates and trustees. For example, legislators distinguish between what voters think is best and what is "really" best for the district—a common description of a trustee orientation. "I do what my people would want me to do if they had the information I have" (interview notes, scaled response = 5.5).

Other legislators claimed that they vote based entirely on constituent preferences—a strong delegate orientation, even while expressing reservations about doing so. "I run surveys. We are now doing one on gun control and seatbelts with respect to the primary enforcement issue. But I'm not sure if constituents understand this" (interview notes, scaled response = 1).

More interestingly, some respondents volunteered information about their efforts to resolve the conflicts posed by these questions. For example, when explaining how they handled the tension between what they thought best and what their constituents wanted, about 10 percent of our respondents said they would explain their vote to constituents if they voted against the district's wishes. "If I go home and can convince over 50% of any group in the district that what I did was right then I did the right thing" (interview notes, scaled response = missing–refused).

Other respondents challenged the meaningfulness of the conflict between what the district wants and what they think is best, in particular objecting that there is no will of the district. Interestingly, respondents who explicitly said that there is *no will of the district* represent constituents who are neither more nor less heterogeneous than others. So we infer that this reflects their views on the nature of representation rather than an assessment of their individual district.

Many respondents objected to using a scale, preferring to describe their approach in their own words. Only 325[5] of our respondents answered our question about representational style using the response scale we provided to them. Some of these legislators said emphatically that other factors mattered too much for them to adopt an overarching role orientation. One of these pragmatic respondents chose all values on our response scale, saying, "All of the above. Don't go purely on poll results—that is not representative government. Move to what people in the district want. On Education: my own beliefs. On business: business people. Other issues: people call—get a sense of what they want" (interview notes, scaled response = missing–refused).

Despite their objections to these questions, some respondents still provided a scaled response, but typically one toward the middle of the scale. One legislator explained that "the hypothesis [implicit in the question] assumes there's a direct conflict and it's rarely that clear" (interview notes, scaled response = "a 4 maybe a 3").

Fewer respondents objected to using a scale to answer the question about representational focus (i.e., conflicts between the state and the district). So we have 347 responses to this question. A comment typical of those who refused to use the scale follows: "Good public policy makers look to get a low bad impact on the district and the overall good of the state. This is a real tough question because of its ambiguity" (interview notes, scaled response = missing–refused).

Some respondents protested that the welfare of state and district are interdependent (9%). As one legislator explained, "Sometimes people don't understand the value of the state—if Detroit hurts, the state hurts" (interview notes, scaled response = 5).

Issues involving budget appropriations were particularly salient. Some respondents' concerns about money motivated a greater district rather than a statewide focus. Just as we found with representational style, some respondents said that their focus depended on issues and on political considerations. But this contingent approach was voiced less frequently for representational focus (23%, or 101 respondents, compared to 35% for representational style).

Overall, we conclude that there is some utility in using these questions and the accompanying response scales, but it oversimplifies representation, providing a crude estimate of a much more nuanced process. In this we concur with Cavanagh (1982), who reports that U.S. legislators expressed frustration regarding questions about their representational style, objecting to the question as too elementary to describe the complex balancing act they perform. At the same time, these questions are provocative and encourage legislators to more fully explain their approaches. The opportunity that open-ended comments provided for respondents to expound on their approach to representation helped many of them tolerate these questions. Often the comments and the scaled responses bear some resemblance to each other. Thus we use these scaled responses to analyze representation in the remainder of this chapter, but with the caveat that some of the difficulty we have predicting legislators' approach to representation might reflect the limitations of measuring representation in this way.

Open-Ended Comments Add Nuance That Numerical Reponses Miss

Based on their open-ended comments, 58 of our respondents asserted that they rely on themselves alone, but their open-ended comments indicated that they did not integrate or synthesize competing information as one would expect of a Burkean trustee. A *trustee style*, to be true to the role orientation Burke ([1774] 2005) defined, should reveal deliberation and consultation with others (see also Guinier 2008; Pitkin 1967; Urbinati 2000; Williams 2000). So, we describe these respondents as *Burkean Cowboys* to distinguish them from *Burkean Trustees*. They made comments such as "I am my district (interview notes)" or "Voters knew what they were getting when they elected me" (interview notes). Yet they represent districts that are nearly 7 percent points more—not less—heterogeneous than the rest of the chamber, so claims of "I am my district" seem unrealistic. Additionally, we find that the average level of electoral competition in these districts is nearly 3 percent percentage points higher than the average for other districts. So these claims are inconsistent not just with the mixed partisan composition of the district but also with voters' affinity for their opponent.

Yet when we look at empirical measures of the approach these Burkean cowboys adopt, their distinctiveness is muted. They expressed only a somewhat stronger tilt toward a trustee representational style compared to their colleagues (4.9 versus 4.2 on our seven-point scale sig. $p < 0.05$). We find that the voting mismatch between Burkean cowboys and their constituents is only a few percentage points larger than the average for their colleagues (22.5% compared to 18.7%, sig. $p < 0.05$). Despite their statistical significance, these differences are not substantively large—7/10ths a point on a seven-point scale and not quite 4 percent on a variable with a range of 72 percentage points.

The comments of the Burkean cowboys reveal the source of their trustee style. They rely upon deeply held moral convictions, issues they campaigned on, or other situations in which their minds were made up. Although scaled-response questions and roll call voting hint at our Burkean cowboys' representation style, it is open-ended comments that distinguish their approach.

Open-ended questions are difficult to code, so their value needs to be weighed against their costs. We suggest using open-ended comments from a small sample of legislators to develop more nuanced questions about representation. More extensive questions might distinguish Burkean cowboys from other trustees[6] among our respondents. Relying on just the two scaled-response questions moderates their distinctiveness. Yet these questions and the voting mismatch calculations do capture some of the Burkean cowboys' approach to representation, reinforcing our conclusions that the scaled response questions about representational roles are valid, albeit blunt, measures of a legislator's approach to representation.

Representational Role Orientations across Time

In this section, we explore the consistency across time of legislators' self-reported representational roles. Our study includes some legislators that we interviewed in consecutive sessions, including a total of 67 legislators who answered the question about representational style twice in a row (of these, 24 answered three times) and 78 legislators who answered the question about representational focus twice in a row (of these, 30 answered three times).[7] If respondents' role orientations remain stable across interviews, it suggests that the questions we asked reveal an enduring tendency toward a particular representational style and focus. This tendency might be a pragmatic, middle-of-the-scale approach, or it could involve a preference for one or the other pole.

To make sure that these repeat respondents are typical of all our respondents, we examined the correlation between their representational style and focus at the first interview. It is 0.38—identical to the correlation we reported above for all respondents. Moreover, the means for their first response about representational style and about representational focus differ by less than 1/10th of a point from the means for all respondents. We conclude that these especially cooperative respondents are typical of all our respondents with respect to their representational role orientations.

We find statistically significant associations across time in the role orientations reported by our repeat respondents ($p < 0.01$). The correlation between the first and second response about representational style is 0.34. This increases to 0.60 for the second and third responses. For representational focus, the correlation is larger, about 0.49 between the first and second responses and 0.80 between the second and third responses. These results imply that legislators' representational role orientations appear to stabilize as legislators gain more experience in the job. A legislator's representational focus tends to be more consistent than his or her representational style, revealing a difference between these two role orientations that is reinforced throughout the rest of the chapter.

Comparing Representational Roles and Roll Call Voting Behavior

Last, but not least, we address the relationship between representational roles and voting behavior. We find that self-described delegates are only very slightly more likely to vote in ways that match the partisan ideology of their district, as indicated by a very small association between representational style and voting mismatch (0.11, sig. $p < 0.10$). We find a similarly small association between legislators' voting mismatch and their representational focus (0.11, sig. $p < 0.05$). It seems plausible, based on these weak associations, that role orientations and voting behavior reflect different, albeit equally important, facets of legislators' attempts to represent their district. We speculate that representational roles measure a legislator's intentions with respect to his or her constituents, while roll call votes reflect the realities of partisan pressures, pragmatic politics, and legislative compromise. Measures of each of these facets of representation can add to our understanding of this multifaceted, complex process.

Question Two: Can We Predict Representational Role Orientations and Voting Behavior?

A basic assumption of term limits advocates is that changing the political context (e.g., removing incumbency advantages) and altering experience and personal characteristics (e.g., attracting citizen legislators) would produce legislators who approached representation differently. Petracca (1991) assumes that term limits will make legislators more responsive, while Will (1992) predicts that term limits will produce a Burkean shift. But in both cases they assume that limiting tenure and removing incumbency advantages will alter legislators' approach to representation. If either of these assumptions is accurate, voters might want to know which personal qualities or contextual factors influence legislators' approaches to representation.

To shed light on this assumed link between context and representation, we examine several factors likely to predict legislators' role orientations and voting behavior. We especially want to understand whether a legislator's approach to representation is more susceptible to context and circumstances (i.e., electoral competition, term limits, the chamber) or reflects personal characteristics (i.e., gender, ethnicity, personal motives for seeking office).

The dependent variables we examine are the scaled responses about the *style* of representation—Delegate (1) versus Trustee (7)—and the *focus* of representation—District (1) versus State (7)—and the percentage of *voting mismatch*—computed as the absolute value of the difference between a legislator's votes and the district's partisanship. Given the mixed results of prior research on legislators' role orientations, we did not expect to explain how all legislators perceive the job of representing constituents all of the time, but we had hoped for more success than we achieved.

As we discuss shortly, we explain only 6 percent of the variation in style and 13 percent for focus. We have more success with *voting mismatch*, explaining a bit more than a third of its variation. We had the most success identifying variables associated with representational focus—nine are associated with representational focus. Only six variables in our model help to explain representational style and seven for voting mismatch. It appears that representational focus is more strongly influenced by the political and social environment that legislators confront. Voting mismatch appears to be more sensitive to institutional and political context. Representational style reflects legislators' personal characteristics and experiences a bit more.

Political and Institutional Context

There are two reasons that we expect context to influence legislators' approach to representation. First, social science research on role theory highlights the importance of the social environment and the expectations of relevant others, referred to as the role set,[8] in maintaining one's role orientation (see, for example, Lieberman 1956; Kahn et al. 1964, Pfeffer 1982; Shivers-Blackwell 2004). The role occupant's expectations for him- or herself are a key part of this role set. But so too are the expectations of other actors, such as colleagues and, in this case, constituents and caucus leaders. Moreover, Jewell (1982) finds that legislators' role orientations may be influenced by political cultures (norms and expectations) in specific legislatures or states. Exemplifying this, Davidson (1969) finds a district focus in the United States as a whole, and Cooper and Richardson (2006) find a trustee focus among several state legislatures.

Second, we expect political context to matter because theories of ballot box accountability emphasize the power of elections to persuade legislators to adapt to constituents' views. Some scholars demonstrate that electorally vulnerable legislators embrace a delegate style and district focus as well as "voting their district" to demonstrate attentiveness to their constituents (Jewell 1982; Jones 1973). Consistent with this, our interview respondents told us that the party caucus releases vulnerable legislators (those representing heterogeneous districts) from party votes whenever possible to facilitate their reelection and maintain party control of the chamber. Therefore, we anticipate that political context will affect representation, especially voting mismatch. The facets of political context we examine are term limits and two measures of political vulnerability: votes cast against the legislator in the primary and in the general election.

Given that a role set reflects the views of a web of actors in a social context, voters logically are part of a legislator's role set. We assume that the social context of a legislator's district should produce different voter expectations for legislators' behaviors. Therefore we explore effects of the level of need in the district (measured by the district's poverty rate), the social distance between legislators and their constituents (measured by the difference between the average education level in the district and the legislator's education), and the heterogeneity of the district, measured by chamber. Senate districts, given their size, tend to be more diverse with respect to a host of factors, including partisan ideology. If these factors predict legislators' approach to representation, it implies that the same legislator would solve the puzzle of representation differently if he or she confronted different district contexts and pressures.

Findings about the Political Environment and Social Context of the District

As we see in table 3.1, a few contextual factors affect representational focus and the voting mismatch, including term limits and electoral competition. Only one of these factors affects representational style—the chamber.

Effects of Term Limits

Term limits have inconsistent effects on representation. They increase legislators' district focus but they expand the voting mismatch, and there is no term limits effect on representational style. Moreover, term limits interact with primary election competition to attenuate its direct effects on repre-

TABLE 3.1. Factors That Predict State Legislators' Role Orientations and Voting Record

Variables in the Model	Delegate or Trustee	District or State	Size of Voting Mismatch
Term limits and its interaction effects			
Term limits	–0.25 (0.45)	**–0.76**** (0.38)	**3.64***(2.09)
Interaction limits and general competition	0.01 (0.1)	0.01 (0.01)	0.05 (0.05)
Interaction limits and primary competition	–0.00 (0.01)	**0.02**** (0.01)	0.003 (0.05)
Interaction limits and chamber senate	–0.29 (0.67)	**0.13** (0.58)	**–10.62***** (2.81)
District characteristics			
General election competition	–0.02 (0.01)	–0.01 (0.01)	**0.33***** (0.06)
Primary election competition	–0.00 (0.01)	**–0.02****(0.01)	–0.04 (0.04)
Percent of district in poverty	0.02 (0.02)	0.01 (0.01)	0.04 (0.08)
Legislator and district similarity—education	–0.14 (0.09)	**–0.13*** (0.08)	–0.58 (0.43)
Chamber (Senate = 1)	**0.85*** (0.50)	0.11 (0.44)	**11.44***** (2.06)
Legislator personal characteristics			
Minority group member	**–0.73*** (0.38)	**–0.80**** (0.32)	1.30 (1.84)
Gender: Female	–0.02 (0.23)	0.15 (0.20)	1.69 (1.12)
Party (Democrat = 1)	0.11 (0.22)	–0.20 (0.19)	**–5.60*****(1.09)
Legislator experiences and behaviors			
Lame duck	–0.14 (0.24)	0.03 (0.20)	0.41 (1.11)
Political ambition	–0.09 (0.21)	0.16 (0.18)	0.17 (1.00)
Time spent on legislative tasks	**–0.66***** (0.23)	**–0.71***** (0.20)	**–2.78***** (1.14)
Prior political experience	0.26 (0.24)	**0.39****(0.20)	0.62 (1.14)
Consulting with constituents	**–0.19**** (0.09)	–0.11 (0.07)	**0.99**** (0.40)
Reasons for running for office			
To represent the district	–0.41 (0.30)	–0.06 (0.25)	1.16 (1.43)
To make a difference	**0.35*** (0.20)	**0.41**** (0.16)	**–1.77***(0.95)
To work on specific issues	**–0.37*** (0.21)	**–0.29*** (0.17)	0.15 (0.95)
Uniquely qualified	0.32 (0.23)	0.23 (0.18)	**1.88*** (1.10)
Constant	**6.61***** (0.97)	**5.55***** (0.80)	**14.64***** (4.59)
Adjusted *R*-squared	0.06	0.13	0.37
F statistic	1.89**	3.24***	11.59***
Observations	289	309	373

Note: Coefficients with standard errors in parentheses. Due to our high response rate, 85%, we discuss results with at least a 90% probability of rejecting one- or two-tailed null hypotheses.

*$p < 0.10$, **$p < 0.05$, ***$p < 0.01$ (two-tailed tests).

sentational focus, as we discuss below. Although term limits effects are not straightforward, it appears that they tend to make legislators less responsive to their voters' views. Even though post-term-limits legislators' votes are less closely aligned with their constituents' preferences, we hesitate to say that this represents a Burkean shift given the null findings about term limits effects on representation style and their contingent effect on district focus. All we can say with certainty is that after term limits, legislators' votes diverge more from their constituents' partisan preferences even as they focus more on the district's rather than the state's welfare.

Effects of Electoral Competition

Overall we find that electoral competition has unexpected effects on our three measures of representation. General election competition only affects voting mismatch. Primary competition affects only representational focus, encouraging legislators to focus on their district. Term limits appear to neutralize the effect of primary competition on representational focus, however. Given the potential for term limits to alter electoral competition by removing the incumbency advantage, we were surprised to find only this one interaction between term limits and electoral competition. It seems logical that an electorally vulnerable legislator would be more responsive to voters, and others have shown this effect (Jones 1973; Jewell 1982). Therefore, we were even more surprised to find that general election competition has no effect on representational style or focus and makes voting mismatch larger not smaller. Moreover, term limits do not change this.

More broadly, our findings cast serious doubt on the power of the ballot box to encourage legislators to respond to their voters, especially after term limits. When legislators are vulnerable they often represent a marginal district in which voters' views are divided—whatever pleases some constituents is likely to displease almost an equal number. Confronted with this dilemma, theories of ballot box accountability suggest that a reelection-seeking legislator would move toward the middle, pleasing each cohort of constituents some of the time rather than one cohort all or most of the time. And with respect to representational style and representational focus, ballot box accountability would predict a tilt toward the district for both conflicts. We find no evidence of this increased responsiveness.

Indeed, legislators who encounter more general election competition have a larger voting mismatch. The effect is large. At its maximum value (50%), this variable could account for a 16.5 percent increase in the voting mismatch. At its average (32% of the votes cast against the legislator), general election competition would be expected to increase the voting mismatch by 10.5 percent. This implies that once a legislator is elected, party discipline trumps constituents' preferences even in a marginal district.[9] Term limits do not alter this. Many constituents may vote against the legislator, but the legislator does not moderate his or her voting behavior.

District Characteristics

Senate districts are much larger than House districts and constituents in these districts tend to be less homogeneous. Only 6 percent of the Senate districts have more than 90 percent Democratic voters compared to 10 percent of House districts.[10] It is harder for a legislator to match the preferences of voters who disagree among themselves. Consistent with this, we find a chamber effect on two of our three measures of representation (representational style and voting mismatch), tilting both away from the district. Before term limits, representatives more closely matched their district's partisanship, while senators tended to adopt a trustee style. After term limits, senators and representatives are nearly equally responsive to their district—or, more precisely, unresponsive, given that term limits increase the voting mismatch by nearly 4 percent.

District Social Context

Looking at table 3.1 again, we see that a legislator's approach to representation is largely impervious to the social context they confront in their district. Social context appears to matter even less than the political or institutional context. Although legislators who are more personally different from their constituents have been shown to adopt a delegate style (see Eulau et al. 1959, 748), presumably in an effort to compensate for the social distance between themselves and their constituents, we find only a small increase in the district focus of legislators whose level of education diverges more from the average education of their constituents. We find no evidence that social distance alters either representational style or voting behavior.

It seems logical that legislators whose constituents have greater need might advocate for their welfare by, for example, focusing on the district rather than the state. Consequently, we consider district poverty rates.[11] We find this has no effect on any of the three measures of representation.

Individual-Level Predictors of Representation

The debate about whether elected officials' orientation toward representation is a function of their personal characteristics has a decades-long history (Lasswell 1960), but it is rare for empirical evidence to shed light on this. Our data provide an opportunity to test a few propositions about personal characteristics, life experiences, and a handful of reasons for running for office. If there is a strong association between a legislator's approach to representation and these characteristics and experiences, it implies that representation is an individual trait rather than a pragmatic calculation based on political or district contexts.

Personal Characteristics of Legislators

Common experiences and socialization could draw minority legislators toward their constituents (Burden 2007; Burrell 1994; Hawkesworth 1990). Based on this, scholars speculate that minority representatives may feel a stronger need to bring their constituents' voices into halls of power that have historically been closed to them (see Burden 2007; also Mansbridge 1999 on descriptive representatives opening channels of communication). Indeed, there is some empirical evidence to suggest this (Cooper and Richardson 2006; Johnson and Secret 1996). Supporting this we find that minority group legislators lean toward a delegate style and a district focus, but we find no effect on their roll call voting.

Other scholars (Johnson and Secret 1996; Cooper and Richardson 2006) find that gender affects representation. We find no gender effects on our three measures of representation. We cannot isolate the effects of gender from the effects of ethnicity due to the paucity of minority women among our respondents—a total of 13 across seven sessions—which might explain our null findings.

Personal ideology reflected by a legislator's political party does not affect either representational style or focus, but it does affect voting mismatch. Democrats' voting records are aligned more closely with their constituents, about 5 percent closer than Republicans. It is likely that some of this greater mismatch for Republican legislators arises from the partisan mixture of voters in the districts they represent.[12] We cannot control for the confounding influence of district maps in the model examined in table 3.1 because post-term-limits Senate elections occurred under the same map. But we revisit the issue of district boundaries and voting mismatch later in this chapter.

Experiences and Behaviors of Legislators

Occasionally some personal characteristic or life experience is associated with some facets of representation, but here again we find it difficult to predict a legislator's approach to representation. On the whole, we report mostly null findings and inconsistent effects. So, with one exception, voters are unlikely to be able to select candidates with a particular approach to representation merely on their personal characteristics or life experiences.

Our only clear and unambiguous result is that especially hardworking legislators (those who spend more time on 11 legislative tasks) are more likely to be delegates, to focus on the district, and to vote in ways that more closely match the views of their voters. This work ethic effect implies that it requires a lot of time and effort to engage with constituents to determine their needs and preferences.

Our other consistent findings refute effects that one would expect based on the political science literature. Much is written about legislators' voting behavior when the electoral connection is severed and they become lame ducks (see Bender and Lott 1996 for a review of this literature and Rothenberg and Sanders 2000 for recent research). Under term limits, lame ducks are almost always more experienced than their colleagues and have had more time to formulate their own judgment on issues. Therefore, we anticipated that these more experienced legislators, with their electoral connection unfastened (Herrick, Moore, and Hibbing 1994), would drift away from their constituents and district. But unfastening the electoral connection for lame ducks does not affect any of our three measures of representation.

We also assumed that political ambition might attenuate ties with current constituents if legislators' attention turns to their future constituents—those they hope will support them in their next political office. This seemed reasonable given that Maestas (2000) demonstrates, at the aggregate level, a connection between political ambition and legislator responsiveness. We find, however, that political ambition has no effect on any of our three measures of representation.

Remaining effects are mixed and inconsistent. Some scholars find that a trustee style is more common among political careerists (Jewell 1982). We find no support for this. But we do find that respondents with prior political experience (a dichotomous variable) are a bit more state-focused. This might indicate that more government experience broadens one's perspective to the state as a whole. Where one seeks information about issues could either reflect or alter one's approach to representation. The only effect we find is that legislators who rely more heavily on constituents for information report a more delegate-oriented style.

Reasons for Running

Finally, we expect that the reasons legislators gave for seeking elected office (their motivations) will be related to their approach to representation. These were open-ended comments to a question asking, "When you first ran for office, what were your reasons for running?" We test four comments that seem likely to affect representation: running to represent the district, running to make a difference, running to work on some specific issue, or running because of special qualifications.

It seems almost tautological that legislators who said explicitly that *they ran to represent the district* would be more delegate-oriented, district-focused, and vote in ways closely aligned with constituents' views. Contrary to our expectations, this reason for running does not affect any of our three measures of representation.

We were uncertain whether running to make a difference would reflect a difference on local issues or a difference on statewide issues. And we still are unsure, because running to make a difference has mixed effects. Respondents who *ran to make a difference* adopt a trustee style and tilt toward a state focus, which suggests that they want to make a difference for the state as a whole. But legislators who ran to make a difference have a smaller voting mismatch with their district. This latter result implies that they want to make a difference for their district's voters.

Similarly respondents who said they *ran to address specific issues* could be thinking either of statewide or local issues. We find that those who ran to work on specific issues expressed a delegate style and a district focus. Running to work on specific issues does not appear to affect roll call voting at all. So we conclude that district-focus legislators who adopt a delegate style ran to resolve local issues.

We assumed the trustees would express more confidence in their own capabilities. They are after all acting as if they know what is best for other people—a fairly self-assured position. This reason for running appears to affect only one facet of representation however—voting mismatch.

Based on these findings, it appears that legislators' reasons for running for office provide only a little information about how they will approach representation. Here again, the message is mixed, and the relationships are much weaker than we expected. Therefore, asking candidates about their motivation for seeking office provides little help to voters who want to select a candidate with a particular approach to representation.

Summary of Our Ability to Predict a Legislator's Approach to Representation

We conclude that it is very difficult to predict legislators' approach to representation based on either context or circumstances or on personal motives, characteristics, and experiences. We find very little support for the numerous theories we described throughout this section. As we noted earlier, scaled responses to questions about representational roles provide crude approximations of the comments legislators make in response to these questions. That obviously complicates our task and may increase null findings. But if imprecise measurement accounted for the entire problem, we would not expect results that contradict predictions of these theories. And we find a handful of those as well. Much of the problem appears to be that representation is multifaceted and just hard to predict.

Term limits advocates who thought that they could alter legislators' orientation toward representation by altering the context in which legislators serve are likely to be very disappointed. Even electoral vulnerability appears to have little effect on legislators' responsiveness to voters, and removing the drag of incumbency through term limits has mixed and inconsistent effects. Our only definitive advice is that voters who seek a responsive legislator should assess the candidate's work ethic. Hardworking legislators are more likely to respond to constituents and to the district and to align their votes with the partisanship of the district.

District Boundaries and Roll Call Voting

As we discussed earlier, ballot box accountability rests on the assumption that vulnerable legislators will be more responsive to constituents in the hope of winning reelection. Limiting tenure allegedly heightens legislators' sense of vulnerability by removing the advantages of incumbency. But so far we find little evidence to support this assumption. Assessing this is complicated, however, by changes in district maps. This alters the fit between legislators and voters because maps drawn by one political party tend to create a small number of very homogeneous districts for the opposing party and many more marginal, but "winnable," districts for the party drawing the map. It is easier to follow to voters' wishes in a homogeneous district, so district boundaries can change a legislator's voting mismatch.

Michigan Republicans controlled the process of drawing these boundaries after the 2000 census. The previous map, drawn after the 1990 census, involved both political parties. That map included 20 competitive districts, 7 that leaned Republican and 13 that leaned Democratic. The subsequent map drawn after the 2000 censuses consisted of 44 competitive Republican leaning districts and 17 competitive Democratic leaning districts. All of our pre-term-limits respondents served under the more bipartisan 1992 map. Most of our post-term-limits respondents ran under the 2002 map. Therefore some term limits differences in voting mismatch could reflect more Republican leaning, but competitive, districts in the later map. It is harder to balance the demands of party leaders and of constituents if one represents a heterogeneous district.

To avoid the confounding effect of two different maps, we use a subset of our data—the 1997, 1999, and 2001 House sessions—to test the prediction that term limits alter legislators' voting mismatch. Veterans were expelled from Michigan's lower chamber in 1999, so we have a pre-term-limits baseline in 1997 and two post-term-limits House sessions (1999 and 2001), all of which occurred under the 1992 map.

We summarize in figure 3.1 the average levels of voting mismatch for these three House sessions using a simple analysis of variance. It is clear from this chart that the size of the voting mismatch for both political parties increases after term limits. It is also clear that there is a partisan difference, with Democrats representing their constituents' preferences more closely both before and after term limits.

To explore whether these voting mismatches arise from an over- or under representation of the liberalness of their district, we substitute the dependent variable, *partisan disparity*, in the same analysis. This measure does not use the absolute value to measure the difference between voters and their legislators—it considers the direction of the mismatch. After term limits each party moves farther toward the ends of the spectrum—more conservative than their voters for Republicans and more liberal than their voters for Democrats. This supports assertions by our respondents that Michigan, always somewhat polarized, became more so after term limits. It also provides strong evidence that after term limits legislators' voting behavior is less aligned with their constituents' views and that more extreme candidates are winning elections. Term limits advocates were correct—changing the electoral environment alters representation, but legislators became more extreme than their voters rather than more consonant with them.

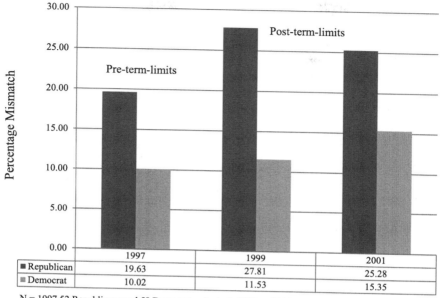

	1997	1999	2001
■ Republican	19.63	27.81	25.28
▩ Democrat	10.02	11.53	15.35

N = 1997 52 Republicans and 58 Democrats; for both 1999 and 2001 58 Republicans and 52 Democrats

Fig. 3.1. Effects of Term Limits on Voting Mismatch in the Michigan House

Question Three: Does a Legislator's Approach to Representation Affect Other Behaviors?

Historically, political scientists have disagreed about whether representational role orientations affect legislators' behaviors (Wahlke et al. 1962, 17). More recent evidence suggests that role orientations matter. For example, Cavanagh (1982) found that state-focused representatives in the U.S. Congress report spending more time doing committee work, studying legislation, mobilizing support for legislation, and participating in floor debates and votes, while district-focused representatives report spending more time doing casework and meeting with constituents. Similarly, Cooper and Richardson (2006) find that trustee-oriented legislators spend less time holding district office hours.

In table 3.2 we provide correlations between our three measures of representation (style, focus, and voting mismatch) and the emphasis our respondents place on 11 legislative tasks (see appendix A, questions 20.1 through 20.11). Results are reported separately for legislators serving before and after term limits. One and only one activity, *Talking to Voters*, is associated with all three measures of representation before term limits, and another, again only one, *Getting Pork*, is associated with all three after term limits. Both logically increase when legislators are more responsive to their voters and their district.

A very clear pattern emerges in table 3.2. Different facets of representation are more and less important in predicting legislators' other behaviors. Representational focus provides the most information and the only consistent information before and after term limits about legislators' behaviors. Representational style provides the least. Voting mismatch provides more information after term limits about legislators' behaviors than it did before, but still lags behind representational focus.

TABLE 3.2. Correlations between Representation and Priority of Tasks

	Representation before Limits			Representation after Limits		
	Style	Focus	Mismatch	Style	Focus	Mismatch
Study legislation	.086 (.41)	.056 (.59)	.037 (.69)	**.153*** (.02)	.051 (.43)	**.131*** (.02)
Develop new laws	.061 (.56)	.068 (.51)	**.167*** (.06)	.029 (.66)	.059 (.36)	–.064 (.25)
Own party coalitions	.085 (.41)	.143 (.16)	.046 (.61)	.032 (.64)	**.135*** (.04)	.000 (.99)
Cross party coalitions	.113 (.27)	.103 (.27)	–.018 (.85)	.019 (.78)	**.125*** (.05)	**–.209*** (.00)
Monitor state agencies	.063 (.54)	**.195*** (.05)	–.085 (.34)	.030 (.66)	.016 (.80)	.011 (.84)
Talk to voters	**–.172*** (.09)	**–.267*** (.01)	**–.151*** (.09)	–.061 (.36)	**–.106*** (.10)	.035 (.53)
Attend district meetings	.007 (.94)	**–.171*** (.09)	.093 (.30)	–.068 (.31)	**–.142*** (.03)	.043 (.44)
Casework	–.082 (.43)	**–.163** (.10)	–.055 (.54)	–.059 (.38)	–.092 (.15)	–.025 (.656)
Getting pork	–.016 (.88)	**–.300*** (.00)	.012 (.90)	**–.19*** (.01)	**–.35*** (.00)	**–.135*** (.02)
Fundraising	–.016 (.88)	.118 (.24)	–.035 (.70)	.002 (.97)	.016 (.81)	**.123"** (.03)
Attend Lansing events	**–.177*** (.09)	.108 (.27)	–.003 (.97)	.086 (.20)	**.21*** (.00)	.086 (.13)
No. of responses (range)[a]	93–99	98–102	123–27	226–27	242–44	321–24

Note: Values are Pearson correlations with the statistical significance for a two-tailed test in parentheses below. Bold type also identifies statistically significant correlations.

[a]Some respondents did not answer a particular question.

*p < 0.10, **p < 0.05, ***p < 0.01 (two-tailed tests).

Specifically, representational focus is associated with five of the 11 behaviors before term limits and 6 of the 11 afterward. Moreover, representational focus affects three of the same behaviors before and after term limits. Before and after term limits state-focused legislators spend less time talking to voters, less time attending meetings in the district, and less time bringing resources (pork) to the district. There is no overlap before and after term limits in the behaviors associated with either of the other two measures of representation.

Representational style has the least influence on legislators' behaviors, affecting only 2 of the 11 behaviors both before and after term limits—and not the same two. Representational style throughout this chapter is the most problematic of the three facets of representation both to measure and to predict. The tenuous link between representational style and other behaviors reinforces this impression.

Voting mismatch also affects only two behaviors before term limits—more time developing laws and less time talking to voters. After term limits, a legislator's voting mismatch expands and is associated with four behaviors—all of which differ from the two pre-term-limits behaviors. After term limits a larger voting mismatch is associated with getting less "pork" for the district, less time spent building bipartisan coalitions, and more time studying legislation. The other association (e.g., increased effort on fundraising) may reflect a legislator who is thinking about the next job rather than current constituents' views.

We conclude that there are some behavioral consequences arising from the way legislators resolve dilemmas of representation. Knowing a legislator's representational focus is more useful for anticipating his or her other behaviors than either of the other two measures of representation, however. The behaviors associated with larger voting mismatch seem consistent with a legislator who is less responsive to constituents, while representational style provides very little information about a legislator's other behaviors.

Conclusions

We discovered in this chapter that representation is not only a complex concept to describe theoretically (Pitkin 1967), but that a legislator's approach to representation is tough to predict empirically. We argue that representation is not one thing, but many. Furthermore, we conclude that representation tends to be contingent rather than overarching, compounding the problems involved in measuring and predicting it.

Despite these difficulties, we find that all three facets of representation (representational style, representational focus, and voting mismatch) have some effect on legislators' behaviors, most notably the priority they place on talking to voters and on bringing resources to the district. So it appears that a legislator's approach to representation has consequences for constituents and the district, a theme we pursue in chapter 4. These behavioral consequences heighten the importance of understanding how a legislator approaches representation.

The weakest of the three ways we measured representation is representational style—the traditional delegate/trustee continuum. Representational style is the most difficult of our three measures to predict and also provides the least insight into other facets of a legislator's behavior. Moreover, legislators object more vigorously to scaled-response questions about their representational style. Clearly, there is much room to improve the questions political scientists ask about representational style. A one-dimensional continuum ranging from delegate to trustee fails to do justice to the highly nuanced balancing act legislators perform when they weigh concerns of heterogeneous voters, conflicting information about issues, and the pressures of party and personal views. Representational style appears to be highly contingent on a host of factors, so it is inherently hard to measure.

Representational focus appears to have greater value empirically than does representational style. Questions about balancing the interests of the district versus the state elicited fewer objections from our respondents. We had more success predicting legislators' representational focus than their style. Moreover, representational focus is associated in a logically sensible way with a consistent set of behaviors before and after term limits. It appears that representational focus is a more useful measure of representation, at least from a research standpoint. It also may be more valuable to voters who wish to anticipate the behavior of their elected officials.

Although we had some success predicting a legislators' voting mismatch, the evidence we found is disquieting. It appears that the electoral connection is weak, even when we control for lame ducks and political ambition, neither of which affected any of the three measures of representation. How are voters to hold elected representatives accountable if not through the ballot box? This reinforces concerns we raised in chapter 2 about candidate recruiting and the selection process. Our findings about voting mismatch also heighten concerns about the impact of district maps on representation. We conclude that term limits have unfastened the electoral connection in ways that leave voters with even less, rather than more, influence on legislators' voting.

Our results underscore how challenging it is to conduct empirical research about representation. Despite extensive debates among political scientists about representation, we produce null or inconsistent findings about most of these assumptions and hypotheses. We discovered only two variables among the many in our model that affect all three measures of representation: the work ethic, measured as time devoted to the job, and running to make a difference. And only time devoted to the job (the work ethic effect) moves all three measures in the same direction—increasing responsiveness to constituents. Clearly political scientists need to ask better questions about representation, but a contingent, multifaceted construct is inherently hard to measure and to predict, despite its importance in understanding representative democracy.

FOUR

Legislators' Behaviors

Term limits activists wanted a new breed of legislator, not as an end in itself, but because they expected these legislators to act differently. They base this on the assumption that career legislators' actions are driven by a single goal—reelection. Shorter terms of service prevent legislators from making a career of their job. Freed from the pressures of reelection seeking, legislators should, according to term limits backers, behave differently—motivated by different goals (Will 1992; Petracca 1991). Although our findings in chapter 2 challenge these assumptions about legislators' motivations, it seems plausible that changes associated with term limits, such as increases in political ambition and the unique status of lame ducks, could alter legislators' behavior.

In this chapter we explore legislators' behavior before and after term limits based on 11 tasks that legislators typically do. But we also examine factors associated with term limits, such as increased political ambition, to determine whether these are the source of any behavioral changes that we discover. Examining legislators' behaviors also reveals their job priorities more generally. For example, we find that Michigan legislators place a higher priority on casework than on legislating. Although we discuss 11 legislative tasks in this chapter, we concentrate on three categories of activity that have attracted considerable scholarly attention: helping constituents with problems (aka casework), getting projects and money for the district (aka pork), and legislating (in which we include four specific tasks: studying legislation, developing legislation, and building partisan and bipartisan coalitions to pass legislation). In subsequent chapters we provide details about two other important tasks: fundraising and oversight of the bureaucracy.

First, we examine all 11 tasks, separately by chamber, to see whether term limits alter legislators' behaviors. Then we examine the behaviors of three key cohorts of legislators that we identified in chapter 2: lame ducks, newcomers, and politically ambitious legislators. Next we test multivariate models of the three activities that we highlight in this chapter: casework, getting pork, and legislating. Finally in this chapter, we examine changes in legislators' behaviors across time. We conducted multiple interviews with some respondents, so we can compare the way these repeat respondents' task priorities change. We also compare the mismatch between legislators and their voters across time to see whether their voting behavior changes.

Data and Methods

Our analyses in this chapter rely on a series of questions, 20.1 to 20.11 in appendix A, that ask legislators to report the time they spent on 11 specific tasks, such as studying proposed legislation or helping voters with problems. Responses ranged along a five-point scale from "An enormous amount (4)" to "None (0)." In the interviews we handed respondents a printed copy of this scale and asked them to specify their response. Although we accepted values anywhere along the scale, most respondents selected whole numbers.

To compute measures for time allocation, we calculate the difference between each respondent's time on a specific task and his or her average time spent on all 11 tasks. This produces approximately normally distributed interval values and controls for the tendency of modest respondents to report a little time on all tasks and exuberant ones to say they spent an enormous amount of time on nearly everything. The resulting difference measure can be thought of as the relative priority placed on any particular task—about average (values near zero), less than average (negative values), or more than average (positive values).[1]

In our multivariate models we include several factors that seem likely to affect legislators' behaviors. We explain some of these as we present the results of these models, but two of them appear repeatedly. So we explain them here to avoid repetition.

Electoral vulnerability is chief among these given the concerns of term limits proponents about the power of reelection seeking to influence legislators' behavior. We consider both the safety of the general election seat for one political party as well as the amount of primary competition a legislator encountered. We measure district safety using the partisan composition of the district produced by *Inside Michigan Politics*. Details of this measure are explained in chapter 3. We use data from the Michigan Secretary of State's office to measure primary competition, tallying all votes cast against the legislator in the party's primary election.

Additionally, we include gender in all our multivariate models given the prevalence of political science scholarship arguing that gender affects legislators' behavior. For example, Kathlene (1994) finds that larger cohorts of women in legislatures alter the process of governing. Volden, Wiseman, and Wittmer (2013) claim that this is because women are more likely to compromise, negotiate, and collaborate across party lines, especially when they find themselves in the chamber's minority. Additionally, evidence indicates that women are motivated by interpersonal relationships and helping constituents (Thomas 1992). The number of men in Michigan's legislature increases after term limits. So if women do behave differently than men, then electing fewer of them could have implications for the behavior of Michigan's legislators after term limits.

Time Allocation

Before we begin our discussion of term limits effects on legislators' behaviors, we point out that much scholarship about legislatures assumes that legislating and voting on bills are central activities. Ellickson and Whistler (2001) and Elling (1979) provide empirical evidence that legislating is indeed a vital and time-consuming task for legislators. But there is conflicting evidence about the importance of legislating, especially as legislative service has changed over the years (Moncrief, Thompson, and Kurtz 1996). Goodman et al. (1986) report that 46 of the Ohio state legislators they interviewed describe their job as an ombudsman, saying that they help constituents with problems that often arise from encounters with state bureaucracies. These authors describe a state-level version of the shift in Congress described by Fiorina (1977) in which he attributes some incumbency advantages to the casework U.S. representatives provide to constituents.

We find evidence that legislating is not a high priority for many of Michigan's state legislators while casework is. Based on the priority legislators place on these tasks, we classify them as high priority, moderate priority, low priority, and avoided. The average of all legislators' difference from their personal mean (hereafter referred to as the *differenced measure*) appear in parentheses. High priority tasks are communicating with voters (0.70), attending meetings in the district (0.57), and helping voters with problems, or casework (0.54). Moderate priority tasks are getting money and projects for the district (0.18) and studying legislation (0.17). Low priority tasks are developing new legislation (–0.11), building coalitions in the party to pass legislation (–0.11), building coalitions across party lines to pass legislation (–0.23), and attending functions in the capital (–0.39). Avoided tasks are fundraising (–0.62) and monitoring state agencies (–0.70).

Term Limits Effects on Time Allocation

Term limits have statistically significant effects on only four of the 11 tasks we explore: developing legislation (legislators spend less time on this task after term limits), building coalitions across party lines to pass legislation (less time), monitoring state agencies (less time), and communicating with voters (more time). We examine these by chamber next, assuming that the influx of newcomers in the lower chamber is a major factor in these changes and expecting to find more post-term-limits changes by examining the House separately.

Looking at figure 4.1 we see a highly consistent rank order in the House for 10 of these tasks before and after term limits. Unexpectedly, we see a lot more change in the Senate. This suggests to us that term limits do more than simply reduce the experience of legislators, because, if that were the only effect or even the dominant effect, then the House, with its waves of newcomers, should exhibit more behavioral change than the Senate.

There is only one shift of two or more places in the rank order of tasks in the House with the advent of term limits (reduced time devoted to building bipartisan coalitions). There are four shifts of this size between the pre- and post-term-limits Senate: attending district events (less time), developing new laws (less time), talking to voters (more time), and studying proposed laws (more time).

If we compare the two chambers after term limits, we find that they are almost identical in the priority they place on these 11 tasks. We see in figure 4.1 that only one task—helping voters (i.e., casework)—differs by two or more places between the rank order of tasks for the post-term-limits House and Senate. The pre-term-limits Senate differs most from the other three panels in figure 4.1. Pre-term-limits senators place a higher priority on developing new legislation and a lower priority on communicating with voters, distinguishing themselves from the three other cohorts. Thus, before term limits, the two chambers differed more than they do afterward.

After term limits the Senate is almost exclusively populated by House

High Priority Tasks

House Before Term Limits	Mean Diff.	House After Term Limits	Mean Diff.	Senate Before Term Limits	Mean Diff.	Senate After Term Limits	Mean Diff.
1 Talk to Voters	0.65	1 Talk to Voters	0.78	1 Attend District Events	0.68	1 Help Voters	0.59
2 Help Voters	0.48	2 Attend District	0.62	2 Help Voters	0.53	2 Talk to Voters	0.57
3 Attend District	0.46	3 Help Voters	0.56			3 Attend District Events	0.48

Moderate Priority Tasks

House Before Term Limits	Mean Diff.	House After Term Limits	Mean Diff.	Senate Before Term Limits	Mean Diff.	Senate After Term Limits	Mean Diff.
4 Study Proposed Laws	0.15	4 Get Money for District	0.20	3 Develop New Laws	0.39	4 Study Proposed Laws	0.22
		5 Study Proposed Laws	0.17	4 Get Money for District	0.38	5 Get Money for District	0.16
				5 Talk to Voters	0.33		
				6 Study Proposed Laws	0.12		

Average Priority Tasks

House Before Term Limits	Mean Diff.	House After Term Limits	Mean Diff.	Senate Before Term Limits	Mean Diff.	Senate After Term Limits	Mean Diff.
5 Get Money for District	0.07	6 Own Party Coalitions	-0.07	7 Bipartisan Coalitions	0.03	6 Develop New Laws	0.01
6 Bipartisan Coalitions	-0.06						
7 Own Party Coalitions	-0.06						

Low Priority Tasks

House Before Term Limits	Mean Diff.	House After Term Limits	Mean Diff.	Senate Before Term Limits	Mean Diff.	Senate After Term Limits	Mean Diff.
8 Develop New Laws	-0.13	7 Develop New Laws	-0.18	8 Own Party Coalitions	-0.39	7 Own Party Coalitions	-0.23
		8 Bipartisan Coalitions	-0.31			8 Bipartisan Coalitions	-0.35
		9 Attend Lansing Events	-0.35				

Avoided Tasks

House Before Term Limits	Mean Diff.	House After Term Limits	Mean Diff.	Senate Before Term Limits	Mean Diff.	Senate After Term Limits	Mean Diff.
9 Attend Lansing Events	-0.41	10 Fundraising	-0.65	9 Attend Lansing Events	-0.62	9 Fundraising	-0.45
10 Monitor Agencies	-0.52	11 Monitor Agencies	-0.79	10 Fundraising	-0.72	10 Attend Lansing	-0.47
11 Fundraising	-0.60			11 Monitor Agencies	-0.73	11 Monitor Agencies	-0.55

Number of Respondents: House Before Limits 89 to 91; After 240 to 256 and Senate Before Limits 31 to 33; After 52 to 54

Bold type denotes statistically significant change in the differenced measure of legislators' activities

Italicized type with shading denotes a shift in the rank order of the source of two or more ranks.

Fig. 4.1. Priority Legislators Place on Tasks before and after Term Limits by Chamber

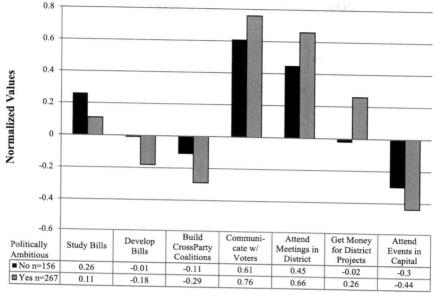

Fig. 4.2. Priorities of the Politically Ambitious Legislator

members moving into the upper chamber, so they have some legislative experience. But we speculate that they bring the norms and routines they acquired in the House with them to the upper chamber. Without a cohort of veteran Senators to resocialize them into the norms and routines used in a much smaller chamber, the post-term-limits Senate comes to resemble the House more than the pre-term-limits Senate did. This is reflected in a similar ranking of tasks in the post-term-limits Senate and House.

Political Ambition: The Big Change

Politically ambitious legislators plan to use their legislative service as a springboard to another office, possibly a statewide office or U.S. Congress or a big city mayor or a judicial position. This may intensify rather than reduce their concerns about elections. Given the proliferation of political ambition after term limits (see chapter 2), we are especially interested in whether these legislators prioritize legislative tasks differently from their less ambitious colleagues. Figure 4.2 summarizes the seven statistically significant differences we find between the priority placed on a series of legislative tasks by politically ambitious legislators and their less ambitious colleagues.

Three tasks carry a higher priority for politically ambitious legislators than for their colleagues: communicating with voters, attending meetings in the district, and getting resources (money and projects) for the district. These three tasks are likely to produce a political payoff. From this we infer that politically ambitious legislators are motivated by election seeking.

Four others are lower priority tasks for politically ambitious legislators than for their colleagues: studying legislation, developing new legislation, building coalitions across party lines to pass legislation (hereafter called *building bipartisan coalitions*), and attending events in the capital (Lansing). Three of these tasks are instrumental facets of legislating. Thus, it appears that politically ambitious legislators are less inclined to devote time and effort to legislating. Given the sharp increase in the number of politically ambitious post-term-limits legislators, this implies that a smaller cohort in each chamber may exercise outsized influence on legislating after term limits—those who do not plan to run for another office are instrumental in making the laws.

Lame Ducks: Do They Make a Difference?

Term limits not only swell the ranks of newcomers, but they boost the number exiting—the so-called lame ducks. Evidence indicates that lame ducks behave differently. For example, lame duck members of Congress maintain less contact with constituents, make fewer trips back to the district, and forego staff resources (Herrick, Moore, and Hibbing 1994). But these same authors find that the "batting average" (a ratio of bills passed to bills introduced) of lame ducks improves as they concentrate their energy on unfinished work, presumably seeking a legislative legacy. And as we noted in chapter 2, with term limits everyone knows who the lame ducks are well in advance of their departure, spawning a unique breed of lame ducks. We are particularly interested in the behavior of these legislators.

In the previous chapter we report that legislators serving their last term do not change their voting behavior nor do they change their representational role orientation. But in this chapter we find that lame ducks allocate their time differently among competing demands, and these differences are statistically significant. There are six tasks, illustrated in figure 4.3, upon which lame ducks place a different priority than their colleagues do.

Michigan's lame ducks place a lower priority on district activities such as communicating with voters and attending meetings in the district, consistent with the behavior of U.S. representatives that Herrick, Moore, and

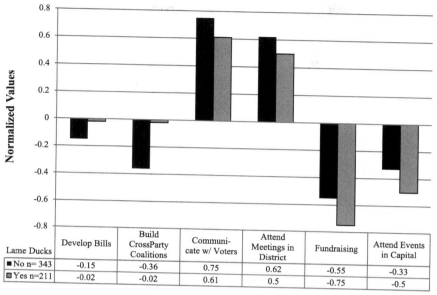

Lame Ducks	Develop Bills	Build CrossParty Coalitions	Communi-cate w/ Voters	Attend Meetings in District	Fundraising	Attend Events in Capital
■ No n= 343	-0.15	-0.36	0.75	0.62	-0.55	-0.33
▣ Yes n=211	-0.02	-0.02	0.61	0.5	-0.75	-0.5

Fig. 4.3. Priorities for Lame Ducks

Hibbing (1994) studied. Quite logically they spend less time fundraising, a very unpopular task even for legislators seeking reelection. And they spend less time attending events in the capital. But not all the lame duck effects involve shirking.

Two tasks assume a higher priority in a legislator's final term, or more accurately a less negative priority. These are developing new legislation and building bipartisan coalitions to pass legislation. This is also consistent with the Herrick, Moore, and Hibbing (1994) finding that departing legislators have a more focused, effective legislative agenda. So, despite early and public knowledge of their imminent departure, Michigan's term-limited lame ducks appear to behave in the ways one would expect any lame ducks to behave. But as we discover later in this chamber, their behavior is contingent on their future political plans.

Newcomer Effects: Less Difference Than Anticipated

Another obvious change with term limits is the number of freshman entering term-limited legislatures. Yet the search for effects from this influx, in both our own work and that of others, has produced limited results. Our findings here are no different. The priorities of freshmen differ from their colleagues on only three behaviors: building coalitions within one's party (less time), building bipartisan coalitions (less time), and attending events in Lansing (more time).

It is possible that freshmen spend less time building coalitions because they do not know who to collaborate with. It is also possible that they do not yet understand the value of this activity. Given that one of these tasks, building bipartisan coalitions, is something lame ducks prioritize at a higher level than their colleagues, it appears that this is part of the learning curve that legislators master just in time to be termed from office.

Freshmen place a higher priority on attending events in the capital. In comments about their time allocation our respondents told us that they attend a lot of these events when they first arrive in Lansing because they need to get to know people. After they propelled themselves up this networking learning curve, they tend to skip these events unless they know that a constituent will be attending (interview notes). This suggests an ephemeral newcomer effect.

Being a freshman has fewer effects than political ambition and lame duck status have, and these effects appear transient. At least two of the three newcomer differences that we find appear to be part of their learning curve rather than a fundamental institutional shift in the behavior of post-term-limits legislators. There are more freshmen so we see more "learning" behavior, but even these few effects dissipate after their first session in office—as we demonstrate later in this chapter.

Casework

As we saw in figure 4.1, helping voters with problems is among the three highest priority tasks in both chambers with or without term limits. Our respondents spend much more than their average effort on this task—and many respondents said their staff spends even more time on this. While investigating legislators' goals Goodman et al. (1986) discovered that 91 percent of Ohio legislators identified constituent service among their top goals—much higher than the next most frequently mentioned goal, good public policy at 64 percent. Kurtz et al. (2006) report that casework accounts for the largest proportion of the difference across states in the time legislators report spending on their job.

Given the importance legislators attach to casework, we felt it was important to understand more about who does it, when, and why. We selected variables for our analysis based on the political science literature and on comments by our respondents. As one suburban legislator told us, "people representing Detroit get a lot more requests for help because their constituents do not have other resources to resolve their problems" (interview notes). He pointed out that if his suburban constituents faced some of these problems, they would just hire a lawyer instead of asking him for help. Therefore, we include district poverty rates in our model, expecting that legislators representing districts with more need would prioritize casework.

Electoral vulnerability feeds into a broader debate among political scientists about whether casework provides an electoral payoff. Freeman and Richardson (1996) find no evidence from their four-state survey that vulnerable legislators perform more casework, challenging the connection with election seeking. Ellickson and Whistler (2001) find that politically ambitious respondents spent less time on casework, suggesting minimal political payoff. Yet others find that politically ambitious legislators might spend more time on casework to enhance one's reelection prospects (Rosenthal 1993; Patterson 1990). Fiorina (1977) attributes the rise in casework to the expansion of the bureaucracy during the 1960s and beyond. He explains that casework is a way to make friends without making enemies, and so he argues that vulnerable legislators who prioritize casework can pick up enough votes to retain their seat.

To add to the debate about the political payoff from casework, we include lame duck status, political ambition, primary and general election competition (measured as the percentage of the vote received by opponents), and how safe the district is for one political party. We assume that more electorally vulnerable legislators and more politically ambitious legislators would prioritize casework to gain voter support. Conversely, lame ducks should avoid casework given that they no longer seek voter support.

Findings about gender differences in casework are mixed. Ellickson and Whistler (2001) find that gender does not alter the amount of time legislators spend on casework. This is consistent with the work of Reingold (2000) on gender. In contrast, Richardson and Freeman (1995) report that women in the four states they studied received more casework requests than their male colleagues. Additionally, they find that women in their sample are twice as likely as men to say that they do more casework and three times as likely as men to say that if they had more staff they would expand their casework efforts. We include gender in our model to explore this effect.

We test our multivariate model predicting the *priority of casework*, and find a negative R^2. Our model explains nothing—indeed, less than nothing. We also replicate to the extent possible with our data the Ellickson and Whistler 15-variable model (2001) that they used with some success to predict casework. In a single state study such as ours, three of their variables are held constant: district population, legislative staff resources, and legislative professionalism scale. We have measures for nine of their remaining 12 variables. Our replication of their model also produces a negative adjusted R^2.

Given the resounding failure of our efforts to predict the *priority of casework*, we explore bivariate relationships to make sure that effects are not hidden by competing variables in the model. Here too we find no relationships between any of our independent variables and the priority our respondents' place on casework. We conclude that variation in the priority placed on casework cannot be explained by the usual cast of suspects.

We do, however, manage to shed some light on the behavior of lame duck legislators with respect to casework. Consistent with the work of Herrick, Moore, and Hibbing (1994), we find that lame ducks shirk with respect to casework, but this is true only for those serving in the upper chamber and who are not politically ambitious.[2]

So, the basic story we can tell about the priority placed on casework is that almost all legislators do it, and they do a lot of it. We remind readers that, as we pointed out earlier in this chapter, when we divide our data by chamber and term limits casework always appears among the top three priorities (see figure 4.1). We speculate that differences other scholars find in the priority legislators place on casework are driven by the institutional resources, such as staff, supporting this task rather than by the characteristics of individual legislator or the district. In a single state study such as ours, these are nearly constant.[3]

The motivation for the popularity of this activity appears to reflect legislators' changing perceptions of their job (Moncrief et al. 1996). Many state legislators see their ombudsman role as a way to represent constituents' interests (Goodman et al. 1986). This suggests an additional line of inquiry into legislators' approach to representation that could complement the traditional inquiry into role orientations and voting records that we explored in chapter 3. From this perspective, constituents are represented through individual attention to their problems, casework, by their legislator rather than by voting on behalf of the district or the state. Our findings are consistent with this perspective.

Constituents who seek help from their elected officials might rejoice that so many of them prioritize casework. Politically ambitious lame ducks remain helpful even as their days in office dwindle. Given that there are a lot more politically ambitious legislators in Michigan's post-term-limits chambers, most Michigan citizens can expect their state legislator to be helpful and attentive to their individual problems even as these legislators exit office.

Public Resource Allocations (aka Pork)

Term limits proponents argue that legislators' craving for pork increases the longer they serve in elected office, but unfastening the electoral connection will trim their appetite (Will 1992). Despite the attention pork barrel spending receives in the popular press (for example, the latest installment of the *Pig Book*, by Citizens against Government Waste, available at http://cagw.org), relatively little academic work examines state legislators' efforts to bring money or projects (aka pork) to their districts.

Carey et al. (2006) report that legislators in states that had adopted term limits spent less time getting pork for their district. But referring back to figure 4.1, we see that getting money and projects for the district is an activity with a moderate priority for all our respondents—lower than helping constituents and communicating with voters, but higher than developing new legislation. Additionally, we find that the priority placed on this task increases in the House after term limits, although it decreases in the Senate.

Once again, there are questions about the political payoff from bringing resources to the district (Mayhew 1974). Although it seems reasonable that legislators might try to run for reelection by taking credit for these projects, they might not succeed. Some authors find that voters lack knowledge about who brought them what benefits (Samuels 2002; Stein and Bickers 1994). As Chen (2010) demonstrates, attributing credit for these resources is a complex task for voters when lower and upper chamber legislative districts only partially overlap, so multiple elected officials might have worked to bring a project to the district.

Yet procuring resources for the district appears valuable. Tate (2003) reports that African American constituents evaluate their representatives less on their ideological voting record and more on the resources they direct to the district. So getting pork may be yet another way to represent their voters' interests. If electoral payoff motivates legislators to bring home the bacon, we expect lame ducks to shirk on this task. Consistent with this political ambition, both primary and general electoral competition should raise the priority placed on bringing projects to the district.

In a legislature such as Michigan's, with strong majority control of the chamber, the chamber's majority leaders control access to these resources. Both Thompson (1986) and Gamm and Kousser (2013) find majority party membership affects allocation of resources (pork) to districts. So, we control for this in our model because we assume members of the minority party will place a low priority on a task with so little chance of any payoff—political or otherwise. On the other hand, we assume that legislators who represent districts with higher poverty levels will prioritize bringing resources to the district because the need is acute, motivating them to engage in this activity regardless of the probability of success.

Ellickson and Whistler (2001) find that seniority has a small but significant positive effect on time spent getting pork. Therefore, we assume that term limits will dampen legislators' emphasis on this task. Additionally, these authors find, as we did at the end of in chapter 3, that representational role orientations affect procuring these resources. Thus, we include our measures of representational style and focus in the model.

As we see in table 4.1 our model predicting the priority legislators place on *getting pork* has some modest predictive strength, and several coefficients are statistically significant. Controlling for other factors, we find that term limits have no statistically significant effect on the priority of bringing resources to the district. This contradicts the work of Carey et al. (2006), who report that legislators in term-limited states spent less time bringing

TABLE 4.1. Getting Pork for the District

Model Predicting the Priority Placed on Bringing Money and Projects to the District	Unstandardized Coefficients		*t*	Sig.
	B	Std. Error		
(Constant)	**0.65**	.20	3.21	.001
Term limits	−0.10	.14	−0.71	.477
Chamber (Senate = 1)	0.09	.13	0.68	.499
Politically ambitious	**0.36**	.09	4.21	.000
Safe district	−0.003	.002	−1.49	.138
Poverty % in district	**0.01**	.01	1.86	.064
Lame duck	0.15	.09	1.60	.112
Chamber minority party	**−0.47**	.15	−3.08	.002
Chamber minority post-TL	**0.45**	.19	2.33	.020
Representational style rely on self (high)	−0.02	.03	−0.79	.428
Representational focus on the state (high)	**−0.15**	.03	−4.86	.000
Gender (female = 1)	**−0.17**	.10	−1.77	.077

Note: Bold type indicates statistically significant coefficients.
F = 6.56; Adjusted R^2 = 0.17; n = 293.
Dependent Variable: mean = 0.18; range −2.3 to 1.9; Skewness = −0.48; Kurtosis = 0.11.

home the bacon, but we are able to control for more individual legislator and district-level factors, which might account for this difference.

Political payoff appears to energize the quest for pork. At least politically ambitious Michigan legislators act as if bringing resources to the district provides a political payoff. By swelling the ranks of political ambitious legislators, we suspect that term limits trigger a surge in the quest for pork. Lame ducks show no signs of shirking on this task. Indeed, they might place a slightly higher priority on it, but the effect is just shy of statistical significance. At least we can say that their status is unlikely to dampen requests for pork.

District need as well as political reward appears to drive the pursuit of pork. Legislators who represent impoverished districts prioritize bringing resources to their constituents. This is true even though many impoverished urban districts are represented by Democrats—the minority party during most of our study period. Before term limits members of the chambers' minority party recognized that to the victor go the spoils.[4] After term limits, the increasing priority that the chambers' minority party members place on getting pork seems to fly in the face of this conventional wisdom. Given that they do not control the budget, they probably find success elusive. Yet it appears that they try hard anyway—perhaps this is part of the learning curve for freshmen.

So what are the characteristics of the pork avoiders? Based on our results, if term limits proponents want to reduce pork barrel spending, they should seek female legislators, who are not politically ambitious and tend to focus on the interests of the state as a whole rather than the district. On the other hand, voters who want their representatives to bring home the bacon should elect men who are politically ambitious, who have a district focus when interests of the district and state collide, and who may be serving their last term in office.

Lawmaking

As we reported earlier in this chapter, our respondents place an average or below average priority on most facets of legislating that we asked about. Pre-term-limits senators are the exception to this pattern, however. This contradicts the work of others (Ellickson and Whistler 2001; Elling 1979) who find that legislating occupies a lot of legislators' time. In general, our findings more closely resemble those of Goodman et al. (1986), who find that casework is more important than making good public policy and developing issue expertise.

The effect of term limits on the priority placed on legislating is ambiguous. Initially Carey, Niemi, and Powell (1998) reported that newly elected legislators in term-limited states spent more time developing legislation than did newly elected legislators in non-term-limited states. In their subsequent work, however, Carey et al. (2006) find no difference among term-limited and non-term-limited states with respect to time spent studying proposed laws or developing new legislation. This is consistent with our findings.

The academic literature is unclear about the association between reelection-seeking and legislating. Gamble (2007) determines that electoral vulnerability, institutional roles, district characteristics, and time in office affect the amount of time legislators devoted to some facets of legislating. Herrick, Moore, and Hibbing (1994) argue that a lot of legislating involves symbolic activity designed for credit claiming and reelection fodder. These authors find that when the electoral connection is severed by retirement, lame ducks formulate a more cohesive legislative agenda and work harder to pass laws rather than simply introducing bills in order to take credit for them. We probe the political payoff of legislating in our model using electoral vulnerability and political ambition. We also examine the effects of experience and expertise on legislating.

It appears that legislating is one of the more challenging activities legislators engage in. Gamm and Kousser (2013) discover that legislators with more expertise in the law (lawyers) gravitate toward legislating. Consistent with this, Michigan's most expert legislators, its pre-term-limits senators, placed a higher priority on developing new legislation than post-term-limits senators or representatives. We include the chamber as well as three other measures of expertise in our model: prior political experience, ranking committee member, and career as a lawyer.

Our preliminary analyses reveal that the various district and legislator characteristics described above influence only two facets of legislating: *developing new legislation* and *building bipartisan coalitions*. Very few individual legislator characteristics are associated with the priority placed on *studying legislation* or on *building coalitions within one's own political party to pass legislation*. Therefore, we concentrate our efforts on explaining the priority our respondents place on *developing new legislation* and *building bipartisan coalitions*.

Developing New Legislation

We report in table 4.2 the results for our model predicting the priority placed on developing new legislation. The model has modest predictive power and several coefficients provide interesting insights into the priority placed on developing new legislation.

Expertise seems to be the most important factor in predicting the priority placed on developing new legislation. Lawyers and respondents with prior political experience prioritize this task. Senators also place a higher priority on this task than representatives do. Although we find no direct effect of term limits, we find that after term limits, the difference between lawyers and other legislators diminishes. This indicates that even legal experts need some experience to develop their potential for legislating.

We also find several indications that developing new legislation is politically fraught. First, legislators who prioritize this task tend to hold safe general election seats. This implies that legislating is a politically risky business unless one's constituents are a homogeneous lot. Yet legislators who experienced a serious primary challenge appear to respond by developing new legislation. Second, politically ambitious legislators eschew legislating, seeming to concentrate on safer activities. Finally, lame ducks, relieved of their reelection concerns, focus more effort on developing new legislation, but only before term limits. After term limits, lame ducks behave no differently than their colleagues with respect to this facet of legislating. This implies that pre-term-limits lame ducks had a legislative agenda that they wanted to finish while post-term-limits lame ducks may not.

TABLE 4.2. Developing New Legislation

Model Predicting Priority Placed on Developing New Legislation	Unstandardized Coefficients			
	B	Std. Error	t	Sig.
(Constant)	−.056	.15	−3.68	.000
Term limits	0.07	.12	0.57	.569
Chamber (Senate = 1)	**0.26**	.10	2.69	.007
Political ambition	−0.12	.07	−1.65	.100
Primary votes against (percent)	**0.003**	.002	2.08	.036
Safe district (0 to 93.2%)	**0.006**	.002	3.06	.002
Lame duck	**0.35**	.14	2.52	.012
Interaction of term limits and lame ducks	−0.32	.16	−1.95	.052
Prior political experience	**0.33**	.09	3.85	.000
Lawyer	**0.56**	.18	3.16	.002
Interaction of term limits and lawyer	−0.36	.21	−1.66	.098
Ranking member of a committee	0.10	.07	1.40	.161
Member of the chamber's opposition party	**−0.20**	.07	−2.84	.005
Percent of poverty in district	**−0.01**	.01	−2.62	.009
Gender (female = 1)	0.02	.08	0.29	.773

Note: Bold type indicates statistically significant coefficients.
F = 5.75; Adjusted R^2 = 0.14; n = 410.
Dependent Variable: Mean = −0.108; Range 4, from −2.09 to 1.91; Skewness = −0.024; Kurtosis = −0.39.

We find that the chamber's minority party legislators place a lower priority on developing new legislation. This probably reflects a rational calculation about the unlikely prospect of getting even a committee hearing, let alone a floor vote, on a minority-sponsored bill.

Given the extensive literature on gender and legislative behavior and the image of women as more issue-oriented, we consider our null finding about gender important. It reinforces evidence that we presented in chapter 2 that women are not more likely than men to have run to address some specific issue or to work on issues in general. (School reform is the one exception we found to this pattern.)

So who do we predict will develop new legislation? It is likely to be a senator, especially before term limits, trained as a lawyer, representing a homogeneous district (a safe seat), but who faced a serious primary challenge prior to his or her landslide victory in the general election. The image of a legislator who places a low priority on developing new legislation is a politically ambitious member of the chamber's minority political party who represents an impoverished district, who is relatively free from a primary challenge, but who is vulnerable in the general election. Developing new legislation appears to be the privilege of electorally secure veterans in the majority party, as well as the purview of experts, such as lawyers.

Bipartisan Coalition Building

Given the stated preferences of the public for more bipartisanship, we think that understanding what thwarts and facilities *building bipartisan coalitions* may have both practical and theoretical value. As we noted above, building bipartisan coalitions is the other facet of legislating that seems sensitive to individual and district characteristics and institutional positions. Therefore, we hope to be able to predict who will prioritize this task and under what circumstances.

Our overall model predicting the priority placed on bipartisan coalition building has modest explanatory power,[5] and we find interesting results for several key independent variables. We report these in table 4.3. Term limits are just shy of statistical significance, but if they do have an effect it is to dampen efforts to work across the aisle.

We find that electoral vulnerability and political payoff are important predictors of bipartisan coalition building, but not necessarily in the ways we would expect. Surprisingly, if legislators are electorally vulnerable, they do not appear to reach across the aisle. Legislators running for safe seats are the ones who prioritize bipartisan coalition building, although the coefficient just misses statistical significance. We expected legislators holding competitive seats to tout their bipartisan achievements to appeal to moderates and independents—about one-third of Michigan's voters. But electoral vulnerability appears to intensify the exodus from the middle. Presumably, vulnerable legislators respond to their base and their party rather than appealing to the independents and moderates.

Legislators who have faced a serious primary challenge also place a lower priority on bipartisan coalition building. We expected this result given the efforts of groups like the Tea Party and MoveOn.org to purge any moderates from seats that are safe for their favored party. Thus both general election and primary election safety spur bipartisan coalition building, suggesting that this is a very risky task.

Reinforcing our speculation about these political risks, lame ducks increase the priority they place on bipartisan coalition building, but not if they are politically ambitious. Politically ambitious lame ducks place a lower priority on bipartisan coalition building, possibly to ingratiate themselves to their fellow partisans.

Minority party members cannot hope to achieve any of their policy goals without the support of the majority party, which in Michigan dominates the committee and floor processes. So it is not surprising that members of the chamber's minority party place a higher priority on bipartisan

TABLE 4.3. Building Coalitions across Party Lines to Pass Legislation

Model Predicting the Priority Placed on Building Cross Party Coalitions to Pass Legislation	Unstandardized Coefficients			
	B	Std. Error	*t*	Sig.
(Constant)	−0.01	0.11	−0.03	.977
Term limits	−0.13	0.09	−1.57	.118
Chamber (Senate = 1)	0.01	0.01	0.09	.927
Primary votes against (percent)	**−0.003**	0.002	−2.02	.044
Seat in safe district	0.003	0.002	1.64	.101
Political ambition	−0.06	0.01	−0.65	.514
Lame duck	**0.45**	0.13	3.56	.000
Interaction of political ambition and lame duck	**−0.33**	0.15	−2.17	.031
Member of the chamber's minority party	**0.24**	0.07	3.56	.001
On Appropriations Committee	0.11	0.08	1.34	.180
Gender (Female = 1)	−0.08	0.09	−0.95	.341
Age category (by decade)	**−0.08**	0.04	−2.14	.033

Note: Bold type indicates statistically significant coefficients.

$F = 5.38$; Adjusted $R^2 = 0.11$; $n=411$.

Dependent Variable: Mean = −0.22; Minimum −2.41 to Maximum 1.91 (Range 4.5); Skewness = 0.10; Kurtosis = 0.006.

coalition building. We infer that legislators expend time and energy on activities likely to produce results, and minority party members seem to recognize that any hope they have of achieving policy goals lies in collaboration with the majority party. Their desire to get something done appears to overcome the risks of reaching across the aisle.

We continue to include gender in our models given the discussion in the political science literature about the bipartisan impact of women on the process of governing (Volden, Wiseman, and Wittmer 2013; Kathlene 1994, 1995). We find no gender effect on building bipartisan coalitions. Indeed, the coefficient, although not statistically significant, is in the opposite direction.

We also control for service on the appropriations committee, given that the obligation of passing a budget might encourage legislators to work across the aisle. Although the coefficient is in the predicted direction, the effect is small. We control for age, thinking that the influx of younger, newer legislators might bring a brash, polarizing influence to the legislature.[6] We find that we were quite wrong. Older rather than younger legislators eschew bipartisan coalition building—a curmudgeon effect.

So who do we predict will engage in the elusive bipartisanship that most citizens claim they want from their elected officials? Pre-term-limits lame ducks representing a safe district and serving on the appropriations committee. This sounds suspiciously like the sort of legislator that term limits proponents wanted to purge from the halls of government—careerists who are unlikely to be challenged at the ballot box.

And who is likely to place a low priority on cross-party collaboration? Our answer here is older politically ambitious legislators, especially those who are facing an electoral challenge either in the primary or general election. Political vulnerability combined with political ambition tends to inhibit rather than enhance bipartisan coalition building. And as we found in chapter 2 there is a burgeoning supply of politically ambitious legislators after term limits, so the prospects for bipartisan policy making appear dim.

Changes across Time

The longitudinal design of our research means that we have multiple measures across legislative sessions for a few of our respondents. We have two sessions of data for 119 legislators, and for 61 of these we have three sessions of data. Although we have four and five sessions of data for a few legislators, there are not enough to analyze. The number of repeat respondents varies slightly because occasionally a respondent does not answer a specific question during an interview.

We use these data on repeat respondents to see how individual legislators change their time allocation as they gain more experience. In order to have enough cases to analyze quantitatively, we count the legislator's first interview as time one, regardless of the year in which this interview occurred. In the following analyses, we compare interview one to interview two, interview two to three, and interview one to three. If there is a session gap between our interviews with a legislator, we treat the first interview as time one, the missing interview is treated as a missing value, and the third interview is treated as interview three, even though there are only two interviews total.

Using specific calendar years would reduce the size of our cohort of repeat respondents too dramatically for us to be confident of the results, but using the sequence of consecutive interviews as our unit of time introduces confounding chamber and partisan effects. This also makes it harder to isolate freshman and lame duck effects.[7] This is a necessary trade-off, but given that many of term limits effects are contingent on factors such as party and chamber, we consider the following analyses to be highly exploratory.

First, we address a threshold question: Is the priority a legislator places on a task associated across time? To explore this, we look at simple bivariate correlations between the priority of a specific task in the first and second interview, the second and third interview, and the first and third interview. The clear answer is yes, for most tasks. As we see in table 4.4, six tasks exhibit an association between both the first and second and the second and third sessions. These six are fundraising, building coalitions within the party, developing new legislation, studying legislation, attending events in the capital, and monitoring state agencies—responses are correlated for all three pairs of sessions.

All these correlations are positive, suggesting that a legislator's priority for each of these tasks moves in a consistent direction across the three time periods—high priority tasks remaining high or low priority tasks remaining low. For example, fundraising is an exceptionally unpopular task. The mean for the priority placed on fundraising decreases across each subsequent interview (−0.62, −0.65, −0.73), producing a fairly large positive correlation.

Two tasks, talking to voters and getting pork, are correlated between interviews one and two and also between interviews two and three, but not between interviews one and three. The absence of a relationship between interviews one and three suggests cross currents that shift the direction of the association, but only for some legislators. The third interview would occur during the final term for many repeat respondents. So the lack of correlation could reflect the interaction between lame duck status and political ambition. Lame ducks' behaviors vary depending on their career plans, as we discussed earlier in this chapter.

Three other tasks are correlated between the first and second interview, but not between the second and third or the first and third. These are casework, and attending meetings in the district. For example, the priority of casework for an individual in the first interview and second interview is correlated ($r = 0.58$, $p < 0.01$), but there is no substantively or statistically significant correlation at all ($r = 0.05$) between the second and third interviews or the first and third interviews. This implies competing lame duck

TABLE 4.4. Correlations across Sessions for Priority Placed on Tasks

	Sessions 1 and 2	Sessions 2 and 3	Sessions 1 and 3
Fundraising	**.54****	**.35****	**.32***
	(.00)	(.01)	(.002)
Own party coalitions	**.30****	**.33***	**.30***
	(.001)	(.01)	(.02)
Develop new laws	**.35****	**.39****	**.39****
	(.00)	(.002)	(.002)
Studying legislation	**.40****	**.36****	**.37****
	(.00)	(.01)	(.004)
Attending Lansing events	**.41****	**.34****	**.36****
	(.00)	(.01)	(.01)
Monitoring state agencies	**.43****	**.45****	**.32***
	(.00)	(.00)	(.01)
Getting pork	**.22***	**.39****	.01
	(.02)	(.002)	(.91)
Talking to voters	**.32****	**.38****	.14
	(.001)	(.002)	(.28)
Cross-party coalitions	**.36****	.02	.12
	(.00)	(.87)	(.35)
Casework	**.58****	.05	.06
	(.00)	(.68)	(.66)
Attend district meetings	**.30****	0.01	.13
	(.002)	(0.66)	(.32)
n ranges between:[a]	111 and 109	61 and 59	60 and 59

Note: Values are Pearson correlations with the statistical significance for a two-tailed test in parentheses below. Bold type also indicates statistically significant associations.

[a] Number of respondents varies because some legislators did not answer specific questions.

*$p < 0.10$, **$p < 0.05$, ***$p < 0.01$ (two-tailed tests).

effects given that both tasks involve constituent or district service. Some lame ducks shirk, while politically ambitious lame ducks double down on this. The result is that past behavior is not strongly associated with third term behavior.

Next we use a paired-samples *t*-test to compare the priority for each task for individual respondents for each pair of interviews, one to two, two to three, and one to three. The clear message is that our repeat respondents' task priorities are very stable across three sessions. We find only three statistically significant differences among pairs of sessions among the 36 pairs we tested. First, we find a change in the average time repeat respondents spend on all 11 tasks. Their average time decreases from their first to their second interview and from the first to the third sessions. Second, we find changes that differ from zero in the priority placed on only two specific tasks: building bipartisan coalitions to pass legislation and attending meetings in the district. The priority placed on both these tasks increases between interviews one and three. We note that these are among the three tasks in table 4.4 that are uncorrelated between interviews two and three or between interviews one and three.

The change we find in the average time spent on all 11 tasks could be a learning curve effect or a lame duck effect. We find that there is no statistically significant change between interviews two and three, when most respondents would be lame ducks. Most of the change occurs between sessions one and two. This means that the learning curve effect rather than the lame duck effect is a more convincing explanation.[8] This learning curve effect dissipates quickly, however—after one session—as legislators rapidly learn the basics of the job.

It appears that our repeat respondents are less averse to working across the aisle to pass legislation as their time in office increases. The priority placed on *building bipartisan coalitions* changes from an avoided task (–0.40) to a low priority task (–0.14) for the 59 respondents answering this question in a first and third interview. Most of the change in this task occurs between the first and second interviews, but the trend is in the same direction across all three time periods. Only the combined change across all three sessions is large enough to be statistically significant. Although this is still not a high priority, it does suggest some potential for bipartisan policy making the longer legislators serve. And we know from our findings presented earlier in this chapter that lame ducks who are not politically ambitious prioritize this task.

Values for *attending meetings in the district* change from a high priority (0.46) to an even higher priority (0.65) for the 59 respondents answering this question in a first and third interview. The priority placed on this task increases about equally between interviews one and two and interviews two and three, but here again the differences separately are not large enough to achieve statistical significance. This contradicts evidence, our own and others, that lame ducks shirk with respect to constituents and the district. It could reflect plans to run for local offices, such as county commissioner, large-city mayor, or positions on local courts or for a state senate seat, however. As reported earlier in the chapter, political ambition can overcome lame duck tendencies.

We also compare our repeat respondents who were elected prior to term limits (and might have been socialized by veteran colleagues) and those who were elected after the initial term limits expulsions. To do this we split the data into two cohorts, 25 who were elected prior to term limits and 33 elected afterward. Here again, we find a lot of continuity and not much change. But we do find differences on four activities: building coalitions in their own party, bringing resources (pork) to the district, fundraising, and attending events in the state capital. Two of these affect pre-term-limits legislators and two affect post-term-limits legislators.

Our repeat respondents elected before term limits shift away from building coalitions in their own party and gravitate toward bringing pork to their district. Those elected after term limits increasingly place a higher priority on fundraising, probably due to the sharp increase in political ambition after term limits. They also place a lower priority on attending meetings in the state capital, Lansing.

But once again, the clearest message is that legislators' initial mix of task priorities is remarkably stable. Time in office makes only small differences in legislators' behaviors, with or without term limits. Factors other than tenure appear to be better predictors of legislators' behaviors—for example, their political ambition.

Roll Call Voting Behavior across Time

Finally, we consider whether legislators change their voting behavior when they are freed from reelection seeking—at least for their current seat. There are two possible changes that legislators might make when they are no longer running for their current position. First, they could vote in ways that are closer to their constituents' views, possibly because the pressures of party loyalty are removed. Second, they could drift further away from voters (at least their current voters) as their electoral connection is "unfastened." Readers are reminded that in chapter 3 we found that term limits increase the voting mismatch between representatives and their constituents, supporting the second possibility.

In order to examine this, we need to hold the district map constant because the homogeneity of the district is a key element in the fit between a legislator's voting behavior and the district. This means that we have two cohorts of legislators that we can examine. First, we return once again to House sessions 1997, 1999, and 2001. This provides us with 81 repeat respondents elected under the map drawn after the 1990 census who were interviewed twice and 27 who were interviewed three times. We also have a cohort of 29 senators who were interviewed twice. They were elected to the Senate under the map drawn after the 2000 census. We can compare their voting behavior in the 2003 and the 2007 Senate sessions.

To assess the maximum size of any changes in these legislators' voting behavior we subtract their most conservative voting record from their most liberal one. We find that the average size of the shifts in roll call voting is 8.6 percent (sd 6.9) and the median shift is 6.9 percent. Only 12 legislators shift their voting pattern by more than two standard deviations from this mean (about a 15% shift in voting behavior) and 7 shifted more than three standard deviations away (a 22% shift). So, about 10 percent of the representatives serving in these three sessions alter their voting behavior dramatically. The maximum shift is 35 percent.

Even when the shifts are large, sometimes legislators shift from one side of their voters to the other. For example, the legislator whose roll call voting behavior changed the most shifted from underrepresenting the liberalness of his district by 17.5 percent to over representing it by 17.5 percent—a 35 percent shift in the liberalness of his voting record but consistently the same distance from his voters. The average for the maximum mismatch between these repeat respondents and their voters is 23 percent, the average for their minimum mismatch is 15 percent. Roughly equal numbers of these legislators move toward and away from their constituents between the 1999 and 2001 sessions. However, between the 1997 (pre-term-limits) and 1999 (post-term-limits) sessions about two-thirds of the 45 repeat respondents who served in these two sessions moved away from their voters. This implicates term limits in the migration of legislators away from voters because it coincides with the first forced mass exodus from the Michigan House.

Political ambition appears to have only a small effect on the changes legislators make in their roll call voting, but it is hard to be certain because we lack cases for representatives without political ambition. Of the 101 respondents whose political plans we know (7 missing cases), only 16 are *not* politically ambitious. These 16 change their roll call votes 7.3 percent compared to a shift of 8.9 percent in the roll call votes of our 85 politically ambitious repeat respondents.

We find that senators are less likely to alter their voting behavior as they exit office. The average shift in roll call voting for the 29 Senators we interviewed twice is 4.4 percent (sd 3.2). Only two of these 29 lame duck Senators made major shifts in their voting behavior of more than two standard deviations from this mean. Political ambition is widely distributed among senators, both those making big changes in their voting and those who did not. With so few cases it is impossible to be confident about the effect of political ambition on their voting behavior.[9] But our findings about senators suggest that more than 80 percent of lame ducks do not change their voting behavior much at all even when the electoral connection with their voters is severed.

We conclude that unfastening the electoral connection generally has little effect on voting behavior. The few representatives who do make big changes in their voting tend to be politically ambitious, but with such a small cohort that lacks ambition it is hard to certain about the effect of political ambition on voting. But when we examine legislators' voting behavior across time, we find further evidence that term limits expands the gap between legislators and their voters, as we established in chapter 3.

Conclusions

We were surprised by several results of our investigation of legislators' behaviors. First, many behaviors change more in the Senate than in the House after term limits. We and many others assumed that changes wrought by term limits would arise from a decrease in legislators' experience. Term limits in Michigan reduce the years of experience in the House more than in the Senate, so we expected behavior to change more in the lower chamber. Yet we find more differences in the Senate for the behaviors we examine here. Two changes stand out. Post-term-limits senators place a lower priority on developing new legislation and a higher priority on communicating with voters.

Next, we were surprised that our respondents place only a moderate to low priority on the four facets of legislating that we examine. They appear to place a much higher priority on other parts of the job. This challenges the usual assumption that legislators primarily legislate. In conjunction with this, we find that some tasks (developing new legislation) are the purview of specialists and others (e.g., casework) are generalist tasks that nearly everyone does, and does a lot.

Much of the change we find in legislators' behaviors is contingent on context and circumstances. For example, we find lame duck effects, but these depend on combinations of political ambition, chamber, and term limits. Searching for these contingent effects, we examined various categories of legislators in addition to lame ducks, including gender, newcomers, and the politically ambitious. Differences among these groups are few and far between, with the exception of political ambition, which has major behavioral consequences. So we conclude that lame ducks and politically ambitious legislators behave differently. Term limits, by swelling the ranks of both these groups, indirectly alter legislators' behaviors.

We find that politically ambitious legislators differ in several ways from their colleagues. They place a higher priority on communicating with voters, attending meetings in the district, and getting resources for their district. They place a lower priority on developing new legislation, and they avoid building bipartisan coalitions. They might be prone to making changes in their voting behavior, but it is hard to be certain because we have so few repeat respondents who are not politically ambitious.

Lame ducks appear to shirk only selectively. They spend more time than their colleagues do on some tasks, such as developing new legislation and building bipartisan coalitions to pass legislation, and they maintain their efforts to bring resources to their district. These differences are more pronounced for pre-term-limited lame ducks, however. Finally, even after their electoral connection is severed, most lame ducks maintain their pattern of voting.

A final surprise involves bipartisan coalition building. Attention to this task reflects electoral concerns, but in unanticipated ways. We assumed, consistent with scholarship and pundits, that vulnerable legislators would work across the aisle to attract moderate and independent voters. To the contrary, we find that electoral competition—primary and general—reduce the priority legislators place on this task. Once again electoral accountability does not have the effects we expect. We pursue these questions further in chapter 5.

FIVE

Elections When Open Seats Are
Not a Surprise

What effects do term limits have on electoral competition? Term limits ballot campaigns nationally and in Michigan promised that removing incumbents would increase competition (Niven 2000; see also the archives of the Yes on B Campaign at the Library of Michigan). This expectation seemed reasonable given that open seat elections tend to be more competitive (Gaddie and Bullock 2000), and term limits increase the rate of turnover in most states, creating more open seats. Therefore, many observers logically assumed that term limits would increase electoral competition, presumably giving voters more choice at the ballot box.

But are open seats as competitive when they are extremely common and occur at short predictable intervals? And does boosting competition by a few percentage points give voters a realistic choice among candidates? An election won by a 70 percent margin of victory is technically more competitive than one with an 80 percent margin. But it seems unlikely that the loser of either contest had much chance of winning, barring a major scandal. And even then, an upset is unlikely. In this chapter we examine term limits effects on electoral competition, but with an eye on viable choices for voters, as well as substantial changes in margins of victory.

We begin by considering primary elections. Often primary victors are nearly certain general election winners. Therefore primary elections are a voter's best opportunity for input. Yet little is written about primary elec-

---

Catherine Schmitt-Sands is a coauthor on this chapter.

tions because there are so many candidates involved and the voting rules vary widely among the states. This makes cross-sectional research exceptionally challenging. By concentrating on Michigan only, we can examine the way the political system and term limits interact to alter the candidate selection process. We find that there are two primary election pathways—one for seats that are very safe for one political party and the other for seats that will be competitive in the general election. Term limits affect both, but differently.

After exploring primary elections, we turn our attention to general elections. After examining general election competition nationally, we look at Michigan's general election competition in detail. We make a minor foray into fundraising in Michigan after term limits, a topic that has been covered more extensively by other authors (e.g., Powell 2012). For Michigan's legislators, we have individual-level variables such as recruiting and legislators' fundraising effort. This means that we can add unique information to discussions of fundraising.

Throughout this chapter, we assess term limits effects within the context of Michigan's political system (e.g., the primary election rules and the district maps). In doing this we seek to understand how Michigan's political system filters and mediates the effect of more open seats and shorter terms of service. Conversely, we look for ways that term limits alter Michigan's politics and political institutions.

Data and Methods

In this chapter we combine a variety of publicly available data about election results and campaign fundraising with variables from our interviews. We describe our use of these data prior to each set of analyses, but we provide an overview of these resources and our adaptation of them here.

First, we examine Michigan's primary elections using data available through the Michigan Secretary of State's tabulation of the votes candidates received. We add variables measuring the base party affiliation of voters in the legislative districts, relying on *Inside Michigan Politics* data, to assess how competitive these seats are in the general election.

Next, we rely on data archived at the Inter-University Consortium for Political and Social Research gathered by Klarner et al. (2013). We use these data to examine general election margins of victory nationally. We add to these data a term-limitedness ratio (Sarbaugh-Thompson 2010b) to assess the stringency of limits in states that have them. We also add a categorical variable denoting the states with ballot initiative options that permit citizens to initiate legislation and constitutional amendments, based on information from the National Conference of State Legislatures website. Finally, we add scores measuring the professionalism of the legislature in each state (Squire 2007).

After considering general election competition nationally, we examine general election competition in Michigan. To do this we use data from the Michigan Secretary of State about the votes cast against legislators serving during the sessions in which we conducted interviews.

Finally, we examine the campaign fundraising of legislators serving during the session in which we conducted interviews. We used campaign finance data available through the National Institute for Money in State Politics. We combine the amounts of money raised by those legislators with our interview data so that we can examine the effects of political ambition, fundraising effort, and recruiting by interest groups on the amount of money legislators raise.

The Michigan Electoral Context

Term limits create more open seat elections in Michigan by forcing incumbents out of office before they reach their average pre-term-limits tenure. The effect is especially strong for Michigan Democrats, who typically served longer than Republicans did before term limits. This increase in open seats, which is not necessarily true in all term-limited states (Heberlig and Leland 2004),[1] produces a persistent churning in Michigan's legislature. This is especially true in the lower chamber, as waves of newcomers arrive, termed lame ducks leave, and politically ambitious legislators jump into other electoral contests even before exhausting their permitted time in their current position.

The initial expulsion effects of term limits on the Michigan House were profound—64 of the 110 members were termed out in 1998. Only 41.8 percent of Michigan's representatives were eligible to run in 1998 for another term, and all of them did so. Following this initial surge in open seats, turnover in the lower chamber fluctuated between 21 and 62 seats. More recently, turnover in the House stabilized at a little more than one-third of the membership for each biannual election. There were 39 open seat races for the House in 2014. There will be at least 40 in 2016. But it has taken more than a decade to approach a term limits equilibrium rate of one-third per election.

Taking a before and after perspective, for the three elections immediately before Michigan voters adopted limits, turnover in Michigan's lower chamber averaged 13 open seats per election. After term limits it is higher (39 seats). Term limits clearly increase the number of open seats in the Michigan House. Turnover in the lower chamber is also slightly higher (about 37 seats) than the one-third level mandated by term limits for a chamber with a 3-session maximum. This difference primarily results from politically ambitious legislators leaving early, often to pursue state senate seats, but occasionally an incumbent loses. The mismatched timing of state senate elections (all senators run every four years) and Michigan's House limits of six years appears to motivate some representatives to run for the state senate elections after four years in the House rather than stepping out of politics for two years.

In 1998, nine veteran senators retired strategically from safely partisan districts, sacrificing their final four years of permitted service to provide a pathway into the Senate for a few termed-out House members. This produced a Senate leadership transition team composed of veteran representatives. It also avoided a complete turnover of all 38 Senate seats in 2002.

The 2002 elections for Michigan Senate, the first after veterans were forced from office, featured 31 open seats in the 38-seat chamber—a huge rate of turnover. There were only 9 open seats in the following Senate election (2006). After another spike in newcomers in 2010, the 2014 election featured only 10 open seat races for the Michigan Senate. Even after a decade, turnover in the Senate is punctuated by peaks and valleys characteristic of the transition to term limits (Mooney 2009). It may take decades for this ebb and flow to moderate as the Senate inches glacially toward a 50 percent rate of turnover (19 of the 38 seats) every four years.[2]

Although there appear to be lots of open seats, many districts in Michigan have been drawn to be safe for one party. These are likely to produce newcomers who win by a landslide, just as their incumbent predecessors did before term limits. So it is important to define a competitive election. Whenever possible we treat district competition as a continuous variable calculated taking the absolute value of the difference between the base party voting strength of the two major political parties in the district. We described this in detail in chapter 3.

But occasionally in this chapter we classify elections categorically into those that are competitive and those that are not. Here we use a generous definition of competition. Specifically, we assume that a difference in the base party strength between the two major parties of less than 20 percent means that the district is competitive. We settled on this definition of competitive districts at the outset of our research, when there were only 20 districts that met even this generous definition of competition.

One change that confounds our efforts to assess term limits effect on electoral competition is a shift in the district maps. Seats that tilt toward one party abound in Michigan as boundary drawing becomes more data intensive and hence more precise. The map drawn in 1992 was a bipartisan compromise, but the maps drawn in 2002 and 2012 were both controlled entirely by the Republican Party. Therefore, the maps in effect for most of the post-term-limits elections were designed to pack Democratic voters into a small number of very safe districts for Democratic candidates, while Republican voters were distributed across a sizable number of districts drawn so that Republicans stand a good chance of winning them. Some of these seats fit our generous criterion for competitive seats, but they lean toward one political party.

By our generous definition of competition, the number of competitive districts increases after term limits from 20 to 61, but it is the partisan opportunity to control the chamber rather than term limits that provides the most plausible explanation for this increase in competitive districts. This is readily apparent in the partisan distribution of these leaning districts. As we noted in chapter 4, of the 20 competitive districts under the 1992 map, 7 tilted Republican and 13 tilted toward the Democrats. The 2002 map features 61 competitive districts, with 44 that tilt toward Republicans and 17 that tilt toward the Democrats. The most recent district map in Michigan, drawn in 2012, consists of 60 competitive districts, 44 that tilt toward Republicans and 16 that tilt toward Democrats. To indicate just how finely honed the boundaries are in Michigan's 2012 district map, one state house district is connected by a narrow strip that measures less than the distance from home plate to the outfield fence in Detroit's Comerica Park. In other words, Detroit Tigers star Miguel Cabrera could hit a baseball across the district.

Safe seats in the general election shift the question of competition back to the primary. When one political party repeatedly wins in the general election, primary elections become particularly important because this is likely to be the only time voters can realistically choose among candidates. As we will explain shortly, when general elections are competitive, post-term-limits primary elections often lose importance in Michigan.

Primary Elections in Michigan

Primary elections provide a pathway to general election contests, but there are two distinct trajectories depending on the safety of the seat. Prior evidence (Sarbaugh-Thompson et al. 2002, 2004) suggests that anointed candidates often run unopposed in primaries for competitive seats while candidates flock unimpeded to primaries for especially safe seats. Therefore, voters may have little or no choice among candidates in certain primary elections.

Indeed, we learned that some potential candidates may be "encouraged" to channel their political ambition elsewhere as party elites shield their preferred candidate in the primary and husband campaign dollars for a competitive general election contest. When we asked our respondents who recruited them to run, one respondent asked whether we also wanted to know who asked him not to run (interview notes). One reason candidates are discouraged from running involves Michigan's primary election rules that allow any voter to cast a ballot in either of the two major parties' primaries. This open primary system facilitates partisan mischief, an issue we discuss below.

Term Limits Effects on Primary Elections

As we saw in chapter 2, recruiting quality candidates to run is more challenging after term limits. Thus more candidates are being asked to run, especially by political elites. We already know that term limits can alter Michigan's electoral environment, not just by increasing the number of open seat general elections but also by changing the process of selecting candidates who compete for those seats. Primary elections are the next step in the selection process—a step at which voters might expect to have more input.

In this section we assess whether term limits affect the number of candidates running in primary elections. We analyze primary elections for the Michigan House because term limits have been implemented long enough in that chamber to provide a reasonable estimate of the post-term-limits electoral climate. Michigan's state senators all run for reelection every four years. So there have not been enough elections yet to reveal clear patterns in the upper chamber.

Number of Candidates Running in Primary Elections

With two political party primaries for each of the 110 state house seats, there should be 220 House primaries per election cycle. Sometimes no one runs in a party's primary election, typically because the district is so safe for the other political party that the general election result is virtually guaranteed. The number of these nonexistent primaries is about 1 percent before and after term limits (i.e., two or three per election cycle). Term limits do not appear to change this.

Only one candidate runs in about two-thirds of the primary elections in Michigan. This clearly provides voters committed to one political party no choice among candidates. But we find that term limits reduce the number of these primaries slightly, from 67 percent to 62 percent. So it appears that 5 percent more voters have a choice of candidates during the primary elections after term limits. But the effect of this change for voters is complicated by the fact that we find different effects for primary elections leading to safe and competitive general election seats.

Before term limits, only 11 percent of the primaries leading to competitive elections provided voters with only one choice. After term limits, only one candidate ran in 36 percent of the competitive open seat primary contests. Thus, when a seat is open in a competitive district, term limits more than triple the proportion of primary elections in which voters are confronted with a "choice" of only one handpicked candidate.

We see clearly in figure 5.1 that voters have more choices after term limits only in primaries that lead to safe open seat general election contests. When an open seat occurs in a district that is competitive in the general election, there are fewer primary candidates after term limits. Moreover, when an incumbent is running for reelection, term limits do not increase the number of candidates that primary voters can choose among. This is exactly what we would predict if we assume that the political parties want to avoid partisan mischief in the primary elections and to preserve an anointed candidate's reputation and campaign coffers in the run-up to a competitive general election.

Michigan's primary elections for state offices enable partisan "mischief." Voters merely ask for a ballot from either one or the other political party. They do not need to declare a party affiliation or register as a member of a political party. Independents are welcome to vote in Michigan's primary elections. Voters often vote strategically if they think one political party is assured of a general election victory—a mini-max strategy.[3]

Another strategy that Michigan's primary voters can use, as long as they don't mind skipping the contest in their own party, is to vote for the weakest candidate in the other party's primary. If that candidate wins, it can improve the odds for their own party's candidate in the general election. For example, Democrats might vote for a Tea Party candidate in the Republican primary to improve the chances that a moderate Democrat would win in November. These strategies are most likely to be consequential when the general election is competitive. Therefore, party elites have

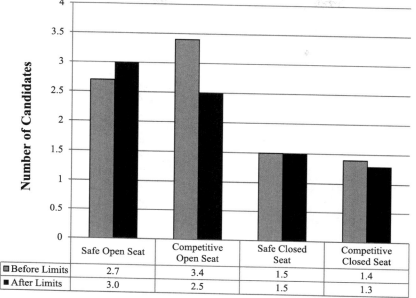

	Safe Open Seat	Competitive Open Seat	Safe Closed Seat	Competitive Closed Seat
▣ Before Limits	2.7	3.4	1.5	1.4
■ After Limits	3.0	2.5	1.5	1.3

The effect of term limits, an open seat, and a competitive general election is statistically significant ($p < 0.01$). n= 2,407 primary elections,

Fig. 5.1. Average Numbers of Candidates in Primary Elections, 1988–2012

an incentive to restrict voters' choices in a primary leading to a competitive general election.[4] This restriction of voters' primary choices appears to be more common after term limits, which means that voters lose some opportunities to participate in the candidate selection process.

Primary elections for safe general election seats are plagued by the opposite problem. They can be inundated by too many candidates for voters to assess. After term limits 17 candidates competed in one primary election—the record number in our data. When voter participation is low and the number of candidates is large, small cohorts of like-minded voters can elect a candidate with only limited popular support. After term limits, these multiperson contests characterize primaries leading to safe seats. Primaries like this produce narrow victories—sometimes less than a 100-vote margin of victory—and winning candidates often receive a total of only one or two thousand votes out of roughly 70,000 to 80,000 possible for the district. The subsequent general election will probably be won in a landslide—sometimes with more than an 80 percent margin of victory. For these seats, the general election contest is largely irrelevant—the primary is decisive.

When safe seats attract many primary contestants, a small number of voters have outsized say within their political party. For example, one winning candidate in our data received only 13.8 percent of the votes cast. We estimate that with a 15 to 20 percent turnout rate, about 2 to 3 percent of the districts' voters selected this candidate, who was funded heavily by a well-connected network cultivated by a former state legislator—the political elite who recruited this candidate. With the primary victory in hand, a general election victory was all but assured. Higher turnout in primary elections could offset some of this effect, however. So we turn now to whether removing the drag of incumbency increases voter turnout.

Primary Election Turnout

We find no evidence that primary election turnout increased after term limits in Michigan. We compared primary election turnout from the Secretary of State's website from 1988 through 2012, eight pre-term-limits and eight post-term-limits primary elections. We find that an average of 18 percent of the voting age population voted before term limits, while 19 percent did so afterward. Although technically this is a slight increase, it is not substantively noteworthy. It is certainly not enough to alter the electoral landscape after term limits.

There are several reasons that Michigan's primary election turnout is so low. First, Michigan schedules its primary elections for local and state offices in early August. This makes voting difficult for college students, families with school-age children, and others who are likely to be away from their voting location. It favors older adults and senior citizens. Second, other than senior citizens, voters in Michigan must give one of a series of acceptable reasons to request an absentee ballot. Third, there is no early voting in Michigan.

Term limits do nothing to overcome these impediments. But, by increasing the number of open seat elections, term limits make turnout more consequential in primaries that lead to safe general elections seats. If the general election is safe for one political party, these open seats typically attract numerous candidates, amplifying the power of small factions of voters to select a nearly certain winner in the general election.

Proportion of Votes Received by the Primary Election Winner

Now we move to our second measure of primary competition—the proportion of the total votes received by the winning primary election candidates, a continuous variable. The smaller this proportion is, the more competitive the election is. We use a multivariate model to test the proposition that term limits will increase primary election competition, reducing the proportion of the vote received by the winner. Our model, presented in table 5.1, explains 69 percent of the variation in the proportion of votes received by the primary winner. As we describe below, most of the independent variables in the model have statistically significant effects, but some of these are so small that they are substantively unimportant.

The number of candidates running makes the biggest impact on the proportion of the vote the winner receives, a finding that is not at all surprising. Obviously, giving voters a choice is a fundamental element of competition. But other variables in the model indicate that a district drawn to be extremely safe for one political party can offset almost all of the additional competition provided by adding another candidate.[5] So the district boundaries matter a lot.

An open seat election increases primary competition. This is also hardly surprising. But the effect of an open seat is surprisingly small, only about 7.5 percent more competition. Clearly there are more open seats after term limits—an indirect effect of term limits. But the direct effect of term limits offsets some of this. We find that the direct effect of term limits decreases rather than increases primary election competition, but only by 3 percent.

Finally, we control for political party given that Republicans single-handedly drew two of the district maps during this time period, and also primary election turnout tends to be lower among Democrats. Winners of Democratic primaries do receive a slightly higher proportion of the votes

TABLE 5.1. Competition in Michigan Primaries, 1992–2012

Model Predicting the Proportion of Primary Votes Received by the Winning Candidate	Unstandardized Coefficients			
	B	Std. Error	*t*	Sig.
(Constant)	**100.62**	.92	110.01	.000
Term limits (Yes = 1)	**2.99**	.90	3.30	.001
Open primary (Yes = 1)	**−1.97**	1.07	−1.84	.066
Term limits x open primary	−0.51	1.32	0.38	.702
Open seat (Yes = 1)	**−7.51**	1.49	−5.06	.000
Term limits x open seat	2.38	1.66	1.44	.151
Safety of seat in general election (0–93%)	**.11**	.01	10.06	.000
Party (Democrat = 1)	**2.20**	.52	4.28	.000
Number of candidates	**−10.75**	.17	−62.39	.000

Note: Bold type indicates statistically significant coefficients.
$F = 671.78$; $R^2 = 0.69$; $N = 2,376$ primary winners (includes one-candidate primaries).
Dependent Variable: Mean = 85.17%; Range, 0–100%; Skewness = −0.31; Kurtosis = 0.09.

cast in their district, a little more than 2 percent larger, indicating less competition. But again this is a very small effect.

On balance primary election competition is contingent on an open seat, district boundaries, and the number of candidates. Safe districts and the number of candidates running have a lot more effect on the level of primary competition than do term limits and even a bit more than open seats. And open seats might be a little less competitive after term limits.

Summary of Term Limits Effect on Primary Elections

There are two types of open seat elections—those that lead to a general election that is extremely safe for one political party and those that lead to a competitive general election. We find that term limits appear to affect each type of primary election differently. After term limits, candidates flock to primaries for safe seats. For open competitive seats, candidates are often winnowed to one handpicked contender per party.

We find that competition in Michigan's elections is a "Goldilocks problem." Too many candidates are just as problematic as too few. And term limits do not alleviate these problems. Indeed, sometimes term limits exacerbate them by reducing the number of candidates running when the general election is competitive and attracting huge numbers of primary candidates when the general election is safe for one political party.

For both safe and competitive seats, the average voters' viewpoint can easily be overwhelmed by the power of well-funded, well-connected candidates recruited and groomed by political elites. The mechanisms differ, but the results are similar for representative democracy. Voters have little input. When they do have a choice in the primary, the general election does not matter. When the general election matters, voters lack choices in the primary elections. Voters appear to lose rather than gain input into the candidate selection process.

Moreover, the potential exists for these effects to fuel partisan polarization of the legislature due to the outsized influence of a few political elites or a small faction of voters. When a handful of committed, possibly ideologically extreme, voters determine the primary result and hence the general election winner, representation of other viewpoints in the district could be distorted or ignored. Similarly, candidates groomed and anointed by political elites or interest groups running in primaries that give voters only one choice could represent their patrons rather than voters. Both these primary election processes could affect the composition of the legislature, roll call voting behavior, and democratic representation in ways that are consistent with our findings in chapters 2 and 3.

General Election Competition, Considered Nationally

Most studies of term limits conclude that landslide victories are the norm in general elections, with or without term limits (Richardson, Valentine, and Stokes 2005; Nalder 2007; Masket and Lewis 2007). These findings are consistent with our previous work on this topic (Sarbaugh-Thompson et al. 2006) in which we found that incumbents were safer in Michigan and California after term limits. Without a risk of losing, it is not clear why small increases in competition would motivate legislators to alter their behavior or their voting patterns. Therefore, we want to know whether term limits increase the viable choices voters can make among candidates.

To explore this question we examine the effects of term limits on general election competition nationally using Inter-University Consortium for Political and Social Research data from Klarner et al. (2013). We created a subset of these data consisting of 63,041 single-member, winner-take-all plurality elections between 1988 and 2010. We analyze these data using robust standard errors clustered on state. Louisiana, which also has term limits, has runoff elections, so we exclude it. This leaves 49 states, 14 of which have term limits. We treat an election as term-limited only if it occurs after the implementation of the limits in the states that have them. The numbers of term-limited elections we examine ranges from a high of 1,488 in Maine, the earliest term limits adopter, to a low of 73 in Nevada, a state whose lenient limits on service just recently expelled a first wave of veterans.

Before term limits were implemented in the states that have them, they had about the same number of candidates running in elections as did the states without term limits. The average was 1.79 candidates per election for the term-limited states before their limits took effect compared to 1.76 for the non-term-limited states. After term limits were implemented, the average number of candidates running rose to 1.93 in term-limited states. So term limits appear to increase the number of candidates. But these additional candidates might run in lopsided elections with little effect on competition. For example, as we described in chapter 2, some candidates run as sacrificial lambs in elections that are so lopsided politically that anyone from the opponent's party is nearly certain to win.

At first glance it appears that term limits reduce the margin of victory in general elections substantively and statistically significantly. The average margin of victory for elections in the states without term limits is 53 percent compared to 37 percent for elections in states with term limits, so it is tempting to infer that term limits increase electoral competition by about 15 percent. But examining these states across time, we find that term-limited states have more competitive elections even without implementing term limits. The average margin of victory prior to the implementation of their term limits is 40 percent in these states.

Thus, the difference between term-limited and non-term-limited states might reflect other distinctive characteristics (e.g., having the ballot initiative). As we argue throughout this book, it is likely that term limits effects are mediated by these state effects. To isolate the effects of term limits from these other sources of electoral competition, we use a multivariate model to control for the effect of other factors, such as the level of professionalism in the state's legislature (Squire 2007).

Looking at table 5.2, we see that a very simple multivariate model predicts 57 percent of the variation in the general election margins of victory across more than two decades of elections (1988 through 2010). But after we control for other factors that affect electoral competition, we find that term limits have no substantively or statistically significant effect on general election competition. To further ensure that this finding is accurate, we examined only the term-limited states across time using the same model. We also find that implementing term limits in these states does not

TABLE 5.2. General Election Margins of Victory Nationally

Model Predicting General Election Margins of Victory from 1988 to 2010	Unstandardized Coefficients			
	B	Std. Error[b]	t	Sig.
(Constant)	**121.26**	6.81	17.81	.00
Term limitedness ratio[a]	−2.84	2.44	−1.16	.25
Number of candidates in election	**−41.30**	3.92	−10.54	.00
Open seat	**−12.44**	0.89	−13.94	.00
State has ballot initiative	−4.09	2.12	−1.93	.06
Squire's professionalism score (0.03 to 0.63)	**41.31**	5.23	7.89	.00
Term limits and open seat interaction	**5.50**	1.85	2.97	.01

Note: Bold type indicates statistically significant coefficients.

[a]Ratio of turnover mandated by term limits to previous level of turnover in the state. See Sarbaugh-Thompson 2010a for an explanation of this measure.

[b]Robust Standard Errors clustered on 49 states (Louisiana omitted).

F = 557.71; R^2 = 0.57; n = 63,040.

Dependent Variable: Mean = 51.01%; Range, 0.01 to 100; Skewness = 0.29; Kurtosis = −1.55.

increase general election competition in either a substantive or statistically significant way.[6]

One important piece of information provided by our model is that ballot initiative states are different (Tolbert, Grummel, and Smith 2001),[7] so it is important to control for this effect. We find that ballot initiative states have slightly more competitive elections, whether they have term limits or not.[8] Two other variables in our model have large substantive and statistically significant effects on competition, but in the opposite direction. More candidates increase electoral competition. Again, this is hardly surprising. More interestingly, elections for seats in states with more professional legislatures are won with larger margins of victory—as much as 25 percent larger.[9]

Term limits also increase the number of open seats in most states, especially those with stringent limits on service, and open seats are more competitive—about 12.5 percent more. But we find that open seats after the implementation of term limits are less competitive than they were without term limits.

Some states with lenient limits might well see little or no increase in the number of open seat contests. For example, Nevada, with its 12-year limit in each chamber, allows its state legislators to serve longer than their pre-term-limits average length of service. So it is possible that term limits might not increase the number of open seats in some states (Heberlig and Leland 2004). It is hard to assess this possibility currently because the states that implemented their limits last are those that are the least likely to see the number of open seats increase. Therefore, this question cannot be answered definitely for a few years yet. The severity of term limits, which we include in our model by using a ratio of term-limitedness, is one way to adjust partially for this.[10] But a definitive answer will have to wait until the discipline can assess where and when term limits increase open seats enough to offset the dampening direct effect of term limits on electoral competition.

Indeed, the best explanation for differences between electoral competition in term-limited and non-term-limited states is that the former have the ballot initiative. Even after we control for their level of professionalism, the number of candidates in their elections, and the number of open seats, elections in ballot initiative states are about 4 percent more competitive.

We conclude that term limits increase the number of open seat elections, which are more competitive contests. But open seat elections produced through term limits are not as competitive as they are otherwise. This is true when we consider all 49 states and also when we consider the

14 term-limited states across time (see endnote 7). So limiting tenure in office is not a silver bullet ensuring that voters have a choice among viable candidates, even though limits typically produce more open seats.

General Election Competition, Considered in Michigan Only

As we pointed out in the introduction to this chapter, one reason to examine electoral competition carefully is that it is a necessary, although not sufficient, condition for ballot box accountability. In theory legislators who do not respond to the preferences of their constituents could be removed at the ballot box. Therefore, in this section we examine individual legislators' voting mismatch in conjunction with general election competition. We want to know whether competitive elections help voters "throw the bums out" when they don't vote for policies their constituents want.

The proposition under consideration here is that after term limits Michigan legislators who won closely contested elections will vote in ways designed to appease their voters—that is, they will behave as if they are vulnerable in coming elections. We test this because it seems likely that shortened tenure could reduce some of the advantages of incumbency, such as name recognition. So the crux of the question we address in this section is whether term limits in Michigan, by reducing the length of incumbency, will increase the responsiveness of legislators to their district, especially if they appear to be vulnerable at the ballot box. Our dependent variable in table 5.3 is the percentage of general election votes cast against the legislator, so negative coefficients represent less competition (fewer votes cast against the legislator). We test this proposition using incumbents rather than newly elected legislators because our key question is whether legislators who won a closely contested election will move to the center, based on their voting record, to match the views of their voters.

First, we find that, if they can run for reelection after term limits, incumbent candidates are safer, not more vulnerable—with about 9 percent fewer votes cast against these incumbents. Voting mismatch (i.e., the difference between a legislator's voting record and the district's partisan orientation) is statistically significant, increasing the votes cast against an incumbent after term limits, and it did not do so previously. This suggests a little greater potential for voters to voice their frustration at the ballot box after term limits. But the effect is fairly small. Even at the maximum value for voting mismatch (a whopping 62.7%), the failure of a legislator to vote with the district does not begin to approach the nearly 10 percent incumbency advantage term limits provide. So on balance post-term-limits incumbents are safer, although it does matter slightly whether their voting record fits their district, but only slightly.[11]

Prior to term limits, incumbent senators were safer than representatives. They lose that advantage after term limits, but there is still a term limits effect that reduces the votes cast against a Senate incumbent. On balance any incumbent in the House or the Senate is safer after term limits. Thus most post-term-limits incumbents can reasonably expect to hold their seat for their maximum permitted tenure whether they vote with their district or not. Once again the safety of the district is the most powerful predictor of general election competition (b = −0.46). Given that this variable ranges from 0 percent to 93 percent,[12] and that the dependent variable ranges from 0 percent to 51 percent, incumbents running in the safest districts face almost no general election competition regardless of how they vote.

Our key finding is that the size of a legislator's voting mismatch seems to have very little effect on the general election competition faced by incumbents—certainly not enough to overcome the protection term limits provide to them. To the extent that term limits advocates believe that truncating tenure increases ballot box accountability, they are likely to be disappointed, because term limits increase Michigan incumbents' electoral safety while they are in office.[13]

TABLE 5.3. General Electoral Competition for Michigan Incumbents

Model Predicting General Election Competition Measured as the Percent of Total Votes Cast Against Incumbent Candidates	Unstandardized Coefficients			
	B	Std. Error	*t*	Sig.
(Constant)	**50.13**	1.95	25.73	.00
Term limits	**−9.39**	2.32	−4.05	.00
Chamber (Senate = 1)	**−6.07**	1.48	−4.11	.00
Interaction term limits and chamber	**7.03**	1.82	3.87	.00
Safety of seat in general election (0–93%)	**−0.46**	.03	−14.58	.00
Interaction term limits and safety of seat	**0.11**	.04	2.98	.00
Representational mismatch (absolute value)	−0.002	.06	−0.03	.98
Interaction term limits and rep. mismatch	.12	.07	1.69	.09
Political party (Democrat = 1)	**−3.14**	.69	−4.55	.00

Note: Bold type indicates statistically significant coefficients.
F = 130.48; Adjusted R^2 = 0.75; n = 344 (incumbents only).
Dependent Variable: mean = 30.8%; Range, 0 to 50%; Skewness = −0.99; Kurtosis = 0.26.

Term Limits and Campaign Contributions in Michigan

Incumbents often raise more money and reportedly amass large war chests to scare off challengers. Therefore, incumbents' financial advantages are often blamed for low electoral competition. In this section we analyze the total campaign funds raised by each legislator for each session during our study period. These data are available from the National Institute for Money in State Politics. We develop a model to explain the variation in the funds raised by these legislators based on the literature and reasoning discussed below.

There is considerable debate about the effect of term limits on the cost of elections. Evidence nationally suggests that term limits reduce the cost of elections (Powell 2012). Many factors unique to individual states, such as campaign finance laws, the cost of media markets, the frequency of special elections to fill vacant seats, population density, and the wealth and strength of interest groups contribute to this. By considering this across time in one state, we are able to neutralize a large portion of these confounding effects.

We have addressed the full cost of Michigan's legislative elections elsewhere (Sarbaugh-Thompson et al. 2002; Sarbaugh-Thompson 2006). In that work, we used the staggered implementation of term limits in Michigan to control for the effects of history and we considered funds raised by all candidates. We found that campaign spending in the House increased abruptly when term limits took effect in that chamber. But the Senate, not yet term-limited, exhibited no similar increase in the cost of campaigns. When term limits took effect in the Senate, we saw a similar jump in the cost of campaigns for that chamber, while the cost of House elections rose only slightly in the same election.

We also found in our prior work that business political action committees (PACs) shift the timing of their contributions after term limits take effect. Instead of giving during the election campaign, they give more money during the campaign finance reporting cycle immediately after the committee assignments have been made (Sarbaugh-Thompson et al. 2002). These PACs target their postelection giving toward members assigned to committees with jurisdiction over issues the PAC cares about. This postelection giving seems like a logical adaptation to the uncertainty of committee assignments in a post-term-limits legislature. Replicating our prior work is beyond the scope of this chapter. We tackle one small part of that major set of questions here.

We focus on the unique contribution we can make to the literature on campaign finance by examining the impact of candidate recruiting, candidate fundraising effort, and political ambition on money that winning candidates raise to fund their elections. We use data from the National Institute for Money in State Politics[14] to determine the amount of money raised by a candidate's campaign committee for the legislators who won seats in Michigan's House and Senate during the time of our interviews in those chambers.

Discussions of campaign contributions often focus on efforts of donors to advance their interests. But candidates do not just passively sit around waiting for cash to fall from the sky, as anyone who receives fundraising phone calls can attest. From the perspective of some donors, "legislators shake them down for cash." Therefore, we expect that legislators who place a higher priority on fundraising, one of the 11 tasks we asked about in our interviews, will raise more money. In this same vein, we examine the effect of political ambition on campaign funds. We assume that politically ambitious legislators work hard to amass a campaign war chest to support their future plans. These ambitious legislators might also be seen as a good long-term investment for donors. Therefore, we assume that politically ambitious legislators will raise more money both through their own efforts and due to their potential value to donors.

We anticipate that campaign costs will differ for the two chambers because state senate districts are so much larger. Additionally, almost all the post-term-limits senators have a track record in the House and have developed expertise on certain committees. Therefore, they are more likely to be a known commodity—a safer investment for donors. In this sense, they might be treated by donors more like one would expect long-term incumbents to be treated. We predict that increased donations to senators is an indirect effect of term limits.

We also examine whether the amount of money raised varies by type of seat (e.g., open seats or competitive seats). With term limits, especially during their transitional phase, open seats arrive in waves, and as we and others have discussed elsewhere, even large interest groups with extremely deep pockets do not have infinite resources. So donors must make choices about when and where to "invest" their money.

There are two likely strategies for donors—gambling on a competitive race to help one political party control the chamber or investing in a safe seat to help a candidate leverage her or his power within the caucus. First, if donors give to a candidate in competitive districts there is a risk that the candidate will lose—providing no return on the investment. This risk is magnified when the seat is open. But the return on the investment could be enormous if this candidate helps the donor's preferred political party to gain or retain control of the chamber.

Second, donors can give to a sure winner to increase their own access to this candidate. Although candidates for safe seats do not need much money for their own campaign, if donors fill their coffers they can use their campaign war chest to help other colleagues (e.g., attending a colleague's $1,000 per plate fundraiser). This increases a legislator's value to his or her colleagues. This can leverage a legislator's influence within the party caucus. But this value diminishes if the candidate's political party does not control the chamber, so a safe seat for the minority party is not likely to attract these strategic donors. Therefore, we control for membership in the chamber's opposition party, a factor that is widely acknowledged to reduce the amount of money a candidate receives.

Our dependent variable, campaign funds raised as reported by the National Institute for Money in State Politics, exhibits a very large positive skew. To compensate for this, we take the log (base 10) of the dependent variable, the campaign contributions in thousands of dollars. Our results are presented in table 5.4. Since we logged our dependent variable, we interpret the coefficients as the percent change in campaign contributions for a one unit change in the independent variable. Although most of the variables in our model are statistically significant, there are three exceptions: (1) an open seat election, (2) term limits interacted with an open seat election, and (3) whether an interest group asked the candidate to run. We do not provide an interpretation of coefficients for those variables here, but rather examine them in a subsequent analysis.

We find that limiting time in office has a statistically significant effect on the amount of money raised in campaigns, but this effect differs by chamber. Term limits reduce the amount of money Michigan's representatives raise and increase the amount that its senators raise. Even before term limits, senators raised more money than representatives, which is logical given that their districts are much larger, and campaigns are likely to cost more. But after term limits this gap swells to more than 150 percent. Money appears to gravitate toward senators. This implies that senators are the new incumbents in the eyes of strategic donors. We remind readers, however, that we are considering the winners only (sitting legislators) rather than the entire cost of the campaign, which would involve the losing general candidates and the primary elections.

Our findings indicate that individual legislator characteristics affect fundraising, but not necessarily in the ways we anticipated. We find political ambition has an effect on legislators' funds, but it runs in the opposite direction from what we expected. A politically ambitious legislator raises about 14 percent less money, all other variables held constant. But candidate effort also appears important in raising money. Legislators who place a higher priority on fundraising are likely to have more campaign money. Each unit of fundraising effort produces a 15 percent increase in funds raised. Given the range for this variable (−3.2 to 2.1), it appears that hard work could provide a 30 percent boost in funds. On the other hand, lackluster fundraising efforts could reduce a candidate's coffers by about 45 percent.

If a candidate is running in a safer district, campaign contributions decline by about 1 percent for every percentage point increase in the safety of the seat, all other variables held constant. The range of the variable for district safety ranges from 0 percent to 93 percent, so donors give a lot less money to candidates running in extremely safe districts. This result implies that donors gamble on control of the chamber by their preferred party rather than helping a sure winner and trying to influence that legislator after the election. This emphasis on partisan control of the cham-

TABLE 5.4. Change in Campaign Contributions for Winning Candidates in Michigan

Model Predicting Log Base 10 of Money Raised in $1,000	Unstandardized Coefficients				Percent Change[a]
	B	Std. Error	*t*	Sig.	
(Constant)	2.127	.045	49.967	.000	
Term limits (Yes = 1)	−.103	.042	−2.453	.015	
Chamber (Senate = 1)	.134	.061	2.193	.029	
Term limits x Chamber	.274	.078	3.517	.000	
Term limits (House)	−.103				−21.1%
Term limits (Senate)	.171				48.3%
Chamber (Term Limits = 0)	.134				36.1%
Chamber (Term Limits = 1)	.408				155.9%
Open seat (Yes = 1)	−.010	.057	−.183	.855	
Term limits x Open Seat	.050	.065	.769	.442	
Safe district (Yes = 1)	−.005	.001	−8.568	.000	−1.1%
Politically ambitious (Yes = 1)	−.064	.031	−2.066	.040	−13.7%
In chamber minority party	−.132	.029	−4.523	.000	−26.2%
Priority of fundraising (−3.2 to 2.1)	.060	.016	3.825	.000	14.8%
Asked to run by interest group	−.010	.040	−.244	.807	

Source: Data from the National Institute for Money in State Politics.

Note: This table shows the raw coefficients as well as the coefficients transformed by the interactions for interpretation.

[a]This column gives the substantive interpretation of these coefficients. We transformed the coefficients from the log scale by taking 10 to the power of the coefficient. This number, differenced from 1 and multiplied by 100, gives percent change for a one unit increase in the independent variable.

$F = 26.834$; $R^2 = 0.42$; $n = 390$.

Dependent Variable: Mean = 1.794; Range, 0.71 to 3.04; Skewness = 0.16; Kurtosis = 0.21.

ber is consistent with the effect of minority party membership. Minority party members raise about 26 percent less money than their colleagues in the majority. Yet, despite indications that donors are giving strategically to control the chamber, we find that candidates recruited by interest groups do not appear to have more cash available than their colleagues do.

Are Open Seats Different after Term Limits?

A major effect of term limits is an increase in open seat elections, so a key question is whether open seats have different electoral effects when they are so numerous. We could not answer this question with respect to fundraising using the model we discussed above because we could not untangle the relationship without multiple interaction terms that introduce a lot of collinearity. But this question is crucial to our understanding of the effect of term limits on fundraising. So to probe this further, we split our data into two cohorts, pre-term-limits and post-term-limits. We present these results in table 5.5. We use the model that we used with the full data set, but separately for our pre-term-limits elections and then for our post-term-limits elections, avoiding the need to measure the interaction of each variable with term limits.

We find that, when we consider only the winners of these contests, open seats repel money before term limits and attract it afterward. Legislators in our pre-term-limits cohort who won an open seat raised 35 percent less money than did their colleagues. Legislators in our post-term-limits cohort who won an open seat raised 18 percent more money than their colleagues. Even though donors may have finite resources, in Michigan their pockets appear deep enough to give more to each open seat even when there are lots of them.

These differences in the strategies of giving to candidates for open seats implies that before term limits donors did not take a risk on open seat races, but focused their giving on incumbents with a track record. After term limits, it appears that donors are more willing to gamble on unknown actors running for open seats given the value of party control in the chamber. The effects of a safe district and of minority party membership are both fairly consistent when we analyze pre- and post-term-limits elections separately. But fundraising effort matters more before term limits, and the sizeable difference between chambers is driven by post-term-limits changes. Senators have become the new incumbents for donors given that they have a track record in the House. But chamber control appears to be the strategy

TABLE 5.5. Effect of Term Limits on the Cost of Winning an Open-Seat Election in Michigan

Model Predicting Log Base 10 of Money Raised in $1,000	Pre-Term Limits					Post-Term Limits					Difference before and after term limits
	Unstandardized Coefficients					Unstandardized Coefficients					
	B	Std. Error	t	Sig.	Percent change	B	Std. Error	t	Sig.	Percent change	
Constant	2.222	.066	33.47	.000		1.996	.050	39.60	.000	206.2	
Chamber	-.002	.067	-.03	.974		.486	.073	6.67	.000		53.4%
Open seat	-.188	.066	-2.87	.005	-35.1	.073	.038	1.93	.054	18.3	0.3%
Safety of seat in gen. elect.	-.006	.001	-5.87	.000	-1.4	-.005	.001	-6.91	.000	-1.1	
Politically Ambitious	-.032	.047	-.68	.499		-.058	.039	-1.49	.139		
In chamber minority party	-.156	.047	-3.29	.001	-30.2	-.127	.037	-3.44	.001	-25.4	4.8%
Time spent fundraising	.097	.027	3.52	.001	25.0	.046	.019	2.45	.015	11.2	-13.8%
Recruited by interest group	.070	.074	.95	.346		-.031	.048	-.64	.524		
Chamber × open seat	.537	.139	3.87	.000		-.136	.099	-1.37	.171		

Pre-term-limits model: $F = 10.167$; $R^2 = 0.43$; $n = 115$. Dependent Variable: Mean = 1.9; Skewness = 0.32; Kurtosis = 1.21.
Post-term-limits model: $F = 26.13$; $R^2 = 0.44$; $n = 273$. Dependent Variable: Mean = 1.8; Skewness = 0.28; Kurtosis = 0.16.
*This is the percentage change post-term limits minus percentage change pre-term limits.

many donors adopt after term limits. At least this interpretation is consistent with the pattern of giving that we find.

These exploratory results suggest interesting and fruitful avenues for more comprehensive investigations of the effects of term limits and open seats on campaign fundraising. Our results indicate that research into term limits effects on fundraising should consider not only the effect of open seats but also the safety of districts for one party (i.e., the effect of the district maps), and chamber differences.

Conclusions

Do term limits make elections more competitive? Yes and no. Term limits are not a silver bullet that can overcome the effects of district maps, candidate recruiting, and the rules and context of the state's electoral system. On balance term limits only affect electoral competition by increasing the number of open seat contests. Moreover, during the time that candidates are eligible to run as incumbents, they are safer than incumbents were before term limits.

Open seat elections are typically more competitive, and in most states term limits produce more open seat elections. But open seats are less competitive when they are produced through term limits expulsions than they are otherwise. Furthermore, even open seats do not increase competition enough to overcome the effect of district boundaries (safety of the district) that reserve some seats for one political party. The district map matters hugely.

In Michigan, where we can control for more facets of the electoral system, we find that term limits' direct effects decrease competition. Although term limits increase the number of open seat elections, which are more competitive, we find that the increased competition from open seats does not offset the decrease in competition that term limits produce. Moreover, a very safe district can produce a whopping 44 percent increase in a candidate's margin of victory. Over and over, questions about electoral competition bring us back to the district boundaries.

We were especially interested in term limits' supposed ability to increase ballot box accountability. We assumed that shorter tenure in office would diminish incumbency advantages enough to make legislators vulnerable if they were not responsive to voters' viewpoint. We find no evidence to support this. Indeed, we identify two ways that term limits may escalate the exodus from the middle of the ideological spectrum. First, term limits reduce the number of candidates in primaries if they lead to a competitive general election. After term limits these are more likely to be candidates who are handpicked by partisan political elites to mobilize the party faithful to win the seat. Second, primary elections for safe seats feature droves of candidates. Often the number of primary candidates for safe seats is so large (17 in one primary in our data) that small, highly active factions could gain outsized influence. Even when these post-term-limits legislators vote in ways that do not match their constituents' ideology, they do not appear to be very vulnerable at the ballot box.

Term limits appear to increase the amount of money raised by winning candidates in Michigan's Senate, although they reduce it in the House. On the other hand, open seats attract more money after term limits, potentially offsetting the dampening effects of term limits on fundraising in the House. Campaign funds are a two-way street with legislators' fundraising efforts substantially affecting the amount they raise. Here again, reformers who hoped that term limits would sever the ties between legislators and donors with deep pockets and well-funded special interests will be disappointed. We find nothing to indicate that this has happened among winning candidates in Michigan, especially not in the upper chamber.

We conclude that reformers who are truly motivated to provide voters with a choice among viable candidates and legislators who fairly represent their voters' points of view should devise less partisan processes to draw district lines. Another way to improve the fit between legislators' voting records and their voters' viewpoint involves designing runoff elections or free-for-all primary contests in which the top two vote-getters face off in the general election. California, which previously had the same stringent term limits as Michigan does, has adopted both these remedies. Commissions draw district lines and the two top primary vote recipients from either political party compete in November. So the general election is a runoff that can pit two candidates from the same political party against each other. It will be interesting to see whether these reforms in California succeed where term limits have failed to reduce the problems of limited electoral competition and lack of ballot box accountability.

SIX

Information Gathering

Legislators confront a dizzying array of policies and issues, yet it is unlikely that they are experts on more than a few. How, then, do they decide what bills to support and to oppose? Evidence suggests that, when legislators make policy decisions, they give and take cues from other sources, especially if they serve in a state legislature (Matthews and Stimson 1975; Songer 1988; Porter 1974). The sources they consult reveal who has access to legislators when they make momentous decisions affecting the economy, the environment, and citizens' well-being. This chapter examines information gathering and vote cuing sources used by Michigan's state legislators before and after term limits.

We organize the chapter using stages of the policy process (the persuasion and satisficing stages) that Mooney (1991) finds affect legislators' information gathering. He divides the policy process into three stages: *initiation*, in which ideas for bills arise; *persuasion*, during which the content of a bill evolves through debate and discussion (e.g., in committee deliberations); and *satisficing*, the final floor vote on the bill during which legislators have no time to double-check information or do research. We have interview data about two of these three stages—committee deliberations and floor votes. We examine information gathering during those stages in this chapter.

Mooney's research links stages in the policy process with legislators' preferred sources of information. He finds that during the initiation stage legislators consult outside sources (constituents, academics, the media, and members of local government). During the persuasion stage, he finds that legislator use midrange sources: those who deal with legislators regularly, but are not part of the chamber (e.g., interest groups and members of the executive branch). And, finally, during the satisficing (floor vote) stage, he finds that legislators rely on sources within the chamber, which he calls inside sources (e.g., trusted colleagues and reliable staff). In this chapter we examine all three of Mooney's three aggregate categories of information (inside, midrange, and outside sources), as well as several individual sources of information (e.g., interest groups, local officials), linking them with the committee deliberations (the persuasion stage) and floor votes (the satisficing stage).

With the advent of term limits, we want to know whether some sources of information have gained or lost influence in policy making. The sources with access to legislators (i.e., those they rely on for information) have a platform from which to influence policy. Given the campaign rhetoric of term limits advocates, we are especially interested in the extent to which legislators rely on information from two sources: organized groups and lobbyists and from local, district sources.

As academics we wish that legislators would consult credible sources of information, use high-quality analyses, and consider aggregate rather than anecdotal information, but evidence is not reassuring (see Danzinger 2001; Kingdon 1989). It appears that politics often drives legislative decisions, and party leaders and other partisan sources make decisions for the entire caucus (Hird 2005). Yet committee members sometimes make policy based on empirical evidence, and their less informed colleagues trust them enough to rely on their judgment during floor votes (Songer 1988).[1] Here we seek to understand which sources of information legislators rely upon at different stages of the policy process and whether term limits change this. Additionally we examine two personal qualities of legislators that have been shown to affect information gathering: gender and party affiliation (Hird 2005).

Data and Methods

During our interviews, we queried respondents about committee deliberations and floor votes—two of Mooney phases of policy making. In appendix A, these are questions 17.1 through 18.8. These 16 questions explore where legislators turn when they need information during committee deliberations about a bill seriously considered in a committee. The specific question is, "How much would you say you relied upon *the specific source* for information and guidance in making up your mind about *the specific issue the respondent described in the previous question?*" In framing questions 17.1 through 18.8, we chose a committee of which a respondent was a member and asked her or him to pick an issue that was seriously considered by that committee. This grounds our questions in actual rather than hypothetical situations (see Kingdon's 1989 rationale for this). To record their answers about these 16 sources of information, we hand respondents a five-point scale anchored by *none* to *an enormous amount*. We accept values anywhere along the scale including between the points, which include, in addition to the anchors, equidistant markings for *a little*, *some*, and *a lot*.

Because both the committee and the issue vary, we normalize their responses, dividing by a legislator's personal average for all 16 sources. As we described in chapter 4, the resulting values are relative and facilitate ranking sources rather than specifying an amount of consulting. We remind readers that values of zero denote a source that is relied upon at the individual's average level. Positive values signify above average consulting, while negative values reflect below average consulting.

In this series of questions, we ask about six sources of information inside the chamber: the chamber's majority party leader, the minority party leader, the committee chair, other colleagues, the party caucus, and subcommittee chairs (used only for appropriations). We combine these and average the normalized responses to create an aggregate measure of *inside sources* of information. We also examine separate effects of three important components of inside information: committee chairs, other colleagues, and the party caucus.

Using this same series of questions, we also ask about five midrange sources of information (i.e., those that interact regularly with legislators in the capital): two nonpartisan support staffs—the Legislative Services Bureau and each Chamber's Fiscal Agency,[2] Organized Groups and Lobbyists, the Governor's Office, and State Agency Officials. We combine these and average the normalized responses to produce a single measure of respondents' use of *midrange sources*. Again we drill down on two specific midrange sources, *state agency officials* and, the most notorious category of midrange sources, *organized groups or lobbyists*. We combine and average the normalized responses for Legislative Services Bureau and the chamber fiscal agency into *nonpartisan staff*, which we also analyze separately.

We also inquire about three outside sources of information (i.e., those that are farther removed from the chamber): key local officials, advisors in the district, and other constituents. We analyze all three of these components separately and also create an aggregate variable called *outside sources*.

We also asked respondents about consulting during floor votes. To do this, we created scenarios in which two hypothetical bills[3] reach the floor of the chamber. Based on evidence that issue salience affects legislative behavior (Price 1978), we use one politically salient and one technical issue. The two issues are school choice, an issue that legislators might have campaigned on, and licensing and regulating health care professionals (hereafter designated by LRHCP), which typically attracts attention only from affected professional groups. In the scenarios, we ask respondents if they would rely on colleagues for information and guidance about a floor vote on a bill about school choice, and if so, who? Next we ask whether there are groups or individuals outside the chamber they would rely upon for information and guidance about such a bill, and if so, which ones? Finally, we ask which of the sources the respondent mentioned would he or she rely on most. We repeat this scenario for a bill about LRHCP. The questions are open-ended, and we code all responses into categories of sources (e.g., colleagues, groups and lobbyists, local sources, and staff). These are questions seven through 12 on the interview schedule provided in appendix A.

The Michigan Context

We remind readers that Michigan's legislature displays many characteristics of highly professional legislatures—unlimited session length, full-time salaries and benefits, personal staff for legislators as well as professional nonpartisan staff (Squire 2007). The reforms that created professional state legislatures were justified as a way to increase state policy-making capacity by expanding the resources available to legislators for making informed decisions (Rosenthal 1996). Not surprisingly, then, Hird (2005) finds variations in information gathering by type of legislature in his comparison on professional, hybrid, and citizen legislatures.

According to Kousser (2005), term limits strip legislatures of experience and expertise, partially deinstitutionalizing them. Based on this, we predict that term limits will alter Michigan legislators' information gathering strategies, producing patterns typical of part-time or hybrid legislatures. Based on interviews with legislators in 11 states, Guston, Jones, and Branscomb (1997) find that lobbyists are a more prominent source of information in states with less professional legislatures. Therefore, in this chapter we test the proposition that as term limits "deinstitutionalize" Michigan's legislature, midrange sources, including lobbyists or interest groups, will gain more access to legislators during policy making.

The Persuasion Stage of Policy Making—
Committee Deliberations

The persuasion phase of policy making, according to Mooney, follows the initiation phase (during which ideas are generated), but precedes satisficing decisions that occur during floor votes. During the persuasion phase, there is time to search extensively, but also to winnow input and to focus on key questions or specific facets of an evolving bill. This resembles committee deliberations during which witnesses are questioned and testimony is given. Therefore, we assume that an issue seriously debated in a committee is in the persuasion phase of policy making. During this phase legislators are expected to rely most on sources from outside the chamber, but with whom they work regularly (e.g., lobbyists and state agency officials)—midrange sources in Mooney's parlance.

Looking at figure 6.1, we see that midrange sources clearly dominate information gathering during the persuasion phase, as Mooney would predict. So, when Michigan's legislators have an opportunity in a committee to deliberate about an issue, they rely most heavily on the network of professionals that they work with regularly (i.e., the various staffs, the executive branch, and lobbyists and interest groups). Although midrange sources are the most popular in both chambers with or without term limits, term limits appear to accentuate senators' preferences for these sources. This produces a statistically significant difference between the chambers, readily apparent in figure 6.1.[4]

With less time to get to know their colleagues after term limits, legislators in both chambers appear to rely less heavily on inside sources of information during the persuasion phase of policy making. The priority placed on all inside sources of information collectively during committee deliberations declines in both chambers after term limits by statistically significant amounts. Here again, the change is larger in the Senate, producing another statistically significant post-term-limits disparity between chambers.

Term limits proponents promised voters that limiting tenure would keep legislators more closely tied to the district. They would likely be pleased to see representatives turning to outside (in this case, local) sources of information during the persuasion phase of policy making. On the other hand, they would be less encouraged by our findings about senators, who turn away from these local sources after term limits.

These opposing shifts between the two chambers produce a third statistically significant post-term-limits chamber difference. To our surprise, these are driven more by shifts in the Senate than in the House. This

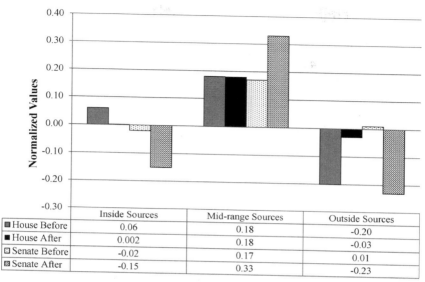

	Inside Sources	Mid-range Sources	Outside Sources
▣ House Before	0.06	0.18	-0.20
▪ House After	0.002	0.18	-0.03
▢ Senate Before	-0.02	0.17	0.01
▨ Senate After	-0.15	0.33	-0.23

Fig. 6.1. Information Sources Used in Committee Deliberations before and after Term Limits

implies that something other than inexperience generates the changes we detect in information gathering. This is reminiscent of the pattern we found in chapter 4 in which the behavior of senators changed more than the behavior of representatives after term limits.

Specific Inside Sources

In the aggregate, neither chamber reveals a strong preference for inside sources of information during committee deliberations, just as Mooney would predict. But several components of this aggregate measure are consulted very rarely—for example, the caucus leaders (speaker, majority leader, minority leader). Their presence in our aggregate measure masks the priority placed on other sources of inside information (e.g., committee chairs, colleagues, and the party caucus). When we examine specific inside sources, we see that each chamber relies heavily on only one or two of them. And we find varied chamber effects with term limits.

In figure 6.2 we see that before term limits the House is more committee dominated and prioritizes individual colleague-to-colleague consulting. Pre-term-limits senators prefer group discussions in the party caucus.[5] These variants could reflect the vast differences in chamber size. As those

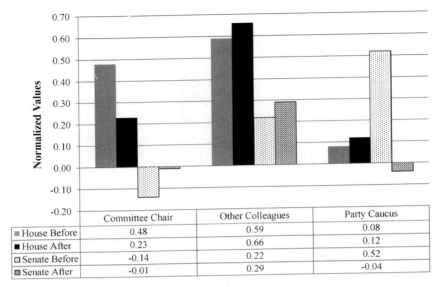

	Committee Chair	Other Colleagues	Party Caucus
▦ House Before	0.48	0.59	0.08
■ House After	0.23	0.66	0.12
▨ Senate Before	-0.14	0.22	0.52
▧ Senate After	-0.01	0.29	-0.04

Fig. 6.2. Inside Sources of Information Used in Committee Deliberations

of us who teach large lectures and small classes can attest, there is a profound difference in class discussions with 50 to 65 students (roughly the size of a House party caucus meeting) and 10–25 students (the size of a Senate caucus). Large lecture classes often rely on small discussion sections in ways that probably correspond to the use of committee meetings in the House. These pre-term-limits chamber approaches look like sensible adaptations to the dynamics of large and small group discussions.

What is more interesting is that these distinctions converge after term limits. Possibly due to their socialization in the House, post-term-limits senators appear to make limited use of the party caucus to gather information during committee deliberations. Senators consult committee chairs more, yet they do not fully adopt the lower chamber's committee-dominated approach. Conversely, House committee chairs lose influence, while the whole caucus makes some minor gains.[6]

Both chambers place a little higher priority on information from chamber colleagues after term limits. Given the influx of newcomers in the lower chamber, we expected consulting among House colleagues to decline precipitously, but we find no evidence of this. Regardless of term limits, colleagues are consulted more in the House than in the Senate, but consulting increases a little in both chambers after term limits.

Specific Midrange Sources

As we already discovered, midrange sources are extremely popular sources of information during committee deliberations. With respect to information gathering from specific midrange sources, we see readily in figure 6.3 that there is a lot more change in the Senate than in the House.[7] Most of this involves consulting staffs. This implies that senators are more fully integrated into the network of professionals in the state capital. We speculate that post-term-limits senators have enough experience to have established relationships with these midrange actors, but that they are new enough to need their help more than their pre-term-limits counterparts did. This produces a statistically significant chamber difference in consulting with state agency staff after term limits where none existed before. Other increases (e.g., senators with partisan staff, for example) are sizeable, but not statistically significant.

Term limits make no difference in the extent to which organized groups and lobbyists are consulted by representatives and only increase this in the Senate, although not at a level that achieves statistical significance. Only consulting with partisan staff matches the priority placed on information from organized groups and lobbyists. This probably dismays term limits advocates and voters who believe that limiting tenure would sever cozy ties between lobbyists and legislators.

Academics, ourselves included, laud the neutral competence of nonpartisan staff (Hird 2005) and hoped that newcomers would rely very heavily upon their expertise to compensate for their inexperience (Polsby 1993). Looking at figure 6.3 we see that nonpartisan staff are consulted infrequently compared to other midrange sources. But we need to keep this in perspective. This source is consulted more than average (a positive value), just not as much as other midrange sources, such as organized groups and lobbyists or partisan staff. This is a fairly high level of consulting compared to inside and outside sources of information, however.

Specific Outside Sources

As figure 6.4 illustrates the House and the Senate again exhibit opposing shifts in their use of local sources of information after term limits. After term limits representatives increase the priority placed on all three components of outside information (constituents, local advisors, and key local officials).[8] None of these is statistically significant individually, but they move in tandem to produce the statistically significant change in our

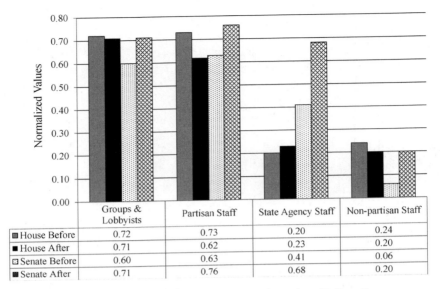

	Groups & Lobbyists	Partisan Staff	State Agency Staff	Non-partisan Staff
House Before	0.72	0.73	0.20	0.24
House After	0.71	0.62	0.23	0.20
Senate Before	0.60	0.63	0.41	0.06
Senate After	0.71	0.76	0.68	0.20

Fig. 6.3. Midrange Sources of Information Used in Committee Deliberations

aggregate measure for outside sources that we noted above. These trends are consistent with the intended consequences of term limits, especially the higher priority placed on information from individual constituents. In the Senate after term limits, none of the components of outside sources gain influence, and two lose a lot (key local officials and advisors in the district). One of these, district advisors' loss of access to senators, is large enough to be statistically significant.

Legislators appear to rely more on individual constituents for the local perspective after term limits. Post-term-limits representatives consult individuals more and post-term-limits senators consult individuals just as much as their predecessors did. So, constituents gain access in both chambers relative to local officials and to advisors in the district, given the declines for the latter sources in the Senate.

Overall, the loss of access for key local officials seems to us to be an especially important change in the Senate. Local officials can explain what policy changes mean in practical terms for different types of municipalities and for citizens. Something that sounds good on paper in Lansing may be difficult to live with in the townships and villages or larger urban centers throughout the state. When key local officials lose access, legislators are insulated from their street-level view of policy impacts. It seems unlikely

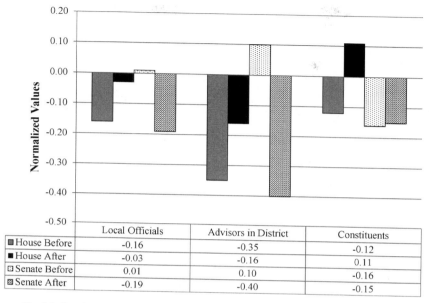

	Local Officials	Advisors in District	Constituents
House Before	-0.16	-0.35	-0.12
House After	-0.03	-0.16	0.11
Senate Before	0.01	0.10	-0.16
Senate After	-0.19	-0.40	-0.15

Fig. 6.4. Outside Sources of Information Used in Committee Deliberations

that the increased access for individual constituents can compensate for this loss. For example, a constituent attending a legislator's coffee hour to complain about school funding is likely to raise different issues than would the president of the local school board or the school district superintendent.

Differential Chamber Effects of Term Limits on Committee Deliberations

Figure 6.5 highlights the massive upheaval in information gathering relationships in the Senate. We readily see that there is more movement in the Senate, and the moves are much larger than in the House. The continuity we find in the House is not what one would expect given the waves of newcomers who wash over the House regularly after term limits.

The biggest "losers" in the Senate are the *party caucus, key local officials,* and *advisors in the district.* After term limits building and maintaining local relationships is probably constrained by short stints of service. One pre-term-limits senator pointed out to us that he had 35 school superintendents in his district, and proceeded to name the one who provided him with the best information on both sides of education issues—his preferred

House Pre-Term-Limits		House Post-Term-Limits		Senate Pre-Term-Limits		Senate Post-Term-Limits	
Rank & Source	Mean	Rank & Source	Mean	Rank & Source	Mean	Rank & Source	Mean
Much More Than Average Level of Consulting (>+ .40)							
1 Partisan Staff	0.70	1 Lobbyists	0.71	1 Partisan Staff	0.63	1 Partisan Staff	0.76
2 Lobbyists	0.70	2 Other Colleagues	0.66	2 Lobbyists	0.60	2 Lobbyists	0.71
3 Other Colleagues	0.57	3 Partisan Staff	0.62	3 Party Caucus	0.52	3 State Agency	0.68
4 Committee Chair	0.48			4 State Agency	0.41		
More Than Average Level of Consulting (>= .10 and < .40)							
5 Non-partisan Staff	0.27	4 State Agency	0.23	5 Senate Fiscal Agency	0.22	4 Senate Fiscal Agency	0.34
6 Senate Fiscal Agency	0.21	5 State Fiscal Agency	0.23	6 Other Colleagues	0.22	5 Other Colleagues	0.29
7 State Agency	0.19	6 Committee Chair	0.23	7 Key Local Officials	0.10		
		7 Non-partisan Staff	0.18	8 Advisors in District	0.10		
		8 Party Caucus	0.12				
		9 Constituents	0.11				
Average Level of Consulting (between .09 and -.09)							
8 Party Caucus	0.08	10 Key Local Officials	-0.03	9 Non-partisan Staff	-0.10	6 Non-partisan Staff	0.07
						7 Committee Chair	-0.01
						8 Party Caucus	-0.04
Less Than Average Level of Consulting (<= -.10 and > -.40)							
9 Constituents	-0.11	11 Advisors in District	-0.16	10 Minority Leader	-0.13	9 Governor's Office	-0.13
10 Key Local Officials	-0.15			11 Committee Chair	-0.14	10 Other Chamber	-0.15
11 Advisors in District	-0.33			12 Constituents	-0.16	11 Constituents	-0.15
				13 Governor's Office	-0.26	12 Key Local Officials	-0.19
Much Less Than Average Level of Consulting (<= -.40)							
12 Other Chamber	-0.44	12 Governor's Office	-0.44	14 Other Chamber	-0.50	13 Advisors in District	-0.40
13 Governor's Office	-0.49	13 Other Chamber	-0.46	15 Majority Leader	-0.62	14 Minority Leader	-0.47
14 Speaker	-0.52	14 Minority Leader	-0.47			15 Majority Leader	-0.65
15 Minority Leader	-0.60	15 Speaker	-0.77				

Response rate except Committee Chair: House Before 89-92; After 245-253 Senate Before 28-30; After 45-50
Chair response rate before and after limits: House 88 and 238; Senate 20 and 37 Some respondents chaired the committee
Italicized type with shading denotes a shift in order of more than two ranks   Bold type denotes statistically significant at p < 0.05

Fig. 6.5. Rank Order of Sources of Information Used during Committee Deliberations

source of information (interview notes). Learning which of 35 superintendents to consult would be exceedingly difficult for post-term-limits senators when time is short, and we found no post-term-limits senators whose answers incorporated this level of detail. Many pre-term-limits Senate veterans named specific local officials, however.

The other major shift in the Senate involves the *party caucus*. As we noted earlier, the pre-term-limits Senate evolved practices befitting a small group in which most members can participate in a discussion. Shifts in the Senate move its structure closer to that of the more formally structured House. In fact, if we compare the priority placed on sources of information in the pre-term-limits House to the post-term-limits Senate, there are only four sources that differ by two ranks or more. And there are no moves of the size we see between the pre- and post-term-limits Senate. The chambers appear to converge, with post-term-limits senators socialized in the House bringing their patterns of consulting with them. The post-term-limits Senate strongly resembles the lower chamber. This is reminiscent of the larger shifts in senators' compared to representatives' behaviors that we described in chapter 4.

Consulting on Floor Votes

We examine consulting about floor votes using the two hypothetical scenarios we described in the data section of this chapter. We remind readers that these are open-ended questions that ask both what sources were consulted and then which among these sources was the most important. In order to manage the demands of coding these open-ended responds, we concentrate on only a few specific sources: colleagues, organized groups or lobbyists, local sources, and staff. To analyze these questions we created a series of dichotomous variables denoting whether the respondent mentioned sources we could classify into these categories.

We asked for a specific colleague, but then accepted groups of categories for sources outside the chamber. Groups or lobbyists most often mentioned by our respondents include professional associations, unions, chambers of commerce, advocacy groups, and religious groups. We treat the following series of actors as outside sources of information: *individual constituents* including individual local experts (e.g., my doctor), friends, family, and *advisors in the district* (e.g., the predecessor in the seat), and *key local officials* (e.g., school superintendents, public health officials). We often refer to these collectively as *local sources* rather than outside sources because it describes them more precisely. Finally, we coded *staff* as a combination of partisan and nonpartisan staff because we often could not distinguish between these in open-ended responses.

According to Mooney (1991) floor votes should reflect a satisficing decision process with heavy reliance on trusted colleagues and others within the chamber—inside sources of information. Wissel, O'Connor, and King (1976) find that highly professional legislatures increase the value legislators place on inside sources. Additionally, time and experience have been shown to increase legislators' willingness to rely on their colleagues (Uslaner and Weber 1977; Arnold, Deen, and Patterson 2000). Thus, before term limits Michigan's highly professional legislature with low turnover should be characterized by lots of consulting among colleagues.

Term limits truncates time in office, which means that there are fewer opportunities to discover which colleagues to trust for information or guidance on a floor vote. Term limits also increase turnover, which is associated with relying less on colleagues for information (Ray 1982). So after term limits we expect to find less consulting between Michigan's legislators on floor votes and fewer respondents rating colleagues as their most important source.

We also anticipate that organized groups and lobbyists will be consulted more during floor votes after term limits. In interviews of legislators in 11 states, Guston, Jones, and Branscomb (1997) find that lobbyists are a more prominent source of information in states with less professional legislatures. Based on the potential for term limits to deinstitutionalize Michigan's legislature (see Kousser 2005), we predict that the proportion of legislators consulting organized groups and lobbyists about a floor vote will increase after term limits, and likewise a higher proportion will name this source as their most important.

According to Mooney (1991), legislators rely on outside sources of information in early stages of policy development, not when a floor vote is imminent. But Price (1978) posits that the political salience of an issue affects information gathering, motivating greater engagement with the public, so we anticipate divergent consulting patterns for the two floor votes we asked about. Specifically, we anticipate that the political salience of school choice will increase legislators' reliance on local sources.

Floor Vote Consulting about School Choice

We find in figure 6.6 that term limits have little influence on representatives' overall consulting about floor votes. They rely about equally on col-

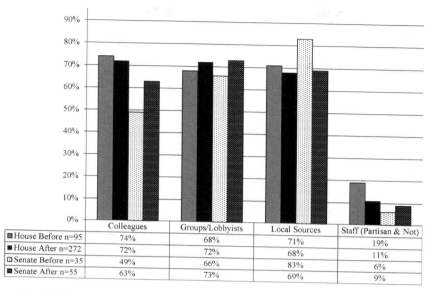

	Colleagues	Groups/Lobbyists	Local Sources	Staff (Partisan & Not)
■ House Before n=95	74%	68%	71%	19%
■ House After n=272	72%	72%	68%	11%
□ Senate Before n=35	49%	66%	83%	6%
■ Senate After n=55	63%	73%	69%	9%

Fig. 6.6. Schools of Choice Floor Vote—Sources before and after Term Limits

leagues, lobbyists, and local sources when confronting a floor vote on the politically salient issue—school choice—before and after term limits.

Once again, term limits alter senators' consulting more. Contrary to Mooney's predictions, pre-term-limits senators did not rely heavily on colleagues when confronting a floor vote. Indeed, before term limits slightly fewer than half of our Senate respondents said they would consult colleagues at all about this issue. Instead, they turned to local sources. According to Mooney, consulting on floor votes reveals close ties. From this we infer that pre-term-limits senators had close ties with local sources, as reflected by a respondent's comment "I've got all my superintendents on the [cell] phone" (interview notes). Local sources appear to lose this access to senators after term limits. After term limits the proportion of senators consulting colleagues rises. The result is that colleagues, interest groups, and local sources have roughly equal access to senators after term limits, whereas before term limits local sources had the most access.

Most Important Sources for School Choice Floor Votes

Consulting a source is different than saying that the source is the most important one. Term limits appear to alter the importance attached to sources. The big message in the House is that after term limits the source

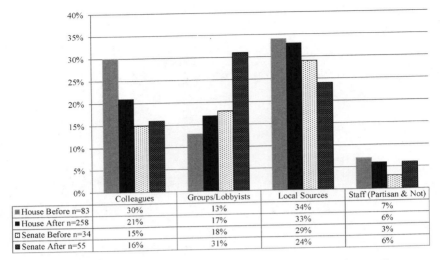

	Colleagues	Groups/Lobbyists	Local Sources	Staff (Partisan & Not)
House Before n=83	30%	13%	34%	7%
House After n=258	21%	17%	33%	6%
Senate Before n=34	15%	18%	29%	3%
Senate After n=55	16%	31%	24%	6%

Fig. 6.7. Schools of Choice Floor Vote—Most Important Sources before and after Term Limits

we would expect to be the most important—colleagues—loses ground. This post-term-limits decline is readily apparent in figure 6.7 and is statistically significant. We speculate that this reflects limited opportunities for term-limited representatives to determine who among their colleagues to trust and rely upon. Local sources remain the preferred ones for representatives, despite term limits. This supports Price's (1978) prediction that salient issues lead legislators to engage the public. It is also consistent with the increased access to representatives for constituents during committee deliberations that we reported earlier in the chapter.

But these ties to local sources may be more tenuous than our results suggest. We say this because this is one of the rare instances in which we find a different pattern between sessions during the transition to term limits (1999 and 2001) and the term-limits equilibrium session (2003).[9] The proportion of representatives saying local sources are their most important on a school choice floor vote drops from 34 percent before term limits to 18 percent in the 2003 House (sig. $p < 0.05$). This could be important in the context of other findings about term limits effects on the relationships between the legislature and local sources. With only one equilibrium session, we cannot establish a long-term pattern, but we can say that the role played by local sources, especially local officials, after term limits warrants further investigation in both chambers.

The big change in the Senate is the rising importance (a 24% increase) of organized groups and lobbyists as trusted sources during floor votes. Nearly twice the proportion of post-term-limits senators turns to organized groups and lobbyists as their most important source compared to the proportion rating colleagues most important. Organized groups and lobbyists displace local sources as the most important ones for post-term-limits senators seeking information about school choice.

Once again, our findings contradict Mooney's prediction about the value of colleagues during floor votes. But our findings about the post-term-limits Senate also contradict Price's predictions about public engagement with local sources on salient issues. Local sources lose access, while interest groups gain after term limits. These results are likely to heighten the disappointment of term limits advocates who hoped to sever legislators' ties with lobbyists and strengthen ties to the local community.

Consulting about LRHCP

Looking at figure 6.8 we see that term limits have only one noteworthy effect on consulting about a technical issue reaching the floor for a vote. The proportion of representatives consulting colleagues increases substantially after term limits, contrary to our expectations. Nearly all our respondents consult their colleagues and organized groups and lobbyists on this issue, but only about half consult local sources. Term limits have no discernable effect on this. As Price (1978) would predict, public engagement on this technical issue is much lower than for the politically salient issue of school choice.

Here again, we find a statistically significant change in consulting with local sources when we compare only the post-term-limits equilibrium session in the House to the pre-term-limits House. The proportion of representatives in the 2003 House session who say they would consult any local sources during a floor vote about LRHCP is statistically significantly smaller ($p < 0.01$) than it was before term limits. Likewise a smaller proportion of the term-limits equilibrium representatives says local sources are their most important ones (sig. $p < 0.10$). Local sources appear to lose access to legislators as term limits reach their equilibrium stage (Mooney 2009). This reinforces evidence that the role of local officials is a promising line of further term limits research, but of course with only one equilibrium session, these results might not be robust.

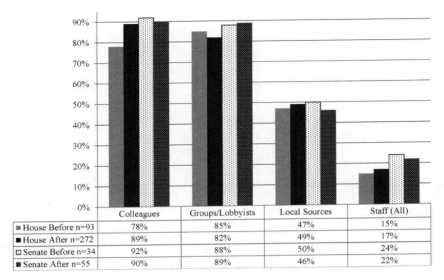

	Colleagues	Groups/Lobbyists	Local Sources	Staff (All)
House Before n=93	78%	85%	47%	15%
House After n=272	89%	82%	49%	17%
Senate Before n=34	92%	88%	50%	24%
Senate After n=55	90%	89%	46%	22%

Fig. 6.8. LRHCP Floor Vote—Sources before and after Term Limits

Most Important Sources for a Floor Vote on LRHCP

Term limits have little effect on the most important sources of information about LRHCP in the House, but there are sizeable changes in the Senate. Comparing figures 6.7 and 6.9 illustrates strikingly similar information gathering patterns in the Senate about LRHCP and about school choice, despite differences in the political salience of these issues. Organized groups and lobbyists make gains in the Senate after term limits, rising from 19 percent to 30 percent saying this is their most important source. This shift almost exactly matches the change in senators' consulting about school choice. Similarly, a smaller proportion of post-term-limits senators say local sources are their most important, but the loss is larger for the technical issue, LRHCP.

Given the relatively small proportion of legislators (less than half) in either chamber who said they consulted any local sources of information about LRHCP, it is surprising that these sources are mentioned as the most important source by nearly a quarter of our respondents for three of our four cohorts. The exception is post-term-limits senators, who repeatedly turn away from local sources after term limits, both on floor votes and during committee deliberations.

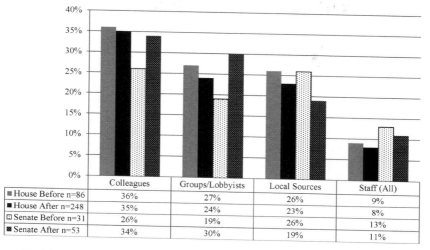

	Colleagues	Groups/Lobbyists	Local Sources	Staff (All)
■ House Before n=86	36%	27%	26%	9%
■ House After n=248	35%	24%	23%	8%
▢ Senate Before n=31	26%	19%	26%	13%
▨ Senate After n=53	34%	30%	19%	11%

Fig. 6.9. LRHCP Floor Vote—Most Important Source before and after Term Limits

We see an increasing proportion of senators saying that their colleagues are their most important source of information (26% before term limits to 34% after). We speculate that this might result from senators migrating in cohorts to the upper chamber. They tend to know each other due to their joint service in the House, so they might value their colleagues' input more than did their Senate predecessors. But we find this only with respect to the technical issue of LRHCP, so we interpret this cautiously.

Discussion of Floor Vote Consulting

Figure 6.10 facilitates comparison across issues of the sources legislators use when anticipating floor votes. Arrows denote shifts of at least two places in the rank order of the sources that arise after term limits, and shading denotes statistically significant changes associated with term limits.

First, as the arrows in the lower panel of the table indicate, the largest changes involve the most important of sources consulted. Specifically, these changes involved colleagues for school choice in the House and in the Senate local sources for both school choice and LRHCP and interest groups or lobbyists for school choice. Additionally, term limits affect consulting about the politically salient issue (school choice) more than the technically

House Any Consulting				Senate Any Consulting			
Before Term Limits		After Term Limits		Before Term Limits		After Term Limits	
Groups LRHCP	85%	Colleagues LRHCP	88%	Colleagues LRHCP	92%	Colleagues LRHCP	90%
Colleagues LRHCP	78%	Groups LRHCP	82%	Groups LRHCP	88%	Groups LRHCP	89%
Colleagues SC	74%	Colleagues SC	72%	Locals SC	83%	Groups SC	73%
Locals SC	71%	Groups SC	72%	Groups SC	66%	Locals SC	69%
Groups SC	68%	Locals SC	68%	Locals LRHCP	50%	Colleagues SC	63%
Locals LRHCP	47%	Locals LRHCP	49%	Colleagues SC	49%	Locals LRHCP	46%
Staff SC	19%	Staff LRHCP	17%	Staff LRHCP	24%	Staff LRHCP	22%
Staff LRHCP	15%	Staff SC	11%	Staff SC	6%	Staff SC	9%

House Most Important Sources				Senate Most Important Sources			
Before Term Limits		After Term Limits		Before Term Limits		After Term Limits	
Colleagues LRHCP	36%	Colleagues LRHCP	35%	Locals SC	29%	Colleagues LRHCP	34%
Locals SC	34%	Locals SC	33%	Colleagues LRHCP	26%	Groups SC	31%
Colleagues SC	30%	Groups LRHCP	24%	Locals LRHCP	26%	Groups LRHCP	30%
Groups LRHCP	27%	Locals LRHCP	23%	Groups LRHCP	19%	Locals SC	24%
Locals LRHCP	26%	Colleagues SC	21%	Groups SC	18%	Locals LRHCP	19%
Myself SC	19%	Myself SC	20%	Colleagues SC	15%	Colleagues SC	16%
Groups SC	13%	Groups SC	17%	Staff LRHCP	13%	Staff LRHCP	11%
Staff LRHCP	9%	Staff LRHCP	8%	Myself LRHCP	13%	Myself LRHCP	6%
Staff SC	7%	Myself LRHCP	8%	Myself SC	12%	Myself SC	6%
Myself LRHCP	6%	Staff SC	6%	Staff SC	3%	Staff SC	6%

* p < 0.10 ** p < 0.05 *** p < 0.01 Shading denotes differences within the chamber that are statistically significant.
Arrows highlight shifts of at least two places in the rank order of sources before and after term limits within the chamber

Fig. 6.10. Rank Order of Sources Used for Floor Votes about School Choice and LRHCP

complex one (LRHCP). Only one shift in the order of the most important sources involves consulting about LRHCP; the others all involve consulting about school choice.

Mooney (1991) characterizes floor votes as satisficing decisions that push legislators toward sources they trust and rely upon when they need immediate information. This means that consulting about these votes should reveal which sources legislators trust. With whom do they maintain a close enough relationship to rely on for information when time precludes checking with multiple sources? Post-term-limits senators frequently report relying on organized groups and lobbyists for floor votes when they lack time to double-check information. Moreover, a higher proportion of post-term-limits senators rely on organized groups and lobbyists not just as a source but as their most important source. Interest groups appear to be trusted sources of information for senators after term limits.

As we noted earlier in this chapter Guston et al. (1997) find that less professional legislatures enhance the influence of interest groups in policy making. By design, term limits reduce the level of professionalism in a legislative chamber. Thus the expanded importance of information from organized groups and lobbyists that we find in the Senate could be a logical, albeit unintended, consequence of term limits.

Comparing floor vote consulting for these two issues, it appears that more legislators rely on colleagues for information about a technical issue (LRHCP) that reaches the chamber floor than about politically salient floor votes (school choice). Approximately one-third of respondents in each chamber identify colleagues as their most important source of information about LRHCP, while less than one-quarter in the House, and less than one-sixth in the Senate, say this for school choice.

We also find issue effects for consulting with local sources. These sources have more access to legislators on the politically salient issue of school choice than on LRHCP. These chamber differences are statistically significant after term limits, which supports Price's predictions about political salience motivating legislators to engage with the public.

The importance of local sources before term limits challenges an assertion of the term limits movement, that legislators who have served for many years lose touch with their district. Our findings demonstrate that local sources were among those that pre-term-limits legislators relied upon when time was short and the need to trust the source was high. After term limits, these local ties appear to fray or never form.

Lost access for local sources is noteworthy because term limits proponents claimed that with limits on their tenure elected officials would be more closely tied to their constituents and their district. We find no evidence of this—indeed, the changes we find are often in the opposite direction. The consulting patterns that evolve in the Senate after term limits often attenuate the ties that term limits advocates wanted to cultivate (local sources) and strengthen the ones they wanted to sever (organized groups and lobbyists). That this occurs at the expense of local sources and of colleagues demonstrates a shift in access and influence for key actors in Michigan's policy-making process. And we add to this the evidence from the equilibrium House session, which indicates that the lower chamber could be following this shift away from local sources now that term limits are fully implemented.

Consulting Staff about Floor Votes

For floor votes we assumed, as does Mooney, that staff is another inside source of information. Michigan Senate staff has a permanent seat on the chamber floor beside their senator's desk, so it seems reasonable to treat this as an inside source. Our results contradict this, as illustrated in figures 6.6 through 6.9. Despite being institutionally part of the chamber and having physical proximity during floor votes and intimate involvement in the day-to-day work in the chamber, staff is not relied upon by legislators at a level that indicates this is an inside source. Given evidence in the state politics literature (Wissel, O'Connor, and King 1976; Hird 2005) about the high quality of information provided by staff, especially nonpartisan staff, we thought that this quasi-inside source of information would provide a way for newly elected legislators to gather information efficiently from a trustworthy, knowledgeable source. So we expected to see newcomers utilize staff more heavily. We find no support for this.

Our key finding here is the small proportion of legislators who consult staff at all and the still smaller proportion that says staff is their most important source of information on either issue. A couple of chamber differences are worth noting. Both chambers consult staff more about the technical issues—LRHCP—than about the politically salient issue of school choice. Representatives consult staff more about school choice than senators do, and the chamber difference is large enough to be statistically significant before term limits (19% in the House and 6% in the Senate). After term limits the chambers converge, because term limits significantly reduce the proportion of representatives who list staff among the sources they consult on school choice (from 19% to 11%, sig. $p < 0.05$). Thus, after term limits, staff losses some of the small bit of clout it enjoyed before term limits on politically salient floor votes.

Lack of Consulting about These Two Issues

We turn now to the narrowest form of search—*myself alone*. Comments that we classify into this category reflect an ideological fervor and distain toward the views of others that we described briefly in our discussion of Burkean cowboys in chapter 3. Politically salient issues are those upon which candidates often take positions during electoral contests and that might be seen as ideological litmus tests with voters. School choice has at various times been a contentious election issue, and so we expect it to exhibit these characteristics.

Ignoring term limits, we find that *myself alone* is specified quite frequently with respect to school choice—20 percent of our House respondents, statistically significantly higher than the 8 percent of senators who say this. In the House consulting *myself alone* is unaffected by term limits—19 percent say this before term limits and 20 percent afterward. This comment rarely arises in consulting about LRHCP in either chamber or for school choice in the Senate. As we would expect, it is the more politically salient issue that drives House members to look to themselves alone. But it also seems that those who advance to the upper chamber are more likely to consult at least some source for information regardless of the political salience of the issue. That should partially reassure any Michigan citizens who favor evidence-based policy making.

We note a qualitative difference after term limits in the responses that we classified into the category *myself alone*. Pre-term-limits representatives more often couch their self-referential information gathering in terms of having heard all the relevant arguments repeatedly for years. For example, "There is nobody I would go to . . . about School Choice. I have enough information. I follow my own position because that is my field. Many look to me. There is nobody else" (interview notes). After term limits, respondents who say they rely on themselves alone often call this a "gut" decision or a core issue. For example: "Me—my own experience, my kids went to Catholic Schools. Competition makes all things better" (interview notes). This post-term-limits comment reflects a more pronounced ideological slant that is difficult to capture using a dichotomous variable.

Effect of Personal Characteristics and Ideology on Information Gathering

Personal characteristics of elected officials affect their information search strategies, according to Hird (2005), who finds that women in legislatures consult more sources than their male colleagues do. Based on his work, we investigate whether the women we interviewed consult more sources of information than do their male colleagues, but our findings contradict his.

One reason gender differences in information gathering are important after term limits is that fewer women, especially Republican women, win seats in the Michigan House, as we reported in chapter 2. If there are major gender differences in the kind of information gathered, then there could be policy implications. For example, if they access a wider array of sources, women legislators might see different policy options. However, given the extremely small number of women in the Senate and the shrinking cohort in the House after term limits, we cannot probe chamber effects nor can we reliably compare consulting before and after term limits. Therefore, we combine our data for both chambers in these analyses.

Gender Differences in Information Gathering during Committee Deliberations

Contrary to Hird's (2005) finding, we find no statistically significant gender difference in the number of sources consulted overall during committee deliberations. The average number of sources for men is 5.6 and 5.5 for women.[10] But we note with interest that women and men have different preferences among the 16 sources we examine here.

First, looking at table 6.1 we see that women place a lower priority on information from the chamber leader (speaker or majority leader), the party caucus, and committee chairs than do their male colleagues. This implies that women shun information from the power structure within the chamber, which is typically dominated by men.[11] Instead, they rely more than men do on partisan staff and on key local officials.

TABLE 6.1. Gender Difference in Consulting during Committee Deliberations

Priority Placed on Sources of Information	Men	Women	F-value
	(Mean with sd below)		
Speaker	**−0.63**	**−0.88**	5.78**
	(0.89)	(0.92)	
Minority leader	−0.46	−0.51	0.23
	(1.04)	(0.82)	
Party caucus	**0.16**	**−0.02**	2.62*
	(0.96)	(0.89)	
Committee chair	**0.30**	**0.05**	3.09*
	(1.18)	(1.22)	
Committee members	0.58	0.54	0.13
	(0.92)	(1.03)	
Partisan staff	**0.60**	**0.87**	5.67**
	(1.01)	(0.93)	
Legislative services bureau (nonpartisan)	0.17	0.16	0.03
	(0.99)	(1.12)	
Chamber fiscal agency (nonpartisan)	0.19	0.39	2.35
	(1.12)	(1.13)	
Governor's office	−0.41	−0.39	0.01
	(0.99)	(0.89)	
State agency staff	0.31	0.20	0.78
	(1.10)	(1.03)	
Members of the other chamber	−0.40	−0.49	0.89
	(0.89)	(0.97)	
Organized groups or lobbyists	0.72	0.66	0.63
	(0.98)	(1.10)	
Key local officials	**−0.13**	**0.12**	4.10**
	(1.10)	(1.06)	
Advisors in the district	−0.24	−0.12	0.82
	(1.06)	(1.03)	
Constituents	0.004	0.04	0.06
	(1.13)	(1.22)	
National Conference of State Legislatures	**−0.92**	**−0.66**	8.25***
	(0.77)	(0.79)	

Note: Number of male responses ranges from 320 to 303; number of female responses ranges from 101 to 97. Bold type indicates statistically significant differences.
* $p < 0.10$, ** $p < 0.05$, *** $p < 0.01$ (two-tailed).

Additionally, the most statistically significant gender difference for any of the sources involves seeking information from the National Conference of State Legislatures (NCSL)—the last row in table 6.1. During committee deliberations, women place a higher priority than men do on information from NCSL. One caveat, however, is that the priority of consulting with the NCSL by women is low, well below their average. So women do not rely heavily on this source, but men rely on it even less. Indeed, this source is used so rarely that we did not include it in other analyses in this chapter.

Gender Differences in Floor Vote Consulting

Once again, contradicting Hird's (2005) work, we find no evidence that women consult more sources on floor votes than men do. Male legislators consult an average of 2.9 sources, while female legislators consult an average of 2.7—a difference that is not statistically significant. For LRHCP, men consult an average of 2.7 sources and women consult an average of 2.1 sources—a statistically significant difference, but not in the predicted direction.

Next we examine gender differences in consulting with specific sources. We find so few of them that we report them here without a table. There is only one source with a statistically significant gender differences in school choice consulting—staff. We find that fewer women (7%) than men (13%) consult staff, and fewer still (2% for women and 7% for men) say staff is their most valuable source of information. Although both differences are significant ($p < 0.10$), these are very small proportions.

With respect to LRHCP, we find two gender differences. First, more women (32%) than men (23%) say that *organized groups or lobbyists* are their most important source of information about LRHCP ($p < 0.10$). This is the only source that we find that women consult more than men in floor votes for either issue. We wonder whether this might result from the increased interest group recruitment of women that we reported in chapter 2.

Second, fewer women (27%) than men (37%) list colleagues as their most important source of information about LRHCP (sig. $p < 0.10$). We speculate that this reflects an "old boys" network in the chamber, given that most legislators are men. If so, this is consistent with women's aversion to consulting committee chairs and others in the power structure during committee deliberations.

Our results simply do not support the hypothesis that women gather more information than men. Still, we find intriguing gender differences in the sources consulted, especially the general tendency of women to eschew

sources from the chamber power structure during committee deliberations, their limited consulting with colleagues on floor votes, and the value
women seem to place on information from organized groups and lobbyists
during floor votes on a technical issue.

Partisan Differences in Consulting

Hird (2005) finds that party affiliation is associated with differences in
information gathering. Specifically, he reports that Republicans rely more
on local sources of information. We find no evidence to support his findings. In fact, we find very few effects, so again we discuss them rather than
provided a table of null findings.

Partisan Consulting of Local Sources in Committee Deliberations

In the House, term limits erase a sizeable pre-term-limits partisan difference. Prior to term limits, Democrats relied upon local sources at about
their average level, and they maintain this after term limits. The priority
placed on information from key local officials rises from a very low level
(–0.31) among GOP representatives before term limits to about average
afterward (–0.02)—a change that is large enough to be statistically significant. The difference we find before term limits contradicts Hird's work,
and there is no partisan difference afterward due to the increased consulting of local sources by the GOP.

    In the Senate the parties differ before term limits with the Senate GOP
placing a moderately low priority on local sources while the Senate Democrats placed a moderately high priority on these sources—again contrary to
Hird's work. After term limits both parties decrease their consulting with
local sources during committee deliberations. For Senate Republicans the
decrease is modest, for Senate Democrats it is a dramatic decline ($p < 0.10$).
This reveals that the pattern we observed in the full chamber reflects pre-
term-limits ties between Democrats and key local officials (government)
and, to a lesser extent, between Republicans and advisors (nongovernmen-
tal) in their district. Term limits untie both sets of relationships in the Senate. And we find no support for the partisan differences Hird reports.

Partisan Consulting on Floor Votes

We find some support for Hird's partisan findings in floor vote consulting,
however. Republicans consult any local source slightly more often about

LRHCP than Democrats do, and they also say local sources are their most important ones for information on LRHCP. But the difference is statistically significant only after term limits and only in the Senate. Additionally, Republicans said that local sources were their most important ones on school choice, but only before term limits and only in the House. This inconsistent pattern does not support the existence of overarching partisan differences, especially given the contradictory findings we report for committee deliberations.

Conclusions

Access matters in policy making, and term limits in Michigan alter access, and hence the potential policy influence of some sources of information. Some actors win, while others lose. But term limits effects are contingent, varying by issue, by chamber, and by stage in the policy process. So determining the winners and losers is complicated. We summarize our three major findings below.

First and foremost, we discover that term limits help organized groups and lobbyists gain access. They are more important sources of information on floor votes in both chambers and for senators during committee deliberations. Floor votes, according to Mooney, involve satisficing decisions under time constraints that preclude checking information. He argues that legislators consult trusted inside sources on floor votes. The sizeable increases that we find in the proportion of legislators who say an organized group or lobbyist is their most important source for floor votes implies that these sources have become trusted inside sources after term limits.

Second, colleagues lose prominence as a source of information on floor votes after term limits. This is a profound shift in consulting patterns in Michigan's legislature, which traditionally exhibited a strong preference for internal sources of information, according to other scholars (Francis 1985; Wissel, O'Connor, and King 1976).[12] Decades later, we find that pre-term-limits Michigan legislators preserved their preference for internal sources (e.g., committee chairs in the House and the party caucus in the Senate) in two stages of the policy process. But term limits change this. We find that term limits reduce the relative importance of and priority placed on colleagues, especially committee chairs, compared to organized groups and lobbyists in both chambers during both floor votes and committee deliberations.

Third, local sources also lose access after term limits. Most of this is occurs in the Senate, but evidence from the equilibrium House session indicates that this may be spreading to the lower chamber as well. The shift away from local sources of information in the post-term-limits Senate is one of the biggest chamber differences we find.

Prior to term limits, there were no statistically significant chamber differences for the three aggregate categories of sources during committee deliberations: inside, midrange, and outside sources. After term limits chamber consulting patterns during committee deliberations diverge for all three of these aggregate categories. Disparities between the two chambers on both inside and midrange sources of information are driven entirely by shifts in the Senate, although differences for outside sources reflect opposing shifts in each chamber after term limits. Term limits apparently trigger a lot more change in the Senate than in the House, especially when individual sources of information are considered.

For floor votes, too, we find more change in the Senate after term limits. In the House we find only one shift in the rank order of sources with respect to either the frequency of consulting or the importance of the source. In the Senate there are three similar shifts. The only loser in the House is colleague-to-colleague consulting about school choice. Information from colleagues on school choice becomes more important in the Senate, but local sources lose clout in the Senate on both issues—school choice and LRHCP.

These chamber differences in the effect of term limits underscore the importance of following term limits until they are implemented in both legislative chambers. Often the literature considers term limits effects mainly in the context of inexperience or newness. Consequently we and many scholars who study these limits assumed that upper chambers would be less profoundly affected by term limits. It appears we were wrong.

Pre-term-limits senators had many years and multiple opportunities to establish relationships with local officials. After term limits time is scarce, and local ties may be a casualty. The lack of time is compounded in the Senate by vast differences in size and geographic dispersion between districts in the two chambers. House districts, especially those embedded within an urban areas, might have one school superintendent and one mayor (key local officials), and a small number of potential advisors. In sprawling Senate districts, there are multiple townships and villages and often several counties as well as multiple school districts. Thus, detailed knowledge of the key local officials is much harder to acquire for a senator than for a House member.

A second plausible reason for these chamber differences reflects campaigning in sprawling rural districts. Attending village meetings, school board meetings, county commission meetings, and other local government events is one effective way to campaign when a district is too big for door-to-door canvassing. These events also provide an opportunity for Senate candidates to get to know the numerous key local officials and other important actors in their district. Prior to term limits, attending these events made a lot of sense for campaigning in large Senate districts, especially those in rural parts of Michigan. After term limits winning Senate candidates in Michigan raise a lot more money (see chapter 5) and can run an election campaign using phone banks, mailings, advertising on TV and other media, and paid staff. This could reduce the need for senators to attend local events where they meet and greet local officials as well as voters. An unintended consequence might be that they miss opportunities to form ties with local officials and others with street-level and local knowledge.

A third explanation for these larger effects on the Senate is that nearly all post-term-limits senators learn the job of legislator in the House. That was less common prior to term limits. Also, when newly elected senators arrived (in ones and twos), there was a critical mass of veteran senators to socialize them into the norms of the Senate. Cohorts of newly elected senators appear to bring remnants of the hierarchical committee-based consulting patterns of the House with them to the Senate. Approaches that work well in a small chamber like the Senate are replaced by approaches that are more effective in the much larger House. The advantages of small group interaction apparent in the pre-term-limits Senate are lost. For example, senators rely less on caucus discussions about issues, shifting to a more committee-based system.

Null findings in lower chambers may have distracted scholarly attention from some of the more profound changes of term limits. As we discover here, institutional changes may overshadow newness and inexperience. These may become more apparent when term limits are disentangled from inexperience, as they can be in upper legislative chambers.

Not only do we find differential effects on the chambers, but we find varying impacts of term limits on our two issues. Consulting about the politically salient issue—school choice—seems to be affected more by term limits than does the technically complex issue—LRHCP. Only one of the statistically significant differences on floor vote consulting involves LRHCP. The others all demonstrate differences for school choice. This suggests that issues with high political salience are more susceptible to term limits effects, but these effects also vary by chamber. We continue to examine these varying issue effects in the next chapter.

SEVEN

Floor Vote Consulting

Consulting colleagues within the chambers remains important among post-term-limits legislators, even as they rely more on organized groups and lobbyists for information. Here we delve more deeply into floor vote consulting among colleagues, probing term limits effects at two levels: the individual and the chamber. In the previous chapter, we treated consulting with colleagues as a pair of binary variables. Colleagues were either consulted or not, and they were either the most important source or not. Now we measure the number of individual consulting relationships—the volume of consulting.

At the individual level, we measure the average amount of consulting among individual legislators—their volume of consulting. We compare the average number of times legislators consult colleagues as well as how often an individual colleague is consulted, paying particular attention to whether this occurs across party lines or not. We compare consulting by veterans and newcomers when freshman are rare and veterans are seasoned (before term limits) to its effects when massive turnover generates surges of freshman and veterans have limited experience (after term limits).

At the chamber level, we explore the cohesiveness and centralization of consulting networks within the legislative chamber—the institutional structure of consulting. In using the term *institutional structure*, we do not refer to an organizational hierarchy that might be portrayed using a chart of the formal organization. Rather we treat institutional structure as the informal, "sedimented" practices that are revealed by reported patterns of interaction.[1] These practices evolve among legislators over time, and hence are likely to be sensitive to changes in tenure and turnover. When these structures involve consulting, they provide insight into the diffusion of information among colleagues within the chambers.

In exploring changes at the chamber level, we extend our prior work (Sarbaugh-Thompson et al. 2006) here by comparing consulting patterns in the two legislative chambers and by adding another post-term-limits House session—one with term limits fully implemented. Previously, based on the first three House sessions, we found that after term limits legislators consult a narrower range of experts about issues. Some of these experts are uniquely positioned to facilitate or to limit the diffusion of information. In this chapter we contrast consulting in the Senate and the House and also focus on representatives in the 2003 House session. This session is the first in which legislators were not socialized or mentored by the cohort of pre-term-limits veterans. It typifies the post-term-limits equilibrium in Michigan, to use Mooney's (2009) terminology.

Finally, we explore the characteristics of legislators considered to be experts by their colleagues. We explore whether expertise gained inside the chamber or from prior professional experience outside the chamber is more or less valuable after term limits.

Data and Methods

This chapter explores two interview questions, questions 7 and 10 in appendix A, which ask legislators to name specific colleagues they would consult about the two hypothetical floor vote scenarios we described in chapter 6. Question 7 asks which colleagues the respondent would look to for information and guidance if a bill about school choice reached the floor of the chamber. Question 10 asks this for a bill about licensing or regulating health care professionals (LRHCP).

We begin by looking at dyadic relationships—ties connecting pairs of legislators. We compute the average number of colleagues consulting with a legislator (revealed expertise) and also the average number of times legislators consulted other colleagues (information search). To calculate the average for information searching we include only legislators we interviewed, but we calculate the average for revealed expertise using all members of the chamber because our respondents could name experts (someone they consulted) that we were not able to interview.

We use these data to explore questions about the amount of consulting by and of newly elected legislators before and after term limits. After term limits, newness and experience are relative concepts, with post-term-limits legislators, at least in the House, amassing very limited experience by pre-term-limits standards. Therefore, the difference in experience between veterans and newcomers is very narrow.

Next we construct a matrix for each issue for each chamber during each session in which we conducted interviews—a consulting network. There are 14 matrices in all, two for each of the four House and three Senate sessions—one for each issue (i.e., school choice and LRHCP) per session and chamber. Each matrix consists of a row and column for each member of the chamber. Values in the cells of the matrix are one if the respondent in the row consulted the person in the column and zero if not.

We analyze these consulting networks to understand institutional flows of information. In this we consider legislators as conduits of information connected to various members of the chamber. To analyze these connections in the consulting networks, we rely on several measures of the pattern for the whole network, such as network centralization. We used UCINET 6.46 to analyze these networks. The specific measures we use might be unfamiliar to some readers, so we describe them as we work through our analyses.

Volume of Individual Consulting about Issues

In this section, we consider term limits effects on two individual-level aspects of consulting: first, the average amount of consulting and, second, the influence of partisanship on consulting (i.e., consulting across party lines). We consider how many colleagues a legislator consulted, calculating an average volume of consulting rather than whether a legislator consulted any colleague or not, as we did in chapter 6.

As we noted in the preceding chapter, other scholars (Mooney 1991; Uslaner and Weber 1977; Arnold, Deen, and Patterson 2000) demonstrate that time and experience increase legislators' willingness to rely on colleagues when decisions must be made quickly and satisficing is necessary. Under term limits, legislators have less time to become policy experts, so logically their need for information is greater. Yet their limited experience with each other makes it harder to know who is knowledgeable about an issue and who provides unbiased advice. So this greater need for information confronts more uncertainty about whom to rely upon. The pull of these competing tendencies seems likely to vary by issue depending at least in part on the issues' political salience and technical complexity (Price 1978).

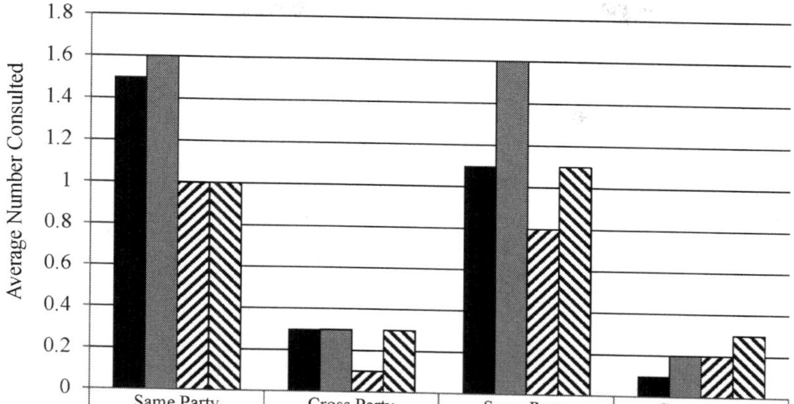

	Same Party Consulting SC	Cross Party Consulting SC	Same Party Consulting LRHCP		Cross Party Consulting LRHCP	
■ House Before	1.5	0.3	1.1	*	0.1	*
▥ House After	1.6	0.3	1.6	*	0.2	*
▨ Senate Before	1.0	0.1	0.8		0.2	*
◥ Senate After	1.0	0.3	1.1		0.3	*

Starred pairs denote statistically significant changes. Averages are based on 95 pre-term-limits and 275 post-term-limits House respondents and 35 pre-term-limits and 55 post-term-limits Senate respondents.

Fig. 7.1. Average Numbers of Colleagues Consulted on Floor Votes

We find that the need for technical information appears to overcome uncertainty about whom to trust and rely upon for information. As we illustrate in figure 7.1, term limits have almost no effect on the amount of consulting about school choice, but the volume of consulting about LRHCP increases after term limits. These effects are generally consistent across both chambers, and the increase in the volume of within-party consulting in the House about LRHCP is statistically significant.

Other scholars demonstrate that political party is a powerful predictor of consulting in state legislatures (Ferber and Pugliese 2000). Hird (2005) reports that directors of nonpartisan research organizations say that term limits increase legislators' tendency to rely on colleagues within their own party and follow the party caucus position. They attribute this to the greater ideological intensity of newcomers. So one might expect term limits to magnify the power of political parties, but principally in the lower chamber.

Although we find that most consulting occurs within the same political party, our results do not demonstrate that cross-party consulting declines after term limits. Indeed, we find evidence to the contrary, which we report in figure 7.1. Cross-party consulting, although rare with or without term limits, increases or remains stable after term limits. These increases are statistically significant for consulting about LRHCP in both chambers. This might reflect the lower political salience of this issue.

Before we leave figure 7.1, we note that in chapter 6 we reported a large increase (14%) in the proportion of senators consulting colleagues about school choice after term limits. Yet here we report only a small increase in the volume of cross-party consulting about school choice in the Senate and no change in same-party consulting. This implies that pre-term-limits senators who consulted any colleague about this issue consulted several colleagues, while most post-term-limits senators who consulted anyone about this issue appear to consult only one source. We explore this change more extensively when we consider institutional-level effects of term limits later in this chapter.

Effects of Experience on the Volume of Consulting

We turn our attention now to newcomers' information search. We expect to find differences in the information search of newcomers and veterans based on the work of other scholars. For example, Porter and Leuthold (1970) find that newly elected legislators rely more heavily on members of their own political party for information. Veteran legislators rely not just on co-partisans, but on colleagues with a proven track record and a reputation for honesty and expertise according to Caldeira, Clark, and Patterson (1993).

Not only is it plausible that newcomers and veterans search differently for information, but we assume term limits will change this. The question we explore in this section is what happens to consulting when newcomers arrive in waves and even veterans can only amass limited experience?

We are especially interested in chamber differences given that the House is most affected by legislators who are new to any legislative service. For example, most senators gain experience and establish reputations in the House prior to moving to the Senate in groups, so newcomers and veteran senators may not differ much, if at all, after term limits. And post-term-limits senators may bring relationships established on the other side of the capitol dome with them when they migrate in cohorts to the Senate. Newcomers to the House on the other hand may have a hard time learning each other's names because there are so many new faces.

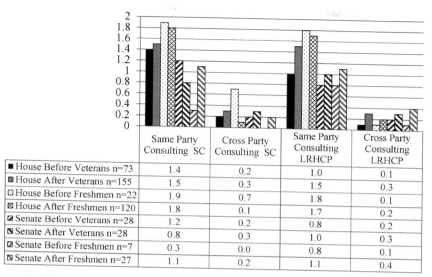

	Same Party Consulting SC	Cross Party Consulting SC	Same Party Consulting LRHCP	Cross Party Consulting LRHCP
■ House Before Veterans n=73	1.4	0.2	1.0	0.1
▦ House After Veterans n=155	1.5	0.3	1.5	0.3
▢ House Before Freshmen n=22	1.9	0.7	1.8	0.1
⊠ House After Freshmen n=120	1.8	0.1	1.7	0.2
◪ Senate Before Veterans n=28	1.2	0.2	0.8	0.2
◩ Senate After Veterans n=28	0.8	0.3	1.0	0.3
◪ Senate Before Freshmen n=7	0.3	0.0	0.8	0.1
◩ Senate After Freshmen n=27	1.1	0.2	1.1	0.4

Fig. 7.2. Effect of Experience on Information Seeking on Floor Votes

Newcomers' and Veterans' Information Search on School Choice

Looking at figure 7.2, we see clearly that House newcomers seek more information than veterans on both issues both before and after term limits. After term limits, differences between House newcomers and veterans diminish slightly for both issues. Moreover, before term limits newcomers sought information across party lines about both issues more than their veteran colleagues did. This result contradicts work of others about the ideological intensity of newcomers—at least pre-term-limits newcomers. With relatively small numbers of newcomers before term limits, we hesitate to make too much of this finding. And cross-party consulting is rare before and after term limits for both issues.

In contrast to the pattern we observed in the House, before term limits Senate newcomers consult far fewer colleagues about school choice than veteran senators do (veterans average 1.2 colleagues compared to 0.3 for newcomers, sig. $p < 0.05$). But figure 7.2 illustrates that some chamber differences for the politically salient issue of school choice vanish after term limits. Post-term-limits Senate newcomers consult more colleagues on school choice than post-term-limits veterans do. Cross-party consulting about this issue by Senate newcomers was nonexistent before term limits, but newcomers after term limits consult across party lines almost as much as veterans do—which is still infrequently. These post-term-limits changes seem likely to reflect migration to the Senate of cohorts of legislators who served together in the House. They appear to bring their relationships with them.

Newcomers' and Veterans' Information Search on LRHCP

Returning to figure 7.2, we examine consulting about the technical issue—LRHCP. Once again, newcomers' greater need for information seems to overcome any lack of familiarity with colleagues, but experience appears to reduce the need to consult multiple sources about LRHCP for pre-term-limits House veterans. So the information-seeking difference for LRHCP in the pre-term-limits House between newcomers and veterans is more extreme. This pattern is not evident in the Senate. The average number of colleagues consulted in the Senate by veterans and newcomers differs only slightly both before and after term limits.

Most of the consulting about LRHCP is with members of the legislators' own political party. Neither experience nor term limits alter this preference for consulting co-partisan. These are small numbers, and consulting across party lines is very rare, so we interpret this cautiously. But we fail to find definitive evidence that newcomers after term limits hew more consistently to their own co-partisans when they seek information. We find evidence for the Senate that hints at the opposite effect.

The Effect of Experience on School Choice Expertise

We consider next the other side of the relationship—who is consulted for information. This reveals which legislators are considered issue experts by their colleagues. Quite predictably we report in figure 7.3 that veteran representatives are consulted much more often with or without term limits in the House. Before term limits House veterans received an average of more than five times as many requests for information as newcomers did. The gap between these newcomers and veteran experts narrows considerably after term limits—with veterans receiving an average of not quite two times the requests that newcomers receive. That newcomers after term limits are consulted this frequently implies that they must have outside experience or other sources of expertise that are valued more after term limits. Although these changes are substantively noteworthy, they are not statistically significant.[2] But, as we discuss shortly, it still appears that time

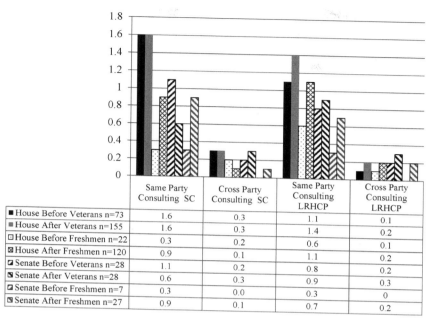

	Same Party Consulting SC	Cross Party Consulting SC	Same Party Consulting LRHCP	Cross Party Consulting LRHCP
■ House Before Veterans n=73	1.6	0.3	1.1	0.1
▥ House After Veterans n=155	1.6	0.3	1.4	0.2
▢ House Before Freshmen n=22	0.3	0.2	0.6	0.1
⊠ House After Freshmen n=120	0.9	0.1	1.1	0.2
◪ Senate Before Veterans n=28	1.1	0.2	0.8	0.2
◣ Senate After Veterans n=28	0.6	0.3	0.9	0.3
◪ Senate Before Freshmen n=7	0.3	0.0	0.3	0
◣ Senate After Freshmen n=27	0.9	0.1	0.7	0.2

Fig. 7.3. Effect of Experience on Floor Vote Expertise (Being Consulted)

in office or experience on the Education Committee or other experience acquired inside the chamber contribute to expertise even after term limits.

We find another chamber difference in school choice consulting here. In the pre-term-limits Senate, newcomers are predictably consulted very rarely about school choice. But after term limits newcomers are consulted *more* than veterans. This is another indication that after term limits many newcomers and veterans who recently served together in the lower chamber have ongoing relationships established on the other side of the capitol. They have knowledge about who has amassed expertise and know their colleagues' reputations for honesty or other attributes. And their accumulated experience varies only slightly.

Consulting across party lines is rare in both chambers, but on the issue of school choice veterans in both chambers with and without term limits are consulted a little more by colleagues from the opposite party. This suggests that veterans are able to establish a reputation as experts given some time in office. That this pattern persists after term limits suggests that it is possible to establish a reputation as an expert quickly when almost everyone is relatively new, and that this reputation can cross the partisan divide.

The Effect of Experience on LRHCP Expertise

The pattern we find for LRHCP expertise before term limits in both chambers is similar to the ones for school choice expertise, but differences between newcomers and veterans are more muted for this issue. Specifically, we see in figure 7.3 that House newcomers are consulted about half as often as veterans on LRHCP compared to only one-fifth as often about school choice. This might indicate that prior professional experience in the health field elevates newcomers more quickly to expert status with or without term limits. After term limits, there are even fewer differences in the perceived expertise of newcomers and veterans in both chambers, and there is no chamber difference for this issue.

Although we expected that the low political salience of LRHCP might facilitate the flow of information across party lines, cross-party consulting on this issue appears to be at least as uncommon as it is for school choice. Experts might establish their reputations more quickly after term limits, but their expertise on both issues is still recognized primarily within their own political party.

Structure of the Consulting Networks

The relative influence of key actors and the structure of the relationships in a legislature can all be explored using several network analysis techniques (Hanneman and Riddle 2005). These measures convey the information that a diagram could provide in a smaller network. But even a network with low density (all our consulting networks have low density) cannot be portrayed visually when it is large. It becomes a tangled mass of lines from which the eye can distinguish little or no information. We recognize that some readers may not be familiar with the terms we use in this section. We, therefore, use the more intuitively obvious network measures available, and describe these measures in some detail before explaining our findings.

We describe 14 matrices in the following analyses. Each matrix is a set of relationships for one legislative session in one chamber about one issue, either school choice or LRHCP. We describe each legislative session separately rather than combining them into pre- and post-term-limits categories. This is partially a function of the nature of network analysis. But it is also, we believe, theoretically valuable to understand the dynamics that occur in the transition to term limits as well as the equilibrium that evolves after term limits are fully implemented (Mooney 2009).

Network Measures

We explore the structure of consulting using two network measures: *network centralization* and *betweenness*.[3] We also touch lightly on *reach centrality* here, but return to it later in the chapter. First, network centralization compares an observed network to a star (i.e., everyone is connected to one central actor and only to that actor). A star is 100 percent centralized. That is, one actor is involved in all the relationships, the remaining actors are involved in only one relation—the one with the central actor. So, in the star network, the central actor's score diverges as much as possible from the score of the other actors. Most networks are not a perfect star, so there is a range of scores among actors. Therefore, network centralization measures the prominence of the experts compared to other actors in our consulting networks—the extent to which the actors' scores diverge from each other.

In directed networks, there are two measures of network centralization: one for indegrees, which measures how central the "experts" are, and one for outdegrees, which measures the concentration or diffusion of the contacts radiating from information seekers—the search strategy. The disparity between indegree and outdegree centralization is important because the closer a network is to a star the bigger the difference between the indegrees (100% for a perfect star) and the outdegrees (1% in a perfect star with 100 nodes). Generally one expects that as indegree centralization increases, outdegree centralization decreases. In the networks we examine, however, we find a few instances in which the centralization measures move in the same direction (both less centralized). In the data we analyze below, high network indegree centralization indicates that there are fewer experts that many colleagues or most colleagues turn to directly for information about an issue. Outdegree centralization indicates agreement on who the experts are—similar search strategies.

The second network measure we use is betweenness. Betweenness indicates the potential for a node in a network (or a person in our data) to connect other nodes that do not interact directly. Intuitively, betweenness can be thought of as the capacity of a particular legislator to facilitate or to thwart the flow of information throughout the consulting network. The sum of the betweenness scores for all actors in a network, total betweenness, provides one way to assess the overall connectivity of a network. The portion of total betweenness attributable to the legislator with the highest betweenness indicates whether the network has many or few pathways for sharing information.

The formal definition of betweenness is the sum of the proportion of the geodesics (shortest paths between two points) connecting two colleagues that pass through that legislator. For example, if there are exactly two geodesics (equally short paths) between legislators A and B and legislator C is on one of those paths, then 1/2 is added to C's betweenness value. If on the other hand, there are five paths connecting legislators D and E, and C is on one of those geodesics, 1/5th is added to C's betweenness sum. If no actor in a network has high betweenness, it could mean that the network is well connected at the dyadic level (little need for third party connections) or it could mean that it is disconnected. Therefore, betweenness needs to be interpreted in context.

Liaisons and bridges are two somewhat familiar network roles that tend to produce high betweenness scores (Farace, Monge, and Russell 1977). For those unfamiliar with these concepts, a liaison is a member of two groups and is the only member in common between those groups. A bridge consists of two connected actors, each of whom is the only member of a group to have any ties with anyone from another group. Liaisons and bridges can facilitate or block the flow of information between clusters of otherwise fragmented actors. Reflecting this, actors playing these or similar roles have high betweenness scores.

In our data, legislators with high betweenness could be key conduits for information or they could provide choke points that might impede the flow of information. We can envision them as spigots that can be turned on or off. Thus we want to know the proportion of the total betweenness provided by the legislator with the highest betweenness. That is to say, how critical is this legislator to the flow of information through the chamber?

Legislators with high betweenness are not necessarily the experts, but they connect experts. For example, committee member A, who is friendly with both the chair and minority vice chair of a committee (both assumed to be experts), could gather information from both and relay it to others in the committee and to the chamber as a whole. Committee member A has high betweenness. So it is possible to have multiple experts, but only one legislator connecting more of them, which gives this linchpin high betweenness.

Networks with high total betweenness (the sum of every member's betweenness) can be envisioned as a series of interconnected segments. Often several members have high betweenness. Thus one individual legislator might not be as crucial in disseminating information. In networks with low total betweenness, a legislator with high betweenness is in a position to control information. There are very few alternative channels along which information can flow. Therefore, the proportion of total betweenness attached to the most connected legislator provides useful evidence about patterns of information dissemination in these consulting networks.

As we noted above, networks with lower betweenness could be open systems if many or most of the actors are connected directly, which we assess using network centralization. But if a network is not well connected and the sum of the betweenness is low, it might be so loosely connected that it is decoupled. Information will not flow freely, if it flows at all. The meaning of network centralization and betweenness are contingent on each other. Therefore quantitative measures of a network need to be interpreted collectively to provide a complete and accurate portrayal of the structure of the network (Prell 2012). In keeping with this, we provide an overall image of the consulting networks first, and then support our description with specific network measures.

Discussion of School Choice Consulting Networks in the House

We find that term limits create a more fragile network in the House for consulting about school choice because information dissemination depends more heavily on fewer legislators. After term limits there is less agreement about who the experts are, but more importantly there is little connective tissue linking these experts into a cohesive network through which information can flow. We base this assessment on evidence summarized in table 7.1.

The pre-term-limits House school choice consulting network is a decentralized system with some clearly accepted experts (about 36% of the chamber) and a moderate number of bridges and liaisons holding the network together (maximum betweenness of 28.5 and total betweenness of 161), and 50 percent of the chamber can be "reached" by the most connected actor (see reach centrality measures). Not only is this network well connected, it is fairly open, based on low network centralization (13.5% indegree). This suggests that information can flow relatively freely throughout the chamber. Key experts are relatively accessible either directly or through several linchpins. There are only a few choke points that could impede information dissemination. We base this on the ratio of the maximum betweenness to the total betweenness. Only 18 percent of the betweenness in the network involves a crucial linchpin legislator, suggesting that there are many others who provide connective pathways (bridges and liaisons) along which information can flow.

The school choice network in the 2003 House, with term limits fully implemented, becomes decentralized (indegree centralization drops to 5%). The amount of consulting falls only slightly, and 6 percent more legislators are consulted for their expertise. This indicates that there are more experts but less consensus on who these experts are. Each expert is likely to have a subgroup of colleagues consulting them. This indicates the potential for factions and a need for connections between information hubs within the network. Therefore, the shortage of legislators playing the key roles of bridges and liaisons connecting other legislators into a system is a critical piece of information. This is reflected in the decline in total betweenness to 101. More than one-third of this betweenness is contributed by one legislator. Additionally total reach centrality declines, supporting lower connectivity generally in the network. This network appears fragmented and decoupled, in stark contrast with the pre-term-limits House.

Thus the 2003 network is characterized by isolated clusters of legislators revolving around somewhat disconnected experts. These multiple experts have few options to disseminate their knowledge to the majority of the chamber or probably even within their own caucus. This makes it difficult for outside experts to educate House members on the issue of school choice. Lobbyists and experts alike need to use a scattergun approach to disseminating information because it is unlikely to flow eas-

TABLE 7.1. School Choice Consulting Networks by Session and Chamber

	House				Senate		
	1997	1999	2001	2003	1999	2003	2007
Possible Consulting (respondents*chamber size)	10,450	10,230	10,230	9,680	1,292	1,064	1,026
Amount of Consulting Reported (% of possible)	1.7	1.9	1.8	1.4	3.0	3.1	3.5
Representatives Consulted (% of chamber)	36.4	53.6	43.6	42.7	39.5	28.9	28.9
Respondents who report consulting (% of respondents)	73.7	74.2	69.9	73.9	50.0	64.3	63.0
Number of respondents	95	93	93	89	35	28	27
Network centralization							
Indegree centralization (%)	13.5	12.6	10.6	5.2	11.3	8.9	8.7
Outdegree centralization (%)	30.3	18.0	18.1	26.9	17.0	23.2	28.7
Reach centrality							
Chamber maximum	45	32	34	40	9	12	15
Percent of chamber reaching top expert	50	50	47	46	24	32	43
Total reach centrality for the chamber	339	472	517	292	94	78	90
Betweenness							
Chamber Maximum	28.5	155.5	406	33.3	19.5	7.5	20
Total betweenness for the chamber	161	1,012	1,463	101	68	14	55

ily throughout the chamber after term limits. They may need to contact many experts individually.

The two sessions during the transition to term limits (the 1999 and 2001 House sessions) include a lot of experts (54% and 44% of the chamber, respectively), but again there is not much agreement on who they are (lower indegree centralization). This leads to segmented networks held together by a few legislators with extremely high betweenness (maximum betweenness of 156 and 406 and total betweenness of 1,012 and 1,463, respectively).

Thus, for both the transition and the equilibrium term limits session, the school choice consulting networks after term limits consist of the multinucleated hubs revolving around multiple competing experts. The variation after term limits appears to be whether these hubs are connected into a more cohesive system. During the transition to term limits, there were still many bridges and liaisons connecting the system. By the final equilibrium House session, very little connective tissue holds the network together. Fragmented networks can limit legislators' exposure to alternative perspectives, producing an echo chamber effect. This is consistent with the post-term-limits decline in building bipartisan coalitions to pass legislation that we reported in chapter 4.

Discussion of School Choice Consulting Networks in the Senate

We find fewer differences between the pre- and post-term-limits Senate than we did in the House. The most obvious difference is that the number of experts declines after term limits from 40 percent of the chamber before term limits to 29 percent afterward. Correspondingly, more post-term-limits senators (63% of the chamber) consult at least one colleague compared to 50 percent of the pre-term-limits senators (consistent with evidence we presented in chapter 6). So, after term limits there are more senators seeking information about this issue, but they consult fewer experts.

Michigan's Senate, with 38 senators, is much smaller than the 110-member House. Therefore, it should be easier to connect its members directly. This reduces the need for conduits of information and provides fewer opportunities for senators to act as liaisons or to participate in bridges. Therefore, it is not especially surprising that before term limits the Senate was dependent on only a few liaisons and bridges to connect the segments of its consulting network (total betweenness of 68).

The pre-term-limits senator with the maximum betweenness (19.5) accounts for less than one-quarter of the connective tissue holding the network together. Total betweenness falls to 14 during the transition to term limits. In this network the chamber could dissolve into two decoupled subunits if anything happened to the one senator who accounts for more than 50 percent of the total betweenness (7.5 of 14). This concentration of connectivity in one senator subsides in the 2007 post-term-limits session, although the senator with the maximum betweenness (20) accounts for more than one-third of the total betweenness of 55.

So, just as we found in the House, the post-term-limits Senate depends more heavily on fewer conduits of information. But this might reflect more direct (dyadic) contact given that total reach centrality is stable and the proportion of the chamber that is "reachable" by the most central actor increases substantially by the 2007 Senate session. This combination of measures indicates that the post-term-limits Senate is a little bit more vulnerable to fragmentation than it was before term limits. The tendency is similar to the pattern we found in the House, but the effect is much smaller. Here again, relationships established in the House could facilitate consulting among senators after term limits.

Discussion of LRHCP Consulting Networks in the House

In table 7.2 we present network measures for consulting about LRHCP. Here again, we provide an overview of the networks before discussing specific network measures. As the House moves toward full implementation of term limits, the LRHCP consulting networks increasingly resembles a star that revolves around one or a few key experts. More legislators seek information about LRHCP, but fewer colleagues are consulted. Moreover, there are fewer pathways along which information can flow. One representative provides nearly half of all the betweenness holding the 2003 network together, so the flow of information is very sensitive to the behavior of this legislator.

Turning to the specific measures, we see in table 7.2 that the proportion of expert colleagues on LRHCP shrinks from 32 percent in the pre-term-limits House to 23 percent in the 2003 House, a decrease of nearly 9 percent across the four sessions. Simultaneously, the proportion of the chamber consulting experts on this issue increases slightly, by about 3 percent. So, fewer experts and a little more consulting produce a more centralized network. This is reflected in changes in indegree centralization, which rises from 20 percent before term limits to 34 percent after term limits.

After term limits are fully implemented in 2003 in the House, the maximum betweenness score is low (31.5), but even more telling is the extremely low sum of the betweenness for the entire chamber (69). This means that one legislator is providing nearly half (46%) of all the connective tissue linking segments of this consulting network. This implies that in 2003 the House consulting network for LRHCP can quickly become disjointed or decoupled. It is even more vulnerable to the behavior of one legislator than the school choice consulting network is.

Combining these measures indicates that consulting about LRHCP in the pre-term-limits House is a multinucleated network that starts out with several experts, but the pool of experts dwindles across the sessions as term limits are implemented. In the final post-term-limits House session, there is a shortage of connective tissue linking the segments of the network as well as a shortage of experts. Although the network is centralized, indicating a strong core, the periphery is fragmented and could easily disintegrate if it is not already decoupled. And it appears that one legislator has outsized influence on the flow of information about this issue after term limits.

TABLE 7.2. LRHCP Consulting Networks by Session and Chamber

	House				Senate		
	1997	1999	2001	2003	1999	2003	2007
Possible consulting (respondents*chamber size)	10,450	10,230	10,230	9,680	1,292	1064	1026
Amount of consulting reported (% of possible)	1.1	1.6	1.9	1.4	2.5	3.9	3.7
Representatives consulted (% of chamber)	31.8	31.8	25.5	22.7	15.8	28.9	23.7
Respondents who report consulting (% of respondents)	69.5	77.4	84.9	72.7	67.6	85.7	81.5
Number of respondents	95	93	93	88	35	28	27
Network centralization							
Indegree centralization (%)	19.6	32.3	32.0	34.4	48.9	34.0	37.1
Outdegree centralization (%)	3.7	3.3	4.9	3.5	6.1	11.2	5.7
Reach centrality							
Chamber maximum	25	49	53	49	21	14	16
Percent of chamber reaching top expert	23	66	62	54	59	35	43
Total reach centrality for the chamber	279	378	398	274	75	82	79
Betweenness							
Chamber maximum	49	120.5	104.5	31.5	7	2	2.5
Total betweenness for the chamber	211	354	241	69	11	8	7

LRHCP Consulting Network in the Senate

We find a completely different pattern in the Senate. In the Senate the LRHCP consulting network moves from the most centralized of any chambers' network on either issue to one that becomes less centralized as term limits are implemented. Before term limits, this Senate consulting network appears to be dominated by an expert or a couple of experts to whom the rest of the chamber defers. After term limits a much larger proportion of the chamber consults at least one colleague on this issue. And the number of experts consulted expands. Reflecting this proliferation of experts, indegree centralization falls from 49 percent to levels ranging between 34 percent and 37 percent after term limits. The pre-term-limits chamber on the other hand reveals one or a few clearly agreed upon experts.

The level of cohesiveness in the pre-term-limits Senate networks is reflected in reach centrality measures, indicating that prior to term limits the top expert was accessible to more than half of the chamber (59%). After term limits, top experts are accessible to a smaller, but still substantial, proportion of the chamber (43%). Both reach centrality and betweenness measures indicate that one or a couple of senators have outsized influence in the pre-term-limits LRHCP consulting network, however.

After term limits, there appears to be greater need for connective tissue because there are more experts who are consulted. So it may be difficult to integrate the information, and it may not flow easily throughout the chamber. Yet in the smaller chamber the connective tissue might not be as important because the experts are more accessible to a larger proportion of the chamber directly. We base this on a substantial increase in the percentage of consulting (more than a 1% increase). Although we find once again that the post-term-limits consulting networks may be more vulnerable to fragmenting, in the smaller Senate direct contact appears to ameliorate this risk.

Discussion of Consulting Networks

We find a consistent pattern in the consulting networks on both issues after term limits in both chambers. There is less connectivity, with a smaller number of legislators linking the segments of the network together after term limits—sometimes one legislator is an especially important linchpin sustaining the network. Often there is less agreement after term limits about who the experts are. With more hubs of expertise, the connective tissue gains importance. But there tends to be fewer actors linking colleagues together. Hence these post-term-limits consulting networks are more vulnerable to disruptions along the rare connective pathways carrying information.

Interest groups, lobbyists, and other advocates need to consider the fragmented structure of the post-term-limits consulting networks in both the Senate and the House when they try to disseminate information or to educate legislators about this issue. They should not assume that diffusion of information throughout the chambers will occur without an extensive multipronged approach. They would be advised to seed the network at various points to increase the probability that information will diffuse throughout the chambers, especially in the post-term-limits House.

This multipronged approach is difficult but more feasible for the large multiclient lobbying firms, whose resources can meet these demands for multiple contacts. Smaller grassroots advocacy groups tend to cultivate one or a few legislators that they educate and rely on to disseminate their information throughout the chamber in a "two-step" information process described by Porter (1974). The need for a multiprong education strategy is challenging for these resource-strapped groups.

The terms *centralized* and *hierarchical* can elicit negative images of closed or constrained information sharing. We point out, however, that legislators may establish a reputation and amass experience that qualifies them as widely recognized experts, even by members of the opposite political party. Network centralization indicates some level of agreement about who the experts are, and this may be valuable. It is interesting to note that, as a percentage of the chamber, there are fewer experts consulted about LRHCP in the pre-term-limits Senate than any other session/chamber combination. That network has the most experienced members and also is the most centralized of any we examined here.

More experienced legislators serving in a smaller chamber might target their information seeking efforts more efficiently—a positive trait when evaluating an Internet search algorithm (Kleinberg 1999). By the same logic, one might assess a legislative chamber's search efficiency by its ability to identify and consult fewer key experts. This of course assumes that these are "successful" searches that produce comprehensive and accurate information. In other words, we need to exercise caution in interpreting our findings—more centralized is more efficient. But efficient searches that produce biased information can hardly be considered "good." Time and experience may cull the faux from the genuine experts based on their reputation. The qualifications and reputation of the expert matters, and they matter more when experts are scarce and time to judge them is short.

Therefore, we turn our attention next to the characteristics of the key experts from whom legislators seek information.

Characteristics of Experts

There are many ways that legislators can acquire valuable knowledge about issues. In legislatures with continuity in committee assignments (e.g., Michigan before term limits), committee members typically learn about an issue by listening to testimony and asking questions during hearings. They also receive written and verbal information from lobbyists, committee staff, and other professionals. They become experts through training by interest groups (Porter 1974) and other advocates. As we learned in chapter 6, they consult a wide array of sources when an issue is seriously considered in a committee. Especially in states like Michigan with extensive committee powers (Hamm, Hedlund, and Martorano 1999, 2006; Battista 2011), committee chairs use their agenda control as well as their knowledge to influence policy. Chairs historically are considered especially influential in policy making in the Michigan House (Francis 1985). Thus we expect chairs and to a lesser extent committee members will figure prominently in issue consulting networks that lead to floor votes. As Songer (1988) demonstrates, state legislators rely on the judgment of committee members during a floor vote on an issue.

Proponents of term limits claim that, with limits on their time in office, legislators will rely on sources of information with real world experience rather than special interest groups in the state capital. With less time to amass experience in the chamber, it seems reasonable that legislators with relevant prior professional experience will be consulted more extensively. By inference this should reduce the importance of committee members and chairs as a resource for the rest of the chamber.

In this section, we examine the characteristics of key experts that colleagues consulted during floor votes on two issues. We consider the same issues we have discussed throughout this chapter, examining first a bill about school choice and then a bill about LRHCP. We test a model using standard OLS regression to predict these experts' qualifications. This allows us to compare a politically salient issue versus a technically complex issue both before and after term limits.

We predict that before term limits committee leaders and members will be consulted extensively by their colleagues, but this will decrease after term limits. We include committee members, the committee chairs, and the minority vice chairs of both the policy committee and the appropriations subcommittee with jurisdiction over the issue. We control for the effect of chamber and also the interaction between term limits and the other variables in the model.

The dependent variable is the normalized reach centrality indegrees for each legislator. The normalized value of reach centrality indegrees is the proportion of consulting contacts received by an individual legislator divided by the maximum possible consulting contacts in the network. Therefore, the regression coefficients can be interpreted as percentages. The normalized measure allows us to compare values across networks of different sizes, in this case the 110-person House of Representatives and the 38-person Senate.

Often legislators with professional experience are assigned to the committees with jurisdiction over their area of expertise. Given this intersection of committee assignments and prior professional experience, we examine the correlations between prior professional experience and committee leadership and between prior professional experience and committee membership to make sure that it is appropriate to include these variables in our model. We find that they are statistically significant associated, but the magnitude of both of these relationships is relatively small, about 0.2. We believe that regression is robust enough to handle this departure from the ideal orthogonal relationships among independent variables.

Results of the regression equation exploring the school choice consulting appear on the left side of table 7.3. Results for LRHCP appear on the right side of the same table. Comparing the two issues, we find direct effects of term limits are limited on school choice and nonexistent on LRHCP. Yet there are several indications that term limits interact with other effects to alter the characteristics of the experts legislators consult. Two of these stand out. First, the importance of prior professional experience increases substantially for LRHCP expertise after term limits. Second, committee chairs and minority vice chairs are important experts on both issues prior to term limits. But after term limits these committee leaders gain clout on school choice and lose it on LRHCP.

Characteristics of Experts on School Choice

Making decisions on a politically risky issue such as school choice seems to motivate legislators to rely on a fairly predictable set of institutional actors—mostly committee leaders, somewhat on rank and file committee members, and, to a lesser extent, on veteran colleagues and colleagues with prior professional experience. As we see in table 7.3 our model identifies committee leaders[4] as having the greatest reach in the school choice consulting networks (a 10% advantage over other legislators), as we would expect. Committee chairs, unexpectedly, increase the reach of their expertise after term limits (5.5% more). This is the only group that benefits from term limits.

This suggests that after term limits actors who could be seen as surrogates for the chamber leadership in each party (chairs and ranking minority members on relevant committees) gain influence, potentially indicating a greater partisan component for consulting about a politically salient issue. Based on this, we would advise efficient lobbyists to concentrate on educating a committee's majority and minority party leaders after term limits rather than spend time on the entire committee—at least for a politically salient issue.

Rank and file members of the relevant committees (both the policy and appropriations subcommittee) lose clout after term limits. Moreover, professional experience in education has a much smaller effect than does com-

TABLE 7.3. Factors That Predict Consulting

Issue:	School Choice			Licensing/Regulating Health Professionals		
Model Predicting Consulting about an Issue	Normalized Reach Incoming			Normalized Reach Incoming		
	B	Std. Error	t	B	Std. Error	t
Chamber (Senate = 1)	**0.031**	0.009	3.360	**0.016**	0.009	1.788
Professional experience	**0.019**	0.011	1.716	**0.113**	0.025	4.592
Committee leader	**0.100**	0.016	6.466	**0.116**	0.014	8.067
Committee member	**0.041**	0.012	3.440	0.015	0.011	1.369
Lame duck (veteran)	**0.025**	0.008	3.027	0.011	0.008	1.341
Term limits (TL = 1)	**0.021**	0.008	2.690	0.006	0.007	0.771
Interaction TL and chamber	**–0.024**	0.011	–2.132	0.006	0.011	0.576
Interaction TL and professional experience	0.007	0.013	0.518	**0.078**	0.027	2.902
Interaction TL and committee leader	**0.055**	0.021	2.578	–0.072	0.017	–1.601
Interaction TL and committee member	–0.023	0.014	–1.663	–0.004	0.013	–0.317
Interaction TL and lame duck	**–0.021**	0.010	–2.115	–.011	0.010	–1.155
Constant	–0.002	0.007	–0.274	0.005	0.007	0.696
Adjusted R^2	0.392			0.566		
F-statistic	33.064			69.439		

Note: Bold type indicates statistically significant coefficients; n = 544.

mittee membership or leadership—increasing an experts' reach to only about 2 percent more of the chamber, and term limits does not alter this. Predictably, in the smaller chamber, expert senators are recognized as such by more of their colleagues, but only about 3 percent more. Expert senators lose most of this small advantage after term limits.

Characteristics of Experts on LRHCP

Turning to the right-hand panel of table 7.3, we find that term limits increase the importance of professional experience in the health care field in establishing one's expertise. Before term limits committee leaders have just slightly more reach centrality than do legislators with professional experience in health care. After term limits, legislators with professional experience catapult into first place in a dramatic shift as they gain (+8%) and committee leaders lose (–7%) of their clout. Committee leaders are a distant second to professional experts in the post-term-limits LRHCP consulting network. Rank and file members of the relevant committee and subcommittee are only slightly more sought after experts than anyone else, and this does not change after term limits.

These results suggest that after term limits a technically complex issue might become driven less by partisan politics and be less dominated by leaders or the caucus. Prior career experience appears to contribute heavily to expertise on this sort of issue, especially after term limits. Given this, issue advocates might want to recruit one of their own professionals to run for the legislature to create an inside expert. Based on our findings in chapter 2 about interest group recruiting, it is plausible that some groups may already be actively involved in recruiting candidates to do this. An alternative information dissemination strategy might involve using citizen members of a professional association to contact legislators with prior professional experience.

Conclusions

We conclude that term limits clearly affect consulting in the Michigan legislature, but these effects are not always straightforward. We discuss five effects and their implications for governing below.

First, we find that prior to term limits, legislators, especially in the House, sought more information about the politically salient issue—school choice—than they did about the technically complex issue—LRHCP. This gap diminishes after term limits, reflecting an increase in consulting about LRHCP and no change in consulting about school choice. The increase in consulting about LRHCP in the lower chamber can be attributed to waves of newcomers arriving without prior experience dealing with this complex issue. But a corresponding change in the Senate suggests that there is a more profound shift in consulting patterns. After term limits, senators almost without exception served first in the House, so newly elected senators are not newcomers to the state capital and have some legislative experience and presumably exposure to these issues. Yet they still seem to feel a greater need for information about LRHCP.

On this technically complex issue, this additional consulting is directed away from committee leaders and toward colleagues with prior professional experience. Based on this shift in the characteristics of experts, term limits proponents can claim victory in augmenting the influence of members with prior professional experience and diminishing the influence of ranking committee members, who are often seen as allies of special interests. We point out, however, that legislators' *prior professional experience* could include membership in some of these interest groups. On the other hand, institutional actors within the chambers, such as committee chairs, gain clout on the politically salient issue of school choice even though the volume of consulting remains constant.

Second, being a newcomer to the chamber when newness is common and veterans have only slightly more experience appears to affect newcomers differently than it does when a handful of newcomers enter a chamber dominated by veterans with decades of experience. Before term limits newcomers generally consulted their colleagues more about issues and were less likely to be seen as experts by their colleagues—not surprisingly. We were told by several respondents that the advice given to newcomers before term limits was to "sit down, shut up, and listen." This seems to have motivated pre-term-limits newcomers in the House to actively solicit advice on both issues and in the Senate to retreat into isolation on school choice—perhaps simply accepting the party position. After term limits, veterans and newcomers appear to seek similar amounts of advice. Moreover, on the technical issue—LRHCP—the expertise of legislators with professional experience is increasingly sought after over the advice of veterans.

Third, being the most experienced members of the chamber—lame ducks—also means something different after term limits. Although veterans are consulted slightly more, especially on school choice before term limits, their additional clout evaporates after term limits. When everyone knows that a colleague is a lame duck, he or she is less likely to retain prized committee assignments and may lose a committee leadership position. Several respondents mentioned this during our interviews with them. This means that even though Michigan's House members have six years to amass experience and knowledge, they are shunted to the side after four years, effectively compressing the learning curve into an even shorter time span. This truncates an already brief opportunity for legislators to learn the nuances of complex issues and exercise influence. It is a dynamic unique to term limits, because only under conditions of explicit limits on service is a legislator's lame duck status apparent even before his or her final term. Wave elections avoid this.

Fourth, after term limits, the prominence of committee leaders increases substantially in school choice consulting, while rank and file committee members lose clout. Newcomers are unlikely to chair committees in major policy areas, such as education, even after term limits. So the influence of newcomers diminishes when information seeking focuses on committee leaders rather than committee members. This is also likely to reflect greater control by the party hierarchy over this politically salient issue.

Fifth, the changes in the institutional structure of the consulting networks are profound, especially in the House, but also in the Senate. In the House, both before and after term limits these networks tend to be multinucleated, typically populated by several experts. Before term limits, there are consistent indications that the segments of these networks are connected by several key actors. In the transition to term limits, we see a unique and possibly transient pattern with lots more actors weaving an increasingly fragmented network together.

In the final post-term-limits session in the House, our data indicate that the networks are decoupled or nearly so. The tendency toward multiple experts persists, but linkages between them vanish. The core and periphery are detached and very few legislators hold the network together. This is especially true for the network about LRHCP. This fragmentation suggests that information gathering may link small subsets of legislators, reinforcing their views and making it harder to negotiate compromises that integrate the needs of a highly diverse state. Some of these small subsets of actors could reflect rural/suburban/urban factions rather than simply partisan divisions.

Both Senate consulting networks look a lot more like the House networks after term limits than they did before. The highly centralized LRHCP network in the Senate becomes more decentralized and less tightly coupled. The loosely connected school choice consulting network in the pre-term-limits Senate appears to fragment into factions after term limits, each revolving around a few key experts after term limits. We speculate that this reflects the socialization of legislators into the behavior patterns that work in the lower chamber.

Without veteran senators to resocialize them after they move to the smaller, upper chamber, the House patterns appear to persist. Representatives and outsiders entered the Senate in ones and twos prior to term limits, allowing veterans to maintain chamber norms and socialize newcomers. The migration of representatives to the Senate in herds instead of as individuals or pairs would be likely to alter the standard operating procedures in the upper chamber even if there were a few veterans left to socialize them.

Although we find both individual and institutional effects, it is the changes in the institutional structure of consulting that we argue are the most likely to affect governance in the state of Michigan. Declining cohesion demonstrates that these networks are vulnerable to isolated pockets of information gathering that can reinforce biases rather than broaden legislators' perspectives about these issues. The decoupled networks that evolve after term limits, particularly in the House, could easily produce an echo-chamber effect in which homogeneous clusters of people tend to assume that their views are more prevalent than they are (Bienenstock, Bonacich, and Oliver 1990). This is likely to undermine bipartisan policy making, which we saw in chapter 4 is an activity performed primarily by lame ducks. Michigan is a culturally and ethnically diverse state. Historically Michigan thrives when state government is driven by consensus and compromise rather than entrenched factions (Browne and VerBurg 1995). But the post-term-limits consulting networks seem likely to thwart rather than facilitate compromise.

EIGHT

Friendship

What happens to friendship in a legislature with stringent limits on service, like Michigan's? Friendships not only ameliorate partisan conflict (Patterson 1959) and facilitate compromise, they can build substantive policy influence as well. But friendships, especially those that cross party lines, evolve slowly, and, as Francis (1962) demonstrates, social interaction only gradually matures into influence. In pursuing this notion, we follow the pattern we established in chapter 7 of examining individual-level and institutional-level effects. In this we consider the average number of friendships as well as the structure of friendship groups within each chamber. In this chapter we focus especially on bipartisan friendships, clusters of highly connected friends, and the role friendship plays in information gathering.

In our prior work (Sarbaugh-Thompson et al. 2006) we found that post-term-limits representatives report more, not fewer, friendships, contradicting our assumption that waves of newcomers would reduce these ties. Consistent with the work of other scholars (Ray 1982; Caldeira, Clark, and Patterson 1993), our earlier work demonstrated that many friendships among newcomers tend to be regional and partisan. Most of these arise from prior local government service at the municipal and county levels. This is important because it is likely to produce more homogeneous friendship networks that could fuel partisan or regional polarization on issues.

Here we extend our previous work to our final post-term-limits session in the House and to the upper chamber. We also consider whether the influx of newcomers and the institutional changes wrought by term limits alter the frequency, distribution, and structure of friendship in each chamber of the Michigan legislature, and, if so, how. We extend this exploration of legislative relationships to include influence in the chamber in chapter 9.

Finally, in this chapter we explore connections between friendship and issue consulting. In their 50-state survey of legislators, Uslaner and Weber (1977) find that friends are often chosen over expert colleagues as sources of information.[1] To investigate whether term limits alter this, we examine correlations between friendship and consulting networks. Additionally the longitudinal design of our research allows us to investigate the temporal order in which these relationships develop across legislative sessions. Specifically we explore whether having lots of friends—popularity—increases the amount a legislator is consulted (an indicator of expertise) or alternatively whether this sort of expertise increases popularity.

Data and Methods

In our interviews we asked whether our respondents had any especially good friends[2] among their colleagues. If so, we followed up by asking them to name each of these especially good friends. This is question 6 in appendix A. From these data we construct a matrix of close friends for each session in each chamber. Each matrix contains one row and one column for each legislator. A value of one in a cell of the matrix denotes that the respondent (the row) names a colleague (the column) as a friend. Cells with zeros denote absence of friendship between pairs of legislators. We use UCINET 6.46 to conduct network analysis of these matrices and to compute some values that we later use in standard statistical analyses.

Network analysis is sensitive to missing data and some techniques that we use in this chapter, such as clique analysis, are especially so (Knoke and Kuklinski 1982, 34–35). Though we did not attain a perfect response rate, we came close, with rates ranging between 71 percent and 92 percent per chamber and session and an average response rate of 82 percent. As a result, we believe that we reduced the problems posed by missing data as much as one can reasonably expect in fieldwork. Furthermore, when missing values are likely to provide misleading results, we focus on indegrees,[3] which are more robust in the face of missing data than other network measures (Costenbader and Valente 2003).

But still even a few missing values can produce very misleading results when identifying clusters in a network. For example, even with just a few missing cases, connected subgroups such as cliques can appear decoupled. We minimized this problem when identifying subgroups for the friendship networks by using information about nonrespondents provided by those legislators we did interview. We did this by treating directed friendship ties as undirected. This means that if only one member of a dyad says that the pair are friends, we link both of them when analyzing clusters of friends. In the jargon of network analysis, we symmetrize the friendship matrices,[4] but only when we analyze clusters of friends. Although this is not an ideal solution, it is better than omitting actors from the network when identifying cliques or other subgroups, which risks decoupling groups of actors who in reality are connected. But to avoid inflating the total number of friendships reported by our respondents, we treat all ties as directed when we enumerate friendships or calculate the mean number of friends or when we measure network centralization.[5]

The Average Number of Friends for Individual Michigan Legislators

Long-term friendships are reputed to increase legislators' ability to negotiate solutions and resolve disputes because they build mutual trust and personal respect, key ingredients in dispute resolution (Carson 1998). Because friendship takes time and repeated interaction to develop, we predicted that term limits will reduce the number of friends, especially among legislators with differing viewpoints or different party affiliations. Although we proved this expectation wrong during the transition to term limits (Sarbaugh-Thompson et al. 2006), we still consider it to be a plausible outcome after term limits are fully implemented, and we test that here. We expect that these effects will be mitigated in the Senate because under term limits representatives tend to move as cohorts from the House to the Senate. So they already know each other.

On the other hand, some of the senators' history with each other might undermine friendships. For example, winnowing candidates from the 110-member House into the 38-member Senate pits fellow partisans against each other in primaries and members of opposing parties against each other in general elections. This could erode friendships that existed in the House. For example, one's colleague in the Senate might have defeated one's especially close friend in the House during a brutal primary or general election campaign. This could make it harder, not easier, to be friends in the Senate.

Overall, we find that the volume of friendship is very stable. Term limits apparently have very little noteworthy effect on the average number of

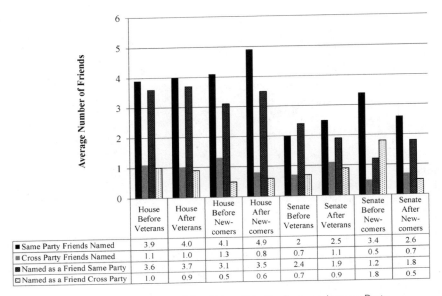

	House Before Veterans	House After Veterans	House Before New-comers	House After New-comers	Senate Before Veterans	Senate After Veterans	Senate Before New-comers	Senate After New-comers
■ Same Party Friends Named	3.9	4.0	4.1	4.9	2	2.5	3.4	2.6
▨ Cross Party Friends Named	1.1	1.0	1.3	0.8	0.7	1.1	0.5	0.7
■ Named as a Friend Same Party	3.6	3.7	3.1	3.5	2.4	1.9	1.2	1.8
▢ Named as a Friend Cross Party	1.0	0.9	0.5	0.6	0.7	0.9	1.8	0.5

Fig. 8.1. Effect of Experience on Friendship within the Party and across Party Lines

friends per legislator in either chamber. Representatives report an average of about 5 friends in the House with or without term limits and between 3 and 3.5 friends in the much smaller Senate before and after term limits. Cross party friendships average about one per legislator in the House and a little less than one friend in the Senate, and term limits do not change this. We do find, however, that the friendship patterns of newcomers and veterans differ after term limits. And with an influx of newcomers, term limits amplify these effects.

We see in figure 8.1 that cross-party friends are rare in both chambers with or without term limits. But this is especially true for newcomers to the House. House newcomers are named as friends by opposing party members about half as often as veterans are. Term limits do not change this statistically significant difference. Similarly, post-term-limits Senate newcomers average about half as many friends in the opposite political party as their veteran colleagues do, a difference that is also statistically significant. We hesitate to say much about pre-term-limits Senate newcomers because they are such a rare breed.

Turning to same-party friendship, we find that post-term-limits House newcomers claim a lot of members of their own political party are their friends. In the post-term-limits House, amid a sea of new faces, newly elected representatives name almost one more friend within their own political party (4.9) than their veteran colleagues do (4.0), a statistically significant difference. But these House newcomers may overestimate their friends because they are named by others as friends much less often (4.9 friends named compared with 3.5 colleagues who name them as friends).

This tendency to overestimate one's same-party friends seems fairly common among newcomers in the upper chamber, too. Thus we find this overly optimistic estimate of one's friends among newcomers in both chambers with and without term limits. This implies that newcomers as a group believe they have more friends than they do. Term limits do not alter this, but there are a lot more newcomers after term limits. Therefore, this overestimate of friendship is likely to be more widespread after term limits.

After term limits Senate newcomers and veterans claim to have about the same number of friends within their own political party—an average of about 2.5 friends each. When post-term-limits senators are first elected to the upper chamber, they have spent up to six years working together in the House. This time appears to be long enough to equalize same-party friendships that senators name, even though for newcomers fewer of these friendships are reciprocal. Yet even this amount of time is not enough to shrink the difference in the number of cross-party friends named by Senate newcomers and veterans. Senate veterans are the cohort with the most cross-party friendships. It appears to take six years in the House plus four years in the Senate (approximately 10 years total) to develop an average of one additional cross-party friend.[6] This provides a rough estimate of the amount of time it takes to develop bipartisan relationships.

The Structure of Friendship—Analyzing Friendship Networks

Based on the work of other scholars described in the introduction to this chapter (Ray 1982; Caldeira, Clark, and Patterson 1993), we assume that propinquity matters in the formation of friendships among newly elected legislators. It is, therefore, likely that regional friendships, friendships with seatmates, or friendships among legislators with offices on the same floor account for the relatively stable average volume of friendships that we report above. But the type of relationships that link clusters of friends together (i.e., cross-party friendships, friendships across geographic regions of the state) are those that take longer to develop, as we just discussed.

And as we saw in chapter 7, when only one or two legislators provide the connective tissue holding a network together, it is very vulnerable to fragmentation. Removing even one or two liaisons or bridges (Farace, Monge, and Russell 1977) can have a dramatic effect on the structure of a network. Even though the volume of friendship is fairly stable overall in both chambers, we predict that friends are less likely to be linked into larger, more cohesive networks after term limits. As a result, we expect that friendship will become more insular.

We provide network measures of the friendship for all four House sessions and three Senate sessions in table 8.1. If we ignore the 2003 Senate session, an outlier given that it reflects a unique opportunity for House members with decades of service to move to the Senate, we find that the House and Senate exhibit similar patterns. Both chambers have exceptionally cohesive friendship networks before term limits that become less so afterward.

The pre-term-limits friendship structure in both chambers is highly connected, and friendship is distributed fairly evenly among the legislators. After term limits, we find that friendship revolves around fewer "popular" legislators. Although both chambers exhibit this pattern, the change is more pronounced in the Senate than in the House. If we were talking about power or influence, we might say that the networks move from egalitarian to hierarchical as term limits are implemented. Given that we are talking about friendship, we can think of this as a move toward greater popularity for a few legislators in the post-term-limits chambers. A detailed discussion of the specific measures follows.

First, we find that friendship ties reported in the House are a relatively constant percentage, varying between 4.6 percent and 4.9 percent of the maximum possible ties, consistent with the stable average volume of individual friendships discussed above. The smaller Senate appears "friendlier" in general, and increasingly so after term limits. We see a fairly large increase, nearly 2 percent more of the maximum possible ties that could have been reported (from 8% to nearly 10%). A 2 percent increase might not sound like a lot, but when the possible number of ties is large—more than 1,000 even in the Senate—this is a noteworthy increase. The rise in friendship in the post-term-limits Senate may reflect the movement from the lower to upper chamber of cohorts of legislators who bring their relationships with them—as we discussed earlier.

Indegree centralization of the friendship networks increases after term limits in both the House and Senate. As we discussed in chapter 7, perfect indegree centralization (100%) means that one focal point is tied to all the other points and that those other points are tied only to that focal point, forming a star. In the House, the change is modest (13% to 18%).

TABLE 8.1. Friendship Networks by Session and Chamber

	House				Senate		
	1997	1999	2001	2003	1999	2003	2007
Possible consulting links (respondents*chamber size)	10,450	10,230	10,230	9,680	1,292	1,064	1,026
Friends Reported							
Total	478	497	498	464	104	94	100
Percentage of Possible	4.6	4.9	4.9	4.8	8.0	8.8	9.7
Number of respondents	95	93	93	88	35	28	27
Network centralization							
Indegree centralization percentage	12.8	15.4	18.2	17.6	12.2	18.6	26.7
Outdegree centralization percentage	11.8	9.8	9.8	11.0	12.2	10.1	12.5
Reach centrality							
Connections of most popular legislator	47	43	45	43	16	14	14
Maximum % for most popular legislator	97	79	83	73	70	73	65
Number of steps to reach maximum	5	5	7	7	4	7	5
Total reach centrality for the chamber	3,240	3,273	3,247	2,733	372	377	334
Betweenness							
Chamber Maximum	2,115	1,401	1,525	1,007	323	215	318
Total betweenness for the chamber	22,020	21,281	22,949	19,327	1,969	2,396	1,453
Clusters of Friends							
Number of cliques with at least three members	9	3	6	7	3	3	3[a]
Cliques with members from both major parties	2	0	0	0	1	0	2
Characterization of the cliques	power brokers	none	tea and sympathy	ideo-logues	minority leaders	power-brokers	minority leaders
K-plexes with 1 missing tie (size: 5 House, 4 Senate)	7	7	3	1	2	3	3
K-plexes with members from both major parties	3	3	0	0	0	0	3

[a]includes one four-member clique.

In the Senate network centralization more than doubles, increasing from 12 percent to nearly 27 percent. These changes in centralization mean that as term limits are implemented friendship in each chamber becomes more concentrated, with a handful of legislators becoming more popular. Yet none of these networks is highly centralized, and most legislators have some friends. Outcasts and isolates are rare.

We also find that the more popular post-term-limits legislators are befriended within fragmented factions. This is apparent from the decline in total reach centrality after term limits and the greater number of steps needed to connect this smaller percentage of the chamber. Reach centrality measures how accessible a focal actor is to all other actors in the network—in this case, the legislative chamber. These connections include linkages through other actors, so that the result is similar to the game "Six Degrees from Kevin Bacon."

As table 8.1 illustrates, in the pre-term-limits House, the most connected actor is connected to nearly everyone (97%) in the House in five steps. This demonstrates an extremely high level of cohesiveness in the friendship network for the pre-term-limits House. As term limits are implemented, we see the proportion of the chamber "reached" decreasing and an increasing number of steps needed to connect this smaller percentage. In the 2003 session, the cohesiveness of the House friendship network falls by 25 percent (to 73%), and it takes seven steps to connect these representatives.

In the much smaller Senate, the number of steps needed to connect the post-term-limits chamber increases from four to five and by the final post-term-limits session only about two-thirds of this small chamber is connected. But that is only 5 percent less than the pre-term-limits Senate. Thus, after term limits, even a relatively small chamber appears to have more marginalized legislators and a little harder time connecting to a smaller in-crowd. But changes in the Senate are more muted than they are in the House.

Betweenness, as we discussed in chapter 7, measures the importance of bridges, liaisons, and other key network actors who provide pathways connecting other members of the network. An actor with high betweenness connects lots of other pairs of actors in a network. In table 8.1 we report that the total and maximum betweenness in all four House sessions is high. It is exceptionally high in the pre-term-limits House, however. The representative with the highest betweenness score (i.e., the person doing the most to link segments of the friendship network) has a score of 2,115. This declines to 1,007 by 2003, meaning that the legislator doing the most to link colleagues is providing less than half the connectivity of his or her pre-term-limits counterpart. If this decline in betweenness were combined with an increase in direct ties in the network, the network would still be well connected. But the final post-term-limits House friendship network is less connected, based on the reach centrality sum. Thus, more connections are needed to link the segments of this network, but there are fewer legislators doing this after term limits. This paints an image of a less cohesive chamber.

We mention one caveat—these changes are relative. Readers might recall that the sum of the betweenness for all actors in both consulting networks (see chapter 7) ranges from a high of 1,463 for the 2001 House consulting about school choice to a low of 69 for the 2003 House consulting about LRHCP. The total betweenness in the friendship network for pre-term-limits representatives is 22,020. Even the last post-term-limits House session (2003) has a total betweenness of 19,327. The least cohesive friendship network is still vastly more connected than any of the consulting networks. Changes in the friendship networks do not imply the demise of these networks, but merely a relative shift in their structure compared to the chamber before term limits.

Turning to the Senate, we find that the most cohesive friendship network in that chamber appears to be the first post-term-limits session—2003. Readers may recall that this transition to term limits produced a chamber led by former House veterans who were termed out of the lower chamber after serving together there for decades. Total betweenness fluctuates from 1,969 before term limits to 2,396 in 2003 before falling in the final post-term-limits Senate session (2007) to 1,453. The contrasting trends between the two post-term-limits sessions indicate that the transition to term limits is an outlier that does not accurately represent the term limits equilibrium conditions, as Mooney (2009) argues. And the friendship structure in the Senate after term limits are fully implemented appears less cohesive, just as it does in the House.

Clusters of Friends—Cliques and K-plexes

The legislative value of friendship stems from its potential to facilitate collaboration, especially across party lines, to pass legislation. Substantial scholarly evidence (beginning with Patterson in 1959 and continuing through Arnold, Deen, and Patterson 2000) supports this. If friendship is to facilitate cross-party collaboration, then it is necessary, albeit not sufficient, that bipartisan clusters of friends exist. Network analysis provides several measures to identify subgroups of friends. We assume that heterogeneous, bipartisan clusters are especially important during periods of divided government, which characterize four of the seven sessions we explore. But with little time to build these relationships it seems likely that these clusters of friends will be a casualty of term limits. Therefore, we predict that after term limits tightly connected friendship subgroups will be smaller in size, fewer in number and more homogeneous, especially in the House.

During the 1990s partisan control of Michigan's lower chamber changed with every election, including the infamous 1993 session with split control, led by the so-called stereo speakers with bipartisan cochairs for all committees. Pre-term-limits House respondents' open-ended comments indicate that this experience encouraged cross-party relationships among representatives. When discussing the role of minority party colleagues, many respondents who served in the pre-term-limits House said that what goes around comes around, to paraphrase their comments. By this they meant that the majority party's treatment of minority party members would be reciprocated when majority control shifted again. Many institutional norms, such as this admonition against mistreating the minority party, eroded over the course of our investigation, as we demonstrate in the coming chapters.

When we gathered the baseline data in 1997–98, Democrats controlled the House, but Republicans controlled the Senate and the executive branch. In all other legislative sessions that we investigated Republicans controlled both chambers. However, in the last House session and the last two Senate sessions, Democrats controlled the executive branch. Therefore, some form of divided government impacts four of the seven chamber/session networks that we analyze below. In one of these sessions, the one before term limits, bipartisan cooperation was needed to pass legislation (the 1997 House), and in the other three sessions (all after term limits) the chambers' majority party needed to avoid a gubernatorial veto (House 2003 and Senate 2003 and 2007). Yet, our interview notes indicate that many legislators in the majority party assumed any shift in partisan control of their chamber would occur after their short stint in office, reducing their motivation to work across the aisle.

Although the volume of friendship is relatively constant during our investigation, we turn our attention here to the structure of friendship. Among other questions, we want to know whether groups of friends include members of both political parties. In our analysis of clusters of friends, we first consider cliques, which are completely connected clusters in which each actor names all other actors in the cluster as friends. Cliques are, as we discussed earlier in this chapter, quite sensitive to missing data. This means that if we did not interview one clique member, the entire group structure could be hidden in our analyses, or if a respondent forgets to name a friend, the clique will be missed. (Some respondents added a friend as an afterthought later in the interview when something about that person came up in another question, so it is realistic to assume that a respondent might have missed naming a friend.)

Given this risk we also explore a type of subgroup that relaxes the requirements for group membership slightly—the k-plex. In a k-plex, subgroup members name almost all of the other members of the group (group size and number of missing ties are chosen by the investigator). Additionally, if one person says the pair are friends, then the friendship is treated as reciprocal.[7] With missing data, cliques probably understate the connectedness of the chamber. By filling in missing values, k-plexes could inflate chamber connectedness, however. We permitted one missing tie in the k-plexes in an effort to limit overestimating. We explored 5-plexes (subgroups with five members) in the 110-member House and 4-plexes in the much smaller 38-member Senate. As we report in table 8.1, the number of k-plexes decreases in the House as term limits are implemented. In the Senate, the number remains almost constant.

The pictures in figure 8.2 for the House really are worth a thousand words in conveying the institutional changes in friendship across time. This figure shows complicated interconnected clusters of friends in the earlier House sessions that gradually unravel into one small k-plex as term limits are more fully implemented.

In the pre-term-limits panel of figure 8.2 we identity an institutional structure in the House that includes a majority party powerbrokers cluster and a separate set of six overlapping k-plexes, three of which have bipartisan members. This extended set of k-plexes includes several representatives who were being groomed for leadership positions (interview notes). The two intervening House sessions (the transition to term limits) illustrate the sequential destruction of the larger friendship structures of the pre-term-limits chamber.

In the 1999–2000 House session, one of the clusters depicted in figure 8.2 reflects regional ties developed before members were elected to the chamber. It consists of representatives from the three most populous counties in the state, most of whom had previously worked together as county commissioners or in other local governments. The other set of intercon-

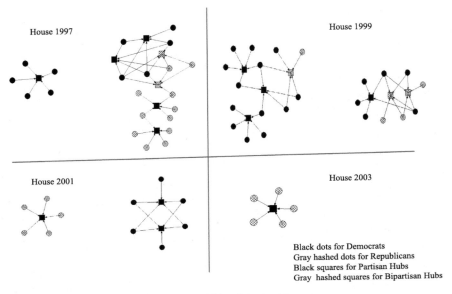

Fig. 8.2. Highly Connected Clusters of Friends in the House

nected k-plexes is composed of several members of the appropriations committee. It retains bipartisan remnants of the pre-term-limits cluster of future leaders.

We call the friendship clusters in the 2001–02 House session the tea and sympathy structure. These consist of two components: one is a cluster of Republican women and the other is a linked pair of k-plexes of Democrats. Members of both groups faced challenging circumstances. The number of Republican women in the chamber fell to about one-third of the pre-term-limits level, and several Republican women (and also men) complained about various forms of gender bias among GOP caucus leaders (interview notes). The other consists of Democrats on the Appropriations Committee, who were engaged in trench warfare to thwart cuts to public programs as Michigan endured its lengthening one-state recession of the early 2000s. These groups of friends might best be viewed as providing solace and assistance instead of aggregating influence.

Moving to the final post-term-limits House session (2003–04) we find only one single 5-plex of representatives, a subgroup composed of the most conservative members of the chamber. These Tea Party Republicans, united in their opposition to almost everything government might do, were a thorn in the side of their own leadership. Some respondents

Senate 1999 Minority Party

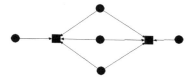

Senate 2003 – Majority Party Powerbrokers

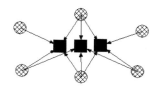

Senate 2007 Bipartisan with Minority Party

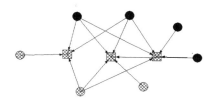

Black dots for Democrats
Gray hashed dots for Republicans
Black Squares for Partisan Hubs
Gray hashed Squares for Bipartisan Hubs

Fig. 8.3. Highly Connected Clusters of Friends in the Senate

described them as bomb throwers (interview notes). Thus, as term limits are more fully implemented, friendship seems to provide reinforcement for peripheral and ostracized legislators rather than a way to build alliances among the central players interested in leveraging their influence.

Changes in the Senate, as we expected, are more subtle. In figure 8.3, we illustrate two 4-plexes in the pre-term-limits Senate. Both are partisan overlapping clusters of minority party members and their leaders. We find also two three-member cliques, both of which are regional and one of which is bipartisan. One of these consists of senators from the heavily populated southeastern corner of the state, and the other is a bipartisan clique from the sprawling northern reaches of the state, areas with very low population density.

The prominence of chamber leaders in the friendship subgroups in the 2003 Senate session is reminiscent of the pattern we found in the pre-term-limits House, in which power brokers bond with other exceptionally influential colleagues. We also find three 4-plexes in the 2003 Senate. Although these include a few members who are not among the majority party leadership, these chums include all of the most influential members of the chamber. This pattern, which melds influence and friendship, may reflect the prior socialization in the House of many key senators during this transition to term limits. They had served together for decades in the pre-term-limits House and in all likelihood brought their camaraderie as well as their understanding of the value of friendship with them to the upper chamber.

The final Senate session (2007) exhibits a pattern of friendship clusters that is even more bipartisan than the pre-term-limits House. Again this could reflect the early socialization into the job of legislator by the House veterans who then moved as a cohort to the Senate. Several of these 2007-session senators served with pre-term-limits House members or had other close ties to pre-term-limits legislators. Only one of the top leaders in the minority party is involved in these bipartisan clusters, so it is not clear how readily these ties could translate into bipartisan policymaking leverage. On the other hand, with a Democrat holding the governor's office from 2002 to 2010, cross-party friendships might have facilitated policy making. So the practical benefits of cross-party ties might have motivated this development.

The Role of Friends in Vote Cuing

As we noted earlier, Uslaner and Weber (1977) identify friends within the chamber and fellow legislators with policy-specific expertise as the two top sources consulted by state legislators, but they find that friends are slightly preferred over expert colleagues. According to Mooney (1991) the reason colleagues are an important source of information in satisficing decisions such as floor votes is that they are trusted and can be relied upon when time is too scarce to double-check information. One key ingredient of friendship is trust. When seeking go-to sources for information, trust among friends enables them to compete with substantive experts because they are seen as honest brokers and truthful conduits for unbiased information. The liability of consulting friends rather than experts with divergent views is the risk that decisions are made in homogeneous groups where shared personal characteristics and attitudes fuel a perception that one's views are more prevalent than they are (Bienenstock, Bonacich, and Oliver 1990).

In this section we probe vote cuing and friendship networks to determine how highly correlated they are and whether term limits alter this association. We anticipate that legislators will solicit information after term limits from friends rather than experts who are not friends. To explore this we correlate the popularity of a legislator and his or her apparent expertise about school choice and LRHCP. Table 8.2 documents these associations.

We find that there is a statistically significant, albeit small, association in the pre- and the post-term-limits House between legislators consulted widely about school choice and legislators with a lot of friends. The number of friends does not appear to be associated with who is consulted about a technically complex issue, however.

These correlations tell us only that popular legislators (those named by many colleagues as friends) are consulted by more colleagues on school choice in the House and in the pre-term-limits Senate. They do not tell us whether the same colleague who designated the legislator as a source for school choice information also said that this same legislator is an especially good friend. To delve into this, we turn again to network analysis.

UCINET 6.46 allows us to correlate pairs of matrices to see whether the specific colleagues that our respondents consult about school choice and about licensing health professionals are the same colleagues that they named as "especially good friends." The recommended test statistic to estimate the strength of these relationships is the Jaccard Coefficient, which simply is the ratio of the intersection of two matrices divided by their union for all cells that are not "empty" in both matrices (Hanneman and Riddle 2005). Using the Jaccard Coefficient eliminates the effect of the correlation between the nonfriends who are not consulted—zeros in both matrices. The column next to the Jaccard Coefficient in table 8.3 reports the probability of observing that level of association based on 2,500 permutations of the matrix. We report the more familiar Chi-square statistic in table 8.3, as well.

UCINET estimates the average value for the Jaccard Coefficient based on 2,500 random permutations of the matrices and reports the probability that the relationship is statistically significant. Comparing the average estimated value to the observed value of the Jaccard Coefficient provides a way to assess the substantive significance of the relationship between two matrices. In other words, how much stronger is the observed correlation than a relationship that we would expect to occur by chance? Given that there are 11,990 possible dyads in the

TABLE 8.2. Correlations between Consulting and Friendship

	House Before	House After	Senate Before	Senate After
Between friendship and school choice consulting	**0.16***	**0.18*****	**0.32***	0.12
Between friendship and consulting about LRHCP	0.03	0.02	0.25	0.14

TABLE 8.3. Correlation between Friendship Networks and School Choice and LRHCP

A. Correlation between Friendship Networks and School Choice Consulting

Chamber and Session	Correlation	Chi-Square	Jaccard Coefficient	Jaccard Average 2,500 Permutations	Number of Friends Reported	Number of Colleagues Consulted	Instances of Friend Consulting	Friends Consulted (%) of All Consulted	Non-Expert Friends[a] Consulted	Respondents
House 1997	0.11	136.6	0.06	0.01	478	138	37	27	5	95
House 1999	0.19	425.0	0.10	0.01	497	130	65	50	19	93
House 2001	0.12	178.8	0.07	0.01	498	137	43	31	9	93
House 2003	0.16	301.7	0.08	0.01	464	96	45	47	11	89
Senate 1999	0.15	32.0	0.09	0.02	104	27	12	44	3	35
Senate 2003	0.17	38.5	0.10	0.02	94	22	11	50	2	28
Senate 2007	0.11	17.9	0.07	0.02	100	27	9	33	2	27

Note: Values for chi-square and for the Jaccard Coefficient are all statistically significant at $p < 0.01$.

[a]Experts include committee members, colleagues with prior professional experience in education, and top caucus leaders.

B. Correlation between Friendship Networks and Consulting about Licensing or Regulating Health Care Professionals

Chamber and Session	Correlation	Chi-Square	Jaccard Coefficient	Jaccard Average 2,500 Permutations	Number of Friends Reported	Number of Colleagues Consulted	Instances of Friend Consulting	Friends Consulted (%) of All Consulted	Non-Expert Friends[b] Consulted	Respondents
House 1997	0.09	100.19	0.05	0.01	478	119	26	22	4	95
House 1999	0.07	64.80	0.04	0.01	497	162	27	17	8	93
House 2001	0.07	51.86	0.04	0.01	498	195	28	14	7	93
House 2003	0.09	104.46	0.05	0.01	464	135	28	21	7	89
Senate 1999	0.17	41.40	0.10	0.02	104	33	12	36	0	35
Senate 2003	0.07	7.30	0.06	0.02	94	41	7	17	1	28
Senate 2007	0.13	21.80	0.08	0.02	100	38	10	26	1	27

Note: Values for chi-square and the Jaccard Coefficient are all statistically significant at $p < 0.01$ except for the 2003 Senate, where $p = 0.015$.

[b]Experts include committee members, colleagues with prior professional experience in health care, and top leaders.

House matrices (110 × 109) and 1,409 (38 × 37) in the Senate, even very small associations are likely to be statistical significant. Indeed, with only one exception, the correlation between the pairs of matrices is statistically significant at $p < 0.01$ for all seven legislative sessions. Yet, as one can see from table 8.3, the magnitude of these associations is small, ranging from 0.07 to 0.19.

Correlations between Friendship and School Choice Consulting Matrices

Consulting with friends about this politically salient issue appears to increase when newcomers flock into the chamber in large numbers—a turnover effect. We find the highest correlations between the friendship and school choice consulting matrices during the 1999 session, with 56 percent turnover, and 2003, with a 45 percent turnover. Interestingly, this association shrinks in the 2001 session, which has only 23 newcomers. There were 25 newcomers in the pre-term-limits House, and the correlations between the friendship and school choice consulting matrices are nearly identical during these two sessions (1997 and 2001).

We see this pattern replicated when we calculate consulting with friends as a percentage of all consulting. Prior to term limits, a little more than a quarter of the colleagues consulted about school choice were the respondents' especially good friends. This nearly doubles after term limits, but only in the two sessions with high turnover (1999 and 2003). During the 2001 session with low turnover, friends are only 31 percent of the colleagues consulted about school choice. Thus turnover rather than the institutional effects of term limits appear to motivate legislators to consult friends on school choice.

In the Senate, we find a similar, although less pronounced, increase in school choice consulting directed toward friends when turnover rises. The correlation between the matrices is higher overall in the smaller chamber, but here again the size of these associations tracks the number of newcomers to the chamber rather than term limits. Prior to term limits, 44 percent of the consulting on school choice involved senators' friends. This rises to 50 percent with the wave of 30 newcomers in 2003 before receding to 33 percent in the 2007 post-term-limits Senate, which had only 9 newcomers. This reinforces the interpretation that turnover spawned by term limits rather than the institutional changes of term limits prompt legislators to rely on their friends for information.

Some of the friends consulted might be issue experts, serving on the relevant committees or bringing prior professional experience to the chamber. Exploring this, we find that turnover primarily increases legislators' tendency to consult nonexpert friends. In the House for the two years with lower turnover, 1997 and 2001, only 5 and 9 nonexpert friends, respectively, were consulted about school choice. Yet in the high turnover years, 1999 and 2003, more nonexpert friends were consulted about this issue—19 and 11 nonexpert friends, respectively.

Based on these comparisons, we suggest that higher turnover in the lower chamber seems to motivate legislators not just to rely on friends, but on friends who are not substantive experts. In the Senate almost all of the friends consulted also have expertise in the area of education. So this effect is isolated to the House, seeming to arise when spikes in turnover deplete experience.

Correlation between Friendship and Consulting about LRHCP Matrices

Overall the correlations between friendship and consulting about LRHCP are smaller than those for school choice consulting. The relationships are statistically significant, however, despite their small size. Beyond the smaller association between consulting and friendship, the relationship between turnover and consulting friends about LRHCP is inconsistent. The proportion of House colleagues consulted about LRHCP who are also friends fluctuates from 22 percent before term limits to values between 17 percent and 21 percent in the post-term-limits House sessions. In the Senate this proportion oscillates from 36 percent down to 17 percent and back up to 26 percent across the three sessions we investigate.

Neither turnover nor term limits seem to affect this relationship. And we find that turnover diminishes rather than increases consulting with friends about this technically complex issue, at least in the Senate. This suggests that turnover has a different effect on consulting about a technically complex issue than it does on consulting about a politically salient issue. Additionally, it appears that the expertise of friends matters more with respect to consulting about LRHCP. In the House, the amount of consulting with nonexpert friends about LRHCP is lower than it is for school choice. And in the Senate, it is almost nonexistent, ranging from zero to one instance per session. This reinforces findings we report in chapter 7 that suggest legislators prefer to consult experts on this technically complex issue, especially those with professional experience. And even during periods of high turnover, expert sources are preferred.

Summary

Consulting expert friends can be an efficient way to gather information when time is short. It is consistent with a process that Porter (1974) describes as a two-step system of information dissemination in which committee members become experts through training by interest groups and staff and by listening to testimony and working on a wide range of issues in the policy area. Then these institutional experts serve as a conduit for information, disseminating it to their colleagues who are not on the committee, possibly through friendship networks. Our findings suggest that the choice of information sources is often based on a combination of friendship and expertise, but we find that consulting with nonexpert friends rises in tandem with turnover for politically salient issues in the lower chamber. This suggests that high turnover compromises the quality of information gathered about some issues. This tendency should be carefully considered by academics, lobbyists, and others who seek to improve the quality of policy making through evidence and information.

The Evolution of Expertise and Friendship

Several scholars have explored friendship in state legislatures. Some focus on the effect of friendship on voting behavior (Patterson 1959; Arnold, Deen, and Patterson 2000; Peoples 2008). Others consider the factors that predict friendship formation (Caldeira and Patterson 1987). Wayne Francis's (1962) in-depth study of the Indiana legislature deconstructs several legislative relationships, exploring the connections between substantive expertise, interaction, and general influence. He argues that social interaction is associated with substantive expertise and also with general influence in a legislature. In his work social interaction includes going out to dinner and socializing outside the chamber. These are activities that one often associates with friendship. We explore next the temporal order between friendship (social interaction) and consulting members with substantive expertise.

None of the other scholars mentioned above have longitudinal data, although some of their hypotheses and discussions imply temporal order—generally, that friendship leads to shared roll call voting behavior, for example. We use our longitudinal data to initiate a highly exploratory probe of the evolution of these relationships. The question we address is does friendship predict which colleagues legislators rely upon for substantive advice, or does consulting with a substantive expert evolve into friendship? Our data include information about people who served in as many as five legislative sessions across the two chambers. The 460 interviews in the four House and three Senate sessions we investigate provide data on friendship and issue consulting from two interviews for 150 legislators. Of these 150 legislators, we have data for a third session for 91. The stringent limits on service imposed by term limits, a three-term maximum in the lower chamber combined with the small size of the Senate, constrains the number of cases with more than three interviews to 26 legislators, too few to analyze.[8]

Even though we have longitudinal data, it is difficult to isolate causality, so we explore whether popularity (measured by number of times a legislator is named as a friend) is a leading indicator of issue expertise (measured as the number of times a legislator is consulted), or whether more issue expertise is a leading indicator of popularity. We assume that legislators who are consulted extensively by our respondents are substantive experts in our two issue areas: school choice and LRHCP. However, as we just demonstrated in correlating the friendship and consulting matrices, there are occasions when nonexperts are consulted by individual legislators. Nevertheless, legislators who are consulted more tend to be those with committee positions or prior professional experience in the field, as we demonstrated in chapter 7.

We develop a simple model to examine three dependent variables for two sets of interviews.[9] These variables are the normalized indegrees[10] for school choice consulting, consulting about LRHCP, and friendship. Our independent variables of interest are the normalized indegrees in the preceding interview for all three of these relationships: school choice consulting, LRHCP consulting, and friendship. We also measure the interaction between these variables and the status of term limits at the time of a respondent's first election.

In order to maximize the number of data points, we focus on the number of interviews with a legislator rather than the specific session of each interview; that is, interviews one and two for some legislators might be the 1997 and 1999 House and interviews one and two for some other legislator might be the 2001 and 2003 House, and for some cases interview one might be in the House and interviews two and three in the Senate. Treating the interview as our unit of analysis provides enough data points to support two sets of longitudinal analyses—the first for interview one predicting interview two, the second for interview two predicting interview three.

The disadvantage of treating the interviews as our unit of analysis is that our models are complicated by the need for a series of control variables. We demonstrate in this chapter and elsewhere that the chambers differ and that the Senate is a friendlier chamber. We speculate that shifting chambers could depress a legislator's consulting relationships and friendships at least in the initial session after the shift. So we create a categorical variable to control for these shifts. We also control for consulting with top chamber leaders because they hold unique positions of influence and expertise.[11]

Finally, we create a categorical variable, *elected post-term-limits*, based on whether the legislator was first elected prior to term limits or first elected after term limits purged veterans. Those who served, even if only briefly, prior to the implementation of term limits were socialized by veteran legislators and formed friendships and consulting relationships within an institutional structure characterized by a clearly defined hierarchy of colleagues with established reputations. In contrast, legislators first elected after the massive turnover precipitated by term limits encountered a different, possibly chaotic, pecking order populated by colleagues about half of whom were complete strangers. To give readers a sense of the impact of repeated wave elections that term limits produce, we were told that legislators began wearing buttons that identify them as a legislator to avoid embarrassing situations of mistaken identity among chamber colleagues (interview notes).

The Evolution of School Choice Expertise

Looking at table 8.4, we find that legislators who were consulted heavily at interview one about school choice were more likely to be consulted about this issue at the subsequent interview. Additionally, the model for school choice consulting explains more than twice the variation at interview three as it did for interview two. Thus it appears that legislators' reputations for expertise tend to amplify across time. On the other hand, we find that having more friends is not a leading indicator of being consulted more about school choice at the time of the next interview. That is, popularity does not appear to increase one's reputation as an expert on school choice.

Only one control variable has an impact on school choice consulting—top leaders. By interview three top leaders are consulted more than other legislators about school choice. Interestingly, this is not true for top leaders at the time of interview two. This, in combination with results we discuss below, implies that top leaders become more important as term limits move to fuller implementation.

TABLE 8.4. Evolution of Expertise and Friendship across Time

Dependent Variable: Normalized Indegrees	SC Consulting				LRHCP Consulting				Friendship			
Independent Variables for First Session 150 Valid Cases Predicting 2nd Session	B	Std. Error	t	sig.	B	Std. Error	t	sig.	B	Std. Error	t	sig.
First elected after term limits (postTL)	-0.73	0.88	-0.83	.41	-1.01	0.99	-1.02	.31	**-1.29**	0.74	-1.74	.09
Moved from one chamber to the other	-0.84	0.80	-1.05	.30	**-1.51**	0.90	-1.67	.10	-0.79	0.68	-1.16	.25
Holds top leadership position session 2	0.90	0.99	0.91	.36	-0.81	1.11	-0.72	.47	0.73	0.83	0.88	.38
Normalized indegrees SC consulting	**0.45**	0.17	2.65	.01	0.16	0.19	0.82	.40	0.01	0.14	0.05	.96
Interaction postTL and SC consulting	**0.39**	0.22	1.81	.07	-0.30	0.24	-1.21	.23	0.18	0.18	1.00	.32
Normalized indegrees LRHCP consulting	-0.08	0.17	-0.47	.64	**0.49**	0.19	2.55	.01	0.10	0.14	0.72	.47
Interaction postTL and LRHCP consulting	0.04	0.18	-0.25	.80	**0.48**	0.20	2.39	.02	-0.08	0.15	-0.54	.59
Normalized indegrees friendship	**-0.13**	0.14	-0.95	.34	-0.08	0.16	-0.52	.61	**0.37**	0.12	3.14	.00
Interaction postTL and friendship	-0.06	0.18	-0.30	.76	0.21	0.21	1.03	.30	0.23	0.16	1.51	.13
Constant	**1.92**	0.65	2.97	.00	**1.34**	0.73	1.84	.07	**3.05**	0.54	5.60	.00
Adjusted R^2	0.30				0.62				0.25			
F-statistic	8.01		sig.	.00	28.01		sig.	.00	6.63		sig.	.00

Independent Variables for Second Session 91 Valid Cases Predicting 3rd Session	B	Std. Error	t	sig.	B	Std. Error	t	sig.	B	Std. Error	t	sig.
First Elected after Term Limits (PostTL)	-0.91	0.98	-0.93	.36	1.89	1.80	1.05	.30	-2.16	1.44	-1.49	.14
Moved from One Chamber to the Other	0.13	0.65	0.19	.85	1.94	1.20	1.62	.11	**2.34**	0.96	2.44	.02
Holds Top Leadership Position Session 3	**2.30**	0.87	2.65	.01	**3.66**	1.60	2.29	.03	**6.54**	1.29	5.09	.00
Normalized Indegrees SC Consulting	**0.59**	0.09	6.94	.00	-0.10	0.16	-0.67	.51	-0.04	0.13	-0.31	.76
Interaction PostTL and SC Consulting	**0.83**	0.13	6.29	.00	0.08	0.24	0.33	.74	**0.39**	0.19	1.99	.05
Normalized Indegrees LRHCP Consulting	0.08	0.17	0.46	.64	**0.74**	0.32	2.34	.02	-0.09	0.25	-0.35	.73
Interaction PostTL and LRHCP Consulting	-0.08	0.18	-0.41	.68	0.39	0.33	1.18	.24	0.18	0.27	0.69	.49
Normalized Indegrees Friendship	-0.23	0.15	-1.52	.13	0.34	0.28	1.21	.23	0.24	0.22	1.08	.28
Interaction PostTL and Friendship	0.23	0.18	1.24	.22	**-0.56**	0.33	-1.67	.10	0.20	0.27	0.74	.46
Constant	1.09	0.76	1.43	.16	-1.20	1.40	-0.85	.40	**3.33**	1.13	2.95	.00
Adjusted R^2	0.77				0.60				0.36			
F-statistic	34.22		sig.	.00	15.80		sig.	.00	6.55		sig.	.00

Note: Bold type denotes statistically significant coefficients.

The Evolution of LRHCP Expertise

We find similar results for LRHCP. Once again being consulted about this issue is a leading indicator of being consulted more at the time of the subsequent interview. This is true both for interviews one and two and for interviews two and three. One's reputation as an expert appears to accumulate over time.

Just as we found for school choice consulting, by interview three a larger number of colleagues consult top leaders about LRHCP. And again we find that this association between top leaders and expertise on LRHCP is absent at the time of interview two.

We find evidence of a "nerd" aspect of expertise on technically complex subjects leading to an inverse relationship between consulting on LRHCP and popularity. Having a lot of friends at interview one is not associated with being consulted more about LRHCP at interview two. More popular legislators at interview two appear to be less, not more, likely to be consulted about LRHCP by interview three. This is consistent with the matrix correlations, which show that expertise rather than friendship prompts legislators to consult a colleague about this technical issue.

One control variable—shifting chambers—statistically significantly decreases the amount of consulting about LRHCP directed toward a legislator. But this only applies to chamber shifts occurring between interviews one and two. This might reflect the transition to term limits in which a few veterans termed out of the House moved to the Senate prior to expulsions in the upper chamber. They would have encountered Senate veterans with established reputations as experts on health care, and, relatively speaking, they would have been less likely to be consulted in the upper chamber than they were previously in the lower chamber. This pattern does not appear to persist for interviews two and three, however, reinforcing our interpretation of this as a transient phenomenon— potentially part of the transition to term limits. Once again, our findings reinforce Mooney's (2009) admonition to wait until term limits are fully implemented before evaluating them.

The Evolution of Friendship

It appears friendship becomes transient as term limits are more fully implemented. We find that having more friends at the time of interview two is not a leading indicator of having more friends at interview three. On the other hand, there is some relationship between friendship at interview one and interview two. Therefore, we conclude that the continuity of friendship declines as term limits are more fully implemented.

We find that having substantive expertise is occasionally a leading indicator of accumulating more friends. But this only applies to the politically salient issue—school choice—and only after term limits are more fully implemented. This is consistent with the difference between the politically salient school choice issue and the technically complex LRHCP that we described above and earlier in the chapter. When political risk is higher, it appears that post-term-limits legislators increasingly trust friends for advice. But technically complex issues seem not to exhibit this association—a potential nerd effect, as we suggested above. Thus expertise can in some politically risky circumstances help expand one's friendship network, but making friends is not likely to increase one's importance in consulting about issues, at least not for the issues we investigate here.

Interestingly, moving from one chamber to another appears to increase friends in the subsequent session. We revisit this result when we consider the evolution of friendship and influence in chapter 9. But here we simply note that it reinforces our suspicion that legislators moving from the lower to the upper legislative chamber bring their relationships with them—at least with respect to friendship.

As term limits become more fully implemented, top leaders are named more often as friends and, as we noted above, as sources of information. This implies that top leaders are becoming more important as term limits are implemented. The associations between interview three top leaders and our dependent variables are large, positive, and statistically significant in all three equations. Holding a leadership position has the smallest effect on being consulted about school choice, a bit larger effect on being consulted about LRHCP, and the largest effect on friendship. Despite its statistical significance by the time of interview three, being a top leader has no statistically significant effects at the time of interview two. We revisit the changing role of top leaders in greater detail in the next chapter.

Summary

Our analyses suggest that having more friends is not a leading indicator of expertise on a specific issue. In fact, we find indications of the opposite effect for the technically complex issue, LRHCP. On the other hand, recognized expertise can in some instances contribute to popularity—at least for politically risky issues.

It appears that legislators are able to expand their colleagues' recognition of their expertise fairly quickly after term limits. Popularity on the other hand often does not accumulate across interviews as term limits become more fully implemented—by the time of the third interview.

Based on our findings, we speculate that people who are eager to move up in the chamber are likely to become involved in politically salient issues and eschew involvement in technically complex issues—even if they have some prior involvement and experience with an issue. We speculate further that as term limits are implemented, legislators try to form friendships with people likely to succeed within their caucus. Those are also likely to be people who are well positioned to move to the upper chamber, explaining the increase in friends among those who shifted chambers between their second and third interviews.

Finally, the role of top leaders seems to change as term limits are more fully implemented. Top leaders are increasingly consulted more about both issues when we predict the third interview relationships. Additionally, top leaders become more popular as term limits become more fully implemented. The control variable, top leader, is measured during the same interview period as the dependent variable, so this does not predict future friendships, but rather controls for these uniquely positioned respondents.[12] Top leaders do not differ from others when we use our model to predict these relationships at the time of interview two, but the top leader effect is quite strong when we apply our model to relationships at the time of interview three. This difference between sessions implies the increasing importance of holding a position in the caucus hierarchy after term limits—a topic we probe in the next chapter.

Conclusions

Nowhere are the institutional effects of term limits more evident in our data than in our diagrams of the friendship clusters in the lower chamber. Clusters of friends within the lower chamber fragment as the chamber assimilates waves of newcomers. Before term limits chamber leaders were well represented among the friendship clusters. In the 2003–04 post-term-limits House, the opposite is true—top leaders vanish from the clusters of interconnected friends. That the post-term-limits friendship clusters we identify so conspicuously omit these top leaders indicates that the institutional structure of friendship has changed. Although top leaders still appear to have lots of friends after term limits, they have friends in twos and threes. They are no longer part of larger clusters of actors in the post-term-limits chambers.

Pre-term-limits clusters of friends that might be described as power brokers vanish, replaced by support groups for the disenfranchised and ostracized. The sole remaining cluster in the 2003–04 House consists of ultraconservative members of the majority party, whose obstruction often placed them at odds with their leaders. Although they may band together to leverage their individual influence, it is highly unlikely that they are considered by anyone involved or observing the chamber to be the movers and shakers of the institution. These friendships reveal stunning differences in the institutional structure of the House before and after term limits.

Despite profound changes in the institutional structure of House friendships after term limits, we find that term limits have no statistically significant effects at the individual level on the average number of friends within the same party or across party lines. We find only a few effects of being a newcomer, such as fewer friendships that cross party lines and overestimating one's friends, but these are fairly predictable.

Once again term limits have different effects on the two legislative chambers. Legislators who move to the upper chamber appear to take their friendships with them. Yet post-term-limits friendship networks in the Senate are less inclusive than the pre-term-limits networks. Clusters of friends in the Senate before and after term limits reveal a role played by minority party leaders, and there are members of both parties in the Senate in these friendship groups after term limits. Institutional changes in the Senate are more subtle than those in the lower chamber.

Our longitudinal data provide a unique opportunity to investigate the evolution of legislative friendships and expertise. While we find that newcomers sometimes turn to friends for information about issues, we find that substantive expertise combined with political salience leads to more friendships. Yet we find that it is more common after term limits for inexperienced legislators to consult colleagues about a politically risky issue *solely* on the basis of their friendship. Moreover, school choice consulting with nonexpert friends increases when turnover is higher. This could lead legislators to make satisficing decisions based on available heuristics—friendship—rather than a reputation as an honest broker of high-quality information.

We do not find this same pattern for consulting about LRHCP. Popularity is inversely related with substantive expertise on our technically complex issue. These issue differences suggest that the political salience of an issue might lead legislators to seek information from those who will reinforce rather than challenge their ideological position. A technically complex issue in contrast appears to motivate legislators to seek information from issue experts. As we learned in chapter 7, after term limits legislators prefer that these experts have professional experience in the health care field.

Top leaders are consulted more on issues as term limits become more fully implemented, based on our analyses of the evolution of friendship across time. And as we noted earlier, leaders have many individual friends. What does fray with term limits, however, is the institutional structure, the tightly knit, reciprocal friendships. Top leaders are absent from clusters of friends, and they no longer hold these groups together. It appears that something has changed in the nexus of friendship and influence after term limits. We attempt to illuminate this shift as we examine the influence side of this relationship in the next chapter.

We argue these structural changes are the most profound effects of term limits and the most likely to affect the process of governance in the State of Michigan as a whole. The changes we find in the institutional structure of friendship could easily undermine bipartisan negotiations about policy, especially in the highly polarized political climate of Michigan's post-term-limits legislature. Post-term-limits friendship networks are less cohesive, and popularity appears unstable from one session to the next. This bodes poorly for major legislative achievements, especially those that are based on bipartisan deal-making. These are often nurtured by caucus leaders and other key actors who can persuade colleagues to compromise. The effects we find could be relevant for citizen legislatures that meet so infrequently that a reputation for expertise is hard to establish and friendship networks are hard to cultivate. This might apply especially in a large state where legislators are scattered far and wide when they are not in session.

NINE

Influence among Legislators

We seek in this chapter and the next to understand how term limits affect the acquisition, distribution, and use of influence in Michigan's legislature. Influence is notoriously difficult to define and to distinguish from related concepts, such as power and control (see, especially, Bachrach and Baratz 1962; March 1966; Tannenbaum 1968, 1986; Raven 1990, 2008; Battista 2011; Mooney 2013). But the underlying processes and dynamics represented by these terms are central to the work of a legislature. Therefore we would be remiss if we let the challenge of distinguishing between them deter us from examining them. Legislators in our conversations with them use power and influence somewhat interchangeably, seemingly recognizing that they overlap in practice. We follow their lead in our discussion, with apologies to scholars whose precise usage articulates subtle distinctions between them. For the most part, we use the word *influence* in the following discussion because that is the term we used in our interview questions.

In this chapter we examine influence among legislators at both the individual and the institutional (chamber) levels. First we assess the effects of term limits on the average number of colleagues who attribute influence to a legislator in each chamber. Then we rely once again on network analysis to explore changes in the distribution of influence in each chamber before term limits, during the transition to term limits, and when the chambers reach their post implementation stage. In these analyses we build on our previous work (Sarbaugh-Thompson et al. 2006) about influence in Michigan's House during the transition to term limits, adding data on the term limits equilibrium stage in the House (2003–04) and also data on the upper chamber before and after term limits.

In addition to this extension of our previous work, we also seek information about various sources of influence and whether some of these are more or less sensitive to the effects of term limits. In conjunction with this, we examine the relationships between influence and friendship and between influence and expertise (measured using the issue consulting networks described in chapter 7). Finally, following in the path set by Francis (1962), we attempt to inform the academic discussion about which came first, friendship or influence. That is, does influence arise from social interaction—from a legislator's friendship network? Alternatively, does substantive expertise provide a foundation upon which influence accumulates? We are uniquely positioned to probe these questions using information provided by our repeat respondents.

Although the rules of a legislature bestow influence by assigning various prerogatives and tools to anyone holding formal positions (e.g., speaker), some influence is also derived from an individual's personal qualities (e.g., charisma or knowledge). In our discussion we treat this distinction as *formal* versus *informal* influence. We do not consider formal and informal influence to be mutually exclusive. The personal qualities (e.g., charisma, knowledge, trustworthiness) of a legislator holding a leadership position (i.e., speaker) enhance or constrain his or her ability to utilize the tools and prerogatives of the position. For example, pre-term-limits committee chairs and caucus leaders were highly experienced veterans with extensive substantive expertise, who were often personally respected and admired by their colleagues, combining formal and informal influence.

Term limits seem likely to undermine informal influence rather than formal influence. Informal influence, based on personal reputation and expertise, usually evolves slowly over time, but time is severely truncated with term limits. Therefore we predict informal influence will decline after term limits. This is a fairly safe prediction given our previous work (Sarbaugh-Thompson et al. 2006). But this change is likely to ripple through the distribution of influence in both chambers and also to affect the ways that legislators acquire influence after term limits. We explore the linkage between these individual and institutional changes in influence in this chapter.

Michigan provides an excellent opportunity to examine term limits effects on influence because Mooney (2013) finds that legislative leaders are perceived as more influential when chamber turnover is higher and when "lawmakers' seats are insecure and valuable" (567). Both turnover and the value of the seat are especially high in Michigan. Seats in professional legislatures are generally assumed to be more valuable given the salary associated with them, and Michigan's legislature is among the best paid in the nation, even after they cut their salary in 2011. As we demonstrated in chapter 5, turnover increased dramatically in Michigan after term limits. These dynamics imply that legislative leaders should gain influence after term limits, despite having access to the same tools and prerogatives of office as their predecessors. Yet Mooney (2013) also indicates that more skill and experience in formal leadership positions appear to be associated with greater perceived influence, possibly indicating that it takes practice to use the tools of office. Thus, legislators holding formal leadership roles might be adjudged less influential by their colleagues after term limits.

In our prior work, we demonstrated that fewer representatives were identified as influential after term limits. But we found that informal influence declined more precipitously than did formal influence. Consistent with Mooney's assessment, influence gravitated toward top leaders after term limits, indicating the increasing importance of formal influence. Although this was based on only the first three of the House sessions we examine here, we see no reason for these trends to attenuate in our final post-term-limits House session (2003).

We expect the Senate to diverge from this pattern, however. Most state senators served together in the House. Therefore, they have had more time to build their personal reputation and to acquire expertise and experience. Consequently, we expect fewer pronounced changes in the volume and distribution of influence in the post-term-limits Senate. But as we found in previous chapters, our assumptions about the Senate are often misguided.

Data and Methods

In addition to the conceptual and theoretical problems with the terminology related to influence, there are problems measuring it. Various measurement techniques have strengths and limitations (see March 1957 and Hall 1992 for excellent discussions). Most important, however, different approaches produce divergent results. Battista (2011) discovered that legislators' influence[1] measured based on the tools or prerogatives available to leaders is poorly correlated with their colleagues' perceptions of their influence.

We rely here on an open-ended reputational approach to measure influence. When we ask about influence, we do not restrict respondents to specific people or specific leadership positions. We ask our respondents, "Who do you consider to be the most influential members of the chamber?" This is question 5 of appendix A. Most respondents freely designated several colleagues they considered to be highly influential. If the respondent initially named only formal chamber leaders, we used a neutral prompt of "Anyone else?" (i.e., we probed for informal influence).[2]

We use these responses to calculate the average amount of influence per legislator and to construct matrices for network analysis as we did for consulting and for friendship, with one difference in coding. We consider self-reports of influence to be valid when analyzing these matrices. In network analysis jargon, we include values on the diagonal in our calculations. Initially, we simply assess the influence reported by and attributed to individual legislators. These involve the now familiar *outdegrees* and *indegrees*. Then we consider other structural measures of the influence networks, such as *centralization*.

We also probe the reasons legislators are viewed as influential by asking our respondents why they consider their colleagues to be influential (e.g., formal position such as speaker, knowledge, and personal qualities such as honesty). We framed this as an open-ended question and coded all responses. In our post-term-limits interviews we asked, "What makes someone influential in a term-limited chamber?" Both these open-ended queries appear in questions 5a in appendix A. We combine responses to both questions into open-ended coding categories adapted from the work of French and Raven (1959). Although they discuss their categories using the terminology *bases of power*, these categories bear a strong resemblance to the reasons our respondents most often said their colleagues were influential. We translate their terminology about the bases of power into bases of influence for consistency with our interview questions and to avoid confusion in the following discussion.

Effects of Term Limits on the Volume of Influence

As we noted in earlier chapters, term limits often change the structure of networks (e.g., friendship and consulting) even when there is no difference in the average volume of these relationships. But, with influence, the effects of term limits are so dramatic that they are readily apparent even in the average amount of influence. In the House after term limits the average number of influential colleagues named by respondents (outdegrees) decreases sharply from about 7.3 to 4.5. This pattern is consistent within the same political party (4.5 influential colleagues before term limits and 3.4 after) and across party lines (2.5 before and 1.5 after). The differences for the lower chamber are statistically significant.

Thus, legislators are naming fewer colleagues as highly influential, producing a chamber-level decline in the amount of influence. After term limits the House loses more than 2 percent of the maximum possible influence (i.e., if everyone thought everyone else was influential), dropping from 5.5 percent to 3.3 percent. Although this might not seem like a big difference, the maximum possible number of influence designations is 440^2 or 193,600 given that we permit self-designations of influence. Even a small percentage of a number this large is a substantial change.

In the Senate, we find no statistically significantly differences in influence after term limits either overall, within the same party, or across party lines. Moreover, the Senate loses only 1 percent of the maximum possible number of ties (1,444 in the 38 member chamber). This suggests that senators' shared House experience is sufficient to attenuate term limits effect on the amount of influence in the upper chamber. And this difference between the chambers implies that influence is sensitive to experience.

Effects of Experience on the Volume of Influence

Regardless of term limits, newcomers lack influence in the House. These results are quite predictable and straightforward, so we discuss them rather than providing a table or figure. Pre-term-limits House newcomers were much, **much** less likely to be named as influential colleagues (indegrees). House veterans were named as influential by an average of 7.6 colleagues while newcomers were named by an average of 1. More interestingly, this pattern persists even after term limits (5.7 for veterans versus 1.5 for newcomers). Newcomers arrive after term limits with a plan to move rapidly into leadership positions (interview notes). It appears that these ambitious newcomers' plans collide with similar plans already implemented by their slightly more experienced colleagues, who are capitalizing on their brief opportunity to exercise their influence. These differences between newcomers and veterans are replicated within their own party and across party lines, and all are large enough to be statistically significant.

After term limits, it appears that the time senators shared together in the House ameliorates the effect of being new. But we still find evidence that being a newcomer in the upper chamber inhibits one's influence. But the contrast between Senate veterans and newcomers was clearer before term limits (4.5 for veterans and 1.0 for newcomers) than after (4.1 for veterans and 2.5 for newcomers). Given the small size of the chamber, statistical significance is elusive, but the gap between Senate newcomers and veterans appears to shrink after term limits.

Volume of Influence—Comparison of Chambers

Stereotypes of upper legislative chambers, implicit in the term *upper*, imply that they are more influential than lower chambers. We compare the mean indegrees and outdegrees for the House and Senate both before and after term limits to assess their relative influence. In order to compare across two chambers that are different sizes, we need to adjust for their size by normalizing the observed *indegrees* (colleagues who say a legislator is influential) and *outdegrees* (colleagues the same legislator names as influential) as a proportion of the total possible indegrees and outdegrees for the chamber.

We find that there is more influence in the upper chamber compared to the lower chamber before term limits, and this gap widens after term limits. This reflects a post-term-limits decline in influence in the House and a relatively stable volume of influence in the Senate. Specifically, before term limits in the House the normalized mean for outdegrees is 6.4 and for indegrees 5.5. In the Senate, the normalized mean for outdegrees is 10.4 and for indegrees 9.5. Hence, prior to term limits, the ratio of the average influence of a representative to the average influence of a senator is about 60 percent for both measures of perceived influence. This comports with other research on disparities between upper and lower legislative chambers (Cain and Levin 1999; Carey et al. 2006; Appolonio and La Raja 2006).

Term limits appear to amplify the discrepancy in influence between the Senate and the House, and this effect is statistically significant and substantively large. After term limits, mean normalized outdegrees and indegrees in the House both decrease (falling from 6.4 and 5.5 to 4.4 and 3.7). In the Senate, the changes are minor. The result is that after term limits the ratio of the average representative's influence to the average senator's drops to 40 percent. In Michigan, it appears that the stereotype of the upper chamber as stronger is justified even before term limits, but more so afterward. If, as Tannenbaum (1961) argues, more total influence (in his words *control*) within an organization enhances its effectiveness, then the Senate might be expected to legislate more effectively. This is consistent with the higher priority placed on developing new legislation by pre-term-limits senators (see chapter 4), but it is less clear whether the Senate capitalizes on its greater volume of influence after term limits. We examine this disparity in greater detail in chapter 11, when we consider the relationship between the two legislative chambers.

The Institutional Structure of Influence

The distribution of influence as well as the amount of influence is important in understanding how an organization, in this case a legislative chamber, operates (Hanneman and Riddle 2005). As we demonstrate in the previous section, as the lower chamber increasingly absorbs waves of novices, the amount of influence in that chamber decreases. Tannenbaum (1956, 1961, and 1986) finds an association between the amount of "influence" and the distribution of "influence" in an organization. Specifically, as the amount of "influence" declines, the size of the cohort exercising "influence" shrinks. Thus we predict that House leaders will gain influence at the expense of rank-and-file House members given the declining volume of influence that we just reported in the House. Moreover, if Tannenbaum's findings are supported, then influence in the lower chamber will become more centralized, with chamber leaders gaining influence despite declines in overall influence. Additionally, the level of centralization in the Senate influence networks would be expected to remain stable, given the upper chamber's fairly constant volume of influence overall.

In table 9.1, we report evidence that supports these predictions. Prior to term limits, influence in the House is widely distributed in an open, equalitarian structure. This type of network is sometimes referred to as a concom (Farace, Monge, and Russell 1977) or a circle (Hanneman and Riddle 2005). As term limits are implemented in the House, indegree centralization increases steadily, albeit modestly, and outdegree centralization falls dramatically. This indicates that influence is concentrated in fewer hands immediately after the implementation of term limits and the trajectory continues through the 2003 House session. Consistent with this, nearly 30 percent fewer representatives have any influence in the chamber, according to their colleagues, in the final post-term-limits session (dropping from 90 in 1997–98 to 67 in 2003–04).

The picture is more complicated in the Senate. We treat the 2003–06 session, led by termed-out House veterans with decades of experience, as an outlier because it is a unique creature of the transition to term limits. Prior to term limits, the indegree influence network is centralized in the Senate. It becomes less so after term limits (declining from 66% to 48%). Thus, although influence declined slightly in the Senate, from 9.7 percent to 8.7 percent of the maximum possible (i.e., if everyone thought everyone, including themselves, was influential), it is more broadly distributed (i.e., less centralized) after term limits. This decrease in influence centralization in the Senate contradicts the pattern Tannenbaum's work predicts, but this might involve the distinction between formal and informal influence, which we explore next.

Formal versus Informal Influence

As early as the 1930s, students of organizations recognized that the formal side of an organization provides an incomplete picture (Barnard 1938; Mayo 1946). As we explained earlier in this chapter, informal influence in organizations arises from personal characteristics such as charisma, knowledge, trustworthiness, and quite possibly friendship. Consequently informal influence assesses the extent to which highly qualified group members can share their expertise even when other, more senior or more fortunate colleagues hold formal positions of authority, such as being elected to caucus leadership positions. The difference between informal and formal influence is likely to explain at least some of the discrepancy that Battista (2011) finds between measuring influence based on the rules of the chamber and on the judgment of colleagues.

Yet Cooper and Brady (1981) find that the institutional prerogatives available to legislative leaders and partisan majorities in the chamber (for-

TABLE 9.1. Influence Networks by Session and Chamber

	House Sessions (110 Members)				Senate Sessions (38 Members)		
	1997– 1998	1999– 2000	2001– 2002	2003– 2004	1999– 2002	2003– 2006	2007– 2010
Number of influence designations reported							
Total	667	428	508	404	140	121	126
Percent of possible ties	5.51	3.54	4.20	3.34	9.70	8.38	8.73
Number of legislators with influence	90	68	91	67	25	28	28
Maximum ties received a legislator	68	68	71	71	28	26	21
Network centralization							
indegrees[a]	57%	59%	61%	62%	66%	62%	48%
outdegrees[b]	50%	19%	33%	11%	31%	24%	24%
Formal influence: *People holding top positions (top 5 in House; top 5 in Senate)*							
Total formal	210	170	195	164	69	67	64
% of total	32	40	38	41	49	55	51
Informal influence: *People without formal positions*							
Total informal	457	258	313	240	71	54	62
% of total	69	60	62	59	51	45	49

[a]indegrees refer to the number of times a legislator is named as influential by colleagues.
[b]outdegrees refer to the number of colleagues a legislator named as influential.

mal influence) empower leaders more than do personality, skill, or leadership style (informal influence). Similarly, Anderson and his coauthors (2003) find that influential representatives in the 103rd Congress were likely to be members of the chamber's majority party and hold formal leadership positions or chair committees. Moreover, Meyer (1980) finds that seniority and leadership positions are instrumental sources of influence in the North Carolina legislature. Thus, formal influence, arising from the tools and prerogatives available to someone holding a formal role, is extremely important in legislative organizations. It seems likely to play an even larger role after term limits given the limited time available to demonstrate one's positive personal qualities (i.e., honesty and expertise) and to establish one's reputation—the bases of informal influence.

As table 9.1 illustrates, top leaders are seen as highly influential by their colleagues in all sessions and both chambers. In the pre-term-limits House nearly one-third (32%) of the total influence accrues to the five top representatives. This increases by 10 percent after term limits. Simultaneously, the proportion of their colleagues without formal positions to whom representatives attribute influence decreases by 10 percent. So, after term limits the volume of influence in the House declines, and remaining influence is concentrated in the hands of top chamber leaders. We conclude that it is informal influence that decreases after term limits.

In the Senate, formal leaders account for an even larger proportion of the total influence—about half of the total. Term limits have little or no effect on this. Despite a small decline in the amount of influence in the Senate, the proportion of influence attributed to the top leaders is nearly constant. Correspondingly, informal influence declines only slightly in the Senate even after term limits, reinforcing evidence that during their time together in the House legislators develop the ingredients of informal influence—knowledge, expertise, personal credibility—and carry these forward into the Senate.

Reasons Colleagues Are Influential

Given the findings we report so far, it is tempting to assume that the altered balance between formal and informal influence explains the effect of term limits on influence in the chambers. But there many sources of influence that legislators, including top leaders, draw upon. Open-ended comments provided by our respondents specify these. In order to organize these reasons into a manageable framework, we adapt categories developed by

French and Raven (1959) and Raven (1993) into the words we use in our interview questions by replacing the word *power* with the word *influence*.[4] As we noted earlier in this chapter, the categories these authors describe closely match the reasons our respondents say their colleagues are influential. The first of these categories is *legitimate* sources of influence, which arises primarily through holding formal positions. The second is *referent* sources of influence, reflecting interpersonal admiration or admirable personal qualities of an individual or possibly friendship. The four other categories of influence are based on *coercion, rewards, expertise,* and *persuasion.* Using this framework, we explore the frequency with which our interview respondents attribute influence to these various sources within the chambers before and after term limits.[5]

Table 9.2 shows that the two most frequently mentioned sources of influence are legitimate influence and expertise. Legitimate sources of influence are the most commonly mentioned sources even before term limits. After term limits the proportion of respondents who say that a formal role or position is the source of their colleagues' influence increases in both chambers, but especially in the Senate. Although this is consistent

TABLE 9.2. Sources of Legislators' Influence

Bases of Influence or Power	House			Senate		
	Pre-Limits	Post-Limits	Sig.	Pre-Limits	Post-Limits	Sig.
Legitimate	**83%**	**92%**	0.01	**71%**	**95%**	**<0.01**
Expert	**82%**	**67%**	**<0.01**	71%	75%	0.68
Life Experience	17%	19%	0.67	30%	33%	0.92
Experience in Government	4%	10%	0.10	**27%**	**13%**	**<0.10**
On an Important Committee	**50%**	**33%**	**<0.01**	12%	20%	0.33
General Knowledge	**26%**	**13%**	**<0.01**	24%	16%	0.37
Issue-Specific Knowledge	**33%**	**22%**	**<0.05**	23%	29%	0.54
Procedural Knowledge	17%	18%	0.83	12%	22%	0.25
Persuasion	**22%**	**47%**	**<0.01**	34%	47%	0.22
Referent	45%	49%	0.50	**34%**	**62%**	**0.01**
Reward	**3%**	**12%**	**0.04**	14%	15%	0.90
Coercion	**2%**	**17%**	**<0.01**	**20%**	**6%**	**0.03**
Number Making Comments	95	275		33	55	

Note: Bold type denotes statistically significant differences.
Difference of Proportions Test: significance of two-tailed probabilities reported.

with our network analysis findings about the distribution of influence after term limits in the House, it is surprising in the Senate. This indicates that holding a formal position enhances the influence of senators outside the top leaders (e.g., committee chairs) more after term limits than before. Moreover, this implies that before term limits Senate committee chairs and others relied more on informal sources, such as expertise or personal qualities like honesty, to establish their influence.

Prior to term limits expertise was as important a source of influence, mentioned nearly as often as legitimate sources in both chambers. After term limits, there is a 15 percent decline in the proportion of respondents mentioning expertise in the House. In the Senate, the proportion of respondents mentioning expertise as a source of influence is fairly stable. But expertise is less prominent relative to the larger proportion of post-term-limits senators attributing a colleague's influence to legitimate sources. Relatively speaking, expertise loses ground in the Senate after term limits.

Given the steep decline of expertise as a source of influence in the lower chamber and in the Senate compared to legitimate sources of influence, we examine in detail the six categories of comments that we classified as expertise: serving on an important committee, life experience, prior government experience, procedural knowledge, knowledge in general, and issue-specific knowledge.

The decline in expertise as a source of influence in the lower chamber is fueled by a decline in three individual components of this category. First, the portion of our House respondents who mention serving on an important committee as a source of influence declines by 17 percent after term limits. Second, general knowledge is mentioned by half as many representatives. Third, issue-specific knowledge is mentioned by only two-thirds as many respondents. Thus, knowledge gained within the chamber appears to bestow less influence on legislators after term limits. These trends appear to intensify as term limits are fully implemented.

Moreover, knowledge acquired outside the chamber appears to confer more influence on representatives after term limits if we compare only the pre-term-limits and 2003–04 (term limits equilibrium) sessions. The percentage of respondents saying that life experience explains a colleague's influence nearly doubles from the pre-term-limits House by the last post-term-limits session (2003–04), rising from 17 percent to 33 percent. We note that this is consistent with the effect of prior professional experience on consulting about LRHCP that we reported in chapter 7. The proportion of respondents who say that influence accrues from prior government experience jumps fivefold (4% to 21%) between these two sessions. But even these sharp increases are not enough to overcome the magnitude of the decline in expertise acquired within the chamber. So expertise is a less common source of influence among post-term-limits legislators.

Expertise in the Senate is less prominent only in relation to the gains made by legitimate sources of influence—the value of holding a formal position. We find that limiting service only slightly alters the importance of expertise in conferring influence on senators. Their years of service in the House appear to fill the void in expertise created by high turnover in the lower chamber. Yet one component of expertise stands out. Post-term-limits senators mention government experience as a source of influence less frequently than their predecessors did. The government experience of most post-term-limits senators is less extensive than it was for their predecessors, so this seems reasonable.

Other Bases of Influence

We speculate that persuasion may replace expertise as a source of influence after term limits in the House. Turning again to table 9.2, we see that the proportion of representatives attributing influence to colleagues' ability to persuade other colleagues doubles. The increase for senators is smaller and not statistically significant.

As Raven (2008) discusses at length, it is difficult to segregate expertise and persuasion empirically. We coded comments such as builds consensus, speaks his or her mind, and makes good arguments into the category of *persuasion*. We also included comments about shares my views, effort and motivation on an issue, and has relationships with powerful actors. We interpret these comments as an indication of efforts to convince a colleague to adopt a particular position on grounds other than knowledge, which we coded as expertise. Given that we were consistent in our coding, comparisons across time should be valid.

The proportion of senators attributing influence to admirable personal qualities (referent sources of influence) approximately doubles after term limits. Examples of traits mentioned are honesty, trustworthiness, respected, and quick learner. Some respondents even mentioned that a colleague is influential because he or she is "nice" (interview notes). Moving as a cohort from the lower to the upper chamber may enhance the importance of referent sources of influence among senators who have similar degrees of experience and past office holding. Regardless of its origins, this increase in the Senate suggests that when term-limited legislators have the time and opportunity to work together, influence becomes intertwined with personal relationships. We detected hints of this in chapter 9 when we found that more legislators consult friends about a politically salient issue when turnover is higher.

Binder, Lawrence, and Maltzman (1999, 815) find that leaders have an array of procedural and financial tools at their disposal to influence their colleagues' positions and behaviors. These tools provide rewards that can be distributed or withheld (coercion), but these sources of influence are rarely mentioned by our respondents. Yet both are mentioned more often by our post-term-limits House respondents. Comments about rewards as a source of influence, which quadrupled in the House after term limits (from 3% to 12%), often mention campaign funds. We were told by several respondents that representatives seeking influence and key committee positions must raise large sums of money for the caucus (interview notes). This means that legislators from safe districts who need only limited money to finance their own campaign are well positioned to amass influence by donating money to the caucus. It also suggests that influence gravitates toward legislators who have relationships with large donors or who are rich themselves.

We were told about specific instances in which legislators' donations to the caucus were rewarded with chair positions on important committees. For example, one legislator said that he gave the caucus between $10,000 and $15,000 in an effort to secure a chair position, but lost out to a colleague from a richer part of the state who gave between $80,000 and $100,000 (interview notes). In another interview, we were told of one representative who gave $40,000 to the caucus and was rewarded with the position of chair for a powerful committee (interview notes). Respondents both implied and stated that these were quid pro quo arrangements, but that is impossible to verify. It underscores, however, that caucus leaders have valuable resources to distribute as rewards, and this contributes to their influence.

In our coding of coercion, we included statements about suppression of dissenting voices as well as tales of bullying and physical intimidation. Some respondents talked about female colleagues leaving in tears from private meetings in leadership offices, of a committee chair who turned off the microphone of an opposition party member during a committee meeting, of "discussions" in the parking lot that included shoving someone up against a car, and of a legislator whose parking space and office staff budget were reassigned by his caucus leaders after he cast a key vote opposing them.

As titillating as these stories are, the most common comments about sources of influence that we coded as coercion involved suppressing dissent within the caucus. For example, one respondent said that "Prior to term limits there were more individual thinking members. There was no notion to go with caucus on every vote. Caucus [influence] is greater now. They want robots, not people in the caucus" (interview notes).

The proportion of House members mentioning coercion quadruples after term limits from 2 percent to 17 percent, but in the upper chamber influence attributed to coercion decreases after term limits from 20 percent to 6 percent. We suspect that it might be harder to coerce term-limited senators serving their final term, many of whom realize that there are few if any electoral opportunities available to them. Threats of dire future consequences are ineffectual when senators have no future in the chamber and begin to realize that they have few prospects for any future political office, despite their earlier political ambition. Logically under these circumstances their concern about opposing the caucus or the party wanes.

The Relationship of Influence to Friendship and Expertise

These changes in the sources of influence, especially those involving personal qualities and expertise, pique our interest in the next set of questions. What is the relationship between friendship and influence in a legislature? What is the relationship between substantive knowledge and influence in a legislature? And do term limits alter these connections?

Based on the work of Francis (1962), Patterson (1959), and Arnold, Deen, and Patterson (2000), which we described in detail in previous chapters, we expect friendship and influence to overlap among legislators who serve together for decades. In table 9.3 we report evidence to support this. Popular legislators also appear to be influential legislators, but less so after term limits than before. The size of the association decreases substantially in both chambers after term limits, but especially in the Senate.

We also expect influence and knowledge about issues will be correlated. We find that the relationships between issue expertise (measured as being consulted about the issue) and influence are inconsistent and contingent on the issue and chamber. Before term limits influence is correlated with both issues in the Senate but neither are in the House. This could occur because there are fewer senators (38) across whom influence can be distributed and a larger proportion of the chamber serves on the committees with jurisdiction over these issues.

After term limits influence is associated with consulting about school choice in both the House and the Senate. The size of these correlations is very small, however. Term limits attenuate the influence of expertise on LRHCP in the Senate and have no effect in the House. Our findings here as elsewhere indicate that developing technical expertise neither wins friends nor influences people in a legislature, but that, at least in the lower chamber, influence and expertise are entwined on politically salient issues.

Correlating Matrices

The foregoing correlations only tell us that someone who is popular is also named as influential by many, but not necessarily the same, colleagues. We want to know whether the same respondents name someone both as influential and as a friend. We also want to determine whether legislators rely more on their own friends, not just popular colleagues, when seeking information and guidance on an issue. To answer these questions, we correlate the matrices to identify joint designations by individual respondents. We explained the procedure for correlating matrices in chapter 8. We simply note here that we used the QAP correlation subroutine in UCINET 6.46 to compare these matrices, producing Jaccard Coefficients as well as more familiar measures of association.

Correlation of Influence and Friendship Matrices

Based on our findings in chapter 8, we expect that the pre-term-limits correlations between the friendship and influence matrices will dissipate in the House, but remain stable in the Senate. In that chapter, we found that

TABLE 9.3. Correlations between Network Indegrees

Correlations between Being Named as Influential and the Other Network Relationships	House Pre-Limits	House Post-Limits	Senate Pre-Limits	Senate Post-Limits
Between friendship and influence	0.59***	0.45***	0.75***	0.41***
Between influence and school choice consulting	0.10	0.14***	0.44***	0.19*
Between influence and LRHCP consulting	0.03	0.03	0.22*	0.02

Note: Indegrees are the ties received by a focal legislator—coming in toward that legislator and being named as a source or named as influential or named as a friend. Bold type indicates statistically significant associations.

*** $p < 0.01$, ** $p < 0.05$, * $p < 0.10$ (one-tailed tests of significance).

friendship clusters in the House revolved around majority party power brokers before term limits, but the sole post-term-limits friendship cluster links ostracized majority party members. Thus we expect friendship and influence to become decoupled in the House after term limits. Yet we found some similarities in the friendship clusters before and after term limits in the Senate, and involvement of power brokers was limited in all three Senate sessions. Therefore, we expect fewer changes in the Senate.

Our findings, which appear in table 9.4, contradict our predictions for the House. Over time the correlation between influence and friendship appears to grow stronger in the House, but the association between friends and influential colleagues is stable in the Senate between the pre-term-limits and final post-term-limits session—as we expected. (We continue to treat the intervening Senate session as an outlier due to its unique leadership team.)

When we correlate the matrices we find a larger correlation after term limits between the friendship and influence in the House, which is inconsistent with the pattern we found in table 9.3. There we found that influential legislators were more popular before term limits than they were afterward. Simply correlating popular legislators with influential legislators produces misleading results if we seek to understand whether legislators claim that their specific friends are also influential in the chamber.

We probe further to see whether legislators befriend influential colleagues or whether they attribute influence to their friends after term limits. To clarify our examination of this, we describe one row of table 9.4 in detail. In the 1997 House, there were 660 influence designations and 478 friend designations made by our 95 respondents. There are also 107 influential friends—colleagues named by the same respondent as both an especially close friend and an especially influential member of the chamber. The frequency of friends and the frequency of influential friends both remain relatively constant for all sessions and both chambers. But the number of influential colleagues identified in the House drops substantially with the advent of term limits, as we reported earlier in this chapter. This means that influential friends become a larger proportion of influential colleagues, rising from 16 percent in the 1997 House to 27 percent in the 2003 House.

Furthermore, in the 1997 House 45 percent or 48 of the 107 joint designations—influential friend—involve the top five leaders. Over time the proportion of formal leaders among the joint designees fluctuates a little around this 45 percent level, but changes are small, and there is no apparent trend. The remaining 59 influential friends in the 1997 House

TABLE 9.4. Correlation between Influence and Friendship Matrices

Chamber and Session	Correlation	Chi-Square	Jaccard Coefficient	Jaccard Average 2,500 Permutations	Number of Influential Legislators[a]	Number of Friends	Number of Influential Friends	Influential Friends as a % of Influential Legislators	Formal Leaders among Influential Friends (%)	Influential Friends among Informal Leaders (%)	Respondents
House											
1997	0.15	272.72	0.10	0.02	660	478	107	16	45	13	95
1999	0.12	175.80	0.08	0.02	414	497	70	17	57	12	93
2001	0.19	412.83	0.12	0.02	496	498	109	22	43	21	93
2003	0.22	591.92	0.14	0.02	395	464	107	27	40	28	89
Senate											
1999	0.27	101.90	0.20	0.04	134	104	39	29	67	20	35
2003	0.19	51.68	0.14	0.04	114	94	26	23	88	6	28
2007	0.25	88.27	0.18	0.04	121	100	34	28	44	33	27

Note: Values for the correlations, Chi-square, and the Jaccard Coefficient are all statistically significant at $p < 0.01$.

[a]We ignore self-designations as an influential legislator because we exclude the possibility of "self-friendship" ties.

are friends who derive their influence from informal sources. Thus friends constitute 13 percent of the colleagues to whom informal influence is attributed in the pre-term-limits House. Over time this increases to 28 percent in the 2003 House, more than double its pre-term-limits proportion. This trend is especially worth noting given the general decline in informal influence. Based on this, we conclude that friendship and informal influence are more closely intertwined in the House after term limits.

Probably due to its smaller size, the Senate is a friendlier chamber than the House, especially prior to term limits. Influence in the upper chamber is relative stable across the three sessions. But we find that formal leaders are a much larger proportion of influential friends—67 percent in the 1999 pre-term-limits Senate session. Friendships with formal leaders, however, decline dramatically after term limits, to 44 percent in the 2007 Senate. If we ignore the transitional Senate session (2003), treating it as an outlier, we find that friends with informal influence form a larger proportion of senators' influential friends, rising from 20 percent to 33 percent after term limits. Once again, we conclude that friendship and informal influence are interwoven after term limits.

This analysis reveals that in both chambers friendship is an increasingly important component of informal influence after term limits. So it appears that many of our post-term-limits respondents consider their friends to be influential, whether they have expertise or can realistically affect policy or not. The size of the increases we find in the House indicates a tendency for less experienced legislators to accord to people that they trust (aka friends) more influence than one would expect for those friends' level of expertise or their role in the chamber. This link between friendship and influence reinforces evidence presented earlier in this chapter that referent sources of influence become more important in the Senate after term limits.

Correlations between Issue Consulting and Influence Matrices

As we noted previously, Francis (1962) discovers that substantive expertise can translate into general influence in state legislative chambers. Meyer (1980) on the other hand finds that seniority and position predict influence, empirically, while issue expertise does not. We have only two issues with which to test the link between issue expertise and influence, school choice and LRHCP. Yet comparing consulting about these issues across time allows us to search for factors that might affect the association between expertise and influence.

By correlating the influence matrix with each of these consulting matrices, we can determine whether a respondent identified a specific colleague as both influential and an expert he or she consults about these issues. As we see in table 9.5, an increase in the House and a very slight decrease in the Senate in the association between colleagues designated both as influential and as a source consulted about school choice.

In chapter 8 we correlated the friendship and school choice consulting matrices. Comparing those analyses with the ones we examine in this chapter, we find that the relationship between influence and school choice consulting is much weaker than the association between friendship and school choice consulting. This indicates that legislators rely upon their friends more than on colleagues with influence when they seek information about a floor vote on school choice, especially in the lower chamber.

There is a very weak, and not always statistically significant, relationship between influence and consulting about LRHCP. In the 2007 Senate this relationship dissipates and is no longer statistically significant. Looking back to chapter 8, we find that the association between friendship and consulting about LRHCP is stronger than the relationship between influence and consulting about LRHCP. Moreover, both friendship and influence are more weakly associated with consulting about this technical issue compared to the politically salient issue, school choice. We conclude that expertise on the technically complex issue, LRHCP, is not associated with general influence. Moreover, our findings in this section support evidence that expertise has decreased as a source of informal influence in the House.

The Evolution of Influence across Time

Francis (1962) argues that both issue-specific expertise and social interaction (i.e., friendship) can evolve into general influence over time. In this section, we investigate the temporal order of these relationships. To do this, we rely once again on our repeat respondents. We consider whether influence is a leading indicator of the amount of consulting on school choice and on LRHCP directed toward a legislator in the next session. Then we test the converse relationship—whether the amount of consulting on an issue is a leading indicator of subsequent influence.

We provided information about our repeat respondents at several points in earlier chapters, so we refer readers back to chapters 4, 7, and 8 for details of our approach. We note here merely that we have data from two interviews for 150 legislators and three interviews for 91 legislators.

TABLE 9.5. Correlation between Influence Networks

A. Correlation between Influence Networks and Floor Vote Consulting about School Choice

Chamber and Session	Correlation	Chi-Square	Jaccard Coefficient	Jaccard Average 2,500 Permutations	Number of Influential Colleagues	Number of Colleagues Consulted	Influential Colleagues Consulted	Influential Colleagues Consulted (%)	Respondents
House									
1997	0.08	83.50	0.05	0.01	660	175	37	6	95
1999	0.10	107.89	0.06	0.01	414	195	33	8	93
2001	0.10	107.98	0.06	0.01	496	180	35	7	93
2003	0.11	144.81	0.06	0.01	395	141	30	8	89
Senate									
1999	0.18	46.15	0.10	0.02	134	39	16	12	35
2003	0.16	36.21	0.09	0.02	114	33	12	11	28
2007	0.14	28.72	0.08	0.02	121	36	12	10	27

Note: Values for Chi-square and the Jaccard Coefficient are all statistically significant at $p < 0.01$ for school choice.

B. Correlation between Influence Networks and Floor Vote Consulting about LRHCP

Chamber and Session	Correlation	Chi-Square	Jaccard Coefficient	Jaccard Average 2,500 Permutations	Number of Influential Colleagues	Number of Colleagues Consulted	Influential Colleagues Consulted	Influential Colleagues Consulted (%)	Respondents
House									
1997	0.04	14.57	0.02	0.01	660	119	16	2	95
1999	0.04	20.33	0.03	0.01	414	162	16	4	93
2001[a]	0.03	12.97	0.03	0.01	496	195	18	4	93
2003	0.07	64.43	0.04	0.01	395	135	21	5	89
Senate									
1999	0.11	16.91	0.06	0.02	134	33	10	7	35
2003	0.10	15.03	0.07	0.02	114	41	10	9	28
2007[b]	0.03	1.03	0.03	0.02	121	38	5	4	27

Note: In the House and Senate sessions, values for the correlations, Chi-square, and the Jaccard Coefficient are all statistically significant at $p \leq 0.05$, except for the 2001 House.
[a]In the 2001 House session, statistical significance is $p = 0.08$.
[b]For consulting about LRHCP, there is no statistically significant correlation with the influence network in the 2007 Senate.

These small numbers make it difficult to achieve statistical significance, but our models generally perform well, as we report in tables 9.6 and 9.7. And several independent variables provide valuable insights into the relationship between expertise, friendship, and influence.

The Evolution of Issue Expertise across Time

Table 9.6 presents results for two dependent variables: (1) normalized indegrees for school choice (consulting on school choice) and (2) normalized indegrees for LRHCP (consulting on LRHCP). The three independent variables we are most interested in are the normalized indegrees for influence and for the two consulting relationships during the previous session. We want to know if they are leading indicators of future consulting or future influence. We also control for the effect of holding a top chamber leadership position, membership in the opposition party, and shifting chambers between the two sessions, and whether the respondent is from the cohort elected after term limits purged the veterans from the chamber (*PostTL*). We consider this latter variable important because legislators who served with the veterans were socialized into an institutional structure composed of stable, well-established relationships. Therefore, we are especially interested in the interaction between each of the three lagged relationship variables (influence and the two consulting relationships) and this *PostTL* cohort.

Our key finding is that issue expertise (measured as being consulted about the issue) accumulates across time. Thus being consulted leads to being consulted more on the same issue. Being more influential does not lead to more consulting on either of the two issues we consider here. In fact, we find some evidence that being more influential can reduce the amount a legislator is consulted about an issue.

Two control variables exhibit effects that are interesting in their own right and provide insight into the effects of term limits, as we discuss below. By the time of interview three, legislators seem to rely more on their current chamber leaders for advice on both these issues. This is not true at the time of interview two. Leaders seem to become increasingly important sources of information as term limits unfold, but these are leaders in the same session as the consulting. This finding is consistent with evidence we presented earlier in the chapter, that legitimate sources of influence play a larger role in chamber influence after term limits.

When a legislator shifts between interviews one and two from the House to the Senate consulting about LRHCP decreases, but it increases

TABLE 9.6. Relationships between Influence and Consulting across Time

Dependent Variable: Normalized Indegrees	School Choice (SC) Consulting 2nd Interview				LRHCP Consulting 2nd Interview			
Independent Variables for First Session 150 Valid Cases	B	Std. Error	t	sig.	B	Std. Error	t	sig.
First elected after term limits (postTL)	**-1.10**	0.61	-1.81	.07	-0.36	0.70	-0.5	.60
Moved to other chamber in time 2	-0.5	0.82	-0.64	.53	**-1.57**	0.94	-1.7	.10
Holds top leadership position time 2	1.30	0.98	1.33	.19	-0.76	1.12	-0.7	.50
Member of the opposition party time 2	-0.1	0.49	-0.11	.91	0.01	0.56	0.02	.98
Normalized indegrees SC consulting	**0.63**	0.20	3.12	.00	0.15	0.23	0.65	.52
Interaction postTL and SC consulting	0.29	0.23	1.24	.22	-0.28	0.27	-1.1	.29
Normalized indegrees LRHCP consulting	-0.1	0.17	-0.66	.51	**0.48**	0.19	2.49	.01
Interaction postTL and LRHCP consulting	0.07	0.18	0.41	.68	**0.48**	0.20	2.39	.02
Normalized indegrees for influence	**-0.2**	0.09	-2.17	.03	-0.02	0.10	-0.2	.85
Interaction postTL and influence	-0	0.14	-0.24	.81	0.09	0.16	0.58	.56
Constant	**1.89**	0.56	3.33	.00	**1.09**	0.65	1.69	.09
Adjusted R^2	0.31				0.62			
F-statistic	7.83				24.77			

Dependent Variable: Normalized Indegrees	School Choice (SC) Consulting 3rd Interview				LRHCP Consulting 3rd Interview			
Independent Variables for Second Session 91 Valid Cases	B	Std. Error	t	sig.	B	Std. Error	t	sig.
First elected after term limits (postTL)	0.58	0.66	0.88	.38	-0.84	1.23	-0.7	.50
Moved to other chamber in time 3	0.05	0.65	0.08	.94	**2.15**	1.22	1.77	.08
Holds top leadership position time 3	**1.81**	0.94	1.92	.06	**5.66**	1.76	3.22	.00
Member of the opposition party time 3	**0.94**	0.54	1.75	.09	-0.16	1.00	-0.2	.88
Normalized indegrees SC consulting	**0.62**	0.09	6.74	.00	-0.02	0.17	-0.1	.93
Interaction postTL and SC consulting	**0.85**	0.13	6.56	.00	-0.03	0.24	-0.1	.91
Normalized indegrees LRHCP consulting	0.01	0.17	0.07	.95	**0.87**	0.32	2.73	.01
Interaction postTL and LRHCP consulting	0.00	0.18	0.02	.99	0.27	0.33	0.81	.42
Normalized indegrees for influence	0.06	0.08	0.70	.48	**-0.25**	0.15	-1.7	.09
Interaction postTL and influence	-0.1	0.08	-0.87	.39	0.19	0.15	1.29	.20
Constant	-0.6	0.61	-0.96	.34	0.78	1.14	0.68	.50
Adjusted R^2	0.78				0.60			
F-statistic	32				14.30			

Note: Bold type indicates statistically significant coefficients.

if the shift occurs between interviews two and three. These mixed results of shifting chambers for consulting about LRHCP could reflect the transition to term limits. Many of our repeat respondents who shifted chambers between interviews one and two were House veterans moving to a Senate still controlled by veterans. Highly consulted experts in the House arriving in the Senate would have had to compete with experts among veteran senators. The increase in consulting on LRHCP that we find for shifting chambers between the second and third interview suggests that as term limits are implemented senators bring some of their consulting relationships with them as they migrate across the capitol dome. But this appears to apply only for the technically complex issue of LRHCP. Shifting to the Senate has no effect on school choice consulting.

The Evolution of Friendship and Influence

Next we examine the chicken and egg question of whether influence begets friendship or vice versa. We also explore the effect of being consulted about school choice and LRHCP on influence and on friendship. To do this, we test models of friendship and influence for two pairs of interview responses. The dependent variables are (1) normalized indegrees for influence and (2) normalized indegrees for friendship. Independent variables and control variables are the same as those we used in the previous section to explore the evolution of consulting about school choice and LRHCP with two additions—a lagged variable for friendship and also the interaction between friendship and being elected after term limits.

Influence

Results presented in table 9.7 indicate that influence becomes ephemeral after term limits. We find that influence during interview one is a leading indicator of influence at interview two, but this is not true between interviews two and three. As we have demonstrated throughout this chapter, legislators elected after term limits are perceived as less influential generally. But we were still surprised to find that influence at interview two is not a leading indicator of influence at interview three. We conclude that term limits disrupt the accumulation of general influence from one session to the next.

Moreover, influence after term limits appears to accrue from holding a position rather than from influence adhering to an individual legislator. We base this on two pieces of evidence. First, influence does not appear to fol-

TABLE ?.?. Relationships between Influence and Friendship across Time

Dependent Variable: Normalized Indegrees	Influence 2nd Interview				Friendship 2nd Interview			
Independent Variables for First Session, 150 Valid Cases	B	Std. Error	t	sig.	B	Std. Error	t	sig.
First elected after term limits (PostTL)	**-3.55**	1.78	-1.99	.05	**-1.37**	0.76	-1.80	.07
Moved to the other chamber at time 2	-1.36	1.61	-0.84	.40	-0.74	0.69	-1.07	.29
Holds top leadership position at Time 2	**21.72**	2.05	10.57	.00	0.57	0.88	0.65	.52
Member of the opposition party at time 2	**-3.27**	1.02	-3.20	.00	-0.33	0.44	-0.75	.45
Normalized indegrees SC consulting	**0.68**	0.42	1.64	.10	-0.02	0.18	-0.11	.91
Interaction postTL and SC consulting	-0.21	0.47	-0.44	.66	0.19	0.20	0.94	.35
Normalized indegrees LRHCP consulting	-0.04	0.34	-0.12	.90	0.10	0.15	0.67	.50
Interaction postTL and LRHCP consulting	0.09	0.35	0.26	.80	-0.08	0.15	-0.52	.61
Normalized indegrees for influence	**0.32**	0.20	1.64	.10	-0.04	0.08	-0.45	.66
Interaction postTL and influence	**0.95**	0.31	3.05	.00	0.11	0.13	0.85	.40
Normalized indegrees for friendship	-0.15	0.29	-0.51	.61	**0.40**	0.13	3.21	.00
Interaction postTL and friendship	0.29	0.41	0.71	.48	0.18	0.17	1.04	.30
Constant	**4.99**	1.42	3.51	.00	**3.24**	0.61	5.33	.00
Adjusted R^2	0.65				0.25			
F-statistic	24.13				5.06			

Dependent Variable: Normalized Indegrees	Influence 3rd Interview				Friendship 3rd Interview			
Independent Variables for Second Session, 91 Valid Cases	B	Std. Error	t	sig.	B	Std. Error	t	sig.
First Elected after Term Limits (PostTL)	**-6.65**	2.90	-2.29	.02	-2.05	1.46	-1.40	.16
Moved to the Other Chamber at Time 3	0.50	1.93	0.26	.79	**2.15**	0.97	2.21	.03
Holds Top Leadership Position at Time 3	**31.43**	2.84	11.05	.00	**6.95**	1.43	4.85	.00
Member of the Opposition Party at Time 3	-0.58	1.60	-0.36	.72	-0.02	0.81	-0.03	.98
Normalized Indegrees SC Consulting	-0.01	0.27	-0.04	.97	0.00	0.14	0.03	.98
Interaction PostTL and SC Consulting	0.50	0.39	1.30	.20	**0.35**	0.19	1.82	.07
Normalized Indegrees LRHCP Consulting	-0.11	0.50	-0.21	.84	-0.05	0.25	-0.18	.86
Interaction PostTL and LRHCP Consulting	0.39	0.53	0.73	.47	0.14	0.27	0.53	.60
Normalized Indegrees for Influence	0.21	0.24	0.89	.37	**-0.20**	0.12	-1.67	.10
Interaction PostTL and Influence	0.04	0.25	0.14	.89	**0.25**	0.13	1.99	.05
Normalized Indegrees for Friendship	**-0.82**	0.46	-1.80	.08	0.35	0.23	1.52	.13
Interaction PostTL and Friendship	**1.24**	0.60	2.06	.04	-0.02	0.30	-0.07	.94
Constant	**6.18**	2.38	2.60	.01	**3.45**	1.20	2.88	.01
Adjusted R^2	0.71				0.37			
F-statistic	19.20				5.31			

Note: Bold type indicates statistically significant coefficients.

low a legislator when he or she shifts chambers. Second, holding a formal leadership position predicts influence in both pairs of interviews, but the effects become stronger as we move from the first pair of interviews to the second pair. This supports evidence presented elsewhere in this chapter that holding a formal position is an increasingly important predictor of influence as term limits are implemented. To be clear, this is a formal leadership position during the same interview period as the dependent variable. It is a one-time effect, not a leading indicator of future influence.

Additionally we find that being consulted about a politically salient issue can be a leading indicator of general influence. That we find this for relationships between interviews one and two, but not for interviews two and three, suggests that as term limits are more fully implemented, they disrupt the evolution of this issue-specific expertise into general influence. Taken together, our findings about the accumulation of general influence, issue-specific expertise, and the importance of leadership positions imply that term limits alter the evolution of influence in Michigan's legislature.

Further illuminating this new pattern, we find that friendship is transformed into influence between the second and third interviews. This is consistent with evidence presented earlier in this chapter that legislators are more likely to view their friends as influential as term limits are more fully implemented. Influence derived from personal qualities (referent influence) appears to replace expertise as a source of influence as term limits are more fully implemented. But this is true only for the cohort of legislators elected after term limits. Friendship reduces influence among those elected before term limits.

Friendship

Results presented in table 9.7 indicate that as term limits are more fully implemented friendship ceases to be a leading indicator of subsequent friendship. Friends in the second interview are not a leading indicator of having more friends in the third interview, yet this association existed between the first and second interviews. Possibly with high turnover one's friends leave and popularity becomes ephemeral, just as we found for influence.

After term limits, consulting on a politically salient issue can result in friendship. We find that consulting on school choice at interview two is related to friendship at interview three. Again, this is not the pattern we found for interviews one and two, suggesting that as term limits become more fully implemented the evolution of expertise into friendship escalates. We found in chapter 8 that the converse is not true—friendship is not a leading indicator of school choice consulting. Thus, we speculate that gratitude for help sorting out a politically risky issue spawns friendship. It appears that the political salience of the issue is an important ingredient of the relationship between friendship and issue expertise because we find no effect on friendship from being consulted about the technically complex issue of LRHCP.

The relationship between general influence and friendship is more complicated. We find support for Francis's (1962) work suggesting the social interaction leads to general influence, but only for legislators first elected after term limits. For the cohort elected prior to term limits, influence in interview two seems to depress friendship in interview three. We add to this evidence that formal leaders are quite popular as term limits become more fully implemented—those holding leadership positions during interview three. Thus influence is not a leading indicator of future friendship, yet legislators holding formal positions are popular in that moment, suggesting once again that the position, not the person, wields influence.

Legislators elected before term limits seem to partition influence and friendship—neither is a leading indicator of the other. But after term limits, the relationships become symbiotic. Friendship in interview two is a leading indicator of influence in interview three and vice versa. Yet the relation is much stronger when we use friendship to predict influence, indicating that friendship is more important for accumulating influence than is influence in accumulating friends. After term limits, legislators seeking influence would be advised to make a lot of friends and to develop expertise about politically salient issues.

Conclusions

Fenno (1973) finds that gaining influence is one of the overarching goals of U.S. House members. In this chapter we probe factors that affect Michigan's legislators' efforts to fulfill this goal. In their quest these legislators, especially those in the lower chamber, encounter a dwindling reservoir of influence, a changing distribution of influence, and different paths to acquiring influence.

Not only does overall influence wane in the House, the decline there disproportionately reduces informal influence. The remaining influence in the House becomes more concentrated in the hands of the chamber leaders, not more evenly distributed. Although the Senate retains more of its pre-term-limits volume and distribution of influence, formal positions become much more promising paths to acquiring influence in the upper chamber as well. This means that the best way to gain influence after term limits in both chambers is to hold a formal position.

There are several other indications that holding a leadership position is a more important source of influence, especially in the House. For example, when we explore the evolution of influence across legislators' sessions of service, the control variable for holding a top leadership position is overwhelmingly the most powerful variable in the model, and its effect increases as Michigan moves further down the term-limits implementation path. Yet influence in one session is not necessarily a leading indicator of future influence. Influence in the post-term-limits legislature appears fleeting, tied to formal positions that legislators occupy briefly. It dissipates even by the subsequent legislative session. In short, the rules of the game change after term limits, especially in the lower chamber.

Prior to term limits legislators in both chambers could gain influence through expertise just as well as through holding official positions. Although this alternative source of influence is less commonly mentioned after term limits, it is still important. As we discussed in this chapter, school choice expertise is a leading indicator of future influence after term limits. And even after term limits, expertise is still the second most frequently mentioned source of influence in both chambers, although it is no longer mentioned by the same proportion of respondents.

This decline in expertise as a source of influence is noteworthy because a legislature can benefit from a multitude of experts. Expertise is non-zero sum. Legitimate influence on the other hand inheres in a handful of formal positions. Competition for those is a zero-sum game. To the extent that formal roles become an increasingly dominant source of influence, the potential to expand a legislative chamber's total volume of influence is constrained. This is consistent with the decline in the volume of influence we find in the House. We were often told by respondents who served before and after term limits that the legislature, especially the House, lost influence in state government more generally after term limits. This could weaken the chamber with respect to other actors, including interest groups, lobbyists, and the executive branch, which we discuss in chapter 11.

Positive personal qualities provide another viable path to influence. Being respected and admired by one's colleagues (i.e., referent influence) is increasingly important for senators seeking influence after term limits, and it remains an important way to acquire influence in the House, too. This is demonstrated both by open-ended comments and an increasing willingness of post-term-limits legislators to attribute influence to their friends even when they hold no formal position in the chamber. This could, however, lead to a conflation of friendship and influence. That is to say, we find that post-term-limits legislators may believe that their friends are more influential than they objectively are. For legislators elected after term limits, friendship and influence are positive leading indicators of each other, so the relationship appears symbiotic. But the effect is larger for friendship as a leading indicator of influence compared to influence as a leading indicator of friendship.[6] Further, expertise on a politically salient issue can build friendship, which might be transformed into general influence, time permitting. So cultivating friends appears to be an increasingly astute move in the new influence game, second only to holding a formal position.

Two other sources of influence, coercion and rewards (often perquisites of formal positions) increasingly offer alternative paths to influence in the post-term-limits House. In the Senate, coercion is no longer a probable path toward influence, but rewards maintain their value as assets for amassing influence. The rewards most often mentioned involved reelection help and appointment to committee and second-tier leadership positions within the chambers (such as speaker pro tempore). The increase in rewards as a source of influence makes allegations that chair positions are "for sale" especially alarming. In addition to the stories we related earlier in the chapter, it was rumored that a Michigan millionaire bought a chair position for a legislator. If this is the whole story, the implications are alarming, and it further challenges the ability of term limits to sever ties between wealthy donors and politicians. This use of rewards means that moneyed interests both within and outside the chamber have more, not less, leverage in the new influence game if they can buy these rewards for their preferred legislator. We remind readers that organized groups more actively recruit candidates to run for office after term limits. If interest groups help legislators acquire formal positions from caucus leaders in exchange for donations, interest group recruiting efforts would be even more persuasive.

The changes in the sources and distribution of influence that we discovered in this chapter encourage chamber leaders to behave differently than they did before term limits. In chapter 10 we consider some of the ways formal leaders, the winners in this new system, use their influence.

TEN

Chamber Leaders and Committee Chairs

How do newcomers decide who to choose for caucus leadership positions, and what difference do these choices make? Caucus leaders typically wield substantial control over the work of state legislatures through the official prerogatives of their positions (Francis 1985; Hamm, Hedlund, and Martorano 2006). As we reported in the chapter 9, these leaders are increasingly influential after term limits. Although much of their influence flows from the positions they hold (i.e., legitimate power), some leaders are described by their colleagues as knowledgeable experts, as exhibiting admirable personal qualities, and as intimidating or generous in dispensing perks (interview notes).

We begin this chapter by examining the factors legislators consider when deciding who to elect to these positions. Given the influence of Michigan's chamber leaders (Francis 1989; Battista 2011), we see their behavior as vital to the work of state government. In Michigan each chamber votes for candidates running for leadership positions in November almost immediately after the general election and before newly elected legislators are sworn in to office. Given the timing of this vote, we are especially curious about how newcomers in the House decide whom to support in these intrachamber elections when they have very little time to get to know the candidates for these positions. We discover that they prefer a new breed of legislative leader, but that they should be careful what they wish for given their complaints about their leaders.

One of the crucial prerogatives of top leaders is selecting committee chairs and minority vice chairs. The choices legislators make in selecting their top leaders ripple through to the next level of leaders—committee chairs. In this chapter we also examine the types of committee chairs the new breed of legislative leaders select. To do this we explore legislators' perceptions of committee chairs by assessing the amount of control chairs have over the work of their committees, the sources of conflict in committees, and the chairs' approaches to dealing with that conflict.

Finally, we examine whether post-term-limits leaders have more or less influence on key decisions about a pair of important issues—school choice and LRHCP. In our interviews we ask chamber leaders to explain where they believe the most important decisions are made about a bill on each of these issues. This is a self-assessment by leaders of their influence over the legislative process.

As Barber (1965) points out, leaders want conformity from their caucus, while legislators want rewards for their compliance. This exchange establishes an opportunity for legislative leaders to use both rewards and coercion. We established in chapter 9 that chamber leaders' use of rewards, and in the House coercion, expands after term limits. For example, caucus leaders use their prerogative to distribute or withhold party campaign funds.[1] Caucus leaders can also induce a recalcitrant colleague to comply by proffering rewards (such as pork for the district, trading "bad" committee assignments for "good" ones, naming the legislator as the sponsor of a bill) or by removing valued perks (taking away an assigned parking space, cutting funds for a legislator's personal staff, removing a legislator from a committee). Use of these specific rewards and sanctions were described to us by interview respondents. We anticipate that term limits will alter the behavior of leaders, chairs, and rank-and-file legislators with respect to these exchanges. For example, in this chapter we examine whether newcomers and lame ducks react differently to threatened sanctions or promised rewards.

We envision another effect of term limits on leadership. Shortening the time that legislative leaders can hold their positions, as term limits do, could enhance their use of harsher tactics to gain compliance from rank and file legislators. When legislators serve together for decades, rank-and-file legislators can hold their leaders accountable for their behaviors, potentially supporting another candidate for their caucus position. Without the option to run for reelection to their leadership position, it seems plausible that term-limited leaders might punish rogue caucus members more harshly and renege on promised rewards more freely.

Term limits establish a known endpoint in what would otherwise be a long-term balance of power between rank-and-file legislators and their leaders. When there is a known endpoint to a "game," some game theory models suggest that there is an incentive to defect (Axelrod1984). With an endpoint on the tenure of their leaders, rank-and-file legislators are poorly positioned to hold lame duck leaders accountable after term limits. Actions of leaders may be less constrained, but also the rewards and threats of leaders may matter less to lame ducks whose ranks swell with term limits. Both dynamics imply that the relationship between leaders and followers will change with term limits. We anticipate that this change in the structure of the leadership "game" will have far-reaching consequences for both leaders and followers in term-limited legislatures.

The Michigan Context

In Michigan, caucus leaders have broad powers to affect the behavior of their colleagues (Hamm, Hedlund, and Martorano 1999, 2006), making Michigan once again an ideal setting in which to examine the effects of term limits on leaders. The House speaker and Senate majority leader assign all members of their respective chambers to committees in proportion to the parties' seats in the chamber. As a courtesy, they may accept input from the chambers' minority leader on committee assignments for minority party members. Chamber leaders also consider requests for committee assignments by members of their own party. But officially the speaker can assign or reassign any members at any time to any committees or remove any member at any time from any committees.

The full chamber does not consider a bill unless a majority of the committee supports it, and the chamber's leader wants to schedule a floor vote, except in exceedingly rare cases of parliamentary maneuvers. Thus, committee chairs act as gatekeepers deciding whether to take up a bill or not. But chamber leaders assign bills to committees and can reassign a bill to another committee if a chair fails to move it or if a majority on the committee does not support it. So the House speaker and Senate majority leader can send bills to unfriendly committees in order to squelch them or to friendly committees to ensure smooth progress or refuse to schedule a floor vote for a bill. In short, Michigan's legislative leaders have an extensive array of tools at their disposal. They can and do use these tools, according to our respondents. For example, we were told that during one House session, the speaker reassigned education bills to the Commerce Committee when Education Committee members did not comply with his wishes (interview notes).

Data and Methods

In our interviews we asked our respondents how they decide on which colleague to support for caucus leadership positions. The exact wording of this open-ended question appears in appendix A, question 19. If respondents omitted the qualities they sought in a leader (for example, some legislators responded by saying simply that they voted for the candidate who would win or they did not feel they had a choice), we probed to determine what qualities legislators want in their leaders. To analyze these data, we code these qualities (or reasons for support) into categories, and we also constructed a series of binary variables based on whether a respondent mentioned specific qualities. Then we use cluster analysis to combine the binary variables, linking them to legislative leadership styles described in an extensive literature on this subject. We provide further details on our methods when we present the results of this analysis.

Also in the interviews, we asked our respondents to assess the chair's control over a committee on which the respondent served. Respondents were given a five-point response scale anchored at the ends by "none" and "an enormous amount." This is question 13 in appendix A. We then asked why the respondent attributed this amount of control to the chair. Respondents typically described behaviors or actions of the chair such as doesn't take up a bill unless (s)he wants to, determines the calendar, or sets the committee agenda. We code these open-ended responses into categories for analysis, and we also classified these using categories adapted from French and Raven's (1959) work, described in detail in chapter 9. Here again, we stick to the terminology we used in our interview questions, referring to committee chairs as *controlling* the work of their committee, but we acknowledge that this blurs distinctions between related concepts, such as power and influence.

The next two questions in the interview, questions 14 and 15 in appendix A, also probe the work of committee chairs. Question 14 asks, "How much conflict would you say there is on the current [____] committee?" The follow-up question asks about the sources of this conflict. Then question 15 asks "How is this conflict dealt with?" In this chapter, we analyze both the scaled responses to question 14 and the open-ended responses to the follow-up and to question 15.

We also consider the perspective of the chamber leaders about the distribution of influence in the legislative process. To do this we asked chamber leaders about where the most important decisions about a particular bill are made. We provided a list of responses, decision-making loci (e.g., in the committee, in the governor's office, and so on), but we also accepted any other responses these leaders provided.

Selecting Caucus Leaders

There is ample evidence that the quality of leadership affects legislatures (Francis 1989; Hamm 1982; Jewell and Whicker 1994). So it is not surprising that many scholars classify legislative leadership styles. Rohdes (1991) divides leaders into two categories: bosses, who control the chamber, versus agents, who serve the interests of colleagues in a principal-agent relationship. Patterson (1963), building on Truman's (1959) middleman hypothesis, describes legislative leaders as brokers, who are likely to act either as agents, building a consensus within the caucus or coordinating factions, or extremists, who would be more ideologically driven and seek to command loyalty to achieve a party's or a faction's agenda (similar to Rohdes's bosses). He finds that empirically leaders mix and match styles. Jewell and Whicker (1994) expand this discussion to include three leadership styles: commanding, coordinating, and consensus building. They find that the command style is more prevalent in less professional chambers and that a coordinating or consensus building style is favored in more professional chambers.

Considering the other side of the relationship, Blanchard et al. (1999) focus on followers' characteristics in their popularized treatment of leadership. They recommend that leaders adjust their actions to followers' levels of competence and commitment. These authors combine these characteristics in a 2 x 2 table that leaders can use to assess whether their followers are likely to respond to *delegating* (highly competent/highly committed followers), *coaching* (highly competent/less committed followers), *supporting* (less competent/highly committed followers), or *directing* (less competent/less committed followers). This typology is useful for our analysis because these characteristics of followers change with term limits.

After term limits, it seems likely that inexperienced followers are less competent legislators (although they may bring other unique skills and backgrounds to the chamber). This means that leaders should choose either directing or supporting behaviors, depending on the level of commitment evidenced by their troops.

Post-term-limits legislators' range of commitment is harder to estimate. As we report in chapter 2, many are politically ambitious, so their commitment initially is likely to be high. But this commitment may be egocentric—focused on their own career path rather than oriented toward helping their caucus, their political party, their district, or the state. The most experienced followers after term limits are also likely to be lame ducks. As the end of their tenure approaches and they begin to recognize the limited opportunities available for them to continue in any elected office, even politically ambitious legislators' commitment may plummet. Therefore, the commitment of the most competent followers is suspect, and leaders would be advised by Blanchard et al. (1999) to adopt a coaching style. We investigate the prevalence of directing, supporting, and coaching behaviors in our analyses.

We also rely upon Jewell and Whicker's (1994) three leadership styles to classify leadership traits. To distinguish more clearly between these styles, we pair them with the actions described by Blanchard and his coauthors (1999): commander/directing, coordinator/supporting, and consensus builder/coaching. We omit delegating, which is recommended to leaders of motivated experts (Blanchard et al. 1999) because Jewell and Whicker did not identify a legislative leadership style that corresponds to delegating even without term limits.

To begin our analysis of leadership, we classify our respondents' comments into 11 reasons for supporting party leaders. We created these reasons by classifying detailed coding of open-ended responses into broader categories of similar comments. Additionally, we group these 11 reasons into the three styles of leadership that we distilled from the work of other scholars described above. We perceive a conceptual linkage between a handful of the 11 reasons and the three leadership style categories. For example, we see a clear association between a commander/directing leadership style and the reason, *Directive or Assertive*. Similarly we link *Negotiator* with a coordinating/supporting leadership style. But we see no obvious tie between some reasons, such as "Admirable Personal Qualities," and these leadership styles. Therefore, we turned to hierarchical cluster analysis. We created 11 dichotomous variables denoting whether a particular reason was or was not mentioned. Then we use Ward's method, which is especially well suited to binary data (Tamasauskas, Sakalauskas, and Kriksciuniene 2012) to cluster these variables into three groups based on their dispersion.

The reasons that clustered into the directing commander leadership style include *Directive or Assertive*, *External Caucus Builder* (which includes comments about keeping the caucus majority, media relations on behalf of the caucus and similar themes), *Experience or Achievements*, and *Political Philosophy*. The second cluster, which we see representing a supporting coordinator style of leadership, consists of *Negotiator*, *Internal Caucus Builder* (which includes comments about inclusiveness and listening to caucus members), *Personal Relationships*, and *Knowledge or Intelligence*. The final cluster, consensus building coach, is a plausible fit but not as intuitively resonant as the other two. The reasons in this final cluster are *Admirable Personal Qualities*, *Leadership Skills*, and a *Political Calculation* (who can win, which we infer means who can appeal to the factions needed to build a winning coalition—consensus building).

We then classified each respondent into one of these three leadership styles, commander (directing), coordinator (supporting), or consensus builder (coaching), based on whether the respondent provided one or more reasons that fell into one of these clusters and did not provide any reason that fell into the other two clusters. This is a stringent criterion. Therefore it is not surprising that many respondents supported a combination of leadership styles. To accommodate this, we create blended pairs (e.g., coordinating commander, coordinating consensus builder, or commanding consensus builder). We classify respondents into these categories if they provide one or more of the reasons that fell into each blended pair of leadership styles, but mentioned no reasons that fell into the third leadership style. Finally, a plurality of our respondents wants a bit of everything in a leadership candidate (i.e., they provide at least one reason that falls into each leadership style category). This produces seven categories of leadership style: three pure styles of commanding, coordinating, and consensus building; three blended pairs of styles of commanding/consensus builder, coordinating/commander, and coordinating/consensus builder; and one hybrid of all three styles.

Given that leaders are elected, there is considerable potential for legislators to select the kinds of leaders they desire—assuming that they are rational actors whose votes are well informed. Although in our analysis we assume that legislators seek the candidates most likely to fit their needs, many legislators may lack the information they need to vote rationally. Newcomers to the chamber vote in caucus leadership elections the week after they are elected—before being sworn in to office and based on little or no firsthand experience working with the leadership candidates. So, it is plausible that they cast uninformed votes.

This suggests that the reasons newcomers support leadership candidates might differ from veterans who have at least some familiarity with the candidates as well as the legislative process. Therefore, we distinguish between votes of newly elected legislators and their somewhat more experienced colleagues in our analyses. We also assume that the effects of newness will be concentrated in the lower chamber. Most senators, after all, do know who they are voting for even after term limits and have experience

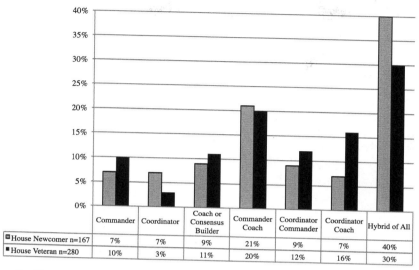

	Commander	Coordinator	Coach or Consensus Builder	Commander Coach	Coordinator Commander	Coordinator Coach	Hybrid of All
House Newcomer n=167	7%	7%	9%	21%	9%	7%	40%
House Veteran n=280	10%	3%	11%	20%	12%	16%	30%

Fig. 10.1. Leadership Style Preferred by Newcomers and Veterans

serving under at least one, probably more, chamber leaders. Therefore, we consider chamber effects in addition to newcomer effects in the analyses that follow.

Preferred Leadership Styles

Term limits themselves do not seem to affect leadership style preferences. But we find that newcomers in the House want different things from their leaders. We see in figure 10.1 that in the House 10 percent more newcomers than veterans seek a hybrid of all three styles. We combine this information with our finding that twice as many veterans as newcomers seek a coordinating coach, omitting the commanding style to conclude that veterans are more reluctant than newcomers about electing a commander who directs them. We infer from this that veterans know not only what they want but what they **do not** want in their leaders. And what they do not want is a directing commander. House freshmen on the other hand want everything in a leader, including a commander. Yet, as we explain later in this chapter, they should be careful what they wish for in their leaders.

The consensus building style is the most frequently mentioned of the three "pure" leadership styles. Yet it is mentioned only slightly more often than the commander style. And the *commanding coach* is the second most frequently mentioned leadership category. Nearly equal numbers of veterans and newcomers seek leaders with this style. So the preference to avoid a commander among veterans is far from universal. Yet, when we explore the individual reasons that we combined in the cluster analyses, it is clear that post-term-limits newcomers' preferences drive a shift toward more directive leaders.

Specific Reasons to Support Leadership Candidates

We want to understand more fully what aspects of directing commanders attract support from many legislative newcomers and some veterans, and we are concerned about losing important information by clustering 11 categories of reasons into only three leadership styles. Therefore, we report in table 10.1 the proportion of respondents who mention each of the 11 categories of reasons. We subdivide these reasons by chamber, by term limits, and by both chamber and term limits. In general our findings indicate that expectations about the role leaders should play evolve in both chambers after term limits. Only three of six term-limits differences are explained by the sizeable influx of newcomers. After term limits it appears that veterans also want different qualities in their leaders.

First, in table 10.1 we compare the qualities members of the two legislative chambers seek in leadership candidates. We find two key chamber differences. Senators care more about a leadership candidate's *Experience or Achievements* and *Intelligence or Knowledge*. A roughly 10 percent larger proportion of senators seek each of these two qualities in their leaders.

Next we combine the chambers to increase the number of responses when dividing our data into pre- and post-term-limits cohorts. Even though term limits do not change the mixture of the three leadership styles, we find that they do affect 6 of the 11 specific reasons for choosing a leader. Four qualities are sought more often and two less often after term limits. The two largest changes in the qualities legislators seek in their leaders both involve the caucus dynamics: an internal caucus builder and an external caucus builder.

After term limits legislators are looking for leaders who will listen to the caucus and are inclusive, qualities that we coded into the category *Internal Caucus Builder*. As we noted earlier, after term limits most leaders are lame ducks who cannot be held accountable through future leadership elections. So a leader's treatment of caucus members could be a problem, and it appears that more post-term-limits legislators consider this when choosing leaders. And when we separate the chambers, as we do in the bottom panel of table 10.1, this reason is especially salient for representatives.

We find an almost equally large change in the proportion of post-term-limits legislators who seek an *External Caucus Builder* as their leader—someone who enhances the public image of the caucus. If we look at the chamber separately, this change in the Senate is the largest change we find in any of our analysis of reasons to support leadership candidates—a 25 percent increase (from 21.9% to 46.9%). The salience of this reason among senators is surprising given that almost all senators have prior legislative experience in the House, and one might assume that they are less concerned about the political environment for their caucus during the next election cycle as the end of their permitted time in the legislature approaches. Perhaps politically ambitious senators see the welfare of

TABLE 10.1. Reasons for Supporting a Candidate for Party Leadership Positions

Reasons for Choice	House (n = 341)	Senate (n = 81)	Sig.	Pre-Limits (n = 121)	Post-Limits (n = 301)	Sig.
Internal Caucus Builder	40.2% (1)	34.6% (5)	0.35	**30.6% (4)**	**42.5% (1)**	0.02
Leadership Skills	39.3% (2)	33.3% (6)	0.32	39.7% (1)	37.5% (3)	0.68
External Caucus Builder	38.7% (3)	37.0% (3)	0.78	**30.6% (5)**	**41.5% (2)**	0.04
Admirable Traits	35.2% (4)	43.2% (1)	0.18	35.5% (2)	37.2% (4)	0.75
Political Calculation	34.6% (5)	35.8% (4)	0.84	28.9% (6)	37.2% (5)	0.11
Experience or Achievements	**30.5% (6)**	40.7% (2)	0.08	31.4% (3)	32.9% (6)	0.77
Political Philosophy	18.2% (7)	18.5% (8)	0.94	**26.4% (7)**	**15.0% (7)**	0.01
Personal Relationship	13.5% (8)	11.1% (9)	0.57	13.2% (9)	13.0% (10)	0.94
Negotiating Skills	12.3% (9)	9.9% (10)	0.54	**6.6% (10)**	**14.0% (8)**	0.04
Decisive or Assertive	12.0% (10)	9.9% (10)	0.57	**5.8% (11)**	**14.0% (8)**	0.02
Intelligence or Knowledge	**11.4% (11)**	**19.8% (7)**	0.05	17.4% (8)	11.3% (11)	0.10

	House Before (n = 89)	House After (n = 252)	Sig.	Senate Before (n = 32)	Senate After (n = 49)	Sig.
Internal Caucus Builder	**30.3% (4)**	**43.7% (1)**	0.03	31.3% (4)	36.7% (4)	0.61
Leadership Skills	41.6% (1)	38.5% (3)	0.61	34.4% (3)	32.7% (6)	0.87
External Caucus Builder	33.7% (3)	40.5% (2)	0.26	**21.9% (7)**	**46.9% (1)**	0.02
Admirable Traits	34.8% (2)	35.3% (5)	0.93	37.5% (2)	46.9% (1)	0.40
Political Calculation	29.2% (5)	36.5% (4)	0.21	28.1% (5)	40.8% (3)	0.24
Experience or Achievements	24.7% (7)	32.5% (6)	0.17	50.0% (1)	34.7% (5)	0.17
Political Philosophy	**27.0% (6)**	**15.1% (7)**	0.01	25.0% (6)	14.3% (8)	0.23
Personal Relationship	15.0% (9)	13.0% (10)	0.72	9.4% (9)	12.2% (9)	0.69
Negotiating Skills	**6.7% (10)**	**14.3% (8)**	0.06	6.3% (10)	12.2% (9)	0.38
Decisive or Assertive	**6.3% (11)**	**14.3% (8)**	**0.03**	6.3% (10)	12.2% (9)	0.38
Intelligence or Knowledge	15.7% (8)	9.9% (11)	0.14	22.0% (7)	18.4% (7)	0.70

Note: The values reported are percentages with rank order among reasons given in parentheses. Bold type indicates statistically significant differences.

the caucus as a partisan advantage that could be connected to their future political aspirations. Or as we see shortly, Senate newcomers are especially eager to win the coming final legislative election.

The other two qualities desired in post-term-limits leaders are negotiating skills and assertiveness. Both are important primarily among representatives after term limits, and we find shortly that this is especially true for House newcomers.

We also find evidence that *Intelligence or Knowledge* becomes a less important leadership quality after term limits. This is one of only two reasons mentioned by smaller proportions of respondents after term limits. (The other is political philosophy.) A merit-based leadership system was one of the promises term limits proponents made when soliciting voters' support for term limits (Yes on B campaign literature). And one would expect intelligence and knowledge to be key ingredients of merit. Therefore, we consider this to be further evidence refuting the promises made by term limits proponents.

We consider next whether newcomers and veterans differ in the qualities they seek in their leaders. When we look at table 10.2 we see that the preference for an external caucus builder is driven by newcomers. Newly elected senators who moved up from the House seem just as motivated as House newcomers to elect a leader who will enhance their political fortunes. That reelection is so important to these senators' contradicts another fundamental tenet of term limits (i.e., the apparently false assump-

TABLE 10.2. Newcomers' Reasons for Supporting a Candidate for Party Leadership Positions

	Both Chambers All Sessions			House Only		
Reasons for Choice	Veteran	Newcomer	Approx. Sig.	Veteran	Newcomer	Approx. Sig.
Internal Caucus Builder	36.1% (2)	43.7% (1)	0.12	39.3% (1)	41.5% (2)	0.69
Leadership Skills	35.7% (3)	41.9% (3)	0.20	37.9% (2)	41.5% (2)	0.50
External Caucus Builder	**34.9% (4)**	**43.7% (1)**	0.07	35.9% (3)	43.0% (1)	0.19
Admirable Traits	37.6% (1)	35.3% (5)	0.63	35.0% (4)	35.6% (5)	0.91
Political Calculation	32.5% (5)	38.3% (4)	0.22	32.5% (5)	37.8% (4)	0.32
Experience or Achievements	30.6% (6)	35.3% (5)	0.31	28.6% (6)	33.3% (6)	0.36
Political Philosophy	20.0% (7)	15.6% (7)	0.25	19.9% (7)	15.6% (8)	0.31
Personal Relationship	13.3% (8)	12.6% (11)	0.82	13.1% (8)	14.1% (10)	0.80
Negotiating Skills	**9.4% (10)**	**15.6% (8)**	0.06	10.2% (9)	15.6% (8)	0.14
Decisive or Assertive	**9.0% (11)**	**15.6% (9)**	0.04	**8.3% (11)**	**17.8% (7)**	0.01
Intelligence or Knowledge	11.8% (9)	15.0% (10)	0.34	9.7% (10)	14.1% (10)	0.22
Number of Respondents	255	167		206	135	

Note: Percentages with rank order in parentheses. Bold type indicates statistically significant differences.

tion that shorter tenure in office reduces reelection concerns). Senators' last term of service appears to be so highly valued that reelection concerns are paramount in their choice of a leader.

Further examining table 10.2 we see that a preference for a leader with negotiating skill distinguishes newcomers and veterans. We assume that all leadership candidates possessed this skill prior to term limits. It seems unlikely that a legislator would be a viable leadership candidate without being an accomplished negotiator during the era when one gradually moved up the leadership ladder. After term limits, however, some candidates may lack this skill. Veterans know who among their colleagues is a good negotiator, while newcomers would seek this information explicitly.

When we subdivide our data by chamber and newcomers, only one reason, *Decisive or Assertive*, is mentioned by a large enough proportion of House newcomers to be statistically significantly higher than other reasons. From this we deduce that this reason drives the newcomers to seek leaders with a commander style. Veterans in general, but House veterans especially, appear less enamored with decisive or assertive leaders, as we illustrate in both tables 10.1 and 10.2.

Legislative Committees and Their Chairs

Experienced veterans chaired committees in Michigan's legislature prior to term limits. Under term limits the most experienced House committee chairs can only amass four years or two sessions.[2] Thus, Michigan's term limits law clearly constrains the experience of chairs, who prior to term limits were experienced veterans. To put this into context, in the 1995–96 session, with Republicans in the majority, House chairs averaged 7.5 years of experience. The most seasoned chair in that session had served for 9 previous House sessions (18 years), and no freshman representatives chaired committees. Under Democratic control in the 1997–98 session, committee chairs averaged 8.9 years of prior service. In 1997–98 the most experienced chair had served for 13 previous sessions (26 years), and one freshman chaired a committee.

In stark contrast to these pre-term-limits levels of chair experience, with the advent of term limits in 1999–2000 House committee chairs averaged 1.9 years of prior service. In this first session after term limits, 11 freshmen representatives chaired committees. In the Senate, however, legislators can have amassed up to 6 years of service in the House. So even when post-term-limits newcomers to the Senate chair a committee, they are likely to have at least served on a committee before chairing one, attenuating this change in the upper chamber.

We find little empirical evidence in the scholarly literature on state legislatures about the behavior of freshman committee chairs because this occurs so rarely, especially in a highly professional legislature. In our own experience watching House committee hearings (Sarbaugh-Thompson 2010a), we observed instances in which post-term-limits chairs asked committee staff what to do next during hearings, were reminded by staff of missed procedural steps, and allowed lobbyists to walk around behind the legislators to converse with some committee members while other witnesses testified. Sometimes committee chairs walked into and out of the hearings while witnesses testified. In other words, some of these committee hearings seemed chaotic.

Based on our observations, pre-term-limits committee meetings chaired by veterans seem much more orderly. Chairs were not observed asking staff what to do, although chairs did occasionally adjourn to caucus with committee members from their party to craft a strategy before voting. Lobbyists stayed in their seats on their side of the room and waited for the chair to call upon them.

These observations are consistent with a growing consensus that term limits undermine the influence of committees or their chairs, or both. Comparing two term-limited states—Michigan and Maine—to two states without term limits—Pennsylvania and Delaware—Brake (2003) found that term-limited chamber leaders, among whom he counts chairs of major committees, lost influence. Moen and Palmer (2003) agree that committees lost power in Maine based on the larger number floor votes that diverge from committee recommendations after term limits.[3] Moen, Palmer, and Powell (2005) report that caucus leaders gained influence at the expense of Maine's traditionally weak committee chairs, supporting this with evidence that leaders initiated more major policy proposals after term limits, whereas before term limits committee chairs did more of this. Cain and Wright (2007) document plummeting committee chair experience in lower legislative chambers in the term-limited-states of California, Michigan, Maine, Arkansas, Ohio, and Colorado. They find no corresponding decline in chair experience in three non-term-limited states—Indiana, Illinois, and Kansas. So they conclude that the decline in chair experience is a term-limits effect, not part of a national trend. They report that inexperienced chairs in Colorado make "mistakes" and report that surveys of informed observers describe term-limited legislators as uninformed and inexperienced.

Control over the Work of the Committee

Based on this scholarship and our own evidence, we were not surprised to find that inexperienced chairs in the House lost some control over their work in Michigan after term limits. Respondents' assessment of House chairs' control over the work of a committee fell from a mean of 3.39 before term limits (about halfway between *A Lot* and *An Enormous Amount* on our five-point scales) to a mean of 2.99 (*A Lot*) after term limits (sig. at $p < 0.01$, F = 11.52). In the Senate the control exercised by committee chairs increased very slightly from 3.34 before term limits to 3.54 afterward—a minor difference.

Moreover, we find that the ranks of weak chairs swell in both chambers after term limits. About a quarter of House respondents before term limits said that the chair we asked about had little control over the work of the committee. This doubles to half of our House respondents after term limits (sig. $p < 0.01$). In the pre-term-limits Senate slightly less than one-third of respondents say that chairs exercise little control over the work of committees. This rises to half after term limits (sig. $p < 0.10$).

Next we explore the ways post-term-limits chairs either succeed or fail to control the work of their committees. We classified reasons respondents gave to explain their scaled response into categories using terms adapted from French and Raven's (1959) work. As part of our adaptation of these categories we also added two categories to explain how chairs lose control: *leaders usurp* control and *outsiders usurp* control.

As we noted earlier, institutional prerogatives give chairs many tools that they can use to control the work of their committee. For example, in Michigan committee chairs can decide not to hold hearings on a bill. Thus we see in figure 10.2 that much of a chair's control over the work of a committee flows from what we described in chapter 9 as legitimate sources of influence—the tools and prerogatives of a formal position. Oddly, legitimate influence appears to be a more important way for chairs in the upper chamber to control the work of their committee, despite the Michigan Senate's reputation as the more collegial chamber. And losses of legitimate influence are bigger in the Senate after term limits.

We consider our most important finding in figure 10.2 to be an increased use of coercion after term limits in both chambers. Forms of coercion become the second most frequently mentioned approach used by committee chairs after term limits—although it lags far behind legitimate influence. Before term limits we find that House chairs combined the legitimate authority of their position with rewards and positive personal qualities (referent sources of influence) to control the work of committees.

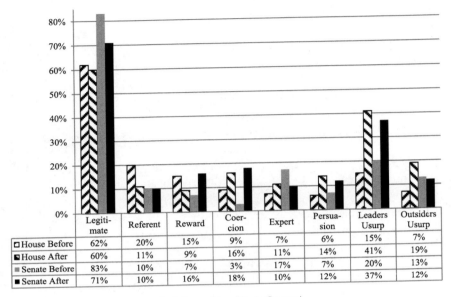

	Legiti-mate	Referent	Reward	Coer-cion	Expert	Persua-sion	Leaders Usurp	Outsiders Usurp
□ House Before	62%	20%	15%	9%	7%	6%	15%	7%
▨ House After	60%	11%	9%	16%	11%	14%	41%	19%
▪ Senate Before	83%	10%	7%	3%	17%	7%	20%	13%
▪ Senate After	71%	10%	16%	18%	10%	12%	37%	12%

Fig. 10.2. Reasons for Level of Committee Chair Control

After term limits House chairs rely slightly less on their legitimate influence, augmenting it with coercion and persuasion. This seems consistent with a more autocratic leadership style in the post-term-limits House. It also suggests a different relationship between leaders and followers that is consistent with concerns about internal caucus dynamics that our respondents revealed in their rationale for leadership choices.

After term limits Senate committee chairs also rely less on legitimate influence to exercise control over the work of their committees, increasingly supplementing it with rewards and coercion. Leaders here as well as in the House seem to intrude on the chairs' prerogatives more freely after term limits. Differences between the sources of influence used by chairs in the two chambers are more pronounced before term limits than afterward. This reinforces evidence that we presented in other chapters that the post-term-limits Senate resembles the House more closely than the pre-term-limits Senate did. Once again, changes that we find in the Senate indicate that lack of experience does not explain all the term limits changes we find. Socialization into the norms of the upper chamber appears to be a casualty of term limits.

The most frequently mentioned reason that chairs in both chambers fail to control the work of their committees is that the party's caucus leaders usurp their control. After term limits the proportion saying this nearly triples in the House, rising to 41 percent. In the Senate the increase is not quite double. This finding adds support to evidence presented earlier in this chapter that caucus leaders have a different relationship with their members after term limits. It appears that the shift toward more directive leaders is consequential. The behavior of leaders combined with the coercive tactics used more commonly by committee chairs paints an image of less collegiality in post-term-limits committees.

Another reason that House chairs appear to lose control over the work of their committee is that the governor or lobbyists or other outside interests interfere with the work of the committees. This comment increases substantively and statistically significantly in the House after term limits (sig. $p < 0.05$), but in the Senate it is virtually unchanged. This suggests that high turnover and lack of experience expose the lower chamber to outside influences, while the more experienced senators are better able to buffer their own internal processes. Here again, the oft repeated promise that term limits would sever the ties between special interests and legislators, freeing elected officials from undue influence, appears to produce the opposite outcome. Lack of experience appears to make the lower chamber more vulnerable to outside influences.

Conflict in Committees

Conflict can make it challenging for committee chairs to control the work of their committees, and it could elicit the aggressive tactics that we find some chairs adopting. Given that term limits decrease chair control of the work of committees, we expected a corresponding increase in the amount of conflict in committees, particularly in the lower chamber, especially with newcomers chairing committees. Contrary to our expectations, term limits appear to increase committee conflict in the Senate, but not in the House.

Prior to term limits, senators report less conflict in committees (mean 1.66) compared to the House (mean 2.14). After term limits the levels of conflict reported in the two chambers are nearly identical, 2.00 for the House and 2.07 for the Senate. The comity and courtesy that traditionally characterized the Senate declined, and the two chambers are equally contentious. Once again we find more change in the Senate than in the House, with the Senate after term limits resembling the House.[4]

To determine whether other variables might account for the differences in the chambers' responses to term limits, we tested a simple multivariate model of committee conflict, reported in table 10.3. We assumed that members of the chamber's minority party would report more conflict in committees, probably reflecting their struggle to thwart or modify the will of the majority party. They do. We thought, based on Fenno's (1973) discussion of Appropriations Committee members in the U.S. Congress (bomb throwers are avoided and team players are chosen)[5] that we should control for Appropriations Committee membership because there would be less conflict on that committee. We were wrong. Appropriations Committee members report more committee conflict. This might reflect the dire economic state of Michigan's economy during most of our study period. Cutting budgets is often contentious. Finally, we find effects of gender and of having more education. These control variables might affect a legislator's perception of conflict. In other words, what one observer considers healthy debate, another might consider conflict based on an aversion to vigorous debate or greater expectations of comity and courtesy. These two categories of legislators do indeed appear to perceive committee conflict differently than their colleagues do.

Even controlling for these other factors, the interaction between the Senate and term limits persists. After ruling out these alternative explanations, we conclude that term limits increase the amount of conflict in committees in the Senate, but not in the already more contentious House. We speculate that as waves of legislators socialized in the House move to the Senate, they bring the norms of the lower chamber with them. The greater collegiality of the Senate appears to be at least partly a casualty of this migration.

TABLE 10.3. Amount of Conflict in a Committee

Model Predicting the Amount of Committee Conflict	B	Std. Error	t	Sig.
(Constant)	**1.63**	.17	9.80	.00
Term Limits	−.16	.11	−1.44	.15
Chamber (Senate = 1)	**−.49**	.19	−2.52	.01
Interaction for Term Limits and Chamber	**.48**	.24	1.97	.05
Member of the Chamber's Minority Party	**.20**	.09	2.22	.03
On Appropriations Committee	**.33**	.10	3.35	.00
Gender (Female = 1)	**.18**	.11	1.64	.10
Education (less than BA, BA, more than BA)	**.14**	.06	2.47	.01

Note: Bold type indicates statistically significant coefficients.

F = 4.14; Adjusted R^2 = 0.05; n = 422.

Dependent Variable: Mean = 2.01; Scaled values range between 0 = none, to 4 = An Enormous Amount; Skewness = 0.07; Kurtosis = −0.52.

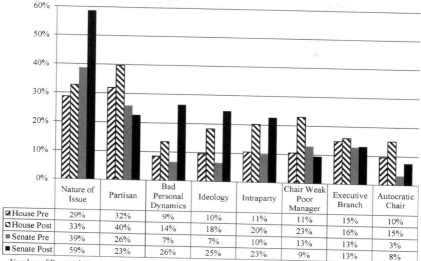

	Nature of Issue	Partisan	Bad Personal Dynamics	Ideology	Intraparty	Chair Weak Poor Manager	Executive Branch	Autocratic Chair
House Pre	29%	32%	9%	10%	11%	11%	15%	10%
House Post	33%	40%	14%	18%	20%	23%	16%	15%
Senate Pre	39%	26%	7%	7%	10%	13%	16%	15%
Senate Post	59%	23%	26%	25%	23%	9%	13%	3%

Number of Respondents: House 82 before and 229 after term limits, Senate 25 before and 38 after term limits.

Fig. 10.3. Reasons for Committee Conflict

Sources of Conflict in Committees

In addition to recording respondents' scaled value for the amount of conflict, we asked them to explain the source of conflict. We prompted for reasons why there was so little conflict if their scaled answer indicated little or no conflict. Alternatively, if the amount of conflict given was *some* to *an enormous amount*, we asked why there was so much conflict. We coded these open-ended responses into categories that we report in figure 10.3.

More post-term-limits senators attribute the committee conflict they report to the nature of the issues rather than to their own behaviors. Typical comments took the form of "issues addressed by this committee do not involve a lot of conflict" or alternatively that "issues addressed by this committee always involve a lot of conflict" (interview notes). We see in figure 10.3 that the proportion of respondents making comments attributing conflict to the nature of the issue ranges from a low of 29 percent in the pre-term-limits House to 59 percent in the post-term-limits Senate. The proportion of House respondents naming the issues as the source of conflict increases only slightly after term limits, while the proportion of senators blaming the issue for the conflict increases dramatically, by 20 percent, a change that is statistically significant. Here again, it is the Senate in which we find the biggest term limits differences.

Partisan conflict increases substantially in the House to 40 percent after term limits. Given the mood of the country, we hesitate to attribute this shift to term limits. On the other hand, partisan conflict decreases slightly in the Senate after term limits. Given the statistically significant chamber difference that we find in the proportion of our Senate and House respondents who attributed committee conflict to partisan differences after term limits, we speculate that experience might reduce partisan conflict, even when the mood of the country is more polarized.

On the other hand, we find that ideological and interparty conflict both increase in each chamber after term limits, and these changes are large enough to be statistically significant. Even the additional experience of post-term-limits senators fails to mute ideological and intraparty conflict in Michigan. Therefore, we cannot distinguish between term limits effects and the national trends with respect to these sources of committee conflict. But we suspect that some of the veteran legislators that we interviewed might have buffered Michigan's state legislature from this national wave of ideological fervor and intraparty conflict given their long-term relationships and their pragmatic view of politics.

Personal dynamics in committees sour after term limits, but with a slightly different twist in each chamber. A bigger proportion of senators report bad personal dynamics among committee members, while House respondents attribute more of the decline to committee chairs, calling the chairs weak, poor managers, or autocratic. Given the stark change in the experience of committee chairs in the House, this likely arises from chairs' inexperience—clearly a term limits effect. But changes in the Senate suggest that after term limits senators are not learning the norms of civility and courtesy for which the chamber was noted before term limits.

Managing Committee Conflict

We explore the ability of a chair to manage conflict among committee members using another open-ended question. Given the comments about House committee chairs reported above, we assume that inexperienced chairs manage conflict differently. Based on the greater experience of Senate committee chairs, we also anticipate fewer term limits effects in the Senate. But once again, it is Senate committee chairs that exhibit substantially altered behaviors, as we report in figure 10.4.

First and foremost, good personal dynamics decline more in the Senate

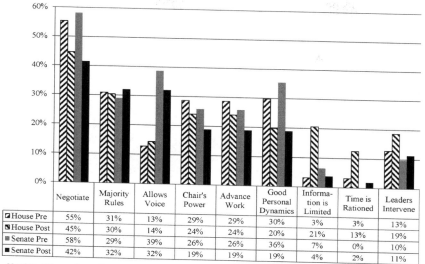

	Negotiate	Majority Rules	Allows Voice	Chair's Power	Advance Work	Good Personal Dynamics	Informa-tion is Limited	Time is Rationed	Leaders Intervene
House Pre	55%	31%	13%	29%	29%	30%	3%	3%	13%
House Post	45%	30%	14%	24%	24%	20%	21%	13%	19%
Senate Pre	58%	29%	39%	26%	26%	20%	21%	13%	19%
Senate Post	42%	32%	32%	19%	19%	36%	7%	0%	10%

Number of Respondents: House 59 before and 244 after limits, Senate 24 before and 43 after term limits.

Fig. 10.4. Managing Committee Conflict

than in the House after term limits. This is consistent with the increases in bad personal dynamics leading to conflicts, as we discussed in the previous section. As we have speculated elsewhere, the absence of veteran senators to socialize incoming legislators into the norms and routines of this smaller, more courteous chamber could explain the prevalence of these institutional changes. Yet as we see in figure 10.4 the Senate continues to allow the minority party to voice its opposition—an approach to managing conflict that differentiates the two chambers both before and after term limits. So some institutional norms of Senate deportment persist.

Although representatives do not report an increase in the amount of committee conflict after term limits, it appears that inexperienced House chairs manage this conflict differently and that caucus leaders intervene more frequently. The weak and autocratic House chairs we identified in the previous section of this chapter seem to show little respect for the legislative process of deliberation, possibly overreacting to the give and take of debate. Respondents report that chairs truncate discussion and constrain their information gathering efforts.

These comments reflect stories we were told about a House committee chair who turned off the microphone of a minority party colleague during committee hearings so that she could not ask questions or make comments (interview notes). It is also consistent with hearings held on a major piece of legislation, distributed without an opportunity for legislators to read the bill (interview notes). One House chair permitted only one question per committee member before calling for the vote to pass a major piece of legislation out of committee (interview notes). As another respondent told us, this vote was taken while the copies of the bill were still warm from the photocopy machine (interview notes).

These tactics are likely to contribute to the 10 percent decline in the proportion of representatives who mention *good personal dynamics* in describing the chair's management style. Comments about chairs' management style are consistent with videotapes of post-term-limits committee hearings that we watched in which witnesses from only one side of an issue were called upon to give testimony during a hearing. Witnesses were called upon in alternating order (pro and con) in the pre-term-limits committee hearings that we viewed.

Although committee relations in the Senate might be less cordial after term limits than they were before, the harsh tactics of House chairs seem to have remained in the House, at least during our study period. The methods we were told about in the House of rationing time and limiting information do not appear to have infiltrated the Senate after term limits.

Prior to term limits more than half of our respondents in each chamber said that chairs managed conflict by negotiating or compromising. The proportion mentioning use of this tactic declines in both chambers (down 11% in the House and 17% in the Senate) after term limits. This decline in committee negotiation could be linked to the desire for negotiating skills among caucus leadership candidates that we reported earlier in this chapter. Committees are a forum in which to learn and to exhibit those skills.

About one-third of respondents in both chambers consistently say that the conflict ends with the majority party voting—"the chair has the votes" (interview notes). This was true both before and after term limits. It is simply the reality of majority rule. It appears, however, that advance work to iron out differences—a prelude to the now rare negotiation and compromise—is used less frequently, especially in the Senate.

Important Decisions about Bills

Readers will recall that we asked our respondents about two hypothetical floor votes—school choice and LRHCP. In conjunction with the questions about these two issues, we also asked any of the top chamber leaders that we interviewed to tell us where the most important decisions about each of these issues would be made. The question wording is "Where are the most important decisions regarding a bill dealing with Schools of Choice likely to be made? [*Record 1, 2, 3 in order of mention*]."

To record their answers, we handed them a list of possible decision-making loci. The list included likely locations, such as committee chairs, chamber leadership, and so on. These are listed in table 10.4. We also accepted any other loci of control a leader mentioned, such as outside interest groups and the other chamber's leaders. We recorded three responses for each leader interviewed (and occasionally a fourth if a respondent reported a tie). We assigned 6 points to their responses in descending order—3 points for the first reply, 2 points for the second, and 1 point for the third (or two values of .5 for responses three and four in the case of a tie). We tallied these values for each decision locus and then divided by the number of possible points (six times the number of top leaders interviewed) during each time period—pre- and post-term-limits—and chamber to produce the values reported in table 10.4. Higher values indicate more important loci of decision making. The top three loci for each time period and chamber are highlighted.

In developing this question we build on the work of Francis (1989) who explores the tension between party leadership and committee control of state legislative policy making. His work provides a historical baseline for the Michigan House and Senate during the 1980s. Based on his 50-state study of legislative control, he develops a typology of state legislatures that includes seven combinations of decision-making control. He classifies the Michigan House as a hybrid of committee and party leader control. This persisted in the pre-term-limits House nearly two decades later, according to the leaders we interviewed. But as we noted throughout this chapter, House committee chairs lose clout after term limits. Francis also found that the Michigan Senate was controlled by the party caucus alone—the only chamber in the 50 states that Francis classified in that category. As we noted in chapter 6, the party caucus becomes less important after term limits, but even the pre-term-limits Senate appears to have shifted substantially away from the party-caucus-dominated model of the 1980s.

Party leaders' responses about loci of important decisions reinforce our broader findings that committee chairs in the House lost influence after term limits. As table 10.4 shows, none of the post-term-limits leaders say that the most important decisions about school choice are made by the committee chair. But before term limits, this locus of decision making was the one leaders mentioned most often. After term limits key decision-making input shifts outside the chamber: to the governor, the other chamber's leaders, and to outside groups.

We find that before term limits the House committee chair is even more important for the technically complex issue (LRHCP) than for the school choice issue. Here again, the pre-term-limits House seems to transact its business in a pattern reminiscent of Francis's 1980s characterization of the chamber—a committee chair/caucus leader hybrid. After term limits, House committee chairs are rarely mentioned as a key locus for making decisions about LRHCP. This reinforces evidence that post-term-limits committee chairs exercise less control over the work of their committees, as we discussed earlier in this chapter. After term limits committee chairs'

TABLE 10.4. Where Are the Most Important Decisions Regarding a Bill Likely to Be Made?

Loci of Policy-Making Control	Schools of Choice				Licensing and Regulating Health Professionals			
	House		Senate		House		Senate	
	Pre-Term-Limits	Post-Term-Limits	Pre-Term-Limits	Post-Term-Limits	Pre-Term-Limits	Post-Term-Limits	Pre-Term-Limits	Post-Term-Limits
Party Caucus	0.08	0.08	0.17	**0.10**				0.07
On the Floor	0.04	**0.12**		0.02		0.04		0.05
In Regular Committee Meetings	**0.21**	0.08	**0.25**	0.07	0.08	**0.17**	**0.29**	0.12
By the Committee Chair	**0.25**			**0.10**	**0.46**	0.09	0.04	**0.26**
In Subcommittee (Appropriations)	0.04							
By the Chamber Leadership	**0.13**	**0.18**	**0.25**	**0.26**	**0.17**	**0.20**	**0.25**	**0.19**
In the Governor's Office	0.08	**0.23**	**0.21**	0.10	**0.17**	**0.17**	**0.21**	0.10
Informal Discussions among Members				0.03	**0.10**	0.04		**0.14**
In Conference Committee						0.04		0.05
Other: Other Chamber's Leaders				0.03	0.02			
Other: Outside Groups			0.10	0.04	0.07		0.04	0.04
Other: State Agency							0.17	
Other: The Community			0.05					

Note: Values denote the proportion of the maximum possible points that could be awarded for a single decision locus for the sessions. This adjusts for the different number of respondents for each session. It does not adjust for respondents who mentioned 2 rather than 3 loci. The first choice received 3 points, the second 2 points, the third received 1 point. If a fourth locus was provided, the third and fourth loci received 1/2 point each. The resulting sum was divided by the maximum points possible if each respondent rated the locus first. Numbers of chamber leaders responding ranges from 2 to 8. Bold type indicates the top 3 (or 4 in the case of ties) choices.

decision-making input on LRHCP seems to diffuse to loci outside the chamber: to the conference committee and to outside actors.

As we noted above, the pre-term-limits Senate is not consistent with the caucus-dominated image of the Michigan Senate painted by Francis in the 1980s. On both issues, leaders in the pre-term-limits Senate assess their own input, that of the governor, and the "regular committee meetings" as the three most important decision-making loci. Although the pre-term-limits senators still placed a high priority on information from their party caucus for school choice (i.e., it is in fourth place), the party caucus appears to have no input into important decisions about LRHCP. For LRHCP state agency officials are in fourth place.

After term limits, decision-making input is dispersed more broadly in the Senate, with committee chairs making major gains on both issues. These committee chairs are locked in a four-way tie for second place as the locus of important decisions about school choice, and they are in first place for decisions about LRHCP. Chamber leaders rate themselves as the most important locus of decision making about school choice and place themselves in second place for decisions about LRHCP. The post-term-limits Senate seems to adopt the pattern that Francis identified in the Michigan House—a hybrid of committee chair and chamber leadership control over policy making. Once again, the post-term-limits Senate resembles the pre-term-limits House.

The governor's office falls in the rankings for both issues in the post-term-limits Senate. We explore the relationship between the executive branch and the legislature more in chapter 11, but our findings here indicate that when governors are term limited, Senate leaders see them as less important in decision making about these issues. This is not true for the House, however.

Looking at the number of decision loci listed in table 10.4, in both chambers it appears that key decisions are made by more participants after term limits. For example, after term limits a decision locus rarely mentioned in either chamber before term limits, *informal discussions among chamber members*, is part of a four-way tie for second place in the Senate for decisions about school choice and is in third place in decisions about LRHCP in the post-term-limits Senate. Comparing the distribution of decision loci before and after term limits in both chambers, we find a narrower range of participants provided by our pre-term-limits respondents for both issues. Pre-term-limits chamber leaders agreed substantially on the loci of decision-making power. Post-term-limits leaders name a much broader set of loci. We find less clarity and less agreement about the locus of these key decisions after term limits.

Conclusions

Legislators are in the unique position of electing (hiring) their own leaders (managers). It is therefore interesting to consider the types of people they choose. Our advice to them is to be careful what they wish for. Newcomers, especially to Michigan's House, appear to embrace leaders who are forceful, decisive, willing to command and control the chamber. Yet harsh tactics by these leaders and the committee chairs they select are decried by those they shut out of the process. And caucus leaders and committee chairs who are more willing to use rewards and coercion elicit complaints from respondents, who bemoan the rough edges of the chamber.

Committee chairs, faced with less sway over their committee members and greater pressure from more directive caucus leaders, seem to rely more heavily on coercion and rewards. Especially in the House, they manage fairly normal levels of conflict in committees by suppressing the opposition and steamrolling legislation through the process. These aggressive tactics do not increase their colleagues' perceptions of their control over the work of the committee, however. They are seen as weak and poor managers, albeit autocratic. Some of their lost influence drifts outside the chamber to the executive branch, outside groups, and the upper chamber. This paints an image of a weakened chamber, especially compared to other branches of government and outside actors.

In the smaller, less hierarchical, and more participatory Senate, committee chairs appear to gain some influence after term limits but this comes at the expense of broader participation of the party caucus. Senate committee chairs appear better able to fend off external actors, but they too are challenged by conflicts within their own party and by caucus leaders' attempts to intervene in the work of their committees. Yet there are still remnants of a more collegial approach to committee deliberations in which the opposition can voice its objections, even though the majority party uses its votes to send bills to the Senate floor. Despite this, civility in the Senate wanes after term limits with an increase in bad personal dynamics, a decrease in good personal dynamics, and more conflict in committees. Institutional norms of conduct appear to change absent a cohort of experienced senators to socialize newcomers. This shift cannot be explained solely by inexperience because all post-term-limits senators we interviewed served in the lower chamber.

Throughout this chapter and the previous one, we examined the influence of caucus leaders and committee chairs from several vantage points using a wide variety of analytic techniques and data. In general, all these efforts produce the same image. The chambers have lost control over their work, influence is concentrated in fewer hands, and influence is exercised more aggressively. These shifting patterns suggest that there are winners and losers in the influence game after term limits. In the Senate the broader membership of the party caucus losses clout to committee chairs and chamber leaders. In the House committee chairs lose and caucus leaders win, but outside actors also gain control over the work of committees. Despite their complaints and frustrations, we find that the type of leader term-limited legislators select—directive, assertive ones—contribute to the circumstances they bemoan.

As we reported in chapter 9, influence is concentrated in the hands of caucus leaders in the House after term limits and to a lesser extent in the Senate. Tannenbaum (1961) demonstrated that concentrating "influence" in the hands of a smaller group of people accompanies a loss of organizational "influence" and lower organizational effectiveness. We find here that Michigan's lower legislative chamber loses some control over its work, especially the work of committees, coincident with centralizing influence in the hands of leaders. Importantly, it is outside actors who apparently gain from the chamber's diminished role in decision making about issues. This is the pattern Tannenbaum's work predicts. But it is not the outcome term limits advocates hoped for.

ELEVEN

Executive-Legislative Relationships in Michigan

How do the effects of term limits spread beyond Michigan's legislative bodies? The effects of legislative term limits appear to ripple beyond an individual chamber. This question of spillover focuses our inquiry as we examine relationships outside Michigan's legislature. We examine three possible spillover effects in this chapter: between the legislature and the state bureaucracy, between the legislature and the governor, and between the two chambers. A key theme involves the redistribution of influence among these actors.

In their surveys of state legislators, Carey et al. (2000 and 2006) find that term limits weaken the legislative branch compared to the executive branch. Our previous work (Sarbaugh-Thompson et al. 2010) provides an example of this loss for Michigan's House. There we show that legislative oversight of the bureaucracy declines and the House assesses its performance on this task negatively. Yet, as we found in chapter 10, governors lose some policy-making input after term limits. Therefore we analyze state agencies and the governor's office separately in this chapter. Consistent with our findings in chapter 9 and the work of others scholars, term limits appear to shift influence from the lower to the upper chamber (Appolonio and La Raja 2006; Cain and Levin 1999). So we examine the two chambers of the legislative branch separately, as well.

In this chapter, we extend our prior work on legislative monitoring to

---

Justin Rex is a coauthor on this chapter.

include the Senate. As we have discovered repeatedly throughout this book, it is risky to assume that the two chambers react in similar ways to term limits. Then we explore factors that alter the quality of the relationships between the governor and the legislature and between the two legislative chambers.

Review of the Political Environment during the Implementation of Term Limits

To provide context for this part of our investigation, we review information about Michigan's state government during our study period. We described this political context in greater detail in chapter 1. Here we merely revisit five key changes relevant to this chapter.

1. Before term limits, Democrats controlled the House. Afterward, Republicans controlled the chamber from 2000–06, but Democrats regained control in 2007–10. We did not interview representatives during 2007–10, but we did interview senators about the House during those years.
2. Republicans controlled the Senate throughout our investigation.
3. A Republican and former Senate majority leader, Gov. John Engler, led the executive branch during the pre-term-limits interviews in both chambers and during the first two-post-term-limits interviews in the House. He was a highly experienced career politician.
4. A Democrat, Gov. Jennifer Granholm, who lacked any legislative experience, led the executive branch from 2003 to 2010. This period covers both post-term-limits Senate sessions and the final post-term-limits House session in our study.
5. Finally, the 2002 implementation of term limits in the Senate enticed many representatives to abandon some of their permitted time in the House and run for open Senate seats. This means that some senators in our second post-term-limits cohort had served only two or four years in the lower chamber. This produced an abrupt decline in the collective experience of the Senate in the 2007–10 session—our final set of interviews. Moreover, this House exodus produced a second wave of freshman in the 2003–04 House nearly as large as the first post-term-limits influx. Representatives continue running for the Senate whenever seats are open despite having more time available in the

House, so it will become the norm for some senators to have only two or four years of prior experience rather than six.

Data and Methods

We have multiple measures for the relationships we examine here: (1) the legislature and state agencies, (2) the legislature and the governor's office, and (3) the two chambers of the legislature. First we asked legislators to grade the chamber on a series of tasks. One of these is *monitoring the implementation of programs*. Another is *working with the governor*, and a third is *working with the other chamber*. Responses to these questions provide us with legislators' self-assessment of their chamber for each of these relationships. We asked respondents to use letter grades, and we invited them to use pluses and minuses. Exact wording of these questions appear in appendix A, questions 21.2, 21.5, and 21.6. We convert grades provided by respondents into numerical values ranging from a zero for an F, one for a D-minus and so on through 12 for an A-plus. (We did not use an F-plus.)

We also have open-ended comments about each of these grades. We classified these comments into categories, creating several categorical variables. We include some of these in our multivariate models of these relationships to control for legislators' attitudes and assumptions.

Next, we have measures of the relative priority legislators place on information from their partners in each of these relationships: information from state agency officials, information from members of the other chamber, and information from the governor's office. We calculate the priority placed on information from each of these sources using a series of questions about the extent to which respondents relied on 16 sources when seeking information and guidance about an issue considered in a committee. To normalize these values we divide the legislator's response for a particular source consulted by his or her average for all sources consulted. This approach is described in greater detail in chapters 4 and 6. We simply note here that positive values denote a higher than average priority placed on the information, zero corresponds to an average priority, and negative values reflect a below average priority.

Finally, we measure the priority placed on one task: monitoring state agencies, (hereafter referred to as either *monitoring* or *oversight*). This measure is a normalized value created by dividing the time each legislator said (s)he spent on oversight by the average time (s)he spent on a series of 11 tasks. Again, positive values reflect a higher than average priority, zero corresponds to average priority, and negative values denote below average priority.

We mention two caveats about the grades for two of the relationships: between the chambers and between the chamber and governor. First, we asked these two questions only of people who had served more than one session, assuming that newcomers would have little basis on which to grade the performance of the entire chamber on its relationship with the governor or the other chamber. Therefore, we have fewer responses to these questions than we do elsewhere in our research.

Second, we added these questions to the interview schedule after our baseline interviews in the House. Therefore, we lack pre-term-limits House baseline data for these. This constrains our analyses. We cannot simultaneously control for the effects of chamber and term limits because we only have pre-term-limits data for the Senate. Therefore, we analyze these two grades by session rather than our usual pre- and post-term-limits categories. For consistency and to adjust for political changes within these analyses, we use session instead of term limits in our bivariate analyses of monitoring state agencies, even though we do have baseline pre-term-limits data for this. Because partisan control of the executive branch changes after one of the three post-term-limits House sessions, looking at the patterns across the sessions clarifies the effect of partisan changes on monitoring and consulting with state agency officials.

Due to the limits of our data, we consider this investigation of the relationship between the two chambers and between the governor and legislature to be exploratory. But even exploratory discussions are likely to provide valuable insights from which others can launch more extensive investigations, given that there is limited scholarship at the state level about these relationships.

Factors Affecting Legislative-Executive Branch Relationships

There are numerous factors likely to affect the relationships we examine here. To avoid redundant discussions of these variables, we describe our rationale for including them in our models in general here and provide necessary details later in the chapter.

Experience for Leaders and for the Rank and File

Consistent with our findings in chapter 10, chamber leaders fulfill multiple roles (Rosenthal 2009) including organizational manager, consensus builder, negotiator, and decision maker. These roles take time to learn. Experienced leaders know more about how to cooperate with a governor and how to steer their chamber during negotiations. Accordingly, we expect legislators who serve under an experienced leader to experience these relationships more positively, reflected in higher grades for these tasks.

Sessions with experienced leaders are the 1997–98 House, the 2001–02 House, the 1999–2002 Senate, and the 2003–06 Senate. Some readers might question the treatment of the 2001–02 House leaders as experienced. The same speaker and leadership team served in the House in 1999–2000 and in 2001–02. Although this is not much experience, it is the most experience any House leaders will have after term limits.

We assume that veteran legislators are more likely to understand their job and the subtleties of their legislative roles. We expect this knowledge to alter expectations about the chamber's performance, thereby affecting grades given. Consequently, we control for respondents' experience in our models.

Specialized Subgroups

Certain tasks are the purview of legislative specialists, as we demonstrate in chapter 4. For example, legal experts, such as lawyers, develop new legislation. Our respondents tell us that the relationships that we analyze here are typically performed by subgroups of specialized experts or those holding formal positions responsible for these tasks. We control for one or more of these subgroups in each of our analyses, assuming their insider knowledge will affect the grades they give.

For example, Appropriations Committee members are a subgroup we consider in the multivariate models. We include this subgroup because Michigan budget negotiations often occur between the two chamber leaders from each political party, each chamber's Appropriations Committee chair and the governor, along with a couple of key budget staff. Additionally Appropriations Committee members do a lot of monitoring of the budget, especially in the House. Governments **must** pass budgets, even if they cannot pass specific policy proposals. Therefore, Appropriations Committee members have more opportunities, but also a more pressing need, to work with the governor and with the other chamber.[1] We assume this will affect their perception of the relationships we explore here.

Political Ambition, Careerism, and Reelection Seeking

Political payoff probably influences legislators' choices about using their time and colors their perceptions of various actions. The motivation to calculate political payoff is likely to be stronger for politically ambitious legislators and those who are politically vulnerable (i.e., elected by a narrow margin). A sizeable literature argues that legislators who are highly concerned about elections (the politically ambitious and the vulnerable) avoid exercising oversight due to its low political payoff (Fenno 1973; Mayhew 1974; Ogul 1976; Rosenthal 1981; Woolley and LeLoup 1989; Elling 1992; Duffin 2003; Woods and Baranowski 2006). As Woods and Baranowski (2006) explain, oversight is labor-intensive, time-consuming work that does not make headlines. The high levels of political ambition among Michigan's legislators could explain the paradox of lax oversight, despite abundant institutional resources to support this task.

Similarly, working with the governor's office is unlikely to provide political payoff in terms of headlines or accomplishments that a candidate can run on either for reelection or to seek another office. In fact, there is likely to be more political payoff from opposing a governor of the opposite political party and undermining efforts of the other chamber if it is controlled by the other party. This sort of partisanship, according to Huber, Shipan, and Pfahler (2001), conditions these relationships nationally, and we assume this extends to state governments.

The governor's office has been shown to be a valuable employment agency for termed-out legislators (Straayer and Drage-Bowser 2004). Therefore, members sharing the governor's political party might defer to the executive branch more readily, especially after term limits when more legislators need future jobs. To assess this we include a variable measuring whether the respondent *Shares the Governor's Party*.

Individual Grading Tendencies

We control for the grading tendencies of individual respondents by including the grade given for *passing good legislation*, another of the activities we asked about during our interviews. By including this grade, we control for respondents who are easy graders and those who are tougher. The effect is positive and statistically significant in each equation. Although the effect is not large—about one-sixth of a letter grade—including it always improves the models' performance.

Relationship between the Legislature and State Agencies

Michigan's state legislators should be proficient in exercising oversight, especially before term limits, because they have broad institutional resources equal to those possessed by Congress (Browne and VerBurg 1995). The literature is quite consistent in pointing out that more professional legislatures, those with institutional powers similar to those in Michigan, exercise more influence over state agencies and bureaucrats (Mooney 1991; Moncrief and Thompson 1992; Baranowski 1997; Potoski and Woods 2000). Michigan's legislature employs full-time partisan and nonpartisan staff in addition to personal staff. The nonpartisan Auditor General's office routinely produces reports for the chamber on state agency finances and performance. Michigan's full-time legislature, with year-round sessions, can "encourage" agency compliance through budget allocations and can scrutinize state agencies' performance during committee hearings.

Logic suggests, however, that term limits could undermine the ability of legislators to wield these tools. If limiting service deinstitutionalizes state legislatures, as Kousser (2005) argues, one would expect legislative influence over the implementation of state policies and programs to wane. Not only does our previous work demonstrate that Michigan's legislature neglects this responsibility, we showed that term limits exacerbate this. In this, our work reinforces that of other scholars (Berman 2004; Farmer and Little 2004; Moen, Palmer, and Powell 2005; Cain and Wright 2007; Green et al. 2007; Kurtz, Niemi, and Cain 2007).

Some Michigan legislators clearly do not understand that they have the authority as well as the responsibility to oversee the executive branch. Based on their comments, we find that 40 percent of them seem oblivious to this responsibility. To represent this we create a variable called *Not Our Job*, which is coded as a 1 for respondents making comments in this vein or 0 otherwise. After term limits, some respondents even "informed" us during interviews that *we* did not understand the difference between the executive and legislative branches of state government, explaining to us that state agencies are part of the executive branch. A typical comment was "the agencies are part of the executive branch so the governor does that, we don't" (interview notes). In a memorable interview moment, a post-term-limits legislator whose position should have involved agency oversight turned to staff after we asked him to grade the chamber on monitoring, saying, "Do we do that?" (interview notes).

Bivariate Analysis: Relationship with State Agencies

Before exploring multivariate models of legislative oversight, we establish the broad contours of the relationship between legislators and state agencies. Looking at table 11.1, we see that monitoring the work of state agencies is a task most legislators avoid—spending far less than their average time on this. Even before term limits, legislators shunned monitoring, and the low grades they gave themselves indicate some awareness of their

TABLE 11.1. Relationship with State Agencies, Including Monitoring

	N	Min.	Max.	Mean	Std. Dev.	F-Statistic
Grade for Monitoring Implementation of Programs (grades A to F)						
House						2.42*
+Before Term Limits	91	0.0 (F)	11.0 (A)	5.08	2.53	
First Session after Term Limits	87	0.0 (F)	11.0 (A)	4.20	2.73	
Second Session after Term Limits	81	0.0 (F)	11.0 (A)	4.18	2.59	
+Third Session after Term Limits	81	0.0 (F)	11.0 (A)	4.64	2.41	
Senate						7.08***
+Before Term Limits	33	0.0 (F)	11.0 (A)	5.12	3.08	
First Session after Term Limits	25	4.0 (C−)	11.0 (A)	7.36	1.85	
Second Session after Term Limits	26	0.0 (F)	9.0 (B+)	4.98	2.44	
Amount of Time Spent Monitoring State Agencies (difference measure)						
House						3.70***
+Before Term Limits	94	−2.55	1.91	−0.52	0.95	
First Session after Term Limits	91	−3.14	1.68	−0.69	0.85	
Second Session after Term Limits	91	−2.64	1.64	−0.94	0.86	
+Third Session after Term Limits	87	−2.22	1.05	−0.73	0.79	
Senate						0.67
Before Term Limits	33	−1.95	0.55	−0.73	0.73	
First Session after Term Limits	28	−2.14	1.40	−0.49	0.88	
Third Session after Term limits	26	−2.14	1.18	−0.61	0.80	
Relying on State Agency Officials for Information (difference measure)						
House						0.33
+Before Term Limits	87	−1.59	2.43	0.20	1.02	
First Session after Term Limits	83	−1.81	2.41	0.26	1.05	
Second Session after Term Limits	83	−2.25	2.41	0.14	1.07	
+Third Session after Term Limits	84	−1.86	2.66	0.28	1.02	
Senate						0.53
Before Term Limits	29	−1.63	2.00	0.41	1.01	
First Session after Term Limits	24	−2.06	3.00	0.61	1.38	
Third Session after Term limits	24	−1.82	2.34	0.75	1.28	

*$p \leq 0.10$, **$p \leq 0.05$, ***$p \leq 0.01$.

omission. These grades tend to fall across time, with the exception of the 2003 Senate. This Senate session, a persistent outlier, shows an increase in the priority placed on monitoring and, correspondingly, these senators give themselves higher grades for this task. This continued consonance between effort and grades reassures us of the usefulness of legislators' self-assessment of their performance.

Translating the numerical values reported in table 11.1 into letter grades, a grade of C in the House declines to a grade between a C and a C-minus as term limits are implemented. Although this seems like a small difference, it is statistically significant. Likewise, the decline after term limits in the relative time devoted to this task in the House is statistically significant. Thus, we find that monitoring—already an avoided task—assumes an even lower priority for term-limited legislators.

One would expect a Republican-controlled chamber to closely scrutinize the performance of state agencies controlled by a Democratic governor, given the potential to embarrass the opposite political party. This is the situation faced by the Republican-controlled House in 2003–04 and Senate in both the 2003–06 and the 2007–10 sessions. The priority placed on monitoring does not reflect this greater scrutiny in the House in 2003–04 or the Senate in 2007–10. But it does in the 2003 Senate, controlled by House veterans who moved to the Senate. We speculate that this pattern reflects legislators' experience or lack thereof. From this we infer that more experienced legislators understand the potential political payoff from monitoring state agencies controlled by the opposite political party.

Apparently experience matters. But when we reach these term limits equilibrium sessions, even the most experienced term-limited legislators (state senators) do not fully grasp the potential political opportunities and risks of monitoring state agencies. Only senators with decades of experience in the lower chamber capitalize on this opportunity during the 2003 Senate session. And even then the motivation appears to be partisan gain rather than a concern for the welfare of the state as a whole. Readers may recall that we found an association between more concern for the general welfare and more monitoring among pre-term-limits representatives in chapter 3 (see table 3.2). Term limits appear to extinguish that motivation for monitoring.

Multivariate Models of Monitoring

Subset of Legislators Likely to Monitor

Monitoring is widely acknowledged as a challenging task that requires specialized expertise (Jones and Barrett 1992). In the Michigan legislature 18 percent of our respondents volunteered that monitoring is performed by a subset of colleagues in their chamber. In some legislatures this is the responsibility of committee chairs (Duffin 2003), but in the Michigan House, Appropriations Committee members are more likely to fulfill this role, according to our respondents. Despite this general pattern, several respondents described one pre-term-limits House committee chair as exceptional at monitoring state agencies under his committee's jurisdiction. Another subgroup with oversight responsibility is the Joint Committee on Administrative Rules, commonly referred to as JCAR.[2] Several senators say JCAR members do most of the monitoring in that chamber.

To adjust for these chamber differences we include two categorical variables for subgroup membership in our models: Appropriations Committee membership and JCAR membership. To control for chamber differences, we also include a categorical variable for the interaction between chamber and Appropriations Committee membership and between chamber and JCAR membership in the models.

Legislators' Attitudes toward Monitoring

As we noted earlier in this chapter, we created a categorical variable, *Not Our Job*, to control for respondents who asserted that "the governor is responsible for that" (interview notes). We predict that these respondents will spend little if any time on monitoring state agencies—giving it a very low priority. To control for two other effects of legislators' attitudes toward this task, we create two categorical variables. We find that 36 percent of respondents feel monitoring is used as a political cudgel in partisan battles or that the executive branch thwarts legislative oversight for political reasons. We created a variable, *Politics Influences Monitoring*, to denote legislators making comments of this sort. We created another categorical variable, *No Time to Monitor*, to control for the 41 percent of our respondents who said that legislators are too busy to monitor or that it just does not happen.

Reelection-seeking legislators, especially those who are politically vulnerable or ambitious, devote considerable energy to filling their political coffers (Kousser 2005; Mooney 2007) and concentrate their efforts on tasks with political payoff, such as bringing money and projects to the district. To see whether reelection concerns deter legislators from channeling their energy toward a task with low political rewards, monitoring, we control for the electoral competitiveness of the district by measuring how safe the district is for one political party. We also control for gender to provide continuity with our exploration of gender differences in behaviors that we initiated in chapter 4.

Multivariate Model of Time Spent Monitoring State Agencies

Even when we control for factors that might reduce legislative oversight, we find that term limits reduce the priority representatives place on monitoring state agencies, as table 11.2 illustrates. In the Senate, however, monitoring increases after term limits. This could reflect partisanship. Confronting state agencies controlled by their own party, logically and prudently pre-term-limits Republican senators expended little effort monitoring the work of state agencies. Pre-term-limits representatives in a chamber controlled by Democrats engaged in slightly more oversight, although this is still an avoided task. After term limits senators placed a

TABLE 11.2. The Priority a Legislator Places on Monitoring

Model Predicting the Priority of Monitoring	B	Std. Error	t	Sig.
(Constant)	−.425	.152	−2.790	.006
Term Limits	−.291	.116	−2.516	.012
Chamber (Senate = 1)	−.391	.210	−1.860	.064
Interaction of Term Limits and Chamber	.518	.226	2.289	.023
On Appropriations Committee	.572	.105	5.457	.000
Interaction of Chamber and Appropriations	−.342	.216	−1.584	.114
On JCAR	−.182	.255	−.713	.476
Interaction of Chamber and JCAR	.873	.359	2.431	.016
Lame Duck	.115	.095	1.208	.228
Politically Ambitious	.026	.092	.283	.777
Safe Districts	−.004	.002	−1.967	.050
Legislators who say this is "Not Our Job"	−.168	.087	−1.93	.054
Same Party as the Governor	−.058	.084	−.684	.494
Gender (Female = 1)	−.282	.103	−2.742	.006

Note: Bold type indicates statistically significant coefficients.

F = 5.42; Adjusted R^2 = 0.14; n = 351.

Dependent Variable: Mean = −0.70; Minimum, −3.14; Maximum, 1.91; Range, 5.05; Skewness = 0.27; Kurtosis = −0.28.

much higher priority on monitoring state agencies. This probably reflects a simultaneous shift to a governor from the opposite political party. The Senate, controlled by experienced Republicans who migrated from the House, seized the opportunity to scrutinize executive branch agencies controlled by the opposing party. Thus, we interpret our results as indicating that in the Senate partisanship rather than term limits is a useful predictor of legislative monitoring.

In the House, on the other hand, experience provides a better explanation of monitoring. Referring back to table 11.1, we see a very low priority placed on monitoring in the third post-term-limits House session despite the shift to an executive branch controlled by the opposite political party. This is not what a partisanship explanation would predict. Legislators who lack experience do not seem to understand the political opportunities and risks oversight provides—an indirect effect of term limits.

How then does this fit with our null findings reported in table 11.2 for the effect of sharing the governor's political party, which we included in order to control for these partisan effects? Our prior work (Sarbaugh-Thompson et al. 2010) provides the missing insight. In that work we compared two House sessions, the 1997–98 (pre-term-limits) and the 2003–04 (fully implemented post-term-limits) sessions. Both these sessions involve a governor from one political party and a chamber controlled by the opposite political party, which means that we are able to hold several potentially problematic interactions constant. We found that, after term limits, representatives from the governor's party prioritized oversight more than those from the opposing party. We concluded that lack of experience in the House led representatives from both parties to a misplaced focus on this activity. Republican representatives missed a political opportunity after term limits, and Democratic representatives risked alienating the governor's office.

We cannot replicate our prior work using the Senate because we cannot isolate term limits effects from changes in the governor's party affiliation. The pre-term-limits baseline for the Senate involves a chamber majority from the governor's political party, and both post-term-limits Senate sessions confront an executive branch controlled by the opposite party. We can only note that in our bivariate analyses the less experienced 2007–10 Republican senators do indeed place a lower priority on monitoring compared to the 2003–06 session led by House veterans who migrated to the Senate after being termed out of the lower chamber. It appears that the less experienced 2007–10 senators as well as inexperienced representatives in 2003–04 missed opportunities to challenge the administration of a Democratic governor.

This discussion assumes that there is some political payoff from monitoring state agencies, an assumption that some scholars dispute, but that our results support. We find that legislators in safe seats place a lower priority on monitoring, and conversely those representing more competitive districts place a higher priority on it. The effect is noteworthy, about one-quarter of a point on a variable with a 5-point range. On the other hand, politically ambitious legislators are not more inclined to prioritize monitoring. Neither are lame ducks, although they also do not shirk with respect to this. So we find mixed evidence about political motivation to perform this activity, possibly reflecting personal circumstances.

As our respondents claim and work of other scholars confirms, oversight is the work of legislative specialists. Our results show that the subgroups named by our respondents as responsible for this task do indeed prioritize it, but these groups are chamber specific. In the House this subgroup is Appropriations Committee members. In the Senate JCAR members prioritize oversight.

Legislators' attitudes and their personal characteristics (gender) appear to affect their effort to monitor state agencies. Women legislators appear to eschew monitoring, a rare instance of gender effects on legislators' behaviors. And those who do not think this is their responsibility, logically, spend less time on the task. The proportion of respondents who claim that oversight is not part of their job increases in both chambers after term limits, from 38 percent to 43 percent in the House and from 35 percent to 38 percent in the Senate. So, reduced awareness of this responsibility is another indirect effect of term limits.

Multivariate Model of Grades for Implementing Programs

We include many of the same variables discussed above to explain the grades legislators give for the chamber's ability to monitor the implementation of programs—a task that state agencies perform. Our dependent variable consists of whole numbers on a scale from 0 to 12 (values of 0 for an F to 12 for an A+), with each number representing about one-third of a letter grade (i.e., the addition of a "+" or a "−" to a letter grade). Our model explains a little more than one-third of the variation in the grades given. Coefficients for 10 of the 13 variables in the model are statistically significant. In general, we assume that more experienced and knowledgeable legislators grade harshly when the chamber performs poorly. We find mixed support for this pattern.

The grade our respondents give themselves for monitoring the implementation of programs, about a C, is lower than grades they give themselves for other tasks. We find, however, that term limits increase the grade both chambers give for this. This effect of term limits is the largest effect in the model presented in table 11.3. Thus, we are left with a conundrum—term limits decrease the effort devoted to monitoring (see the previous section), but raise the grade. This implies that term-limited legislators laud their lax monitoring.

To resolve this puzzle, we consider chamber differences. Grades given by post-term-limits senators increase more than those given in the House. And, we remind readers that during the transition to term limits, senators place a higher priority on monitoring. So their higher grades appear reasonable.

Additionally, the linkage we expected between effort and grades does show up in the open-ended comments. Respondents who said there is *"no time for monitoring"* or that it just is not being done gave lower grades. This effect is the second largest in the model, indicating that lack of effort devoted to this task is perceived negatively. Additionally, other cohorts of respondents grade the chamber's monitoring harshly, especially those in a position to know more about monitoring.

As we noted earlier, the complicated task of monitoring is the purview of specialists—Appropriations Committee members in the House and JCAR members in the Senate. We combined these two groups of experts into one categorical variable assuming that their knowledge would influence their

TABLE 11.3. The Chamber's Grade—Monitoring Agencies

Model Predicting the Grade for Monitoring the Implementation of Programs	B	Std. Error	t	Sig.
Constant	1.779	.584	3.048	.003
Term Limits	.671	.389	1.725	.086
Chamber (Senate = 1)	.066	.517	.127	.899
Interaction of Term Limits and Chamber	1.348	.637	2.115	.035
On Appropriations Committee or JCAR	.736	.440	1.671	.096
Interaction of Term Limits and Appropriations or JCAR	−.996	.515	−1.932	.054
Lame Duck	−.079	.265	−.298	.766
Politically Ambitious	−.607	.252	−2.410	.017
Chamber Leader is experienced	.458	.281	1.632	.104
No Time for Monitoring	−1.085	.238	−4.549	.000
Politics Thwarts Monitoring	−.525	.243	−2.163	.031
Priority Placed on State Agency Information	−.144	.112	−1.293	.197
Same Party as the Governor	.639	.233	2.740	.007
Grade for Passing Good Laws	.438	.045	9.848	.000

Note: Bold type indicates statistically significant coefficients.
F = 14.93; Adjusted R^2 = 0.36; n = 315.
Dependent Variable: Mean = 4.77; Minimum, 0; Maximum, 11; Skewness = 0.12; Kurtosis = −0.53.

grading. After term limits, these specialists give the chamber lower grades, possibly reflecting the dwindling effort devoted to monitoring. We also assumed lame ducks, who have greater experience, would understand the risk of lax oversight. So we thought they too would give low grades for the chambers' underachievement on this task. But we find no lame duck effect. Finally, when a chamber has an experienced caucus leader, legislators grade the chamber's performance more positively. As we explained in chapter 10, leadership matters.

Grades appear to have political overtones. We assumed that legislators with closer ties to the governor or state agency officials would not want the executive branch to be closely supervised. Therefore, we expect them to give a higher grade for lax oversight. This is true for members of the governor's political party. Additionally, we find that legislators who claim that *Politics Thwarts Monitoring* give their chamber a lower grade. This implies that those who give low grades want not only more monitoring, but more effective monitoring. Finally, politically ambitious legislators give lower grades for lax monitoring. Once again we find some evidence that monitoring offers some political payoff in the hands of legislators who recognize this potential. But after term limits, fewer legislators understand this, even if they know that they have the prerogative or the responsibility to oversee the bureaucracy.

Summary

We find that legislative oversight is an avoided task among Michigan's legislators. The priority placed on it is exceptionally low. And term limits exacerbates this problem in the House, although less so in the Senate. We find strong support for the specialized nature of legislative oversight—it is the job of specialists who place a higher priority on it and assess the chambers' performance on this task differently. After term limits, however, even more legislators are not aware that the chamber has the authority and responsibility to perform this task. Our findings indicate that about 5 percent fewer legislators in each chamber after term limits are aware that oversight is part of their job.

This lack of awareness seemingly explains the paradox of lax performance and higher grades after term limits. Knowledge appears to increase legislators' awareness of their shirking. Members of specialized subgroups who are more knowledgeable about monitoring give lower grades, indicating dissatisfaction with their chamber's lax performance.

Increasingly oblivious to this part of their job, term-limited legislators are likely to cede control to state agencies, undermining institutional checks and balances. The checks and balances between branches of government seem to work poorly even before term limits, and often they are used as a political cudgel rather than as a tool for promoting good government and neutral technical competence in the bureaucracy. Term limits appear to exacerbate this situation.

Working with the Governor

As we noted earlier, our research covers the tenure of two governors with very different leadership styles as well as divergent political backgrounds. And as Rosenthal (2004, 2013) notes, the leadership styles adopted by the governor and the legislative leaders affect the tone of legislative-executive branch relationships. As we described earlier, both the governor and legislators lost experience during our study period, and both the House and the executive branch shifted political parties. This clearly complicates our task of isolating term limits effects.

Bivariate Analysis: Working with the Governor

In table 11.4 we see that neither chamber relied heavily on information from Governor Engler's office (through 2002) when considering a committee issue. Indeed, one might say they avoided this source of information. This might indicate the natural tension between the executive and legislative branches, regardless of their partisan affiliation. After Governor Granholm's election (third House session 2003–04 and the second Senate session 2003–06), the priority placed on information from the governor's office increases to almost its average level for legislators in both chambers. This implies that majority party legislators recognized the political realities of a gubernatorial veto from an executive branch controlled by the opposite party, motivating them to consult or negotiate with the governor's office. Moreover, her co-partisans seem inclined to prioritize information from her office. Yet, with the same governor and partisan control, the priority placed on information from the governor's office plummets for senators in 2007–10.

Once again, experience appears to matter. The higher priority placed on information from the governor's office by senators in 2003–06 compared to 2007–10 can be interpreted as demonstrating that House veterans who migrated to the Senate better understood the need to work with a governor from the opposite political party. But we note that higher is a relative term. At its highest, the priority placed on information from the governor's office is only average in the Senate. Clearly the governor's office is not at the top of the list of legislators' sources of information.

Returning to table 11.4, we find the grade for working with the governor's office trends steadily downward in both chambers across the sessions. The pre-term-limits senators, despite complaining about the heavy hand of Governor Engler, gave their relationship with him a fairly high grade of 8.7 (between a B and a B+). This falls to the C/C+ range in the 2003–06 Senate and even further to the D+/C– range for the 2007–10 Senate. With the new governor, some of our respondents protested our question by asking, "What about her ability to work with us?" (interview notes).

The 2003–06 Senate session provides some insight into the shared responsibility for the quality of the relationship between the governor and the legislature. With highly experienced legislators (veterans from the House) controlling the Senate, the grade given by senators for working

TABLE 11.4. Relationship with the Governor

	N	Min	Max.	Mean	Std. Dev.	F-Statistic
Relying on Governor for Information (difference measure)						
						5.35***
House						
+Before Term Limits	89	–2.24	1.91	–.4918	.88	
First Session after Term Limits	83	–2.25	1.66	–.5660	.89	
Second Session after Term Limits	85	–2.47	1.22	–.6498	.90	
+Third Session after Term Limits	85	–2.00	2.75	–.1171	1.07	
						0.71
Senate						
+Before Term Limits	29	–1.65	1.83	–.2553	1.01	
First Session after Term Limits	24	–1.64	2.79	.0277	1.12	
Second Session after Term Limits	24	–1.69	1.44	–.2762	.87	
Grade for Working with the Governor's Office (grades A to F)						
						13.21***
House						
+Before Term Limits	—	—	—	—	—	
First Session after Term Limits	25	0.0 (F)	12.0 (A+)	7.6	4.1	
Second Session after Term Limits	55	1.0 (D–)	12.0 (A+)	8.6	2.6	
+Third Session after Term Limits	43	2.0 (D)	11.0 (A)	5.7	2.0	
						24.62***
Senate						
+Before Term Limits	32	0.0 (F)	12.0 (A+)	8.7	2.4	
First Session after Term Limits	27	0.0 (F)	10.0 (A–)	5.9	2.7	
Second Session after Term Limits	26	0.0 (F)	11.0 (A)	3.7	3.1	

* $p \leq 0.10$, ** $p \leq 0.05$, *** $p \leq 0.01$.

with a novice governor falls, but not that much compared to the coming low point of the 2007–10 Senate session. In this session less experienced senators with the same partisan control of the chamber confront the same governor, and the grade falls nearly a whole letter grade—almost to a D+. This reflects a difficult relationship, as evidenced by a budget stalemate that shut down state government in October 2007. As we discuss in our multivariate analysis, leadership experience matters. Although senators from the two political parties disagree on whom to blame this fraught relationship, they agree on its poor quality.

Multivariate Model of Working with the Governor

As we discussed earlier, all the relationships we examine in this chapter are likely to be the purview of specialists. This time the specialists are the top chamber leaders and Appropriations Committee members, who must work with the governor to produce a budget. We also control for chamber because the Senate after term limits is a reservoir of experience compared to the House.

But we also anticipate that this is a two-way relationship depending on both the governor and the chamber leaders. As Rosenthal (2004) observed, governors have the institutional tools to exert strong influence over their relationship with the legislature, should they have the desire and ability to wield these tools. Rosenthal (2004, 2013) comments further that governors can meld attitudes, ranging from friendly to confrontational, with either a legislative or executive style. Governors with a legislative style excel at relationships, cutting deals, and legislative politicking. Governors with an executive style are more aloof, forming few relationships with legislators. Thus, we control for the effect of governor in our analyses.

In table 11.5 we see that our model explains just over a third (35%) of the variation in the grade for working with the governor. We remind readers that we added this question to the interviews partway through the project and asked it only of experienced respondents. Therefore we cannot effectively use term limits in our model, and we have only 193 respondents.

The most powerful variable in this model is the governor. Although there are several differences between these governors, two important ones are political party and experience. We control for the effect of political party using a variable for sharing the governor's political party. The biggest remaining difference between Governors Engler and Granholm is experience. Legislators, even in her own party, often expressed frustration about working with Governor Granholm, and they attribute much of this to her lack of legislative experience. For example, one legislator said,

> "This governor . . . would have been more successful if she had legislative experience. She didn't know how to work with the House or Senate members with experience and connections to people on the ground . . . She has not utilized the legislature, established friendships to make you want to support her, she has not called on the legislature for experience." (interview notes)

On the other hand, the relationship between the legislature and the governor is a two-way street. And we find that when more experienced legislators led the Senate, respondents gave higher grades for this relationship—during Governor Granholm's first term when she had the least experience. Yet senators, who tend to be more experienced, appear more frustrated with their gubernatorial relationship than are representatives. Similarly, legislators with more experience in their current chamber grade the chambers' relationship with the governor more harshly. The lower grades these more experienced legislators gave could reflect their higher expectations for this relationship and their knowledge of what could and should occur. Members of the governor's political party also assess the relationship between the governor and the legislature more negatively. This could reflect their own frustrations trying to work with Governor Granholm, or their resentment of the partisan way the Republican majority treated her, or both.

Interestingly, members of the Appropriations Committee, a subgroup that works most closely with the governor, grade this relationship the same

TABLE 11.5. The Chamber's Grade—Working with the Governor

Model Predicting the Grade for Working with the Governor	B	Std. Error	t	Sig.
(Constant)	**3.33**	.60	5.56	0.00
Chamber (Senate = 1)	**−0.71**	.43	−1.65	0.10
Chamber leader is experienced	**1.36**	.45	3.04	0.00
On Appropriations Committee	.58	.40	1.46	0.15
Years of service in current chamber	**−0.13**	.06	−2.38	0.02
Governor	**3.69**	.45	8.16	0.00
Same party as the Governor	**−0.90**	.39	−2.30	0.02
Grade-passing good laws	**.29**	.07	4.00	0.00
Is a chamber leader	**1.59**	.65	2.43	0.02

Note: Bold type indicates statistically significant coefficients.
F = 13.96; Adjusted R^2 = 0.35; n = 193.
Dependent Variable: Mean = 6.92; Minimum, 0; Maximum, 12; Skewness = −0.44; Kurtosis = −0.70.

way their colleagues do. On the other hand, top leaders, the legislators who work most closely with the governor, are more favorably disposed toward their relationship with the governor. The effect is fairly large—more than one-half of a letter grade. So in general, despite the bad press and generally negative assessment of this relationship, those who work on a daily basis with the governor's office assess their relationship more positively. Given their partial responsibility for this relationship, their judgment might be biased.

Other Measures of the Legislative-Executive Branch Relationship

Given our limited ability to probe the effects of the partisan shift that coincides with term limits in the Senate using only our interview data, we report the number of vetoes by each governor reported in the *Book of the States*. Governor Engler worked with both the pre- and post-term-limits legislature, so his record provides some opportunity to isolate term limits effects.[3]

Governor Engler averaged almost seven vetoes per year before term limits. His average after term limits was a little less than six per year. During his tenure he never used the line-item veto. This suggests that before term limits, even during periods of Democratic control in the House, an experienced governor and experienced chamber leaders could negotiate compromises much of the time.

Looking at Governor Engler's vetoes after term limits, one would expect them to decrease given that both legislative chambers and the executive branch were controlled by the same political party. But the number of vetoes remains nearly constant. This could reflect the institutional independence of the legislature. On the other hand, this constant rate of vetoes could suggest that even an experienced governor will find it challenging to work with a term-limited legislature. The current challenging relationship in Michigan between a novice Republican governor, Rick Snyder, and inexperienced Republican leaders in both chambers certainly supports our interpretation that experience matters on both sides of this relationship even during periods of one-party control.[4]

Governor Granholm averaged about four legislative vetoes per year, plus a little more than four line-item vetoes per year in eight years. Given that her political party did not control both chambers at any time during her tenure in office, this is a very modest number. Her approach to governing was often characterized as conciliatory, so this could indicate some pragmatic willingness to accept legislation advanced by the opposite political party. If this were the case, one would expect her relationship with the legislature to be graded positively. Clearly it was not. State government briefly shut down in a standoff between the governor, novice House leaders, and somewhat more experienced senators, who were nevertheless new to the job of chamber leadership. This rocky relationship implies that her lack of experience constrained her use of her veto pen.

On the legislative side, there is virtually no difference in the legislative batting averages before and after term limits during Governor Engler's tenure. The pre-term-limits batting average is 22 percent overall.[5] The post-term-limits batting average across both governors' administrations was only slightly lower, 20.5 percent. And the portion of this occurring under Governor Granholm's tenure is 20 percent, barely below the average.

We conclude two things from this discussion. First, even with one-party control of government, the relationship between the executive and legislative branches is likely to be rocky after term limits. A governor as highly experienced as John Engler appears to have had some trouble avoiding this tension, and he faced only one term-limited chamber.

Second, the declining trajectory of the grades is more consistent with increasingly public episodes of conflict than it is with nearly stable rates of bills passed and vetoed. Therefore, we believe that the grades our respondents gave more accurately reflect the relationship between the executive and legislative branches than do the vetoes.

Finally, partisanship clearly matters, but experience is also a crucial factor on both sides of this relationship. Inexperience is the future condition of all the key actors in this relationship. Our prognosis is that tension will persist between the legislature and the governor in the term limits era in Michigan regardless of single-party or divided control of state government.

Working with the Other Chamber

Members of the lower chamber often chafe at what they see as the superiority complex of the upper chamber. As one House respondent put it when we asked about the relationship with the Senate, "You mean the House of Lords?" (interview notes). Given the increasing gap in experience between the chambers after term limits, we anticipate that the House will feel even more like the Senate "lords it over them." And, as we found in chapter 9, the gap in influence between the two chambers expands after term limits. Therefore, we predict that grades given for the relationship between the two chambers are likely to fall among representatives after term limits. The Senate, on the other hand, gains influence, and so senators are likely to be more satisfied with the relationship, giving it higher grades.

Bivariate Analysis: Working with the Other Chamber

Table 11.6 shows that after term limits senators place a higher priority on consulting across the capitol dome. That said, in both chambers and for most sessions, we find that information from colleagues in the other chamber does not have a high priority as indicated by the negative values for this normalized measure. After term limits, senators tend to place a higher priority on information from representatives than representatives on information from senators. We suspect that senators maintain relationships with their former chamber colleagues established during their recent stint in the lower chamber. But with an influx of newcomers who do not know the senators, the effect is muted in the House. We find only a small increase in the final House session in the priority representatives place on information from senators.

Grades tell a different story. Looking again at table 11.6, we see that the grades representatives give for working with senators rise slightly after term limits. During all three of the post-term-limits House sessions Republicans

TABLE 11.6. Relationship between the Two Chambers

	N	Min.	Max.	Mean	Std. Dev.	F-Statistic
Relying on Colleagues in the Other Chamber for Information (difference measure)						
House						2.31*
+Before Term Limits	86	−1.75	1.75	−.45	.85	
First Session after Term Limits	83	−2.37	1.24	−.58	.78	
Second Session after Term Limits	82	−2.33	2.00	−.54	1.00	
+Third Session after Term Limits	83	−2.00	1.69	−.24	.94	
Senate						1.69
Before Term Limits	29	−2.17	1.38	−.50	.81	
First Session after Term Limits	24	−1.64	1.94	−.28	1.06	
Third Session after Term limits	24	−2.19	1.53	−.02	1.01	
Grade for Working with Other Chamber (grades A to F)						
House						2.85*
+Before Term Limits	—	—	—	—	—	
First Session after Term Limits	25	2.0 (D)	11.0 (A)	5.6	2.5	
Second Session after Term Limits	56	0.0 (F)	12.0 (A+)	6.8	2.1	
+Third Session after Term Limits	44	2.0 (D)	11.0 (A)	6.6	1.9	
Senate						6.45***
Before Term Limits	32	0.0 (F)	11.0 (A)	6.1	2.8	
First Session after Term Limits	24	0.0 (F)	10.0 (A−)	6.7	2.2	
Third Session after Term limits	26	0.0 (F)	11.0 (A)	4.2	2.7	

*$p \le 0.10$, **$p \le 0.05$, ***$p \le 0.01$.

controlled both chambers. Grades for working with the House are stable in the Senate until the final post-term-limits session, when they plummet. This steep decline in grades given by senators coincides with the term-limits equilibrium in that chamber (2007–10). But simultaneously Democrats regained control of the House in the 2007–08 and 2009–10 sessions. Therefore, it is difficult to disentangle the effects of inexperienced senators from split-party control of the chambers.

We do, however, have another period of split control between the chambers. During the first two years of their 1999–2002 session pre-term-limits senators worked with House veterans. During the last two years of that session they confronted the first wave of term-limited representatives, about whom they complained vigorously. The following open-ended comments from the pre-term-limits senators imply that a combination of experience and partisanship explains grades senators give for working with the House. One veteran Republican senator separated his grades saying that before term-limits the relationship with the Democratic-controlled House was an A– or a B+, but afterward it fell to a D despite Republican Party control of both chambers. Some senators described the post-term-limits House as chaotic and a tool of Governor Engler, even saying explicitly that it was easier to work with veterans from the opposite political party. Because veteran senators and veteran representatives from opposite political party worked fairly well together before term limits, we infer that experience can overcome the partisan divide. After term limits, split party control of the chambers undermines senators' assessment of their work with the House.

Multivariate Model of Working with the Other Chamber

To untangle factors that might influence the two chambers' ability to work together, we test a multivariate model. Once again we explore the role of a subgroup of specialists—those legislators more heavily involved in working across the capitol dome. To do this we created a variable that adds up a legislator's opportunities to work with the other chamber—giving one point each to service on the Appropriations Committee, being a ranking committee member, being a top leader, and serving on any of several joint House-Senate committees.[6] We called this variable *Work across Chambers*.[7] It ranges from 0 to 4. We expect that legislators with a role that requires them to work with the other chamber will develop greater understanding of their partners and correspondingly give higher grades for their relationship.

Referring to table 11.7, we see that our model explains 22 percent of the variation in the grades given for the chambers' ability to work with each other. We remind readers that once again we cannot include term limits in our model because this question was added after the pre-term-limits House interviews. Moreover, our decision to ask this question only of respondents with at least one term of experience means that we have only 183 respondents for this part of the analysis, making it more difficult to establish statistical significance. Yet the model performs reasonably well, and several independent variables provide interesting insights.

Overall we find that senators have a fairly low assessment of their relationship with the House—lower than representatives' views of the Senate by nearly a full letter grade. This contradicts our expectation that senators would be happier about a relationship that they are better positioned to control. It is consistent, however, with senators' disgust with novice representatives, expressed by many during our interviews. As one Republican senator said of his co-partisans in the House, "The relationship is terrible right now. With term limits the Governor has too much influence over the House and House members don't understand the process" (interview notes). Many Democratic senators expressed even more frustration with statements such as "The House appears in chaos" and "They're an unstable body" (interview notes).

We find that legislators with more opportunities to work across the capitol dome view chamber relationships differently. The senators who do more *Work across the Chambers* soften their harsh judgment of representatives by about one-third of a letter grade. This difference might capture

TABLE 11.7. The Chamber's Grade—Working with the Other Chamber

Model Predicting the Grade for Working with the Other Chamber	B	Std. Error	*t*	Sig.
Constant	**5.82**	.62	9.44	0.01
Chamber (Senate = 1)	**-2.94**	.68	4.35	0.01
Works across the chambers	-.54	.32	-1.71	0.09
Interaction of chamber and work across chambers	**1.01**	.44	2.30	0.02
Priority of consulting colleagues in other chamber	-.13	.17	-0.75	0.45
Normal tension between chambers	-.59	.42	-1.43	0.15
Conflict within the same party	**-1.16**	.39	-2.94	0.00
Blames chamber leaders	-.50	.35	-1.53	0.16
Years of service in current chamber	-.01	.05	-0.18	0.86
Chamber leader is experienced	**0.85**	.34	2.48	0.01
Grade-passing good laws	**.25**	.06	4.07	0.00

Note: Bold type indicates statistically significant coefficients.
F = 6.29; Adjusted R^2 = 0.22, n = 183.
Dependent Variable: Mean = 6.18; Minimum, 0; Maximum, 12; Skewness -0.44; Kurtosis 0.07.

the greater satisfaction of those better able to control the relationship—senators. Conversely, representatives' negative views of Senators appear to harden the more they interact with senators—possibly a reaction to the perceived superiority complex often attributed to the upper chamber. This difference is small and only barely statistically significant, however.

Some legislators do not expect these chamber relationships to be harmonious. For example, some legislators expressed the opinion that much of the friction in the relationship was simply part of the normal tension between legislative chambers. This tension reflects different election cycles, different levels of district homogeneity, and so on. To control for respondents' orientation toward these institutional differences, we created a categorical variable called *Normal Tension between Chambers*. Although this variable was not quite statistically significant, its negative coefficient implies that one should not expect the chambers to be overly solicitous toward each other.

Political parties on the other hand are expected to be internally harmonious. We created a variable, *Conflict within the Same Party*, to control for respondents who complained about partisan conflict between chambers even though one party controlled both chambers. Respondents who made these comments gave lower grades for working with the other chamber. The effect is a bit more than one-third of a letter grade.

Many respondents blame chamber leaders for the chambers' problems. In the eyes of many senators, it is the responsibility of caucus leaders to oversee the deals their caucus members make and make the deal stick. One senator asserted, "A deal is not a deal anymore," after describing three different "deals" made by the House in one day on the same bill (interview notes). One respondent volunteered, "Last term was a disaster because of the speaker. Some people let power corrupt them when they are in leadership" (interview notes). To control for this we created a categorical variable denoting whether respondents *Blame the Leaders* for the chambers' problems. The effect of this variable is very small and not statistically significant.

Chamber leadership, however, appears to be an essential ingredient of the relationship between the chambers. So we include a variable, which we described earlier, that denotes whether these leaders had more than one term of experience in their position. We find evidence that strongly supports the value of experienced chamber leaders in promoting a positive relationship. The effect increases the grade given by almost one-third of a letter grade, implying that experienced leaders improve the performance of the chambers as a whole.

Overall, we conclude that experienced chamber leaders play an important role in the ability of legislative chambers to work well together. It is not clear how Michigan can develop these leaders, however, given its stringent limits on service. Senators are more fully aware of the legislative process of deal making and negotiation, leading them to express their dissatisfaction with novice legislative partners across the capitol dome. Lack of experience appears to exasperate senators more than the different institutional imperatives and different political party positions, some of which they regard as part of the normal tension between chambers.

Conclusions

In this chapter we explored some effects of term limits that extend outside Michigan's legislative chambers. Our most consistent finding is that more chamber leader experience enhances all three relationships we consider here: monitoring state agencies, working with the governor, and working with the other chamber. The increment attributable to leader experience is roughly one-third of a letter grade in all three instances. Term limits severely truncate rungs on the leadership ladder, so this is an indirect effect of term limits.

During the transition to term limits, veterans migrating from the lower chamber are likely to lead the upper chamber. Thus it might take a while for the effect of inexperienced leaders to surface in term-limited states. But once these states reach a term limits equilibrium, inexperienced leaders will be the norm, especially in states with stringent limits. In the Michigan House, a pattern has emerged in which a sophomore legislator moves into leadership, and serves again as a leader, now experienced, in his or her final term if the party retains control of the chamber. This means that the best the House can hope for is alternating between inexperienced and experienced leaders. And even these "experienced" leaders lack overall legislative experience compared to their pre-term-limits predecessors.

It is highly unlikely that a first-term senator would become the leader. So, with only two terms in the Senate, going forward all Senate leaders will lack leadership experience unless they acquire it in the lower chamber. So far, no post-term-limits House speakers or minority party leaders have become senators. So even in the upper chamber, inexperienced leaders and the attendant rocky relationships associated with them appear to be the "new normal" in Michigan.

Legislative oversight and the relationships with the governor and the other chamber seem to be the portfolio of specialists. And those most involved in these relationships often demonstrate a different perspective, awarding grades that differ from those given by their less involved colleagues. Specialized tasks, as we found in chapter 4, appear to be more vulnerable to the effect of limiting tenure. The challenging tasks we examine in this chapter require a skill set beyond the generalists' repertoire. So it is not surprising that working with the other chamber, the governor, and the bureaucracy are graded harshly.

The value of experience, both among the rank and file and their leaders, comes through clearly in this chapter, and it is an important finding about the impact of term limits in Michigan. The value of experienced leaders that we find here supports modifications to term limits that allow legislators to serve in one chamber for their maximum combined length of service in both chambers. This is the reform that California recently adopted in which its legislators can now serve a total of 12 years in either chamber. Previously, California's legislature shared the same stringent limits as Michigan—6 years in the lower chamber and 8 years in the upper. Going forward it will be interesting to observe the impact that this change has on the work of California's legislature. Our findings suggest that the differences will be substantial.

We find political overtones in each of the three relationships that we consider in this chapter. Conflicts within the parties thwart work with the other chamber. Membership in the governor's party colors perceptions of the chamber's relationship with the executive branch. Politics are seen as thwarting monitoring. Yet experience enables legislators to manage the "normal tensions" between chambers and between branches of government. Veteran senators claimed that it was far easier to work with House veterans from the opposite political party while venting frustration about working with novice representatives from their own political party after term limits.

Our findings challenge the perception that legislative oversight does not provide political payoff. Legislators from marginal districts, politically ambitious legislators, and members who do not share the governor's party affiliation all seem to recognize the value in challenging or embarrassing the governor. That said, oversight is an avoided task throughout most of our study period. Therefore, one is tempted, given the dearth of monitoring, to applaud any motivation, even partisan pandering, for performing this task. But monitoring undertaken or suppressed for partisan gain tends not to advance the public welfare so much as score points and produce "gotcha moments."

Consequently, we recommend educating state legislators about their role in overseeing the work of the executive branch. If more realized it was their responsibility, they might spend a bit more time on it. Given the level of expertise needed to perform this task, the value of such training might be nearly universal. Various orientations and training sessions are conducted for the throngs of newly elected legislators in Michigan. We argue that oversight needs to become a substantial part of the curriculum. There are oversight techniques that can be taught, and legislators can be apprised of sources of information to help them monitor. Additionally, while training them, legislators could be normed to regard this task in a manner consistent with our system of checks and balances—a basic tenet of American government that seems to elude increasing numbers of them.

TWELVE

Conclusions

At the outset we compared term limits to a rock thrown into a lake. The rock produces waves. The nature and dynamics of those waves, term limits' direct effects, are interesting and worthy of investigation. But we also learn a lot about the lake (the legislature or state government) while examining the waves. In some cases mere ripples barely break the surface. Other times waves of change fundamentally alter the lake, leaving lasting impacts. From this perspective term limits provide political scientists with an opportunity to test a host of theories and propositions about characteristics of legislative bodies and their impact on governing (Mooney 2009). We embraced that approach throughout this book.

We find evidence that term limits do have effects across time within a single state. Some effects are direct and obvious; others are subtle and indirect. Many effects are contrary to proponents' expectations. But after careful examination, we are convinced that term limits substantially alter Michigan's legislature and its state government.

First, we summarize the most important of these effects here, moving through each chapter sequentially. Then we use crosscutting themes to integrate and synthesize effects that recur throughout the chapters. We use these topics to speculate about overarching changes that affect and reflect Michigan political institutions. Finally, we suggest ways term limits research might proceed, including reforms and corrective actions to ameliorate some of what we consider to be term limits' harmful effects.

Key Findings of Term Limits Effects

In chapter 2 we identify differences and similarities between the new and old breed of legislator. Simply removing the so-called drag of incumbency does not diversify Michigan's state legislature. Our female and minority respondents said that an open seat did **not** motivate them to run. White male legislators often replace women and minority legislators who are termed from office. The net result in Michigan is a "new breed" that is more homogenous, not less. Part of this results from candidate recruiting and part from losing elections.

First, the demand for candidates increases dramatically in Michigan after term limits. To meet this need for candidates, post-term-limits legislators are likely to have been asked to run, most often by political elites, but also, to a lesser extent, by interest groups. Many of these actors recruit candidates who strongly resemble the pre-term-limits legislature. For example, political elites recruit more white men than women or minority candidates after term limits. Therefore, current patterns of recruiting are likely to reproduce the existing levels of gender and ethnic diversity, despite abundant open seat opportunities.

The second impediment to diversifying the legislature is that fewer viable female candidates win their election contest after term limits.[1] More Democratic women enter primary elections after term limits, although fewer Republican women do. So participation is only part of the explanation. In the case of Democratic women, many of them compete against each other in primary elections, reducing their success rate. But after term limits, women are less likely to win even when they make it to the general election. The success rate for women from both political parties drops in general elections after term limits.

The biggest difference between the new and old breeds of legislator is that the post-term-limits breed is vastly more politically ambitious than their predecessors. Political ambition plus stringent term limits transform Michigan's legislature into a springboard to another political office (e.g., big city mayors; judges; county, state, and national office). State legislator is no longer a career, but rather one rung on a political career ladder. Yet our respondents say that they ran for the same reasons that their predecessors did. Making a difference and working on issues are among their top reasons. Thus, the new breed is a little more homogeneous (white men gain) and a lot more politically ambitious, but otherwise quite similar to the old breed.

In chapter 3 we discover wider gaps between constituents' partisan preferences and their legislator's roll call votes after term limits. Term limits do not attract legislators who act as delegates "voting their district." Yet we hesitate to call them Burkean trustees, because rather than weighing evidence to pursue the common good many of them tell us they arrived in the capital with their minds made up. We call them "Burkean cowboys" to depict their disregard for their voters' views. More generally, we find that representation is a multifaceted concept that is difficult to measure and even harder to predict empirically.

Yet voters may want to know how their legislator approaches the complicated job of representative democracy because legislators' approach toward representation affects the priority they place on other parts of the job. Moreover, the connections between a legislators' orientation toward representation and the tasks he or she prioritizes change with term limits. State-focused legislators before term limits emphasized monitoring state agencies, but afterward those with a state focus prioritize attending events in the capital and devote more effort toward building coalitions to pass legislation. Legislators who focus on their district prioritize bringing resources to the district and talking to voters. Those whose voting record does not reflect the district spend more time fundraising after term limits, possibly signaling that their political ambition distracts them from the district. Knowing a legislator's orientation toward representation may help voters choose the type of legislator they want to serve them.

In chapter 4 we learn that some legislative tasks are the remit of specialists, while others are performed by almost all legislators. Casework appears to be a central task for all Michigan's legislators, with or without term limits. Legislating, on the other hand, is not where most Michigan legislators concentrate their efforts, especially after term limits. Only a specialized set of expert lawmakers emphasize developing new legislation—lawyers, for example.

Bringing resources to the district (getting pork) is a popular task that remains prevalent even after term limits. It appears that there is political value in bringing home the bacon, given that politically ambitious legislators (who multiply after term limits) place a higher priority on this than do their less ambitious colleagues. Thus, term limits, by increasing the number of politically ambitious legislators, increase the time devoted to bringing home the bacon.

Political ambition and lame duck status mediate term limits effects on legislators' allocation of their time. Politically ambitious legislators, especially in their last term, prioritize their time differently on more than half the tasks we asked about. They avoid legislating. They concentrate on talking to voters as well as bringing resources (pork) to the district. Given how many post-term-limits legislators are politically ambitious, these differences in their behavior are consequential for the state.

We find that senators change their behavior more after term limits than representatives do. This implies that term limits do more than simply reduce the collective experience in the lower chamber. The task priorities of post-term-limits senators strongly resemble those of representatives before and after term limits. So, there appear to be changes triggered by term limits that ripple throughout the legislative system. Legislators' time allocation seems to be among these institutional changes.

We find in chapter 5 that anyone hoping term limits would provide voters with more choice among candidates or increase ballot box accountability is likely to be sorely disappointed. Term limits effects on electoral competition are trivial—a few percentage points—and sometime term limits decrease rather than increase competition. Moreover, we find that despite limiting tenure, political accountability remains elusive, and Senate election costs rise.

Open seat elections, which are typically more competitive, multiply after term limits. But term limits mute some typical effects of open seats. For example, in competitive open seat contests, term limits decrease the number of primary candidates running because political elites try to restrict the number of candidates, focusing instead on their party's general election prospects. Combined with the recruiting patterns we found, this challenges term limits advocates' image of independent self-starters (people who initiate their own run for office) jumping into elections in which special interests play a smaller role. Instead, we found more candidates are recruited to run, and party elites and interest groups do more of this recruiting.

Term limits make incumbents safer in Michigan, even though they reduce margins of victory when the seat is open. One reason for this is that quality candidates wait for an open seat rather than challenging an incumbent—especially an incumbent within the same political party. This might not be true in states with longer limits, but when limits are short it is fairly easy to wait for an open seat. But, in either case, after winning their first election, legislators can reasonably expect to serve the maximum permitted years. Reducing the drag of incumbency by limiting tenure seems to increase the short-term staying power of incumbents.

This enhanced incumbent advantage is not tied to legislators' responsiveness to constituents. We find that electoral vulnerability does not reduce gaps between a legislator's roll call voting behavior and the district's partisan preferences. Term limits moderate this slightly, but not enough to offset the bonus incumbents receive in post-term-limits elections. In general, our findings challenge assumptions about voters' capacity to hold elected officials accountable through the ballot box. Not only can post-term-limits incumbents anticipate serving all their permitted time, but the way they vote seems to have little impact on this expectation.

In chapter 6 we examine the sources legislators rely upon for information—information that is likely to affect policy making. According to Mooney (1991), legislators lack time to double-check information during floor votes, so they turn to the sources they trust most. We find that organized groups and lobbyists are named more often as the **most important** source of information in floor votes after term limits, especially in the Senate. This suggests that ties between lobbyists and legislators, especially senators, are closer now than they were before term limits.

Additionally, we find that after term limits senators seek information less often from key local officials during the policy-making process. Without this street-level perspective legislators are deprived of information about how policies affect day-to-day life in their local communities. This has potentially profound consequences for the state and its citizens.

Interestingly we find that term limits are associated with more changes in information gathering in the Senate than in the House. This implies that term limits effects are systemic rather than isolated to lower chambers flooded with newcomers.

In chapter 7 we find that term limits not only alter the sources providing information, but they alter the flow of information within a legislative chamber. Post-term-limits legislators, even senators, demonstrate higher information needs, particularly on technically complex issues. Experts within the chamber proliferate, and often newcomers are seen as experts after term limits. But these experts appear more isolated. The two issue consulting networks we explore depend heavily on one or just a few legislators to link experts to the rest of the chamber after term limits.

These less robust consulting networks can easily fracture into decoupled factions. And the few legislators who are information conduits may have outsized influence on who knows what about an issue. They can facilitate the flow of information or cut it off and keep it localized. And there are few, if any, alternative pathways for outside groups to use to educate legislators.

This bodes poorly for information sharing across party lines and across regions in the state. Sources seeking to educate legislators about issues should expect bottlenecks when trying to diffuse information throughout the chambers. Larger resource-rich groups and multiclient lobbying firms can, and should, deploy their resources to seed information throughout the chamber given the potential impediments to the free flow of information. Smaller grassroots advocacy groups will be hard pressed to adopt this strategy given their more limited resources.

We also find that after term limits legislators with prior professional experience become the "go-to" experts on our technically complex issue, while committee chairs become more important sources of information on our politically salient issue. Once again, the effects of term limits are contingent, but this time depending on the issue. The value placed on experts with professional experience means that organized groups may want to recruit professionals in their field to run for office. This could be a winning strategy for disseminating information within the chamber.

In chapter 8 we see that bipartisan friendships erode as the lower chamber absorbs waves of newcomers. Friendship networks are much less cohesive, especially in the lower chamber, after term limits. Clusters of friends who might work together vanish. Moreover, the composition of tightly linked friendship groups is transformed. Before term limits, highly connected friendship groups in the lower chamber provided opportunities for power brokers to leverage their influence. After term limits, where clusters of friends do exist, they consist of legislators who appear ostracized and disempowered.

After term limits, cohorts of representatives migrate en masse to the upper chamber, bringing their social relationships with them. Some especially close friendships flourish in the Senate, and the structure of friendship in the Senate remains relatively stable. There are still bipartisan friendship groups in the Senate after term limits.

Despite these changes in the structure of friendship, legislators turn to individual friends for advice and guidance on issues more after term limits. Some of these friends have substantive expertise, but when turnover is higher (by term limits standards), friends who lack expertise become the go-to sources for legislators. Consulting with friends can produce an echo chamber effect in which like-minded colleagues reinforce each other's views rather than exposing each other to nuances and the statewide impacts of a policy.

We demonstrate in chapter 9 that term limits alter the paths to influence, as well as the structure of influence. Influence in the House becomes more centralized, concentrated in the hands of a few chamber leaders. Formal influence flourishes, while informal influence declines. Informal influence often arises from expertise or admired personal qualities (referent power).

Formal influence stems from holding specific roles or positions (legitimate power). So legislators seeking influence after term limits should seek a formal position rather than cultivating expertise or personal qualities.

That said, influence seekers should also cultivate friends after term limits. Particularly when turnover is high, legislators appear to attribute more influence to their friends than is justified based on their formal influence or their expertise. This suggests a conflation between friendship and influence. Although friendship in the same session predicts influence, popular legislators (those with more friends) do not necessarily become more popular in subsequent sessions. Influence is similarly transient. Term limits seem to undermine continuity, forcing legislators to constantly rebuild their relationships.

In chapter 10 we describe changes in legislative leadership. Newcomers vote for directive leaders, but then protest the heavy-handed treatment they receive from them. House committee chairs lose some control over the work of their committees and adopt harsh tactics in an attempt to manage committee conflict. House committee hearings led by novice chairs often appear chaotic. Outside groups interject themselves and chamber leaders usurp the chair's decision-making prerogatives, particularly if the chair fails to produce the desired results. Conflict in committees mounts after term limits, especially in the Senate, although committees are still more collegial there compared to the House.

Much of this escalating conflict is blamed on the nature of the issues, but individuals' behaviors appear to contribute as well. Respondents attribute conflict to bad personal dynamics between committee members, chairs who are autocratic, and more intraparty conflict, as well as the usual levels of partisan conflict. House committee chairs manage this conflict with rougher tactics than senators do, by shutting off microphones, ramming legislation through while it is still warm from the photocopier, and limiting questions in committee hearings. Senate committee chairs have at least served on a committee previously, so they appear better at managing committee tensions.

Fewer actors influence key policy decisions after term limits in both chambers, with leaders playing a more pivotal role. Hence the ability of novice legislators to choose capable leaders is consequential. Although legislators complain about these tactics, they continue to favor leaders who are directive and assertive, which seems likely to perpetuate more rough edges throughout the chamber. Yet it is hard for newcomers to judge the candidates for caucus leadership when they vote for them before working with them. Additionally, with term limits leaders are more likely to be lame ducks. Game theory models demonstrate that a known endpoint, which term limits provide, encourages defection. So, not surprisingly, it is more difficult for the caucus to hold lame duck leaders accountable for their behaviors. These leaders can and do usurp the control of committee chairs more freely after term limits.

In chapter 11 we find that term limits undermine relationships outside the chamber. Those between the legislature and the bureaucracy, the governor's office, and between the two chambers are all downgraded. But when chamber leaders are more experienced these relationships improve, even after term limits.

Monitoring state agencies is a task legislators avoided even before term limits. But, after term limits, even fewer legislators are aware that they are responsible for overseeing the work of the executive branch. This undermines the checks and balances in our system of government. The subset of legislators who do more of this work downgrade the quality of the chamber's performance on this task after term limits. And even those who are aware that they should be doing this claim they lack the time and resources to do this part of their job. Finally, the few who do monitor state agencies appear to be motivated by political gain. Inexperience and partisanship interact to undermine opportunities to improve the work of state agencies as they implement public programs and deliver services to citizens. Term limits make a bad situation worse.

Intraparty conflicts complicate working relationships between novice legislative leaders and inexperienced governors, as well as relationships between the two chambers. Subgroups of each chamber work with the governor's office and across the capitol dome, developing specialized skills or relationships. Some of these specialists are more satisfied with these external relationships, but the interactions are still evaluated less favorably after term limits. And some legislators blame novice leaders for gridlock and the collapse of bargains made.

These findings underscore the extent to which experience matters, especially the experience of leaders. We find that a steady experienced hand at the helm can overcome partisanship. But lack of experience produces tension even during periods of single-party control. However, after term limits, there is little way for leaders to gain experience.

Overarching Lessons from the Impacts of Term Limits

We turn now to the insights about Michigan's legislature and its state government that we gained from this investigation. The waves of change from term limits, both big and small, act as probes deepening our understanding of Michigan's politics and institutions. Dissecting the forces that produce these impacts helps to portray the basic shape and function of the legislature and some of the larger processes of governing the state.

Conditional Effects Dominate

One clear and consistent finding, both from statements of legislators and from our own analysis, is the highly contingent nature of legislative reality. There may be deep structures where nomothetic laws exist in these political settings, but those are hidden from us and from our respondents. Rather, context predominates in the many areas, including committee conflict, consulting, lame duck behavior, and representational role orientations.

The nature of the issues legislators confront generates variations. For example, when assessing committee conflict, the most frequent answer was that conflict was a function of the nature of the issues addressed by the committee (see table 10.6). Beyond the two specific issues that we investigate, we were repeatedly told by legislators that their representational role orientations depended on the issue, on the intensity of constituents' opposition, on who objects, and on whether the issue involved taxing and spending or was a core religious or moral issue.

We find that the institutional context of the upper and lower chambers mediate term limits effects throughout our analyses. At the individual level, we find that sometimes gender and ethnicity alter term limits effects. And political party conditions term limits effects on women. Similarly we find political ambition and lame duck status interact with term limits.

Given the overwhelming importance of context in our findings, we advise other scholars to design analyses that control for as many contingencies as possible in order to isolate term limits effects from background noise. We discuss several categories of these contingent effects below in greater detail.

District Maps Filter the Effect of Open Seats

Reinforcing our finding that context matters, general electoral competition alters term limits effects on the associated primary elections. One strategy dominates if a primary leads to a safe general election and another if the primary is the prelude to a competitive general election. Both strategies can, however, produce more extreme candidates. Therefore, we conclude that district maps mediate term limits electoral effects.

If a primary leads to an open seat safe for one political party, candidates flock to primaries, multiplying voters' choices. One such primary election featured 17 candidates. In such a crowded field, even a candidate representing a small fraction of partisans can win. The subsequent general election resembles a coronation for the primary winner rather than a contest providing viable alternatives for voters.

If a primary leads to competitive general elections, party elites anoint and finance candidates for open seats, often insulating them from primary competition. Empirically we find that after term limits fewer candidates enter these primaries. If voters are committed to one or the other political party, they have fewer candidates to choose from after term limits in these districts.

These election strategies may contribute to more partisan polarization after term limits in an electoral environment flooded with open seats. Candidates representing small factions can amplify extreme positions. Given the ideological commitment of party elites, these groomed candidates may also fuel polarization. This may explain some the discrepancy we find between the partisan composition of the district and the votes of its legislator—voting mismatch. If legislators owe allegiance either to party leaders (for competitive seats) or to a relatively narrow slice of their partisan voters (for safe seats), then why would they adapt their roll call votes to the partisan characteristics of the district? Their accountability lies elsewhere. Hence it is not surprising that we find that the gap between legislators' voting records and their district's partisan composition expands after term limits. We conclude that term limits and district boundaries drawn for partisan advantages combine to escalate partisan polarization.

Crosscutting Effects of Ethnicity and Gender

Most minority legislators represent urban districts with boundaries drawn to pack many Democrats into a few districts. This means that they occupy an especially safe seat, so they typically compete in multicandidate primary elections. Additionally, most of these districts have very high levels of poverty. Therefore, it is difficult to untangle the effects of the district's poverty level and the competitiveness of the district, and then still control for the respondent's ethnicity. As a result we did not accumulate as much information about minority legislators as we had hoped for in our analyses. Additionally, as we noted earlier, data from the Secretary of State's office do not indicate candidates' ethnicity, so we could not probe their primary election behavior.

But we do find that ethnic minority legislators focus more on the welfare of their district than of the state as a whole. And they tend to use a delegate style when confronting conflicts between what they think is best and what their constituents want. Open seats are rarely mentioned by ethnic minority legislators as the reason they ran for election. With or without term limits they are motivated to represent the interests of the district, more so than their colleagues. And their approach to representation reflects this.

It is district boundaries rather than open seats that offer the best opportunities for ethnic diversity in Michigan's legislature. Minority legislators still only rarely win seats unless the majority of the voters are also minority group members. Term limits and the attendant open seat elections do not overcome these effects. But the subtle differences we find in the style and focus of ethnic minority legislators indicate the value of diverse perspectives and experiences in the legislature.

Gender effects appear highly contingent as well, but it is their political party rather than district boundaries that mediate women's experiences. Women, especially Democratic women, have lower general election success rates, winning fewer state legislative seats after term limits than they did before. So removing the "drag of incumbency" has not increased their ranks in Michigan's legislature. With fewer self-starters, Republican women dwindled to one-quarter their former (pre-term-limits) strength largely because they do not enter primary contests.

When open seats are plentiful and occur in predictable patterns, as they do after term limits, a lower proportion of women say that the open seat motivated them to throw their hats into the electoral ring. As we summarized earlier, after term limits the need to recruit women rises, yet recruiting after term limits, especially among Democrats, targets men. Thus, we conclude that more open seats may well expand rather than erase the gender gap in Michigan's legislature. Concerted efforts to recruit candidates from underrepresented groups are still necessary.

After term limits, a larger proportion of women who win seats are recruited by interest groups. It would be interesting to explore recruiting patterns with a survey of candidates who lost in the general election. We can only speak about those who won. And among winning candidates, interest groups are the rare actors whose efforts might increase the diversity of the chambers. This larger role for interest groups might dismay term limits advocates given their aversion to special interest involvement in government, however.

But does altering the proportion of men and women in the chambers produce change that is more than skin deep? Except in rare instances, women and men act more like each other after term limits. One of these exceptions is bringing resources to the district. Women place a lower priority on this task. But they also avoid monitoring state agencies even more assiduously than their male colleagues do. After term limits, men's motivation for seeking office changes more than women's, but this decreases the gender gap in their reasons for seeking office. We suspect that social changes in gender roles contribute to this convergence. Post-term-limits men are younger than their pre-term-limits brethren, although we find no change in the average age for women. In many ways, a legislator's gender may not make a lot of difference.

On the other hand, women's information gathering choices differ from men's. They consult the formal leaders within the chamber less than men do. In the Republican Party most chairs and caucus leaders are men. After term limits, Democratic women were elected to top minority party leadership positions in both chambers. Women turn to key local officials and partisan staff for information more than men do. This suggests that electing more women to the legislature could soften some of term limits' information-gathering effects, especially the decline in access that local actors experienced. Gender effects appear to be highly contingent and more subtle than we anticipated.

The Effect of Experience—Newcomers and Lame Ducks

Freshmen face a steep learning curve, but we find that only a few newcomer effects endure. Differences in their time allocation and their consulting patterns dissipate after their first term in office. So the individual newcomer effects of term limits appear ephemeral.

On the other hand, we find more enduring institutional effects that result from the collective reduction in experience and expertise that inevitably characterizes a legislature with a steady stream of newcomers. First, not only does the level of expertise in the chamber decrease, but we find that expertise acquired in the chamber is valued less. Prior career experience seems to substitute for expertise developed in the chamber. In this, Michigan's legislature seems to resemble part-time chambers in which legislators' expertise and influence arise from their professional career rather than their capacity as full-time legislators.

Next, we see enduring newcomer effects in the sources of information that legislators consult more and less heavily after term limits. For example, key local officials are consulted less after term limits, possibly because legislators do not know them well enough to trust their judgment, or because newcomers do not realize that a street-level view of a bill provides valuable insight into what will happen on the ground.

The other "freshman" effect that permeates the legislature is the choice of more directive and assertive leaders. This has consequences for the entire chambers by altering the relationships between leaders and committee chairs and between leaders and their caucus. Although freshmen seem to "outgrow" their preference for these leaders, the sheer number of votes cast by perpetual waves of newcomers favors this style of post-term-limits leader. The size of the cohorts of newcomers enables them to change the leadership dynamics for the whole chamber.

Changes for lame ducks are more systemic. Not only are there large flocks of lame ducks, but the nature of being a lame duck changes with term limits. There have always been legislators who lost elections or retired. But there was also some mystery about whether they would run again. Now everyone knows that legislators must retire at a given point in time. Most of the suspense is gone—except for rare electoral defeats or politically ambitious legislators who gamble on another opportunity before exhausting their tenure in their current office. This produces flocks of lame ducks who are often seen as superfluous.

We find stronger evidence that lame ducks are sidelined rather than that they shirk. Previously seen as issue experts who were consulted more extensively about floor votes, lame ducks are consulted less after term limits. They may be stripped of choice committee assignments just as they get a grasp of the issues. Their wisdom, experience, and expertise seem to be devalued by colleagues who shun their advice and shunt them aside. Unlike pre-term-limits lame ducks, these departing legislators do not focus on completing a legislative agenda (Herrick, Moore, and Hibbing 1994). Political ambition seems to be an especially powerful force among post-term-limits lame ducks with consequences for how they allocate their time. They are driven by activities most likely to advance their electoral goals beyond their current job—casework and getting resources for the district, not legislating.

Chamber Differences

The interaction between term limits and chamber is one of the more persistent findings throughout this research. As cohorts of representatives migrate to the upper chamber, they take many of their House patterns of behavior with them. Without veteran senators to resocialize them into the advantages of the small group format of that chamber, those traditions are lost. For example, the policy discussions among Michigan's senators before term limits, capitalized on the advantages of small groups—meeting as the full caucus. The House uses a mass audience strategy of deliberating in committees (i.e., discussion sections). Both chambers change after term limits, with the Senate doing more work in committees and the House yielding more control to caucus leaders. The chambers converge toward a mixture of caucus and committee input, losing the advantages of small group dynamics in the Senate.

Although socialization can explain some of these chamber differences, it cannot account for some of the chamber-specific electoral effects. In additional to effects from chamber size, other chamber interactions with term limits could reflect district size. For example, Senate elections are more expensive than are House races. This is quite reasonable given that senators compete in districts nearly three times as large as House districts. But this spending gap increases after term limits. This might reflect the greater value to interest groups of electing a Senate candidate whose views are well known from their tenure in the House or just the cost of more newcomers campaigning in a large district. These contrasting trends raise interesting questions about campaign finance that term limits can help scholars explore.

Sometimes term limits minimized chamber differences through contrasting effects on each chamber. For example, the average voting mismatch between legislators' voting records and their constituents' partisan orientations is 10 percent larger in the Senate than in the House before term limits. After term limits the difference between the chambers converges because voting mismatch increases about 5 percent in the House and decreases about 5 percent in the Senate. The question is what motivates these contrasting patterns? Party control is one possible explanation that could be explored.

At other times one chamber is more sensitive to term limits. General election competition is lower in the Senate before term limits. After term limits the difference shrinks to a 1 percent difference between chambers, as general election competition decreases by 7 percent in the House, but decreases only 3 percent in the Senate. The result is that after term limits levels of general election competition are nearly identical in the two chambers, ceteris paribus, albeit lower in both. This raises questions about why one chamber is more sensitive to these forces.

The list of chamber differences, as readers are well aware, could go on.

But the point is that term limits effects are contingent. They interact with the existing institutional structures, they are influenced by state election laws, and they interact with norms and assumptions about the appropriate roles and behaviors of a state's legislators. Therefore cross-sectional research about term limits needs to incorporate as much state-level context as possible lest the effects of term limits are overwhelmed by a variety of state political systems, different political institutions, and the differences in term limits laws themselves.

We counsel patience in waiting for term limits full implementation in both chambers before drawing conclusions about their effects. We also advise scholars to be wary of substituting legislator experience for term limits effects. The regularity with which we find greater impacts in the Senate than in the House suggests that using experience as a surrogate for term limits effects ignores important institutional changes. And our findings convince us that institutional changes are among the more interesting and profound effects of term limits.

Different Types of Leaders

Legislators elect their own managers, and the types of individuals they choose reveal interesting priorities. Prior to term limits the largest proportion of senators chose leaders based on experience and past achievement. In both chambers after term limits, the expertise and knowledge of prospective leaders takes a back seat to their decisiveness and assertiveness. This makes it less surprising that chamber leaders deal more harshly with their chairs and caucus members and work less effectively with external partners (e.g., the other chamber and the executive branch).

Across our analyses it is clear that leaders, especially in the House after term limits, acquire more influence, leading to a much more hierarchically driven legislature, facilitating greater use of rewards and punishment. These leaders use their influence to intercede when chairs don't produce the bills they want as fast as they want. Sometimes they intervene directly in the committee, sometimes indirectly by reassigning a bill to another committee. Despite their complaints about the use of coercion by their leaders, legislators are the ones who chose them. Their choices have consequences.

After term limits, legislators also appear inclined to choose leaders whose focus is on external caucus building. That is, they prioritize fundraising for the caucus, promoting the caucus positions in the media, and other external "caucus building" activities designed to enhance members' reelection prospects. This is especially true in the Senate. This emphasis is consonant with continuous campaigning rather than governing. Continuous campaigning makes it more difficult to form bipartisan coalitions to pass legislation (effort on this declines after term limits), and it reduces the motivation to negotiate and compromise on bills seriously considered by a committee (another activity that wanes with term limits).

We find that term limits trigger a seismic shift in the committee system in both chambers. In the House term limits undermine chairs' influence and control over the legislative process. Part of the reason for this loss is attributed to the poor management or weak leadership of the committee chair. These chairs resort to harsher tactics, such as limiting minority party members to one question during hearings or shutting off their microphones. Time to gather information is restricted as a means to control the committee members, and negotiation and compromise are used less frequently to resolve conflicts. The range of options considered narrows, as chairs rely more heavily on majority voting power to "ram" legislation through.

Before term limits, Senate committee members placed a high priority on information from the caucus when deciding how to vote on an issue considered in a committee. Information flowed from debates among the broader caucus membership and the narrower membership of the committee. After term limits, this channel between the caucus and the committee dissipates, and the caucus becomes less influential. The ultimate effect in both chambers is similar. Both narrow the range of participants and concentrate policy influence in the hands of fewer legislators.

Some of the influence lost by chairs in the House shifts to the governor and to lobbyists, but some of it expands the reach of the House leadership. In the House leaders are not shy about stepping in and taking over the committee, if they do not get the results they want. Leaders also appear to undermine relationships outside the chamber (e.g., the executive branch and the other chamber). These behaviors might have had consequences for pre-term-limits leaders, but after term limits leaders are more often lame ducks who will not be running for a leadership position again. In other words, they are not accountable to their colleagues who voted them into their position. Term limits remove constraints from leaders while simultaneously flooding the lower chamber with newcomers who naively "hire" leaders who are more likely to abuse unbridled use of their tools and prerogatives of office.

The Transformation of Friendship and Influence

The steady unraveling of friendship clusters in the House is one of the most dramatic transformations we see in the institutional structure of Michigan's legislature after limits. The pre-term-limits clusters of friends are gone now, and we could no longer identify bipartisan groups that spend time socializing together.

Prior to term limits in Michigan, amateur musicians from both political parties formed a band that played in bars in the capital. There was a bipartisan hockey team that played in the recreational league in the capital. Legislators knew each other and did things outside the chamber together. We were told repeatedly about a transportation committee trip in the late 1990s throughout rural Michigan to assess regional road needs. The whole committee traveled in a state van for several weeks, staying in little hotels in small towns in the Upper Peninsula and along the lake shores, eating together in local diners. They said they really knew each other well at the end of their road trip. These friendships, which facilitated pre-term-limits legislators' ability to work together across party lines, are gone for the large part.

Simultaneously, we find that fewer legislators are considered influential after term limits. This mainly reflects a loss of informal influence (i.e., people who do not hold a formal leadership position, but were widely known for their expertise or credibility). Especially in the House, Michigan's post-term-limits influence structure is far more centralized, with influence concentrated in the hands of the small group of formal leaders.

We discovered that before term limits, expertise and personal qualities such as honesty and candor produced informal influence. After term limits, it is friendship that tends to generate informal influence—those who are popular are more influential.

Because we interviewed some legislators more than once, we can shed some light on the temporal order of these relationships—does popularity translate into influence or does influence attract friends? We find that friendship itself becomes transient after term limits, rather than growing and expanding across time. Friends leave faster than new friendships are formed. Even more interesting, influence also becomes transient. Among repeat respondents, we find a very strong positive association between influence at interviews one and two. But having lots of influence at the time of second interview is not associated with the level of influence at the third interview. With high rates of turnover, relationships are unstable. They require constant re-creation. This instability makes it harder to know who to trust and rely upon for information and expertise, especially across party lines.

Legislative Specialists and Legislative Generalists

As we explored the task priorities of Michigan's legislators, we realized that there are generalist tasks that almost everyone masters and specialist tasks that only a few legislators grasp. Much of the expertise needed for specialist tasks (e.g., monitoring state agencies) is in short supply after term limits, but the generalist tasks (e.g., talking to voters and helping voters) are not affected much at all. Specialized skills are harder to learn. Term limits constrain the time available to develop specialized expertise. So the work of specialists is neglected more after term limits. This restructures the way legislators spend their time, changing the nature of the job.

We discovered that legislating is the purview of experts—lawyers, legislators with prior government experience, and lame ducks before term limits. Before term limits the Senate was a reservoir of specialized expertise. Consistent with this, senators placed a high priority on developing new legislation before term limits—but not so afterward. Not only is developing new legislation a task for experts, it appears to be the privilege of the majority party in a legislature with strong partisan prerogatives. But also, given the probably of alienating at least some constituents, responsibility for legislating falls mainly on legislators holding fairly safe seats. After term limits, legislating has a lower priority in Michigan's legislature, even in the Senate.

Legislating often creates winners and losers, potentially fueling opponents. Motivated by electoral concerns, risk-averse legislators sidestep legislating. Given their short tenure in office, they can kick problems down the road for someone else to deal with. Rather than credit seeking for developing legislation, politically ambitious legislators avoid legislating— and there are a lot more politically ambitious legislators after term limits. Short-term solutions that delay hard choices allow legislators to move to their next job without alienating many voters.

The top tasks for "generalist" legislators include helping voters (case-work), talking to voters, and attending meetings or events in the district. This evidence contributes to a growing literature suggesting that many legislators see themselves as ombudspersons or resource allocators— helping voters through casework or getting pork for the districts. These are win-win situations in which legislators make a few constituents happy without alienating others. They are tasks that any legislator can and most do perform. But they do not resolve state problems, such as crumbling roads and structural budget problems.

Term limits were sold as a way to motivate legislators to prioritize the public welfare instead of their own political fortunes. But most post-term-limits legislators appear risk averse, especially the growing cohort of the politically ambitious. These risk-averse legislators avoid developing legislation or working across the aisle to pass legislation. As term limits expand the size of this cohort, fewer legislators are likely to try to resolve statewide issues, such as road funding, prison reform, chronic municipal revenue shortfalls, and so on. Not only does the motivation to act seem to ebb, but the knowledge and expertise needed to carry out more specialized tasks, like legislating, is in short supply and harder to acquire. This combination of forces means that the prognosis for resolving major public problems is poor. Coincident with this, Michigan continues to slide in national rankings in educational achievement and infrastructure quality, among other measures, due largely to inaction and little political will to make hard choices.

Knowledge and Information Gathering Alter Policy-Making Access

Term limits alter flows of information in both chambers by changing the priority placed on various sources of information and by removing channels connecting legislators to experts within the chambers. Although there are still some issue experts in the House, they are not well connected with the rest of the chamber. So information no longer moves throughout the House as freely as it did before term limits. We also find less consulting across party lines. This probably reflects, as well as affects, partisan polarization, especially in the lower chamber. With little bipartisan consulting, information appears to be processed in an echo chamber. This is especially true for school choice, the politically salient issue that we examined.

Not only do the two chambers display different information gathering responses to term limits, but the changes in information gathering differ by issue. With respect to the politically salient issues, other committee members and lame ducks were consulted more widely before term limits than afterward. The mixture of interest groups, local sources, and chamber sources consulted about a technical issue does not change as much in the House as it does in the Senate. Results indicate that senators shift their attention away from local sources on both issues, and outside groups and lobbyists gain access after term limits.

Key local officials and advisers in the district lose access to legislators, especially senators, after term limits. The decline in access for local sources has had profound implications for policy making in the state. The Michigan Municipal League, displeased with the post-term-limits legislature, tried to pass a ballot initiative limiting the ability of the legislature to pass laws affecting local governments. They failed. Subsequent cuts to revenue sharing, a crucial source of local funding, may be a consequence of senators' fraying ties to the municipal leaders in their districts.[2] More and more municipalities struggle with budget deficits and service cuts after state legislators slashed their share of the state's sales tax, according to the Michigan Municipal League.[3]

After term limits organized groups and lobbyists displace local actors as the top sources of information about a floor vote in the Senate. If, as Mooney (1991) postulates, floor vote consulting reveals the sources that legislators are willing to rely upon when time is too short to fact check, then this shift in consulting indicates that organized groups and lobbyists have become inside sources of information—those that are the most highly trusted and relied upon. Legislators, increasingly recruited to run for office by organized groups, arrive in the state capital more connected, not less, to outside special interests. This contradicts the stated goals of term limits advocates. That this occurs at the expense of local sources in the Senate— the more skillful of the two chambers—raises more questions about who influences policy making after term limits.

Summary

We believe that the contingent effects we discover raise interesting questions and can inform cross-sectional investigations. In state politics research there are risks in overgeneralizing results from multistate and national studies to individual states. State governments have many similarities, but they also differ. Differences lurk beneath chimeras of similarity. It is easier within the context of a single state to isolate factors that may trigger contingent effects. Then, in cross-sectional studies, investigators can control for some of these. The greater nuance of qualitative research can also be valuable in uncovering these effects. These subtle or substantial variations across states are likely to explain some of the differences in our findings from those of multistate investigations (on this point, we agree with Miller, Nicholson-Crotty, and Nicholson-Crotty 2011). Alerting scholars to these factors is a valuable contribution of our study.

Recommendations for Reform

Stepping back from our analyses, we stress six insights that we deem especially important. First, term limits compound the electoral problems created by gerrymandered districts. We have described several effects of gerrymandering that interact with term limits, such as the different electoral strategies for safe and competitive open seat primaries, both of which increase the potential to elect legislators with extreme views. It may be easier to reduce the tools that aid gerrymandering than to alter term limits. Reformers with concerns about electoral accountability and democratic representation would be well advised to take aim at Michigan's system for drawing district lines. Therefore we recommend that Michigan reform the way electoral boundaries are drawn by adopting a bipartisan system.[4] Other term-limited states have led the way (e.g., California and Arizona). The Supreme Court decision in *Arizona State Legislature v. Arizona Independent Redistricting Commission* opens a path to resolve this.

Second, legislators need to develop friendships, whether by working together or socializing. Cross-party friends are especially valuable, but after term limits these friendships are unlikely to develop without concerted effort. Legislator exchange programs in which they share district coffee hours, take road trips, attend social events, although they might seem contrived, need to be incorporated into the schedule. Interest groups in the state could facilitate this by holding events and creating opportunities for legislators from both political parties to interact socially in informal settings—baseball games, concerts, family retreats, and so on. Given the current conditions of Michigan's roads, another road trip around the state would inform legislators, as well as giving them lots of time together.

Third, many tasks requiring specialized expertise are neglected after term limits. At a minimum all legislators should know that the system of checks and balances underpinning our democracy depends on the legislature fulfilling its responsibility for oversight. The founding fathers would be embarrassed by some post-term-limits legislators' limited comprehension of the system. Committee chairs, minority vice chairs, and appropriations committee members need special training in order to acquire the legislative expertise needed for bureaucratic oversight, as well as the skill to develop new legislation.

Fourth, term limits heighten the need to reform Michigan's primary election system. The current system interacts with term limits and gerrymandering to encourage polarization of Michigan's legislature. Runoff elections, which would pit the top two primary vote recipients against each other in November, could reduce the oversized influence of political elites and of small factions of voters to select candidates who win in a landslide in November.

Fifth, term limits has eroded connections between legislators and their key local officials. This may well have contributed to the state legislature balancing its budget on the backs of local government. As a result many municipal governments in Michigan face financial receivership and struggle to deliver essential services. The Detroit bankruptcy grabbed the headlines, but even affluent communities struggle to balance their budgets in the wake of state policy changes. Legislators show no recognition of their role in the plight of local governments. We recommend training sessions for Michigan's legislators by the Michigan Municipal League, county commissions, and other representatives of local governments, and more media attention to this.

Finally, Michigan's legislature needs more experienced leaders, leaders who are accountable to their caucus and their committee chairs, and leaders who are known to the legislators selecting them. This can only happen if the length of service in the lower chamber increases. Term limits remain popular in public opinion polls in the state, although more knowledgeable voters do not like them (Weissert and Halperin 2007). So it is unlikely that voters will repeal them. But elsewhere there have been some successful efforts to lengthen the limits in the lower chamber. For example, California voters adopted new limits in 2012 that permit a total of 12 years of service in either chamber. Previously California's limits were identical to Michigan's—6 years in the lower chamber and 8 in the upper for a combined total of 14 years of service. This compromise reduced the total service for some legislators by two years, but it provides a way to develop expertise in the lower chamber.

Allowing legislators to serve their total permitted time in the same chamber provides several advantages. First, chamber leaders could serve for a few terms, work their way up through chairing minor committees and then major committees, establishing a reputation before their colleagues fresh off the campaign trail vote them into some of the most influential positions in state government. We saw in chapter 11 that experienced chamber leaders enhanced the chambers' performance and in chapter 10 that inexperienced leaders use harsh tactics.

Leaders with the option of serving again have an incentive to treat their colleagues carefully in order to be elected for another term as the caucus leader. And committee chairs might have time to once again become experts on the issues before their committees. As we noted above, there is a need to develop the expertise needed in specialized tasks in the legislature. Twelve years in either chamber would mean that some legislators would have time to learn to perform these highly technical parts of the job, such as oversight and legislating.

In Closing

Naturally occurring quasi experiments arise only rarely in political science. We believe that these opportunities to learn about state government should not be dismissed after a cursory exploration. We see three consequences of discounting term limits effects: two that affect the subfield of state legislative studies and one that more broadly affects the discipline of political science as a whole. First, a rush to evaluate before implementation thwarts careful investigation of the effects of term limits themselves. It focuses heavily on a spike with the first mass expulsion of veterans. Though the equilibrium stage will persist long after the limits are implemented, this phase has received little scholarly attention.

Second, this rush to judgment undermines the potential for a broader investigation of state legislative processes utilizing term limits as a probe. As Mooney (2009) points out, the effects of experience, incumbent effects, and a host of other political factors can be investigated by comparing term-limited and non-term-limited state legislatures. We have tried to fulfill that potential using Michigan's legislative bodies before tenure was limited and then after.

Third, scholars outside the subfield of state legislative studies have largely ignored the opportunities that term limits provide to test broader propositions about representative government. Term limits provide ample opportunities to explore a host of questions, such as what happens to representation when the electoral connection is decoupled, when wave elections occur, when legislative reforms alter seniority systems in a legislature,[5] or the roles legislators play in public policy making and democratic governance.

We learned much about government and governing in this investigation, thanks to the gracious participation of hundreds of state legislators. We have tried to share some of these insights with the public and with other political scientists. We hope that our work renews interest in term limits research so that the discipline capitalizes on this valuable opportunity. Time is of the essence because term limits in some states are already in the equilibrium stage, although other states are only in the transitional phase. But even more important, we hope the insights we provide into Michigan's government generate interest in reforming and improving state political systems in ways that are more likely to achieve some of the noble goals term limits promised, but failed to deliver.

Appendix

Interview Questions for
Members of the Michigan Legislature

There are several versions of this basic set of questions. The versions are tailored to each chamber, whether the member is on the Appropriations Committee, whether we had interviewed the member before, and whether they could run for election again. Differences are minor. This is the basic House newcomer version.

1. When you initially ran for the House, what were your reasons for running?
2. Did some person or group ask you to run?
3. What groups do you consider among your strongest supporters?
4. Did any experienced legislator help you learn the job or coach you when you first came to the House?
5. Who do you consider to be the most influential members of the House? Why?
6. Do you have any especially good friends among the members of the House?
6a. Do friendships affect the work of the House? How?
7. I'd like to find out how you make up your mind on a bill that reaches the House floor. Let's take Schools of Choice, for example. Are there any fellow House members whom you would rely on for information and guidance on a bill about Schools of Choice?
8. I'd like to find out about sources other than fellow House

members. Are there any sources outside the House member-ship that you would rely on for information and guidance on a bill about Schools of Choice?

9.   In making up your mind on a bill about Schools of Choice, which of the sources of information and guidance that you have mentioned would you rely on most?

10.   Let's consider a bill in another area. Let's talk about a bill licensing or regulating heath care professionals. Are there any fellow House members whom you would rely on for informa-tion and guidance about a bill licensing or regulating health care professionals?

11.   What about sources other than fellow House members? Are there any sources outside the House membership that you would rely on for information and guidance on a bill licens-ing or regulating heath care professionals?

12.   Which of the sources that you have mentioned would you rely on most in making up your mind about a bill licensing or regulating heath care professionals?

13.   I understand that you are a member of the ——— Commit-tee. I would like to find out a number of things about the Committee and your work on it. In several of the questions I am going to ask, I would like you to tell me things about the Committee in terms of this continuum [hand the respondent a card with a scale of categories ranging from an enormous amount to none]. How much control would you say that the Chair of the ——— Committee has over the work of the committee?

14.   How much conflict would you say there is on the ——— Committee?

15.   How is conflict dealt with?

16.   What do you think was the most difficult issue that the ——— Committee seriously considered this term? What made that issue difficult?

17.   Thinking about this issue you just mentioned, I would like to know the extent to which you rely on various possible sources of information and guidance within the House in making up your mind on the issue. We will use the continuum we used before. [Hand respondent a card with a scale of categories ranging from an enormous amount to none].

17.1   Let's begin with the Speaker. How much would say you relied upon the Speaker for information and guidance in making up your mind about the issue mentioned above?

17.2   What about the Party Caucus?

17.3   The Minority Party Leader?

17.4   The Committee Chair?

17.5   Other House members?

17.6   The Partisan Staff (Caucus or Committee staff)?

17.7   The Non-Partisan Staff (Legislative Service Bureau)?

17.8   The House Fiscal Agency?

18.   Now I would like to know something about outside sources. Still thinking about the same issue you mentioned earlier, to what extent did you rely upon the sources outside of the House?

18.1   Let's start with the Governor's Office. How much would you say you relied upon the Governor's Office for information and guidance in making up your mind about the issue mentioned above?

18.2   What about State Agency people?

18.3   State Senators?

18.4   Organized groups or Lobbyists?

18.5   Key local officials?

18.6   Advisors in your district?

18.7   Other constituents?

18.8   National Conference of State Legislatures?

18.9   Were there any other external sources that you rely on for information and guidance? Who?

19.   How do you decide whom to support for party leadership positions?

20.   Now I am going to ask you about some things legislators typically spend time doing. Thinking about your work in the House, I'd like you to tell me the amount of time you personally spend on each of these, again using the continuum running from "An enormous amount" to "None." [Again hand the respondent the card with a scale of categories ranging from an enormous amount to none.]

20.1   What about studying proposed legislation? How much time would you say that you spend studying proposed legislation?

20.2   Developing new legislation?

20.3   Building coalitions in your own Party to pass legislation?

20.4   Building coalitions across party lines to pass legislation?

20.5 Monitoring state agencies?

20.6 Communicating with constituents?

20.7 Attending meetings and functions in your district?

20.8 Helping constituents with problems?

20.9 Making sure your district gets its fair share of government money and projects?

20.10 Fundraising?

20.11 Attending events sponsored by groups in Lansing?

21. Now I'd like you to give the House a letter grade (A to F) on the following things. You may add pluses or minuses if you like.

    Passing good legislation

    Monitoring the implementation of programs

    Responding to constituents' needs and concerns

    (asked only of veterans and only beginning with 1999–2000 interviews in the House)

    Working with the Governor's Office

    Working with the other chamber

22. If there were a conflict between what you feel is best and what the people in your district want, what would you do? Would you always do what the district wants, always do what you think is best, or would you be somewhere in between? [Provide the card with scale running from 1 (always do what people in the district want) to 7 (always do what you think best)].

23. If there were a conflict between what is best for your district and best for the state, as a whole, what would you do? Would you always look after the needs of your district, always look after the needs of the state as whole, or would you be somewhere in between? [Provide card with scale running from 1 (always look after my district) to 7 (always look after the state)].

24. What do you think will be the most important impact of term limits on the House?

25. What do you think will be the most important impact of term limits on state government generally?

26. What do you plan to do when you are termed out of the House? Do you plan to run for another public office?

These are the response scales that were handed to the respondent at designated points in the interview:

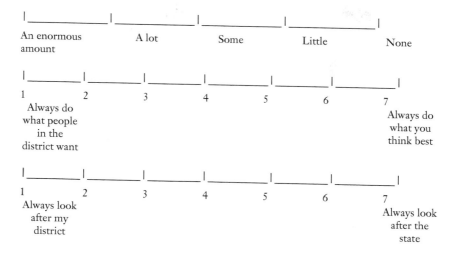

|_____|_____|_____|_____|_____|

An enormous amount   A lot   Some   Little   None

|_____|_____|_____|_____|_____|_____|

1   2   3   4   5   6   7

Always do what people in the district want   Always do what you think best

|_____|_____|_____|_____|_____|_____|

1   2   3   4   5   6   7

Always look after my district   Always look after the state

Notes

1. Numerous other studies share this problem. We chose this one because of the wide interest in roll call voting among political scientists and the overall quality of this author's scholarship. Therefore, it aptly illustrates the problem for the discipline.

2. These ballot initiatives also sought to limit congressional service, but the Supreme Court ruled this unconstitutional.

3. Three state supreme courts, Washington, Massachusetts, and Wyoming, ruled that limiting state legislators' years of service violated their state's constitution. Oregon's Supreme Court overturned its term-limits law after it took effect in the lower chamber. Utah and Idaho repealed their laws through legislative action. These states, by adopting term limits and then reversing course, provide another naturally occurring quasi experiment that can be used to assess the effects of repeatedly changing legislative incentives or of returning to more stability after mass turnovers.

4. Recently California prevailed in its second effort to alter its original highly stringent limits. It did so by shortening the total years of combined service in the two chambers to 12 (down from 14 years under the original law). Now, instead of limiting service in each chamber (6 years in the lower and 8 in the upper), legislators can serve all twelve years in only one chamber or divide them in any combination of years between the two chambers. Altering the length of limits provides yet another quasi experiment.

5. Louisiana has term limits, but not the ballot initiative. It is the only state that did not acquire term limits through the citizen initiative process.

6. http://www.michiganinbrief.org/ (accessed September 20, 2015).

7. Michigan's senators all run for reelection at the same time, every four years.

8. In this same vein, we do not expend extensive effort on clustering to adjust

the standard errors in our analyses, because we are more interested in the size and direction of the coefficients.

9. Ballenger uses a four-year rolling average of the votes cast at the bottom of Michigan's very long ballot to assess partisan identification. Ballot fatigue is very high in Michigan, with many voters casting votes only for candidates appearing at or near the top of the list. Some of the positions at the end of the ballot, including the State Board of Education and the various governing boards of the state's three constitutionally mandated universities, are partisan. Most voters, however, have never heard of them, and vote for them only if they vote a straight party ticket.

CHAPTER 2

1. We used a two-tailed difference of proportions test and a cutoff of *p* < 0.10.

2. Florida, Ohio, Michigan, California, and Nevada.

3. Maine, Colorado, Arizona, Oklahoma, and Louisiana, for example.

4. This pattern is true for ethnic minority legislators, too. There were only 10 Republicans (that is less than 2%) among the 622 African American state legislators nationally in 2008 (All Other Persons 2013).

5. Immediately after term limits in 1998, Michigan's Democratic House caucus included three African American legislators whose districts had fewer than 50% African American constituents—in one case, only 16% were African American. These were safe Democratic seats. All three districts elected white legislators after these incumbents were termed out.

6. We classified candidates based on their given name. When this was ambiguous, we searched the Internet. But occasionally we still could not determine a candidate's gender. In these cases, we assumed the candidate was a man because the majority of candidates are men. This occurred rarely, but it means that we might have slightly underestimated the number of women running. We use averages in our analysis, so a few errors are unlikely to change our conclusions.

7. We asked these questions only during our first interview with legislators because the answer to these two questions should not change for people who were interviewed more than once. Therefore, we have only 295 responses to these questions. We also ask these questions during our first interview with senators even if we had previously asked them these questions about their first election to the House. We did this to explore the reasons they ran for the upper chamber and to see whether they were recruited to run for Senate seats and by whom.

8. We do not know how many losing candidates were asked to run nor do we know who asked them to run.

9. Our earlier work, Sarbaugh-Thompson et al. (2002), documents an increase in postelection contributions to legislators by interest groups based on the legislators' committee assignments and majority party membership—potential vote buying.

10. This difference is shy of statistical significance (*p* = 0.17), however. Only our high response rate justifies treating this as an increase.

11. Given the small size of the Michigan Senate, we do not analyze ethnic and gender subgroups separately for that chamber. Rather, we consider gender and ethnicity without regard to chamber.

12. Although a higher proportion of legislators from both political parties say they were recruited to run after term limits, fewer than 10% of our respondents from either party said that the party organization itself recruited them.

13. In 2015, there were 20 ethnic minority representatives, 19 of whom were Democrats.

14. We find no evidence that this is a bimodal distribution with many younger and older legislators. This could occur if term limits discourage prospective candidates in their late 30s and 40s from interrupting a successful career for a job that offers only a few years of service. We find that approximately one-third of Michigan's legislators are in their 40s and another third is in their 50s with or without term limits.

15. For example, Sandy Lipsey of Kalamazoo, Michigan.

16. For example, Steve Tobacman (white) replaced Belda Garza (Latina) in southwest Detroit, which has large Hispanic and African-American populations.

CHAPTER 3

1. Burke [1790] 1968; Hobbes [1651] 1994; Mill [1861] 2010; Rousseau [1762] 1988; Pitkin 1967.

2. Michigan State's Board of Trustees, University of Michigan's Board of Regents, and Wayne State's Board of Governors.

3. Wahlke et al. (1962) refers to these two dilemmas as representational role (district versus self) and the areal role (district versus state) orientations.

4. Interestingly, results from a statewide survey conducted by the Center for Urban Studies in 2010 show that 10% of voters want to be represented by a state-focused delegate—the rarest combination in our data.

5. We did not ask these questions in the second round of Senate interviews given respondents' objections to them.

6. It is possible that other legislators also rely on themselves alone, but did not volunteer any comments that led us to code them as Burkean cowboys. There are another 108 respondents with a scaled reply of 4.5 or higher who might fall into this category.

7. An occasional legislator was interviewed twice, but with several years between the two interviews, for example, a first interview in the House in 1998 and a second interview in the Senate in 2010. We do not include these because we assume that this could involve a lot more change than it would if we had interviewed this same legislator in consecutive sessions or skipped only one session.

8. Organizational research on professional roles documents the power of the role set (i.e., other actors' expectations of the focal actor) to mold and shape behavior. For a solid description of the basic tenets of role theory and a review of the literature, see Pfeffer 1982.

9. This message is even more powerful because the votes we analyze here include many issues on which vulnerable legislators might move to the middle rather than maintain party discipline.

10. Recent maps were drawn by Republicans who packed Democrats into a few very safe districts.

11. The Center for Urban Studies at the authors' institution subdivides U.S.

Census (e.g., poverty levels and education levels) by each state House and Senate district in the state.

12. Republicans drew the maps and created more districts with mixtures of voters that tilt toward the party, for example 60% Republicans and 40% Democrats. These heterogeneous districts are harder to represent than homogeneous districts comprised of 90% Democratic voters.

CHAPTER 4

1. Despite clear computational and conceptual advantages in using this relative measure, the resulting numbers are difficult to interpret because the range of the values varies for each task.

2. We discover this by using analysis of variance with chamber, lame duck status, and political ambition, producing eight categories of legislator. We find a statistically significant interaction effect of chamber and lame duck and a nearly statistically significant three-way effect.

3. The survey question Ellickson and Whistler (2001) ask about the importance of casework accounts for a lot of the explanatory power of their model, but this information tells us very little—merely that people who think casework is important spend more time on it. And asking respondents to assess the importance of the dependent variable could be endogenous to the dependent variable. This question probably explains the difference in performance of their model and ours.

4. Given that the Democrats were so often the minority party in each chamber during our study period, we wondered if minority party was simply measuring a partisan difference. So we also tried using % *liberal votes* instead of minority party, given the potential for extremely conservative Republicans to shun getting pork. The variable was not even close to statistical significance. Therefore, we consider minority party status the best explanation of this effect.

5. The histogram of the residuals is almost perfectly normally distributed and the skewness and kurtosis for the dependent variable using the difference measure are well within acceptable bounds. We reran this model using the ordinal scale—time spent building coalitions across party lines to pass legislation—as the dependent variable. The coefficients tell the same story, but the histogram of the residual is not well distributed, so we abandoned this approach.

6. This was part of our effort to explain the negative relationship for general election competition (aka safe district).

7. Several of our repeat respondents were first elected many years before our research. These House veterans were termed out of office, but won a state senate seat. This means that their first session in our data is their lame duck session in the House. In their second interview with us, they are Senate newcomers—freshmen. Their final session in the Senate (once again lame ducks) is our third interview with them. Other legislators we interview more than once might be in the House for all three interviews, as freshmen in their first interview and lame ducks in their third. Another cohort of repeat respondents served two sessions in the House and then moved to the Senate. In their third interview they are Senate freshmen.

8. We remind readers that a few third interviews occurred between a respon-

dent's two terms in the Senate—not during their final term in office. So this is not an ideal test of lame duck effects.

9. We have information on political ambition only for legislators we interviewed. We have roll call voting data on all legislators serving in these sessions.

CHAPTER 5

1. Limits in some states exceed the average tenure in office and may encourage longer service.

2. All Michigan senators run for reelection in the midterm elections along with the governor.

3. Many voters privately admit doing this in Michigan's 2010 gubernatorial primary when the more moderate Rick Snyder beat several more conservative Republicans during an election cycle widely predicted to favor Republican candidates (personal conversations with the authors).

4. The following quote reproduced in the news media from an elected officials' Facebook page demonstrates that this sort of mischief does occur. "With the power of my vote diminished (by partisan primaries), I use my head and try to maximize the power of that vote to create the general election I desire most. That is what the system rewards, so that is what I attempt to provide" (*Ann Arbor News*, August 17, 2014, C4).

5. For example, an extremely safe district would be one with a 90% advantage to one political party. So 90 × 0.11 (the coefficient for district safety would increase the victory proportion of the votes by about 10%, offsetting the effect of one more candidate). But in primaries leading to highly competitive general elections, each additional candidate decreases the margin of victory by a bit more than 10%.

6. As a check for robustness, we consider only the term-limited states across time in the same multivariable model (without the ballot initiative variable, which is a constant). We find that implementing term limits does not alter the level of competition in those states ($b = -0.92$, $p = 0.7$). The effect is extremely small and not statistically significant.

7. In our continuous measure of term limits, all non-ballot-initiative states have a value of zero for term limitedness. Ballot initiative states include some without term limits. The range for the term-limits ratio variable is –0.25 for Nevada to 1.96 for Arkansas.

8. All term-limited states except Louisiana have the ballot initiative, but not all ballot initiative states have term limits.

9. This variable, which ranges from 0.03 to 0.63, is multiplied by a coefficient of 41.31.

10. As a check of robustness, we reestimated our model using the more traditional binary measure of term limits instead of the continuous measure of term limitedness. We find that the binary measure estimates term limits' effect on competition at a slightly larger level (–3.36%). This effect, however, is still not statistically significant. The binary measure of term limits reduces the estimated effect of the ballot initiative states and reduces the statistical significance of that coefficient, which one would expect given the higher correlation between those two variables,

an issue we have discussed elsewhere (Sarbaugh-Thompson 2010a). In either case, term limits effects are small and open seats are not as competitive after term limits.

11. We note additionally that if we include all cases, not just incumbents, open seats are more competitive (2%), and term limits do not significantly alter this effect of open seat elections. Moreover, term limits still reduce the percentage of votes cast against a winning candidate (reducing electoral competition by about 4%), with Senate elections remaining less competitive before and after term limits. But in this configuration of the model, we cannot assess the relationship between voting behavior and electoral competition, our purpose in this section.

12. This is a continuous variable measured as the difference in straight ticket voters for the two major political parties. It is calculated and reported in *Inside Michigan Politics*. We described this variable in more detail in chapter 3.

13. Readers will recall that we found in chapter 3 that electorally vulnerable legislators do not vote their district—even as vulnerable freshmen.

14. We adjusted these data when and where we found obvious discrepancies. These problems primarily involved special elections, which we treated as missing.

CHAPTER 6

1. Songer (1988) explores a tort reform bill passed by the South Carolina House. A public report provided evidence about the number of cases, settlement amounts, and so on. Legislators were quizzed about their knowledge of these. The average legislator exhibited little accurate knowledge, but committee members were highly informed. The resulting bill defied the views of most legislators, but passed by a wide margin because, according to Songer, they trusted the judgment of their colleagues on the committee.

2. Mooney (1991) considers staff to be an inside source. Empirically we find no similarity between consulting staff and consulting colleagues. Consequently, we treat staff as a midrange source.

3. Given our longitudinal design we could not anticipate whether an actual bill would pass during the course of our research and become irrelevant. Therefore we picked issues that recur regularly, but we acknowledge that problems arise from hypothetical scenarios.

4. The House might follow the Senate's lead in the future because the equilibrium House session (2003) exhibits a sizeable, albeit not statistically significant, reliance on midrange sources. This is a rare instance in which transitional and equilibrium House sessions differ.

5. This is consistent with Francis's (1985) finding that party caucuses in Michigan's Senate controlled decision making in the 1980s—a unique structure among all state legislatures.

6. These patterns are more pronounced in both chambers if we consider only the equilibrium post-term-limits session, omitting the sessions during the transition to term limits.

7. We find that term limits effects are not statistically significant, but chamber differences are. We discuss term limits effects based on our exceptionally high response rate. Limiting our analyses to equilibrium sessions for each chamber does not change our findings.

8. Analyzing only the equilibrium sessions, we find less consulting with voters in each chamber and less in the House with local officials. We have so few cases when we limit ourselves to the equilibrium sessions that we cannot be confident that these are enduring differences, however.

9. During the transition to term limits, about 40% of our respondents say that local sources are their most important.

10. We counted the ordinal scale values between some (2) and an enormous amount (4). If we include sources consulted a little (1), men consult 7.7 sources and women consult 7.4 sources.

11. Our data include 59 female respondents in the chamber's minority party and 49 women in the majority. This could explain some of aversion to the chamber leadership structure among women, but the imbalance is too small to account for all the differences we find.

12. Wissel, O'Connor, and King (1976) studied eight state legislatures, including Michigan. They assess the value of information provided by internal and external sources to identify a search strategy for each state. They conclude that in the 1970s Michigan's legislators favored internal information.

CHAPTER 7

1. See the work of Anthony Giddens, among many others, for a thorough explanation of this concept. This encourages us to think of institutional structures as sedimentary rocks, which accumulate gradually, almost imperceptibly, as fine layers of sediment are deposited and then built upon by the next layer. Repeated patterns of human behavior can be viewed as sediment deposited in organizations, forming institutional structures over time.

2. The size of the cohorts, especially the small number of pre-term-limits newcomers, makes it difficult in some of our analyses to achieve statistical significance even when there are substantively noteworthy differences.

3. A UCINET tutorial by Bob Hanneman and Mark Riddle is available at http://faculty.ucr.edu/~hanneman/nettext/

4. We included both the committee chair and the minority party ranking member (*Minority Vice Chair*) as leaders.

CHAPTER 8

1. These authors asked respondents to rank order the top five sources from a list of 13 that they might consult to make up their minds about how to vote on a bill.

2. Some politicians will politely say that they are friends with all their colleagues; hence we focused on *especially good* friends.

3. Indegrees, ties directed toward a named legislator, provide information about all members of the chamber. They are based on the responses (ties radiating outward—outdegrees) of the legislators we interviewed.

4. This assumption is only reasonable for the friendship networks. For example, in the consulting networks, there is no reason to assume that if a person consults someone about an issue that the consulting is mutual. With friendship, there is a reasonable chance that if we had interviewed each and every legislator that some

of the missing ties would be reciprocal. Furthermore, given that our response rate is highest for the pre-term-limits sessions in both chambers, using directed ties to analyze clusters of friends would introduce bias, making the post-term-limits sessions appear less connected than they are. One of our hypotheses speculates that connectedness will decline after term limits. Therefore, symmetrizing the networks for some of our analyses is the "conservative" treatment of our data. The betweenness subroutine in UCINET treats ties as undirected.

5. For readers unfamiliar with network analysis, we described these measures in chapter 7.

6. There is a small, but statistically significant correlation (0.18) between being named as a friend within the party and across party lines. So, people with cross-party friends appear to be more friendly in general.

7. In network jargon, the tie is transformed from directed to undirected or data are treated as symmetrical even if, as in our data, they are not.

8. We have the maximum five sessions of data for six legislators who started in the House, serving in 1997, 1999 and 2001, who moved to the Senate for the 2003 and 2007 sessions. Indrees include all colleagues mentioned by repeat respondents.

9. Given the exploratory nature of this portion of our analysis, we tried using a dependent variable calculated by taking the difference between the three relationships at times one and two. The control variables become more complicated when we use the difference variables. Because we find consistent support for the effects of the independent variables of interest for both the lagged and differenced dependent variables, we present the more straightforward results for the lagged dependent variables.

10. Indegrees are the number of ties directed toward a legislator by his or her colleagues. Normalized indegrees adjust for the size of the network so that we can combine House and Senate data.

11. Including this control variable improves the distribution of the residual as well.

12. It is not possible to use top leadership positions to predict friends in the post-term-limits era because top leaders are usually serving their last term.

CHAPTER 9

1. Battista (2011) uses the word power, but we substitute influence to maintain consistent terminology throughout our discussion.

2. When we asked about influence in Michigan's legislature, we were told more than once that if we wanted to know who was influential in the chamber that we should watch the sessions and see who legislators listen to. Although we spent many hours in the gallery observing the sessions, a general hubbub prevailed on the floor when members were speaking. We rarely observed members listening to their colleagues.

3. A story told by Prof. Arnold Tannenbaum in his graduate seminar on the social psychology of organizations describes his colleague Prof. Rensis Likert asking him if he couldn't just call it influence—we adopt Prof. Likert's preference here.

4. In their seminal work French and Raven (1959) articulate bases of what they call power and we refer to here as influence. The original categories are legitimate

power, referent power, coercive power, reward power, and expert power. In Raven's later work, expert power is redefined and one of its facets, persuasion, forms a sixth category (see Raven 2008 for discussion of this sixth category).

5. We include in the category *legitimate influence* any open-ended responses that mentioned the legislators' formal position—top leadership positions or chairing an important committee—as the reason for his or her influence. We coded into the category *expertise* comments related to substantive experience or knowledge from prior government or private sector positions, service on important committees, procedural knowledge (i.e., how to move bills and get things done), and issue-specific knowledge. We treat chairing an important committee as a source of legitimate influence because it allows a chair to exercise his or her official prerogatives. But we view service on an important committee as an opportunity to gain knowledge by sitting through committee hearings and to be educated by committee staff on substantive issues. Clearly, however, chairs sit through hearings, gaining knowledge and expertise, so there is some overlap between these categories. Because we focus on change across time and make this distinction consistently across time, we minimize this problem.

6. These are all normalized indegrees and the respondents are the same, so we can legitimately compare the values of coefficients across the two models.

CHAPTER 10

1. Michigan's legislative chambers each have two caucus campaign accounts that are political action committees (PACs). These are controlled by top caucus leaders of each political party in each chamber.

2. In 1999–2000 one committee chair had been elected in the 1980s for one term, and so had served three previous sessions. But this is the exception, not the rule.

3. Unlike Michigan, in Maine all bills receive a committee vote and then all of those go to the floor for a vote with a committee recommendation to pass or reject.

4. Based on a two-way analysis of variance, the chamber effect is significant at $p < 0.10$ and the interaction between term limits and chamber is significant at $p < 0.05$.

5. Fenno (1962) discusses the logic of selecting U.S. representatives to serve on the congressional Appropriations Committee. He claims that legislators who can work across the aisle to negotiate and compromise will be chosen because passing a budget is mandatory. Bomb throwers could thwart timely passage of budget measures; therefore the Appropriations Committee norms require calm deliberation.

CHAPTER 11

1. We recognize that these observers are not entirely unbiased in their judgment of relationships that they are largely responsible for facilitating.

2. Historically JCAR performed oversight by reviewing any rule promulgated by Michigan's state agencies. Shortly before our interviews with pre-term-limits veterans, Gov. Engler won a Michigan Supreme Court victory that curtailed JCAR's power. Open-ended comments by some pre-term-limits respondents suggest that

this transition influenced their responses, especially the grade they awarded for the quality of legislative oversight. JCAR members report more time spent monitoring, especially in the Senate.

3. Data are missing for one year and duplicate a previous year in another book in the series.

4. Michigan's governor has repeatedly been sent bills he said he did not want to see on his desk. He resorted to political maneuvers to fund an international bridge after the legislature rejected his repeated efforts. He was stymied for months on road funding, among other items.

5. Of the 14,813 bills introduced during Governor Engler's tenure, 3,274 passed, according to various issues of the Book of the States.

6. We considered only committee members, not alternates.

7. We created this variable in response to panel commenters at the 2014 State Politics and Policy Conference. We are grateful for this suggestion.

CHAPTER 12

1. We cannot identify minority group members in Michigan's Secretary of State data. Therefore, we investigate gender only. Furthermore, changes in district maps confound the influence of term limits on minority legislators.

2. Michigan collects a statewide sales tax that is to be shared with local governments and school districts. Local governments are prohibited from levying any sales taxes. Over the past decade, statutory revenue sharing has been cut as the state effectively balanced its budget on the backs of local governments. There is constitutionally mandated revenue sharing that still provides some funding to local governments. But the substantial and persistent cuts in statutory revenue sharing have contributed to financial insolvency at the local level throughout the state, not just in Detroit. Municipal governments complain vigorously about these cuts to no avail. State legislators blithely announce budget surpluses without restoring any of these cuts to local governments—spending the money elsewhere.

3. http://www.mml.org/pdf/advocacy/mml-revenue-sharing-heist-2014.pdf (accessed July 17, 2015).

4. One idea that would make gerrymandering more difficult is to nest House districts within Senate districts. If Michigan were to add one House seat and cut one Senate seat, three House districts could be nested within each Senate district. This makes it harder to gerrymander the boundaries, and it encourages senators and representatives to collaborate on behalf of their shared constituents. Some of these might be bipartisan collaborations.

5. For example, the Gingrich revolution of the 1990s.

References

Aberbach, Joel D. 1990. *Keeping a Watchful Eye: The Politics of Congressional Oversight.* Washington, DC: Brookings Institution.

All Other Persons. 2009. "Factoid: Black State Legislators in 2009." April 16. Accessed May 10, 2013. https://allotherpersons.wordpress.com/

Anderson, W. D., J. M. Box-Steffensmeier, and V. Sinclair-Chapman. 2003. "The Keys to Legislative Success in the US House of Representatives." *Legislative Studies Quarterly* 28 (3): 357–86.

Apollonio, Dorie, and Raymond J. La Raja. 2006. "Term Limits, Campaign Contributions, and the Distribution of Power in State Legislatures." *Legislative Studies Quarterly* 31:359–81.

Arceneaux, Kevin. 2001. "The 'Gender Gap' in State Legislative Representation: New Data to Tackle an Old Question." *Political Research Quarterly* 54 (1): 143–60.

Arnold, L. W., R. E. Deen, and S. C. Patterson. 2000. "Friendship and Votes: The Impact of Interpersonal Ties on Legislative Decision Making." *State and Local Government Review* 32:142–47.

Axelrod, R. 1984. *The Evolution of Cooperation.* New York: Basic Books.

Bachrach, P., and M. S. Baratz. 1962. "Two Faces of Power." *American Political Science Review* 56 (4): 947–52.

Ballenger, W. S. *Inside Michigan Politics.* 2029 South Waverly Road, Lansing, MI 48917.

Baranowski, Michael. 1997. "Executive and Legislative Influence in State Bureaucratic Agencies." PhD diss., University of Kentucky.

Barber, James David. 1965. *The Lawmakers: Recruitment and Adaptation to Legislative Life.* New Haven: Yale University Press.

Barnard, Chester. 1938. *The Functions of the Executive.* Cambridge: Harvard University Press.

Battista, J. C. 2011. "Formal and Perceived Leadership Power in US State Legislatures." *State Politics and Policy Quarterly* 11 (1): 102–18.

Bell, Dawson. 1992. "Term Limits, B Yes: Likely Shake-up Now Likely in Lansing, Congress." *Detroit Free Press*, November 4, 1992, Sec. A.

Bender, B., and J. R. Lott Jr. 1996. "Legislator Voting and Shirking: A Critical Review of the Literature." *Public Choice* 87 (1–2): 67–100.

Berman, D. R. 2004. "The Effects of Legislative Term Limits in Arizona." In *Final Report Joint Project on Term Limits*. Denver: National Conference of State Legislatures.

Bernstein, R. A., and A. Chadha. 2003. "The Effects of Term Limits on Representation: Why So Few Women?" In *The Test of Time: Coping with Legislative Term Limits*, edited by Rick Farmer, John D. Rausch Jr., and John C. Green. Lanham, MD: Lexington Books.

Bienenstock, E. J., P. Bonacich, and M. Oliver. 1990. "The Effect of Network Density and Homogeneity on Attitude Polarization." *Social Networks* 12 (2): 153–72.

Binder, S. A., E. D. Lawrence, and F. Maltzman. 1999. "Uncovering the Hidden Effect of Party." *Journal of Politics* 61 (3): 815–31.

Blanchard, K., R. Hambleton, D. Zigarmi, and D. Forsyth. 1999. *LBA II: Leadership Behavioral Analysis II-Self Questionnaire*. Escondido, CA: Ken Blandard Companies.

Borgatti, S. P., M. G. Everett, and L. C. Freeman. 2002. *Ucinet for Windows: Software for Social Network Analysis*. Cambridge, MA: Analytic Technologies.

Brake, R. A. 2003. "Who's in Charge? The Impact of Term Limits on State Legislative Budgeting in Maine and Michigan." Paper presented at the Annual Meeting of the American Political Science Association, Philadelphia, August 27–31.

Bratton, K. A. 2005. "Critical Mass Theory Revisited: The Behavior and Success of Token Women in State Legislatures." *Politics and Gender* 1 (1): 97–125.

Browne, W. P., and K. VerBurg. 1995. *Michigan Politics and Government: Facing Change in a Complex State*. Lincoln: University of Nebraska Press.

Burden, B. C. 2007. *Personal Roots of Representation*. Princeton: Princeton University Press.

Burke, Edmund. (1774) 2005. *The Works of the Right Honourable Edmund Burke, Vol. II*. Project Gutenberg Ebook.

Burke, Edmund. (1790) 1968. *Reflections on the Revolution in France*. London: Penguin.

Burrell, Barbara C. 1988. "The Political Opportunity of Women Candidates for the US House of Representatives in 1984." *Women and Politics* 8 (1): 51–68.

Burrell, Barbara C. 1994. *A Woman's Place Is in the House: Campaigning for Congress in the Feminist Era*. Ann Arbor: University of Michigan Press.

Cain, Bruce E., and Thad Kousser. 2004. *Adapting to Term Limits: Recent Experiences and New Directions*. San Francisco: Public Policy Institute of California.

Cain, Bruce E., and M. A. Levin. 1999. "Term Limits." *Annual Review of Political Science* 2 (1): 163–88.

Cain, Bruce E., and G. Wright. 2007. "Committees." In *Institutional Change in American Politics: The Case of Term Limits*, edited by Karl T. Kurtz, Bruce E. Cain, and Richard G. Niemi. Ann Arbor: University of Michigan Press.

Caldeira, G. A., J. A. Clark, and S. C. Patterson. 1993. "Political Respect in the Legislature." *Legislative Studies Quarterly* 18 (1): 3–28.

Caldeira, G. A., and S. C. Patterson. 1987. "Political Friendship in the Legislature." *Journal of Politics* 49 (4): 953–75.

Campbell, D. T., and J. C. Stanley. 1963. *Experimental and Quasi-Experimental Designs for Generalized Causal Inference.* Chicago: Rand-McNally.

Caress, S. M., and T. T. Kunioka. 2012. *Term Limits and Their Consequences: The Aftermath of Legislative Reform.* Albany, NY: SUNY Press.

Carey, John M., Richard G. Niemi, and Lynda W. Powell. 1998. "The Effects of Term Limits on State Legislatures." *Legislative Studies Quarterly* 23 (2): 271–300.

Carey, John M., Richard G. Niemi, and Lynda W. Powell. 2000. *Term Limits in State Legislatures.* Ann Arbor: University of Michigan Press.

Carey, John M., Richard G. Niemi, Lynda W. Powell, and G. F. Moncrief. 2006. "The Effects of Term Limits on State Legislatures: A New Survey of the 50 States." *Legislative Studies Quarterly* 31 (1): 105–34.

Carroll, S. J. 1994. *Women as Candidates in American Politics.* Bloomington: Indiana University Press.

Carroll, S. J. and K. Jenkins. 2001a. "Unrealized Opportunity? Term Limits and the Representation of Women in State Legislatures." *Women and Politics* 23 (4): 1–30.

Carroll, S. J., and K. Jenkins. 2001b. "Do Term Limits Help Women Get Elected?" *Social Science Quarterly* 82 (1): 197–201.

Carson, C. 1998. "Public Policy Dispute Settlement: A Best Practice Model." Paper presented at the Dispute Resolution Study Circle, Mediating Theory, and Democratic Systems, Detroit.

Cavanagh, Thomas E. 1982. "The Calculus of Representation: A Congressional Perspective." *Western Political Quarterly* 351:120–29.

Center for American Women and Politics. 2012. "Women in State Legislative Elections: 1992–2012," December 18. Accessed May 10, 2013. http://www.cawp.rutgers.edu/education_training/2012Project/about2012.php

Chen, J. 2010. "The Effect of Electoral Geography on Pork Barreling in Bicameral Legislatures." *American Journal of Political Science* 54 (2): 301–22.

Citizens Against Government Waste. *Pig Book.* Accessed April 15, 2014. http://www.cagw.org/reporting/pig-book

Citizen's Research Council. 2002. *Compensation of Michigan Legislators.* Report prepared by the Michigan Legislative Service Bureau, Legislative Research Division, Research Report 12, no. 5 (revised June). Accessed August 18, 2014, available at http://www.crcmich.org/PUBLICAT/2000s/2002/Ballot/socc.pdf

Cooper, C. A., and L. E. Richardson Jr. 2006. "Institutions and Representational Roles in American State Legislatures." *State Politics and Policy Quarterly* 6 (2): 174–94.

Cooper, J., and D. W. Brady. 1981. "Institutional Context and Leadership Style: The House from Cannon to Rayburn." *American Political Science Review* 75 (2): 411–25.

Costenbader, E., and T. W. Valente. 2003. "The Stability of Centrality Measures When Networks Are Sampled." *Social Networks* 25 (4): 283–307.

Danziger, S. 2001. "Welfare Reform Policy from Nixon to Clinton: What Role for Social Science." In *Social Science and Policy-Making: A Search for Relevance in the Twentieth Century*, edited by D. Featherman and M. Vinovskis. Ann Arbor: University of Michigan Press.

Darcy, R., S. Welch, and J. Clark. 1994. *Women, Elections, and Representation*. 2nd ed. Lincoln: University of Nebraska Press.

Davidson, Roger H. 1969. *The Role of the Congressman*. New York: Pegasus.

Day, J., and K. Boeckelman. 2012. "The Impact of Legislative Term Limits on State Debt: Increased Spending, Flat Revenue." *Politics and Policy* 40 (2): 320–38.

Dolan, J., M. Deckman, and M. L. Swers. 2007. *Women and Politics: Paths to Power and Political Influence*. Upper Saddle River, NJ: Pearson/Prentice-Hall.

Dominguez, C. B. 2011. "Does the Party Matter? Endorsements in Congressional Primaries." *Political Research Quarterly* 64 (3): 534–44.

Duffin, D. L. 2003. "Explaining Participation in Congressional Oversight Hearings." *American Politics Research* 31 (5): 455–84.

Ehrenhalt, Alan. 1992. *The United States of Ambition: Politicians, Power, and the Pursuit of Office*. New York: Three Rivers Press.

Ellickson, M. C., and D. E. Whistler. 2001. "Explaining State Legislators' Casework and Public Resource Allocations." *Political Research Quarterly* 54 (3): 553–69.

Elling, Richard C. 1979. "State Party Platforms and State Legislative Performance: A Comparative Analysis. *American Journal of Political Science* 23 (2): 383–405.

Elling, Richard C. 1992. *Public Management in the States: A Comparative Study of Administrative Performance and Politics*. Westport, CT: Praeger.

Erler, H. A. 2007. "Legislative Term Limits and State Spending." *Public Choice* 133 (3–4): 479–94.

Eulau, H., J. C. Wahlke, W. Buchanan, and L. C. Ferguson. 1959. "The Role of the Representative: Some Empirical Observations on the Theory of Edmund Burke." *American Political Science Review* 53 (3): 742–56.

Farace, Richard V., Peter R. Monge, and Hammish M. Russell. 1977. *Communicating and Organizing*. Reading, MA: Addison-Wesley.

Farmer, Rick, and Thomas H. Little. 2004. "Legislative Power in the Buckeye State: The Revenge of Term Limits." In *Final Report Joint Project on Term Limits*. Denver: National Conference of State Legislatures. http://www.ncsl.org/jptl/casestudies/OHFamer_Littlev2.pdf

Fenno, Richard F., Jr. 1962. "The House Appropriations Committee as a Political System: The Problem of Integration." *American Political Science Review* 56 (2): 310–24.

Fenno, Richard F., Jr. 1973. *Congressmen in Committees*. Boston: Little, Brown.

Ferber, Paul H., and Rudy R. Pugliese. 2000. "Partisans, Proximates, and Poker Players: The Impact of Homophily and Proximity on Communication Patterns of State Legislators." *Polity* 32 (3): 401–14.

Fiorina, M. P. 1977. "The Case of the Vanishing Marginals: The Bureaucracy Did It." *American Political Science Review* 71:166–76.

Fiorina, M. P. 1989. *Congress, Keystone of the Washington Establishment*. New Haven: Yale University Press.

Fiorina, M. P. 1996. *Divided Government*. Boston: Allyn and Bacon.

Fox, R. L., and J. L. Lawless. 2005. "To Run or Not to Run for Office: Explaining Nascent Political Ambition." *American Journal of Political Science* 49 (3): 642–59.

Francis, W. L. 1962. "Influence and Interaction in a State Legislative Body." *American Political Science Review* 56 (4): 953–60.

Francis, W. L. 1985. "Leadership, Party Caucuses, and Committees in US State Legislatures." *Legislative Studies Quarterly* 10 (2): 243–57.

Francis, W. L. 1989. *The Legislative Committee Game: A Comparative Analysis of Fifty States*. Columbus: Ohio State University Press.

Freeman, P. K., and L. E. Richardson Jr. 1996. "Explaining Variation in Casework among State Legislators." *Legislative Studies Quarterly* 21:41–56.

French, J. R., and B. Raven. 1959. "The Bases of Social Power." In *Group Dynamics*, edited by D. Cartwright and A. Zander. New York: Harper and Row.

Friesema, H. P., and R. D. Hedlund. 1974. "The Reality of Representational Roles." *Public Opinion and Public Policy* 2:413–17.

Gaddie, R. K., and C. S. Bullock. 2000. *Elections to Open Seats in the US House: Where the Action Is*. Lanham, MD: Rowman and Littlefield.

Gamble, K. L. 2007. "Black Political Representation: An Examination of Legislative Activity within US House Committees." *Legislative Studies Quarterly* 32 (3): 421–47.

Gamm, Gerald, and Thad Kousser. 2013. "Contingent Partisanship: When Party Labels Matter—and When They Don't—in the Distribution of Pork in American State Legislatures." Paper presented at the Annual Meeting of the American Political Science Association, Chicago, August 29–September 1.

Gill, J. 1999. "The Insignificance of Null Hypothesis Significance Testing." *Political Research Quarterly* 52 (3): 647–74.

Goodman, M. R., D. S. Gross, T. A. Boyd, and H. F. Weisberg. 1986. "State Legislator Goal Orientations: An Examination." *Polity* 18 (4): 707–19.

Guinier, L. 2008. "Beyond Electocracy: Rethinking the Political Representative as Powerful Stranger." *Modern Law Review* 71 (1): 1–35.

Guston, D. H., M. Jones, and L. M. Branscomb. 1997. "The Demand for and Supply of Technical Information and Analysis in State Legislatures." *Policy Studies Journal* 25 (3): 451–69.

Hadley, D. J. 1977. "Legislative Role Orientations and Support for Party and Chief Executive in the Indiana House." *Legislative Studies Quarterly* 2 (3): 309–35.

Hall, R. L. 1992. "Measuring Legislative Influence." *Legislative Studies Quarterly* 17 (2): 205–31.

Hamm, K. E. 1982. "Consistency between Committee and Floor Voting in US State Legislatures." *Legislative Studies Quarterly* 7:473–90.

Hamm, K. E., R. D. Hedlund, and N. Martorano. 1999. "The Evolution of Committee Structure, Powers, and Procedures in Twentieth Century State Legislatures." Paper presented at the Annual Meeting of the American Political Science Association, Atlanta, September 1–5.

Hamm, K. E., R. D. Hedlund, and N. Martorano. 2006. "Measuring State Legislative Committee Power: Change and Chamber Differences in the 20th Century." *State Politics and Policy Quarterly* 6 (1): 88–111.

Hanneman, R. A., and M. Riddle. 2005. *Introduction to Social Network Methods*. Riverside: University of California, Riverside. http://faculty.ucr.edu/~hanneman/

Hawkesworth, M. E. 1990. *Beyond Oppression: Feminist Theory and Political Strategy*. New York: Continuum.

Heberlig, E. S., and S. Leland. 2004. "Term Limits, Opportunity Structures and

Career Development in State Legislatures." Paper presented at the Fourth Annual Conference on State Politics and Policy, Akron, Ohio, April 30–May 1.

Herrick, R., M. K. Moore, and J. R. Hibbing. 1994. "Unfastening the Electoral Connection: The Behavior of US Representatives When Reelection Is No Longer a Factor." *Journal of Politics* 56 (1): 214–27.

Hird, J. A. 2005. *Power, Knowledge, and Politics: Policy Analysis in the States*. Washington, DC: Georgetown University Press.

Hobbes, Thomas. (1651) 1994. *Leviathan*. Edited by Edwin Curley. Indianapolis: Hackett.

Huber, J. D., C. R. Shipan, and M. Pfahler. 2001. "Legislatures and Statutory Control of Bureaucracy." *American Journal of Political Science* 45 (2): 330–45.

Jenkins, S. 2007. "A Woman's Work Is Never Done? Fund-raising Perception and Effort among Female State Legislative Candidates." *Political Research Quarterly* 60 (2): 230–39.

Jewell, M. E. 1982. *Representation in State Legislatures*. Lexington: University of Kentucky Press.

Jewell, M. E., and M. L. Whicker. 1994. *Legislative Leadership in the American States*. Ann Arbor: University of Michigan Press.

Johnson, J. B., and P. E. Secret. 1996. "Focus and Style: Representational Roles of Congressional Black and Hispanic Caucus Members." *Journal of Black Studies* 26 (3): 245–73.

Jones, B. D. 1973. "Competitiveness, Role Orientations, and Legislative Responsiveness." *Journal of Politics* 35 (4): 924–47.

Jones, R. S., and M. Barrett. 1992. "Congressional Oversight: In the Crosshairs and at a Crossroads." *Public Manager* 2:4–8.

Kahn, Robert L., Donald M. Wolfe, Robert P. Quinn, and J. Diedrick Snoek. 1964. *Organizational Studies: Studies in Role Conflict and Ambiguity*. New York: John Wiley.

Kathlene, Lyn. 1994. "Power and Influence in State Legislative Policymaking: The Interaction of Gender and Position in Committee Hearing Debates." *American Political Science Review* 88 (3): 560–76.

Kathlene, Lyn. 1995. "Alternative Views of Crime: Legislative Policymaking in Gendered Terms." *Journal of Politics* 57 (3): 696–723.

Keele, L., N. Malhotra, and C. H. McCubbins. 2013. "Do Term Limits Restrain State Fiscal Policy? Approaches for Causal Inference in Assessing the Effects of Legislative Institutions." *Legislative Studies Quarterly* 39 (3): 291–326.

Kingdon, John W. 1989. *Congressmen's Voting Decisions*. 3rd ed. Ann Arbor: University of Michigan Press.

Klarner, C., W. Berry, T. Carsey, M. Jewell, R. Niemi, L. Powell, and J. Snyder. 2013. "State Legislative Election Returns (1967–2010)." ICPSR34297-v1. Ann Arbor, MI: Inter-University Consortium for Political and Social Research [distributor], 2013–01–11. http://dx.doi.org/10.3886/ICPSR34297.v1

Kleinberg, J. M. 1999. "Authoritative Sources in a Hyperlinked Environment." *Journal of the ACM* 65 (September): 604–32.

Knoke, D., and J. H. Kuklinski. 1982. *Network Analysis*. Beverly Hills, CA: Sage.

Kousser, T. 2005. *Term Limits and the Dismantling of State Legislative Professionalism*. Cambridge: Cambridge University Press.

Kuklinski, J. H., and R. C. Elling. 1977. "Representational Role, Constituency

Opinion, and Legislative Roll-Call Behavior." *American Journal of Political Science* 21:135–47.

Kurtz, K. T., G. Moncrief, R. G. Niemi, and L. W. Powell. 2006. "Full-Time, Part-Time, and Real Time: Explaining State Legislators' Perceptions of Time on the Job." *State Politics and Policy Quarterly* 6 (3): 322–38.

Kurtz, K. T., R. G. Niemi, and B. Cain, eds. 2007. *Institutional Change in American Politics: The Case of Term Limits.* Ann Arbor: University of Michigan Press.

Lasswell, Harold D. (1930) 1960. *Psychopathology and Politics.* New York: Viking.

Lawless, J., and R. L. Fox. 2005. *It Takes a Candidate: Why Women Don't Run for Office.* Cambridge: Cambridge University Press.

Lawless, J., and R. L. Fox. 2013. "Girls Just Wanna Not Run: The Gender Gap in Young Americans' Political Ambition." March. Washington, DC: American University, Women and Politics Institute. Accessed April 4, 2014. http://www.american.edu/spa/wpi/upload/Girls-Just-Wanna-Not-Run_Policy-Report.pdf

Lieberman, Seymour. 1956. "The Effects of Changes in Roles and Attitudes to Role Occupants." *Human Relations* 9:385–402.

Maestas, C. 2000. "Professional Legislatures and Ambitious Politicians: Policy Responsiveness of State Institutions." *Legislative Studies Quarterly* 25 (4): 663–90.

Mansbridge, Jane. 1999. "Should Blacks Represent Blacks and Women Represent Women? A Contingent Yes." *Journal of Politics* 61 (3): 628–57.

Mansbridge, Jane. 2003. "Rethinking Representation." *American Political Science Review* 97 (4): 515–28.

March, J. G. 1957. "Measurement Concepts in the Theory of Influence." *Journal of Politics* 19:202–26.

March, J. G. 1966. "The Power of Power." In *Varieties of Political Theory*, edited by David Easton. Englewood Cliffs, NJ: Prentice-Hall.

Masket, S. E., and J. B. Lewis. 2007. "A Return to Normalcy? Revisiting the Effects of Term Limits on Competitiveness and Spending in California Assembly Elections." *State Politics and Policy Quarterly* 7 (1): 20–38.

Masket, S., and B. Shor. 2014. "Polarization without Parties: Term Limits and Legislative Partisanship in Nebraska's Unicameral Legislature." *State Politics and Policy Quarterly* 15 (1): 67–90.

Matsusaka, John. 2004. *For the Many or the Few: The Initiative, Public Policy, and American Democracy.* Chicago: University of Chicago Press.

Matthews, D. R., and J. A. Stimson. 1975. *Yeas and Nays: Normal Decision-Making in the US House of Representatives.* Hoboken, NJ: Wiley-Interscience.

Mayhew, D. R. 1974. *Congress: The Electoral Connection.* New Haven: Yale University Press.

Mayo, Elton. 1946. "The Social Problems of Industrial Civilization." *Harvard Law Review* 59 (5): 830–32.

McClone, D. J., and J. H. Kuklinski. 1979. "The Delegate Theory of Representation." *American Journal of Political Science* 23 (2): 278–300.

Meyer, K. 1980. "Legislative Influence: Toward Theory Development through Causal Analysis." *Legislative Studies Quarterly* 5:563–85.

Mill, John Stuart. (1861) 2010. *Considerations on Representative Government.* Cambridge: Cambridge University Press.

Miller, Susan M., J. Nicholson-Crotty, and S. Nicholson-Crotty 2011. "Reexamining the Institutional Effects of Term Limits in US State Legislatures." *Legislative Studies Quarterly* 36 (1): 71–97.

Miller, W. E., and D. E. Stokes. 1963. "Constituency Influence in Congress." *American Political Science Review* 57:45–56.

Mitchell, Cleta Deatherage. 1991. "Term Limits? *Yes!*" *Extensions*, Spring 1991. Norman, OK: Carl Albert Research Center.

Moen, M. C., and K. T. Palmer. 2003. "Maine: The Cutting Edge of Terms Limits." In *The Test of Time: Coping with Legislative Term Limits*, edited by Rick Farmer, John D. Rausch Jr., and John C. Green. Lanham, MD: Lexington Books.

Moen, M. C., K. T. Palmer, and R. J. Powell. 2005. *Changing Members: The Maine Legislature in the Era of Term Limits*. Lanham, MD: Lexington Books.

Moncrief, G. F., and J. A. Thompson, eds. 1992. *Changing Patterns in State Legislative Careers*. Ann Arbor: University of Michigan Press.

Moncrief, G. F., and J. A. Thompson. 1993. "Changing Patterns in State Legislative Careers." *American Political Science Review* 87 (4): 1031–32.

Moncrief, G. F., J. A. Thompson, M. Haddon, and R. Hoyer. 1992. "For Whom the Bell Tolls: Term Limits and State Legislatures." *Legislative Studies Quarterly* 17 (1): 37–47.

Moncrief, G. F., J. A. Thompson, and K. T. Kurtz. 1996. "The Old Statehouse, It Ain't What It Used to Be." *Legislative Studies Quarterly* 21 (1): 57–72.

Mooney, C. Z. 1991. "Information Sources in State Legislative Decision Making." *Legislative Studies Quarterly* 16 (3): 445–55.

Mooney, C. Z. 2007. "Truncated Careers in Professionalized State Legislatures." In *Legislating without Experience: Case Studies in State Legislative Term Limits*, edited by R. Farmer, C. Z. Mooney, R. J. Powell, and J. C. Green. Lanham, MD: Lexington Books.

Mooney, C. Z. 2009. "Term Limits as a Boon to Legislative Scholarship: A Review." *State Politics and Policy Quarterly* 9:204–28.

Mooney, C. Z. 2013. "Measuring State House Speakers' Formal Powers, 1981–2010." *State Politics and Policy Quarterly* 13 (2): 262–73.

Nalder, Kimberly. 2007. "The Effect of State Legislative Term Limits on Voter Turnout." *State Politics and Policy Quarterly* 72:187–210.

National Conference of State Legislators. "About State Legislatures." Last accessed July 22, 2016. http://www.ncsl.org/meetings-training/legislativesummit12/overview/general.aspx

National Institute for Money in State Politics. Last accessed April 1, 2016. http://followthemoney.org/

Nicolson-Crotty, J., and Susan M. Miller. 2011. "Bureaucratic Effectiveness and Influence in the Legislature." *Journal of Public Administration Research and Theory* 22(2):347–371.

Niven, David. 2000. "Revolutionary Headlines: Media Coverage of Legislative Term Limits." Paper presented at Coping with Term Limits: Ohio and the Nation conference, Ray C. Bliss Institute of Applied Politics, Columbus, April.

Ogul, Morris S. 1976. *Congress Oversees the Executive: Studies in Legislative Supervision*. Pittsburgh: University of Pittsburgh Press.

Patterson, Samuel C. 1959. "Patterns of Interpersonal Relations in a State Legislative Group: The Wisconsin Assembly." *Public Opinion Quarterly* 23:101–9.

Patterson, Samuel C. 1963. "Legislative Leadership and Political Ideology." *Public Opinion Quarterly* 27:399–410.

Patterson, Samuel C. 1990. "State Legislators and the Legislatures." In *Politics in the American States*, 5th ed., edited by Virginia Gray, Herbert Jacob, and Robert B. Albritton. Glenview, IL: Little, Brown.

Peoples, C. D. 2008. "Interlegislator Relations and Policy Making: A Sociological Study of Roll-Call Voting in a State Legislature." *Sociological Forum* 23 (3): 455–80.

Petracca, M. P. 1991. "The Poison of Professional Politics." October 30. Policy Analysis, Cato Institute No. 141.Accessed July 22, 2016. http://www.cato.org/publications/policy-analysis/poison-professional-politics

Pew Research Center. 2013. "Majority Says the Federal Government Threatens Their Personal Rights." Accessed June 3, 2013. http://www.people-press.org/2013/01/31/majority-says-the-federal-government-threatens-their-personal-rights/

Pfeffer, Jeffrey. 1982. *Organizations and Organization Theory*. Marshfield, MA: Pitman.

Pitkin, Hanna Fenichel. 1967. *The Concept of Representation*. Berkeley: University of California Press.

Polsby, Nelson. 1993. "Some Arguments against Congressional Term Limitations." *Harvard Journal of Law and Public Policy* 16:101–7.

Porter, H. O., and D.A. Leuthold. 1970. "Legislative Expertise in Michigan: Formal and Informal Patterns over Time." *Michigan Academician* 3 (2): 71–83.

Porter, H. O. 1974. "Legislative Experts and Outsiders: The Two-Step Flow of Communication." *Journal of Politics* 36:703–30.

Potoski, M., and N. D. Woods. 2000. "Designing State Clean Air Agencies: Administrative Procedures and Bureaucratic Autonomy." *Journal of Public Administration Research and Theory* 11:203–21.

Powell, Lynda. 2012. *The Influence of Campaign Contributions in State Legislatures: The Effects of Institutions and Politics*. Ann Arbor: University of Michigan Press.

Prell, C. 2012. *Social Network Analysis: History, Theory, and Methodology*. Thousand Oaks, CA: Sage.

Price, David. 1978. "Policy Making in Congressional Committees: The Impact of Environmental Factors." *American Political Science Review* 72:548–74.

Raven, B. H. 1990. "Political Applications of the Psychology of Interpersonal Influence and Social Power." *Political Psychology* 11:493–520.

Raven, B. H. 1993. "The Bases of Power: Origins and Recent Developments." *Journal of Social Issues* 49 (4): 227–51.

Raven, B. H. 2008. "The Bases of Power and the Power/Interaction Model of Interpersonal Influence." *Analysis of Social Issues and Public Policy* 8 (1): 1–22.

Ray, David. 1982. "The Sources of Voting Cues in Three State Legislatures." *Journal of Politics* 44:1074–87.

Rehfeld, Andrew. 2009. "Representation Rethought: On Trustees, Delegates, and Gyroscopes in the Study of Political Representation and Democracy." *American Political Science Review* 103:214–30.

Reingold, Beth. 2000. *Representing Women: Sex, Gender and Legislative Behavior in Arizona and California*. Chapel Hill: University of North Carolina Press.

Richardson, L. E., Jr., and Patricia Freeman. 1995. "Gender Differences in Representation among State Legislators." *Political Research Quarterly* 48 (1): 169–79.

Richardson, L. E., Jr., D. Valentine, and S. D. Stokes. 2005. "Assessing the Impact of Term Limits in Missouri." *State and Local Government Review* 373:177–92.

Rohdes, David W. 1991. *Parties and Leaders in the Postreform House*. Chicago: University of Chicago Press.

Rosenthal, A. 1981. "Legislative Behavior and Legislative Oversight." *Legislative Studies Quarterly* 6 (1): 115–31.

Rosenthal, A. 1993. "The Legislative Institution—in Transition and at Risk." In *The State of the States*, 2nd ed., edited by Carl E. Van Horn. Washington, DC: Congressional Quarterly Press.

Rosenthal, A. 1996. "State Legislative Development: Observations from Three Perspectives." *Legislative Studies Quarterly* 21:161–98.

Rosenthal, A. 2004. *Heavy Lifting: The Job of the American Legislature*. Washington, DC: CQ Press.

Rosenthal, A. 2009. *Engines of Democracy: Politics and Policymaking in State Legislatures*. Washington, DC: CQ Press.

Rosenthal, A. 2013. *The Best Job in Politics: Exploring How Governors Succeed as Policy Leaders*. Los Angeles: Sage/CQ Press.

Rothenberg, L. S., and M. S. Sanders. 2000. "Severing the Electoral Connection: Shirking in the Contemporary Congress." *American Journal of Political Science* 44 (2): 316–25.

Rousseau, Jean-Jacques. (1762) 1988. *On the Social Contract*. Indianapolis: Hackett.

Samuels, D. J. 2002. "Pork Barreling Is Not Credit Claiming or Advertising: Campaign Finance and the Sources of the Personal Vote in Brazil." *Journal of Politics* 64 (3): 845–63.

Sanbonmatsu, K. 2002. *Democrats, Republicans, and the Politics of Women's Place*. Ann Arbor: University of Michigan Press.

Sanbonmatsu, K. 2006. *Where Women Run: Gender and Party in the American States*. Ann Arbor: University of Michigan Press.

Sarbaugh-Thompson, M. 2006. "Effects of Term Limits on Campaign Fundraising." Paper presented at the Southern Political Science Association meeting, Atlanta, January 4–7.

Sarbaugh-Thompson, M. 2010a. "Measuring 'Term Limitedness' in Cross-Sectional Research." *State Politics and Policy Quarterly* 10 (2): 199–217.

Sarbaugh-Thompson, M. 2010b. "The Work of Committees in a Professional Legislature before and after Term Limits: How Can We Unravel the Action?" Paper presented at the 10th Annual Conference on State Politics and Policy, Springfield, IL, June 3–5.

Sarbaugh-Thompson, M., J. Strate, K. LeRoux, R. C. Elling, L. Thompson, and C. D. Elder. 2010. "Legislators and Administrators: Complex Relationships Complicated by Term Limits." *Legislative Studies Quarterly* 35 (1): 57–89.

Sarbaugh-Thompson, M., L. Thompson, C. D. Elder, M. Comins, R. C. Elling, and J. Strate. 2006. "Democracy among Strangers: Term Limits' Effects on Relationships between State Legislators in Michigan." *State Politics and Policy Quarterly* 6 (4): 384–409.

Sarbaugh-Thompson, M., L. Thompson, C. D. Elder, J. Strate, and R. Elling. 2004. *The Political and Institutional Effects of Term Limits.* New York: Palgrave Macmillan.

Sarbaugh-Thompson, M., L. Thompson, L. Marckini, J. Strate, R. C. Elling, and C. D. Elder. 2002. "Term Limits and Campaign Funding in Michigan: More Money, More Candidates, More Wealth." In *Money, Politics, and Campaign Finance Reform Law in the States,* edited by David Schultz. Durham, NC: Carolina Academic Press.

Schlesinger, J. A. 1966. *Ambition and Politics.* Chicago: Rand McNally.

Schraufnagel, S., and K. Halperin. 2006. "Term Limits, Electoral Competition, and Representational Diversity: The Case of Florida." *State Politics and Policy Quarterly* 6 (4): 448–62.

Shivers-Blackwell, S. L. 2004. "Using Role Theory to Examine Determinants of Transformational and Transactional Leader Behavior." *Journal of Leadership and Organizational Studies* 103:41–50.

Shor, B., C. Berry, and N. McCarty. 2010. "A Bridge to Somewhere: Mapping State and Congressional Ideology on a Cross-Institutional Common Space." *Legislative Studies Quarterly* 35 (3): 417–48.

Songer, D. R. 1988. "The Influence of Empirical Research: Committee vs. Floor Decision Making." *Legislative Studies Quarterly* 13 (3): 375–92.

Squire, P. 2007. "Measuring State Legislative Professionalism: The Squire Index Revisited." *State Politics and Policy Quarterly* 7 (2): 211–27.

Stein, R. M., and K. N. Bickers. 1994. "Congressional Elections and the Pork Barrel." *Journal of Politics* 56 (2): 377–99.

Straayer, J., and J. Drage-Bowser. 2004. "Colorado's Legislative Term Limits." *Final Report Joint Project on Term Limits.* Denver: National Conference of State Legislatures.

Swers, M. L. 1998. "Are Women More Likely to Vote for Women's Issue Bills Than Their Male Colleagues?" *Legislative Studies Quarterly* 23 (3): 435–48.

Tamasauskas, D., V. Sakalauskas, and D. Kriksciuniene. 2012. "Evaluation Framework of Hierarchical Clustering Methods for Binary Data." In *2012 12th International Conference on Hybrid Intelligent Systems,* 421–26. Institute of Electrical and Electronics Engineers. http://dx.doi.org/10.1109/HIS.2012.6421371

Tannenbaum, A. S. 1956. "The Concept of Organizational Control." *Journal of Social Issues* 12:50–60.

Tannenbaum, A. S. 1961. "Control and Effectiveness in a Voluntary Organization." *American Journal of Sociology* 67 (1): 33–46.

Tannenbaum, A. S. 1968. *Control in Organizations.* New York: McGraw-Hill.

Tannenbaum, A. S. 1986. "Controversies concerning Control and Democracy in Organizations." *International Yearbook of Organization Democracy* 3:279–304.

Tate, Katherine. 2003. *Black Faces in the Mirror: African Americans and Their Representatives in the U.S. Congress.* Princeton: Princeton University Press.

Thomas, Sue. 1992. "The Effects of Race and Gender on Constituency Service." *Western Political Quarterly* 45:181–99.

Thompson, J. A. 1986. "Bringing Home the Bacon: The Politics of Pork Barrel in the North Carolina Legislature." *Legislative Studies Quarterly* 11:91–108.

Thompson, J. A., and G. F. Moncrief. 1993. "The Implications of Term Limits for Women and Minorities: Some Evidence from the States." *Social Science Quarterly* 74 (2): 300–309.

Tolbert, C. J., J. A. Grummel, and D. A. Smith. 2001. "The Effects of Ballot Initiatives on Voter Turnout in the American States." *American Politics Research* 29:625–48.

Truman, D. B. 1959. *The Congressional Party: A Case Study*. New York: Wiley.

Urbinati, N. 2000. "Representation as Advocacy: A Study of Democratic Deliberation." *Political Theory* 28 (6): 758–86.

Uslaner, E. M., and R. E. Weber. 1977. "Partisan Cues and Decision Loci in U.S. State Legislatures." *Legislative Studies Quarterly* 24:423–44.

Volden, C., A. E. Wiseman, and D. E. Wittmer. 2013. "When Are Women More Effective Lawmakers Than Men?" *American Journal of Political Science* 57:326–41.

Wahlke, J., H. Eulau, W. Buchanan, and L. C. Ferguson. 1962. *The Legislative System*. New York: Wiley.

Weissert, Carol S., and Karen D. Halperin. 2007. "The Paradox of Term Limit Support: To Know Them Is NOT to Love Them." *Political Research Quarterly* 60 (3): 516–30.

Will, George F. 1992. *Restoration: Congress, Term Limits, and the Recovery of Deliberative Democracy*. New York: Free Press.

Williams, Melissa. 2000. "The Uneasy Alliance of Group Representation and Deliberative Democracy." In *Citizenship in Diverse Societies*, edited by Will Kymlicka and Wayne Norman. Oxford: Oxford University Press.

Wissel, P., O. O'Connor, and M. King. 1976. "The Hunting of the Legislative Snark: Information Searches and Reforms in US State Legislatures." *Legislative Studies Quarterly* 1 (2): 251–67.

Witt, L., K. M. Paget, and G. Matthews. 1994. *Running as a Woman: Gender and Power in American Politics*. New York: Free Press.

Woods, N. D., and M. Baranowski. 2006. "Legislative Professionalism and Influence on State Agencies: The Effects of Resources and Careerism." *Legislative Studies Quarterly* 31 (4): 585–609.

Woolley, J. T., and L. T. LeLoup. 1989. "The Adequacy of the Electoral Motive in Explaining Legislative Attention to Monetary Policy: A Comparative Study." *Comparative Politics* 22 (1): 63–82.

Wright, G. C. 2007. "Do Term Limits Affect Legislative Roll Call Voting? Representation, Polarization, and Participation." *State Politics and Policy Quarterly* 7 (3): 256–80.

Index